D1610599

Rwanda's
Popular Genocide

Revised
Social Services

Rwanda's
Popular Genocide

A Perfect Storm

Jean-Paul Kimonyo

Translated from the French by Wandia Njoya

LYNNE
RIENNER
PUBLISHERS

BOULDER
LONDON

Published in the United States of America in 2016 by
Lynne Rienner Publishers, Inc.
1800 30th Street, Boulder, Colorado 80301
www.rienner.com

and in the United Kingdom by
Lynne Rienner Publishers, Inc.
3 Henrietta Street, Covent Garden, London WC2E 8LU

© 2016 by Lynne Rienner Publishers, Inc. All rights reserved
Rwanda's Popular Genocie: A Perfect Storm is a revised and updated version of
Rwanda: Un génocide populaire, © Éditions KARTHALA, 2008.

Library of Congress Cataloging-in-Publication Data
Names: Kimonyo, Jean Paul.
Title: Rwanda's popular genocide : a perfect storm / by Jean Paul Kimonyo.
Other titles: Rwanda, un génocide populaire. English
Description: Lynne Rienner Publishers, Boulder, Colorado, 2016.
Originally published in French in 2008. I Includes bibliographical references and
  index.
Identifiers: LCCN 2015020560 I ISBN 9781626371866 (alk. paper)
Subjects: LCSH: Genocide—Political aspects—Rwanda. I Genocide—Social
  aspects—Rwanda.
Classification: LCC DT450.435 .K5413 2016 I DDC 304.6/630967571—dc 3
LC record available at http://lccn.loc.gov/2015020560

British Cataloguing in Publication Data
A Cataloguing in Publication record for this book
is available from the British Library.

Printed and bound in the United States of America

The paper used in this publication meets the requirements
of the American National Standard for Permanence of
Paper for Printed Library Materials Z39.48-1992.

5 4 3 2 1

UNIVERSITY
OF
GLASGOW
LIBRARY
WITHDRAWN

To Nganji, Keisha, and Cyusa

Contents

Illustrations

Tables

Figure

Maps

Acknowledgments

I am deeply grateful to Bonnie Campbell, Catharine Newbury, Jean-Pierre Chrétien, Alison Des Forges, Franck Chalk, and Chantal Rondeau, whose comments, critiques, and suggestions contributed to improving this work.

Also, I sincerely thank all those in Rwanda—both in and out of prison—and those in Belgium who took time to answer my questions and who shared their knowledge with me.

I am grateful to the African Development Bank for its support of the translation of the book from French to English.

Introduction

From April to June 1994, a genocide of extraordinary magnitude and intensity was perpetrated against the Tutsi minority in Rwanda. The number of victims is still the subject of debate, with estimates in most studies varying between 800,000 and 1 million people killed, of whom the overwhelming majority was Tutsi.[1] More recent research shows that the number of Tutsi living in Rwanda before the genocide was underreported, giving more weight to the higher hypothesized death count.[2] Most of the Tutsi living in the country at the time were exterminated, thus making the genocide against the Tutsi a genocide "in whole," rather than "in part," as defined by Article II of the UN Convention on the Prevention and Punishment of the Crime of Genocide.[3]

In record time, the Tutsi population was under complete physical control; in just a few days, hundreds of thousands of Tutsi were held captive within the small country encompassing only 26,000 square kilometers (just a bit more than 10,000 square miles). There were no special administrative mechanisms set up to physically control the future victims, such as concentration camps; no huge prisons and no plans for transporting the victims or the killers. Most of the Tutsi had gathered within and around churches or government buildings but soon found themselves hedged in and under siege by crowds that included women and children, many armed with machetes, clubs, and sharpened sticks, often accompanied by the din of beating drums and the noise of saucepans and whistles, and possessed by an intense euphoria.[4] The local population was the tool used to prevent any escape and to track down those who attempted to hide. The executions were carried out by soldiers, gendarmes, militias, and grassroots groups mostly of young people but also by older men and women.[5] Based on his list of the different organizers and instigators of the massacres, Gérard Prunier concludes, "Nevertheless, the main agents of the genocide were the ordinary peasants themselves. This is a terrible statement to make, but it is unfortunately borne out by the majority of the survivors' stories."[6]

There were certainly more than two hundred thousand people who killed or were direct accomplices of killing. However, this number does not take into

1

account the many people, sometimes entire communities, who crucially contributed to the physical control of the designated victims, as described above.[7]

As we shall see, a number of studies have tried to explain why so many people participated in the genocide, each providing different answers. However, closer examination shows that most of these studies address the question of how people were mobilized for killing rather than why they responded so strongly to incitement from state agents and political operatives.

The objective of this research is therefore to understand how and why a significant segment of the Hutu population participated in the massacre of Tutsi neighbors and sometimes of their Tutsi relatives, when among ordinary people, hatred between the Hutu and Tutsi had rarely been expressed in the countryside or in the towns.

The research available on the overall causes of the 1994 genocide in Rwanda falls into roughly two camps, typical of comparative study of genocide: the intentionalist and functionalist schools of thought. The first sees the genocide as ideologically driven, whereas the second considers context and circumstances as central to the genocide.

Ideology or Context?

The debate over ideology and context is modeled on the "dispute" of historians of Nazi Germany, otherwise known as the *Historikerstreit*, which pitted "intentionalists" against "structuralists," or "functionalists." Those in the first group held that the "final solution" to the "Jewish question" was an intrinsic component of the policies built around Hitler's personality, underpinned by a pathological anti-Semitism already in existence before the Nazis came into power. By contrast, the structural-functionalists saw the genocide of the Jews as a cumulative process of the radicalization of Nazi anti-Semitism under contextual constraints. These included the nature of power as exercised by Hitler, the power structure within the Nazi state, and the regime's anti-Jewish policies as well as its foreign policy and expansionist ambitions.[8]

When it comes to the 1994 Rwanda genocide, proponents of ideology as the root cause believe the genocide was an intrinsic component of the "Hutu Republic" ideology because it was founded on hatred of the "Other"—that is, the Tutsi. These scholars see discrimination against the Tutsi as the continuity between the otherwise distinct Kayibanda and Habyarimana regimes. They consider the internal political crisis and the political-military crisis following the Rwandan Patriotic Front (RPF) attack in 1990 as largely a result of the regime's anti-Tutsi ideology and the response of the Habyarimana regime to the genocide as consistent with that ideology.[9] They essentially explain the process of mass mobilization deductively, by arguing that the ideology of the Hutu regime since the revolution had strongly permeated the political class as well as the ordinary citizens. On the issue of the mass mobilization, this school of thought emphasizes the impact of the "hate media," the use of state institutions, especially the local authorities, and above all the importance of the spirit of obedience to authority of the Rwandan population.

For those who highlight the external context to the Habyarimana regime, the RPF invasion was the catalyst of the crisis. Combined with a deteriorating economic and social environment and increasing competition among the elites for the shrinking national pie, worsened by political pluralism, the attack crystallized the crisis and its subsequent explosion into extreme violence.[10] Others in the same school of thought replace ideology with ethnicity, which they see as social atavism that turns collective identity into a driving force. They explain the eruption of the genocide as an ethnic reaction to the RPF military aggression, which they ultimately consider responsible for the surge in the violence.[11] The ethnicity argument does not distinguish between the strength of ethnic sentiments among the common classes and those among the ruling class, an ambiguity that in turn supports the theory of Hutu fear, desire for revenge, and intent to wage war in retaliation for the RPF aggression, and thus the entire community's violent reaction, especially after the plane carrying President Juvénal Habyarimana was shot down.

The investigation begun in 1998 by a French judge, Jean-Louis Bruguière, into the assassination of President Habyarimana, revealed by the press in March 2004, led to issuance on November 22, 2006, of international arrest warrants against nine Rwandan RPF senior officers after he consulted French political authorities, including President Jacques Chirac.[12] Judge Bruguière could not indict President Kagame, who enjoys presidential immunity. Not only did Bruguière accuse the Rwandan president of ordering the attack against his predecessor's plane but also he blamed him for the genocide that followed.[13] This accusation against the RPF for being responsible for shooting down Habyarimana's plane gave rise to a more neatly structural-functionalist interpretation of the cause of the genocide. Its proponents contend that the genocide was not planned prior to Habyarimana's death but was a reaction hastily prepared by regime hard-liners in the days following the downing of the presidential plane.[14] In January 2012, a ballistic report commissioned by French judges Trevidic and Proux, who took over the case from Bruguière, established that the missile that destroyed the plane was fired from the area of Habyarimana's presidential guard barracks, inferring that the main suspects were members of the slain president's own guard. The day following President Habyariamnana's death his military inner circle, with the presidential guard at the forefront, sparked off the genocide.[15]

Why Did So Many Ordinary People Participate in the Genocide?

This, as you will recall, is the central question of this study. Three researchers, Omar McDoom, Lee Ann Fujii, and Scott Straus, have attempted to specifically address it, and their answers have been similar on some points and divergent on others.[16] Apart from Straus, none of the others have sought to determine the causes of the genocide at the national level. Broadly Straus defends the thesis of provocation,[17] which holds that the assassination of President Habyarimana, allegedly by the RPF, and the war that followed were the real cause of the reactive violence.

The most balanced and complete contribution is perhaps that by Mc-Doom, who worked on four cells in both the north and the south of the country. McDoom distances himself from the thesis of mechanical obedience to state institutions, pointing to the importance of political and social dynamics at the meso-level (prefectures and communes) and micro-level (sectors and cells) in grassroots mobilization to participate in the killings. His study shows a major difference in the processes of mobilization between the north (Ruhengeri Prefecture) and south (Butare Prefecture). In the north, dominated by the National Revolutionary Movement for Development (MRND), the massacre of the Tutsi population commenced on the day following the death of President Habyarimana, and the killings were carried out by the local state representatives, villagers, Interahamwe ("those who attack together") militia, and military. The political influence of the MRND and the proximity of the war played a major role in this mobilization. "In contrast, in the south the war was distant."[18] In Butare Prefecture in the south, after the political and social intermediaries at meso- and micro-levels had swung to the genocide agenda, the motives for individual mobilization among the grassroots population were coercion, opportunism, habit, conformism, racism, and ideological indoctrination.

The conclusions of a study by Fujii are very similar to McDoom's, except for a slightly different focus, for the former favors the micro- and individual rather than the structural levels. Fujii studied a site in the northern part of the country (Ruhengeri Prefecture) and another in the center (Gitarama Prefecture), where the political dynamics are similar to those in Butare Prefecture and found a difference of dynamics of mass participation between the north and the south similar to the one McDoom identified.

Fujii shows that the general context of the genocide, especially the ethnic narrative as promoted at the highest levels of the state, did not entail automatic and universal compliance by the population. Also, the people's own accounts of the events she presents "do not focus on murderous hatreds or overwhelming fears. Instead, they point to situational factors and personal motives, such as greed and jealousy."[19] Her contribution centers on group dynamics as the major explanation for mass mobilization, which was sometimes voluntary, frequently forced, and at times carried out by the authorities but more frequently by peers motivated by the social and family environment. Motivations for participation also included personal hatred "rooted in specific grievances, such as jealousy over parental favoritism toward another sibling, rivalries with family members over property, resentments over another's better fortune, or the coveting of another man's wife."[20] Fujii concludes her research with her thesis of social interaction: "The mechanisms that were critical to the process were local ties and group dynamics, which exerted powerful pressures on Joiners to join in the violence and powerful new identities for continuing."[21]

As mentioned above, Straus integrates mass participation in the genocide into a general framework of the theory of provocation at the national level. He stresses two main, specific motives for such participation: coercion, essentially by peers in face-to-face interactions, and war-related fear and combativeness against the RPF. When it comes to the main cause of their involvement in the genocide, his respondents overwhelmingly cite the insecurity caused by President Habyarimana's death and the desire to avenge it. Here, Straus agrees with the two points cited above on the issue of pressure exercised by peers, but he definitely differs with Fujii and McDoom with regard to personal motivations for participation in the genocide. He instead cites the Hutu fear caused by the war with the RPF and the desire to fight it along with the entire Tutsi population, then "guilty by association" with the war. Straus's conclusions are mainly based on a survey of 210 prisoners in fifteen prisons throughout the country. In an analysis of Straus's methodology, David Becker statistically demonstrates an 80 percent underestimation of participation in massacres by the respondents in the Straus study—unless some of the killers had killed dozens, if not hundreds, of people, which Straus does not mention. For Becker, this problem of reliability of the responses "precludes arriving at valid, general conclusions from the survey about the reasons for involvement in the genocide."[22]

In his analysis and conclusion Straus unduly emphasizes war related fear and combativeness against the RPF as a motive for participation in the genocide or as a cause for the genocide. He overlooks his own data from the survey or from his interviews pointing to different causes. The other element that mars the validity of Straus's conclusions, especially regarding the war-related motivation, is the fact that he dismisses or downplays, for no good reason, his own data suggesting a strong regional difference between the north and the south/center in the dynamics of mass participation in the genocide related to political allegiances, ideological leanings, and geographical proximity of the war: "These findings are suggestive theoretically but hardly conclusive."[23] Five prefectures out of the eleven prefectures situated in the center and the south, far from the war zones and opposed to the MRND, were home to 66 percent of the country's Tutsi population.[24]

In addition to the issue of fear during war, the contributions of the three authors cited above are mainly drawn from the statements of the killers themselves, which constitute their principal source for elucidating popular motivations for participating in the killings. As discussed regarding Straus's study, we have seen how surveys may pose the risk that respondents may attempt to minimize their share and nature of responsibility as individuals, leading to problems of reliability. A further element that emerges from the work of Fujii and

Straus is the self-avowed importance of intragroup coercion between peasant peers. However, neither Straus nor Fujii tries to systematically unpack the dynamics of this peer pressure in making a clear distinction of nature and motivations between peer groups initially exerting such coercion and those who followed. Finally, Fujii does this to a lesser extent, but Straus's data strongly minimize material motivations for mass participation in the genocide, such as looting or grabbing victims' land.[25] McDoom provides an interesting and broader range of motivations, albeit no clear hierarchal order of importance. All of the three authors largely ignore the striking rise of the level of violent crime at the grassroots before the genocide caused by hunger and intense land pressure[26] and more generally the local historical and sociopolitical contexts that shaped the participation of Rwandan peasants in the genocide. In seeking to determine the causes of mass participation in the genocide, these three authors' approaches, mostly based on interviews of the perpetrators, lead to rather partial answers that do not allow a determination of the contours of the constrained agency of the Rwandan peasant population, particularly in choosing whether to participate in the genocide, whether actively or by following the herd.

A Different Approach

Instead of seeking to determine the causes and modalities of mass participation in the genocide as a specific event at a given moment and merely relying on the genocide perpetrators' statements, this book attempts to write a history of the Rwandan peasant population before and during the genocide and of how it has negotiated the assertion of its agency over time. To this end, it attempts to elucidate the contexts, determinants, constraints, and motivations for the peasants' action over the longer term.

The goal of this research is no longer to find answers to such discrete questions as "Why did you participate in the genocide?" but to try to construct a social and political history of the Rwandan peasants in which participation in the genocide in 1994 constitutes chronologically the latest phase, albeit a very specific one.

My study began with an attempt to theorize this new approach using the dialectics of control, a concept adapted from Michel Foucault's theory of power, which links constraint with freedom and which seems to best capture the behavior of the lower social strata in Rwanda.[27] For the purposes of this study, my primary interest was the idea that an individual or a community occupying the subordinate position in a power relationship still has some leeway in complying with orders. To gain access to certain privileges later, the dominated can feign overzealous obedience and employ strategies such as avoidance behavior, maneuvering, feet-dragging, pretended compliance with or-

ders, work to rule, or passive sabotage. These strategies are part of a contin-
uum that stretches between coerced obedience at one extreme and freely chosen course of action or open rebellion at the other. Strategic behavior is central
to the concept of the "popular modes of political action" as formulated by the
journal *Politique africaine* in the 1980s, which emphasizes the political ration-
ality that guides the behavior of African lower classes. An elucidation of
Rwandan peasants' strategic behaviors should allow us to perceive the constrained agency of these subaltern social classes and how it developed before
or during the genocide.

In this research, three periods captured our attention: first, the decade before the socioeconomic crisis at the end of the 1980s, that is, before the civil
war and the establishment of multiple parties; second, the war and multiparty
period; and last, the period of the genocide. I began at the national level in the
capital, Kigali, and continued in Butare and Kibuye Prefectures at the regional
level, ending within Kigembe and Gitesi Communes, in the Butare and Kibuye
Prefectures, respectively. This research is structured like Russian nesting dolls,
with each level of analysis fitting within another, which allowed triangulations
across different layers of inquiry. Reports from the Rwandan Interior Ministry
headquarters worked in the same manner, in that they dealt with the situation
in Kigali but also gave a summary of information coming from each of the ten
remaining prefectures. The prefectures in turn drew up reports on what was
happening at the administrative center as well as a summary of the information
coming from each of their communes. The communes dealt with each of their
sectors in detail. Years later, these reports still give gripping images of the
communes and the life of their citizens. I also obtained life narratives from interviews with prisoners, survivors, and bystanders to the genocide.

I chose Butare and Kibuye Prefectures for their sizable Tutsi population;
the two prefectures combined were home to 30 percent of the entire Rwandan
Tutsi population. I also chose these two prefectures because of their distance
from the battlefields, which meant that the areas were less directly affected by
the military violence. This distance in turn permits a better understanding of the
underlying dynamics of the implementation of the genocide. Finally, I chose
Kigembe and Gitesi Communes for the distinctly different dynamics within the
communes during both the democratization period and the genocide.

Notes

1. Human Rights Watch (HRW) estimates the number of Tutsi killed at 507,000,
or 77 percent of the Tutsi population living in Rwanda (Des Forges, *Leave None to Tell
the Story*, 1999, p. 15). Gérard Prunier estimates that 800,000 Tutsis were killed
(Prunier, *Rwanda Crisis*, 1997, pp. 261, 265). A census released by the Rwandan Di-
rectorate of Planning lists 1,074,017 declared victims and 934,218 counted (Direction
de la Planification, *Dénombrement des victimes du génocide*, 2002).

2. Verpoorten, "Death Toll of the Rwandan Genocide," 2005, pp. 331–367.

3. UN General Assembly, Third Session, "Resolution 260 (III): Convention on the Prevention and Punishment of the Crime of Genocide," December 9, 1948.

4. African Rights, *Rwanda,* 1995.

5. Des Forges, *Leave None to Tell the Story*, pp. 260–263.

6. Prunier, *Rwanda Crisis*, p. 247.

7. The Gacaca community courts, in the first instance and appeal, sentenced people involved in more than 320,000 cases of the second category of those who killed and their direct accomplices. People were also condemned in more than 50,000 cases of the first category of the zealous killers or those in a position of leadership. However, because one person could be involved in more than one case, the exact number of the killers is difficult to assess from Gacaca data. Republic of Rwanda, National Service of Gacaca courts, "Gacaca Courts in Rwanda," Kigali, June 2012. Straus estimates that between 175,000 and 210,000 people were directly involved in the killings. Straus, "How Many Perpetrators?," 2004, p. 93.

8. Kershaw, *Nazi Dictatorship*, 1992.

9. Chrétien, *Le défi de l'ethnisme*, 1997; de Heusch, "Anthropologie d'un genocide," 1994; Braeckman, *Rwanda*, 1994; Uvin, *Aiding Violence*, 1998.

10. Reyntjens, *L'Afrique des Grands Lacs en crise*, 1994; Maton, *Développement économique et social,*1994; Marysse, De Herdt, and Ndayambaje, *Rwanda*, 1994, p. 82.

11. Reyntjens, *L'Afrique des Grands Lacs en crise*, pp. 10, 257; Lemarchand, "Les génocides se suivent mais ne se ressemblent pas," 2002.

12. Philippe Bernard, "En France, l'enquête sur le Rwanda était suivi en haut lieu," *Le Monde*, December 9, 2010, Wikileaks, http://wikileaks.org /cable/2007/01/07PARIS322.html.

13. Judge Bruguière, judicial ordinance, November 7, 2006.

14. Guichaoua, *Rwanda, de la guerre au génocide,* 2010, p. 20; Straus, *Order of Genocide*, 2006, pp. 42–49.

15. Des Forges, *Leave None to Tell the Story*, pp. 200–201; Reyntjens, *Rwanda: Trois jours qui ont fait basculer l'histoire*, p. 57.

16. Fujii, *Killing Neighbors,* 2009; Straus, *Order of Genocide*; McDoom, "Rwanda's Ordinary Killers," 2005.

17. On the provocation theory of genocides, see Melson, *Revolution and Genocide*, 1991.

18. McDoom, "Rwanda's Ordinary Killers," p. 11.

19. Fujii, *Killing Neighbors*, p.77.

20. Ibid., p. 183.

21. Ibid., p. 185.

22. Ibid., p. 183.

23. Straus, *Order of Genocide*, p. 62.

24. République rwandaise, Ministère du Plan, Service National de Recensement, *Recensement général de la population et de l'habitat au 15 août 1991,* n.d., p. 23.

25. For a different account, see Verwimp, "Economic Profile of Peasant Perpetrators of Genocide," 2005; Verpoorten, "Leave None to Claim the Land," 2012.

26. See André and Platteau, "Land Tenure Under Unbearable Stress," 1998.

27. Foucault, "How Is Power Exercised?," 1982.

1

The Historical Context

The categories of Hutu, Tutsi, and Twa and how they interacted in traditional Rwandan society remain controversial in contemporary debates and among historians. The debates are provoked in part by the contradictions inherent in these identity groups. On the one hand, the Hutu, Tutsi, and Twa are tightly knit into a single cultural entity. They are therefore not ethnic groups in the strict sense of the term. The three groups shared the same language and religious beliefs, coexisted and intermingled within the same territory, belonged to the same clans, and were subject to a single political entity: the Rwandan monarchy. On the other hand, the formation of distinct sociopolitical identities of Hutus and Tutsis from the end of the nineteenth century, and their subsequent polarization, has been well documented.

Granted, the present is not exclusively defined by the past, an idea we must reiterate when it comes to Rwanda. In revisiting the past, however, the key challenge is to identify the continuities and breaking points that could shed light on the broadest contemporary context of mass political and social action.

What are the categories of Hutu, Tutsi, and Twa, and how did they relate to each other historically? Are they social classes, castes, ethnic groups, or even "races," as some have said? For comprehending mass participation in the Rwandan conflict since 1959, it is crucial to understand how the hostility between the Hutu and Tutsi crystallized over time, particularly in relation to the respective roles played by external factors—specifically colonialism—and by internal factors.

The other challenging task in revisiting history is determining the extent of political polarization after the 1959 revolution as well as the extent to which the population was involved in this polarization between the Tutsi and Hutu.

The extensive research on this subject can be divided into three broad schools of thought related to ethnicity in Africa: instrumentalism, essentialism, and constructivism.[1] I situate my study in the constructivist framework given

that I identify the multiple factors leading to the emergence of ethnic antagonism, particularly the political manipulation of ethnic sentiments and the precolonial sociopolitical contradictions that intensified under colonial rule. In
other words, my approach is twofold. On the one hand, I examine Hutu and
Tutsi as distinct sociopolitical identities since the end of the precolonial period
and their polarization under colonialism in the twentieth century. On the other
hand, I outline how both the religious and secular arms of the colonial enterprise propelled a vicious antagonism by introducing to the Hutu and Tutsi
elites the notion of race.

The Precolonial Period

Population Settlement in the Great Lakes Region

Missionary and colonial historiography depicts a rigid and hierarchical image
of settlement in Rwanda by three distinct races arriving at different historical
periods.[2] The first inhabitants of Rwanda were said to be the Twa, who were
related to Pygmies and were hunters and gatherers living in the forest. According to the Hamitic hypothesis, which traces any "civilization" to an origin outside the African continent, and specifically to Hamites, descendants of the
"Caucasian" race, the Twa would have been followed by the Hutu, a Bantu
group arriving from Chad and Cameroon. Finally, the Tutsi would have arrived from Ethiopia between the thirteenth and fifteenth centuries and used
trickery or force to conquer and enslave the Hutu majority and the Twa minority. Based on physical features and the "sophisticated" organization of the
kingdoms in the Great Lakes Region, missionary historiography concluded
that the Tutsi belonged to the Hamitic race, incorporated each of three social
categories as different waves of settlement, and ranked each according to its
level of civilization.

Recent research combines a critique of written sources with archaeology,
linguistics, and genetics in order to offer a more nuanced perspective. The researchers note the heterogeneity of the populations of the Great Lakes Region
but date the encounter and coexistence between different populations to a
much earlier era.[3] They hypothesize the prominence of farming communities
over a long period of time compared with populations that mainly kept livestock.[4] These studies also situate the factors behind the dominance of the
Bantu language communities in the region, from the first millennium to the beginning of the second millennium of this era, in the context of coexistence; intense economic, technical, and cultural exchanges; and integration of the different populations settled in the region starting from the Neolithic age.
However, what remains paradoxical is how certain ancient sociocultural distinctions persisted despite this long shared history. According to David

Schoenbrun, the distinctions would have been accentuated at the beginning of the second millennium, foreshadowing the establishment of the kingdoms.[5]

The Emergence of the Rwandan Kingdoms

From 1000 AD, the area that would come to be known as Rwanda experienced significant climatic and social changes that would lead to increased specialization of skills and the rise in power of the pastoral groups.[6] These changes led to the evolution of new kingdoms ruled by pastoralist groups over the next few centuries. Jan Vansina traces the creation of the kingdom of the Nyiginya Dynasty to the seventeenth century.[7] Until the nineteenth century, the population and herd size of this kingdom continued to grow.[8]

Vansina explains that from the seventeenth century onward, the agrarian and pastoral economies in the hills were intertwined but not integrated, which brought about the need for deliberate political coordination between the two groups. Under normal circumstances, the herders needed food crops, but during the frequent famines, their mobility made them less vulnerable than the cultivators. From this time onward, the country would also be densely populated, a development that would become a potential source of conflict between cultivators and pastoralists. The two groups had to use the same fields in rotation, thereby preventing the emergence of land rights tied to permanent partitioning of the land. Similar conflicts would have arisen over the right of passage for cattle in search of pastures and the implied damage to crops, the use of the margins of the low-lying marshes during the dry season, and the intensifying need for land by both groups as a result of the increase in cattle and human populations.[9] Under these circumstances, dialogue would have been necessary for deciding when to begin burning the vegetation to clear the land and for negotiating access to water, the right of free passage for cattle in search of better pastures, and the annual soil rotation. Political issues therefore had strong implications for daily life.

This detailed description of the social conditions of an era dating this far back relies primarily on a 1958 study, a compilation of pastoralist narratives and vocabulary. But the description of a world "filling up" slightly contradicts other sections of the book in which Vansina explains that central Rwanda was contiguous to the large forest and that the pastoralists moved easily from one region to another. He even lists several areas within and on the outskirts of central Rwanda sparsely populated at the time. Does his portrayal of early overcrowding belong more to the nineteenth century?

Central Rwanda in the seventeenth century was administratively divided into several small territories ruled by kings. In the collective imagination, the *mwami* (king) and his royal drum embodied each of these units. The mwami was, above all, a spiritual leader. Through rituals and with the help of lineage priests, the mwami guaranteed rituals celebrating the fertility of the land, the cattle, and the mwami's subjects. But the mwami was a secular leader as well. According to Vansina, there were two kinds of political entities: the "lineage territory" and the "principality." In the former entity, the mwami's power depended on alliances. He was seen as a descendant of a lineage who arrived first and cleared the land. The other lineages immigrated more recently and were known as *abagererwa* (land-tenure clients); they had received land, sealed marriages, and sometimes made blood pacts that facilitated their assimilation into the founding lineage, otherwise known as *ubukonde*, which was also the foundation of the political organization.[10]

Power in the principalities was held by the herders, ruled by hereditary chiefs called *abatware*, namely, those "not linked by kinship to any of their subjects from the farming community."[11] These chiefs claimed ownership of the land and guaranteed the land tenure of the farmers as well as access to pastures for the herders. Their coercive power relied on the warrior groups composed of young men from the chiefs' own lineages or from Tutsi or Hima families within their chiefdoms, and these groups operated like the herdsmen migrating in search of pastures. Lineage heads accepted the ritualist and military tutelage of the lord-mwami, to whose court they sent one or several sons to be enrolled as "pages" in the king's guard and to be educated. Their families intermarried with that of the mwami, contributed an annual tribute, and sent members for compulsory duty at the court.[12]

Thus we have a general picture that anticipates the well-known situation in the nineteenth century in which the north, ruled by Hutu lineage chiefs who controlled the land within the *ubukonde* system, stood out in contrast to the rest of the country. According to Vansina, Nyiginya Rwanda emerged toward the end of the seventeenth century, at the same time as the other major kingdoms in the subregion. The kingdom's founder was Ruganzu Ndori, who Vansina believes was a Hima pastoralist chief who arrived from the north with a substantial number of cattle.[13] Ndori's wealth would have enabled him to stamp his authority on the smaller pastoral fiefdoms and establish the cattle-clientship system of *ubuhake,* which was more permanent than the previously existing patron and client relationship known as *ubugabire*. The other important institution Mwami Ndori created was the army. He recruited the chiefs' personal guards into his central army with an increasing number of different units. Vansina makes the following observation in this regard:

> The deepest effect of this new military organization was the institutionalization of a glorification of military and martial violence that eventually permeated the whole of Nyiginya culture as the armies became the foundation of the administrative structure of the realm. For the ties forged by Ndori between the army, on the one hand, and the corporations that provided services to the court, managed the herds, and controlled the pastures, on the other, were to flourish during the eighteenth century, so that ultimately all the inhabitants of the realm were incorporated into the military organization.[14]

The oral traditions associated with the royal court recount the history of Ndori as a series of conquests Vansina restricts to the central Rwanda region. From then on, the Rwandan monarchy was apparently given its essential governing institutions: "Ndori succeeded in being recognized as the legitimate king in central Rwanda and created a government that rested on four institutions: the court-capital, the *umurwa* district, the political *ubuhake* clientele, and a true army. The last two of these remained innovations that, from that time on, distinguished the Nyiginya kingdom from all of its neighbors from that time on."[15]

The history of the kingdom is one of gradual expansion in both progress and setbacks, bringing together neighboring autonomous regions and better integrating the remoter regions. Vansina's schema definitely merits further discussion. Above all, it is important to note that the schema generally follows fixist Maquet's "premise" of institutionalized difference, or worse, of social inequality.

The Sociopolitical Situation on the Eve of Colonialism

The situation at the end of the nineteenth century was complex given the contradictions inherent in the numerous changes affecting social relationships at various levels. The sociocultural Hutu-Tutsi divide was held up by customs and institutions of convivial coexistence. The most important of these structures were the clans, which were multiethnic in composition and which encouraged solidarity. They were strengthened by rituals affirming mythical common patrilineal ties such as the *ubuse* ritual ties between clans considered *abasangwabutaka* ("the people found on the land," the majority of whom were Hutu) and the *ibimanuka* ("those who descended," the majority of whom were Tutsi). Through *ubuse*, members of *abasangwabutaka* clans could allow people from other clans to settle in their locality. Clan solidarity embodied both reciprocity within the clan and solidarity with other clans, in accordance with the ties of *ubuse*. According to Gamaliel Mbonimana, "This framework of reciprocity excluded reference to what is today called 'ethnic groups' or the 'social categories' of Hutu, Tutsi, and Twa. *Ubuse* played a major role in maintaining a cohesive and integrated Rwandan society."[16]

The traditional worship ceremony of *kubandwa*, which the Tutsi and the Hutu celebrated together, was yet another affirmation of their religious kinship. During the ceremonies, a ceremonial mwami and a queen were chosen independent of their social status in the real world, thereby rendering the class/caste system impotent.[17] Finally, another form of breaking the social barriers was manifest in blood pacts, many times sworn between a Hutu and a Tutsi. A blood pact tied the two individuals closer than brothers, and breaking the pact was considered taboo.[18] Another source of social cohesion was the powerful ideology and culture upholding nationa unity embodied in the monarchy. Lasly, besides the aristocracy, which was Tutsi, most cattle-keeper and agriculturist lineages and families related to the monarchy in the smae manner and shared the same living conditions.

However, despite these instances of social bonding that cut across hereditary social stratification, the final years of precolonial Rwanda were characterized by a hardening of sociopolitical relations. At the end of the eighteenth century, the increased clearing of land and the growth in the population and herds exacerbated the conflicting interests and needs of the pastoralists and farmers.[19] Within this context the establishment of two institutions greatly contributed to rigidifying social relations: *ibikingi* and *uburetwa*.

Ibikingi was a clientship system in which the mwami granted land for pastoral use to his chiefs or to the people close to him. Everyone, both cultivators and pastoralists, living in a particular *ibikingi* had to pay a tribute to the landholder, who also became their patron. Until around 1880, the *ibikingi* were restricted to vacant land, but after the position of chief of a hill was created, *ibikingi* were imposed on land on which people had already settled, based on their lineage. This new development infringed on ancestral rights and led to the outright dispossession of farmers or small-scale herders by the chief and his cronies.[20] It also led to the emergence of the position of the chief of the pastures, whose duty was to control public pastures not granted as *ibikingi*, whereas the land chief ruled primarily over the agriculturalists. The two chiefs were responsible for collecting, on behalf of the royal court, annual tributes from the populations under their respective jurisdictions, which the chiefs submitted after they had taken their cuts. In the southwest and especially in the northwest, the population experienced *ibikingi* as the plunder of their property by the new administrators, whom they also considered outsiders to the region. Jean-Népomucène Nkurikiyimfura highlights the social impact of this new development as follows:

> Wherever it was implemented, igikingi increased the structures through which the administration authorities oppressed the poor and lower classes. It also helped reinforce feelings of ethnic hatred from the bottom to the top of the social hierarchy. Leaving the proletariat (often Twa and Hutu, and rarely Tutsi) to their own devices, and reckoning that the middle-income groups (which included Hutus and Tutsis) were relatively happy with their fields and pastures, the mwami and his most powerful chiefs figured that any muhutu, mututsi, and mutwa could get integrated into this upper social class, that is, into the Tutsi ethnic group, depending on the individual's talent, property, and ability to form alliances with socially well-situated families. To gain access to the ibikingi, which had become a new source of wealth, one often had to undergo a process of "Tutsification," also referred to by the authors as "ennobling," which blurred the distinction between the few powerful Tutsi lineages with the common Tutsi. . . . Such cases of "ennobling" became more widespread from the time of Rwabugiri [the last mwami of Rwanda, in the second half of the nineteenth century] and the spread of ibikingi. . . . How-

ever, the fact that "ennobling" was initiated by the royal court or powerful chiefs became an obstacle to the development of a class comprising Bahutu chiefs powerful enough to serve as special intermediaries between the royal court and the greater section of the population.[21]

Climbing the social ladder required one to go through the process of "Tutsification" under the political clientship system of *ubuhake*. Those privileged to attain such social advancement were powerful cattle owners, and they did so at the expense of the majority of the Hutu, as well as of the Tutsi, who may have belonged to the same group as the nobility but who still led a precarious existence. Also, many in the most densely populated areas of central Rwanda lost their cattle and became Hutu after failing to get accepted as the client of a powerful chief.[22]

To have access to fields belonging to *igikingi*, poor agriculturist families that could not provide a certain amount of beans and sorghum as payment were required to perform *uburetwa*. For two out of every five days, a family had to provide manual labor on the lands owned by the chiefs, a new requirement that was particularly unpopular. The *ubuhake* and the *uburetwa* started to spread within central Rwanda only later, around the middle of the nineteenth century, and they varied in nature. It is during the colonial time that these institutions will be generalized and become overtly exploitive. The implementation of *uburetwa* was bound to have devastating consequences: the agriculturalists were bonded and exploited for their labor by the land chiefs in return for not getting evicted from their land. The imposition of *uburetwa* exclusively on the farmers and not on the pastoralists became the straw that broke the camel's back. It quickly precipitated the development of the schism that split Rwandan society, from the top to the bottom, into a hierarchy of two opposing categories that henceforth carried the labels Hutu and Tutsi.

In his historical account of the two categories, Vansina traces the origin of the term *Tutsi* to a period before the establishment of the Nyiginya kingdom. According to him, *Tutsi* designated a segment of the pastoralist population, whereas the word *Hutu* "was a demeaning term that alluded to rural boorishness or loutish behavior used by the elite."[23] As the military institution developed, the labels *Hutu* and *Tutsi* would take on new meanings. The army evolved into three distinct companies, two comprising herders responsible for combat and cattle raids, and the other composed of agriculturalists responsible for military logistics. Subsequently, *Tutsi* became the equivalent of warrior, in contrast with *Hutu*, or the servant. Vansina notes, "As most noncombatants happened to stem from lineages of farmers, the elites began to call all farmers 'Hutu' and to oppose this word to 'Tutsi,' now applied to all herders, whether they were of Tutsi origin or not."[24] According to Vansina, it is in this context that the first institutionalized distinction between Hutu and Tutsi appears:

The absolute division between Hutu and Tutsi institutionalized by the daily practice of uburetwa rapidly displaced the older social class consciousness, in spite of the fact that this consciousness itself resulted from a political phenomenon rather than from a pure notion of class. Until then, class consciousness had elaborated a very fine social scale in which families were deemed less "good or bad" according to their occupations and their relative well-being, but it also made a rough distinction between the elite (imfura) and the bulk of the people, or between wealthy and poor people.[25]

Therefore, from 1870 onward, the social identification opposing Tutsi herders to Hutu agriculturalists spread throughout Rwanda. After 1885, several spontaneous revolts against the Tutsi authorities broke out in the center and south of the country. The following summary by Vansina provides a fitting conclusion:

> Their first error was to attribute the Tutsi/Hutu opposition to feelings of racial hatred, as Captain Berthe did in 1898 when he spoke of "Rassenhass," which reveals his opinions about race more than it reflects any reality on the ground. Indeed, it became commonplace for Europeans to equate Tutsi with Hamite and to apply to Rwanda the racist theories that Speke's book had introduced in the Great Lakes Region. From there, it was only a small step to imagine that a Hutu was a special racial designation accepted by all those who were so designated. Yet, at that time, the farmers in the country absolutely did not think of themselves as members of a single ethnic group, and they all rejected the insulting epithet that was bestowed on them. They distinguished themselves as the "people" of Bugoyi, Kinyaga, Nduga, Rukiga. . . . Awareness of their common quality was to arise only as the result of their common experience as Hutu subjects of the same colony and by its registration in all manner of census and identity papers of an awareness that then was openly appropriated and further refined during the political struggles of the 1950s.[26]

Researchers have different views of how these social and political tensions were handled by Mwami Rwabugiri at the eve of colonial rule. Vansina describes the mwami's reign as brutal and unpredictable, and he did not spare even the aristocratic lineages.[27] According to Emmanuel Ntezimana, Rwabugiri was prepared to use the common people instead of the privileged classes to reinforce the power of the monarchy:

> Toward the last decade of the nineteenth century, the aristocracy in general and the nobility from the provinces in particular had become unstable. These groups were disoriented and, worse, alienated from the highest levels of power and from the administration of the kingdom. Numerous historical accounts tell of exile and of Rwabugiri forcing the displacement of families and entire lineages to hostile regions that had recently come under occupation. These accounts suggest that ultimately, the beneficiaries of Rwabugiri's administration were initially unknown people from lowly backgrounds, be they abahutu, abatutsi, or abatwa, who in fact came from the newly conquered territories. The monarch drew them from very poor backgrounds and placed them in high positions of responsibility.[28]

The aristocratic lineages did not waste time in taking their revenge. During the Rucunshu coup after Rwabugiri's death in 1895, a section of the aristocracy killed Rwabugiri's legitimate successor and crowned instead a prince they could control. This faction, perceived as having usurped power, relied on the military might of the German and then of the Belgian colonists to reclaim and protect its privileges and power.[29] Under Rwabugiri the use of force had begun to overtake mysticism as the defining link between the people and the monarchy.[30]

The Colonial Period

The Rucunshu Coup and the Installation of the German Protectorate

Rwanda came under German control following the Anglo-German agreement of 1890 on partitioning East Africa. In 1894, the first official contact between the Rwandan monarchy and the German colonial authorities took place when Mwami Kigeli IV Rwabugiri received German emissary Gustav-Adolf von Götzen at the royal court. In 1895, Rwabugiri died after thirty-five years on the throne, leaving behind a kingdom at the height of its power.[31] Rutarindwa, Rwabugiri's designated successor, was killed at Rucunshu by his maternal uncles from the Abega-Abakagara clan. His step-brother Yuhi Musinga took over as mwami.[32] Among those who fiercely resisted this takeover were several Hutu-ruled provinces. In 1912, Ndugutse, a man from the north, organized a multiethnic revolt that included Rukara, a Hutu chief, and Basebya, a Twa chief, as well as Tutsis from regions opposed to the new royal court. The Germans came to Musinga's aid and crushed the rebellion,[33] thereby solidifying a hatred for Tutsi chiefs from central Rwanda.[34]

Throughout Germany's presence in Rwanda (1897–1916) and during the majority of Belgian rule (1916–1931), all kinds of exactions were levied against the people. Despite numerous ups and downs, the collaboration between the colonial administration and the Tutsi aristocracy remained close. The colonial system—which included the church—sought to subdue the population to obtain food and, above all, labor. For the royal court and Tutsi nobility, gaining favor with the colonial invaders became the practical thing to do in the face of the latter's invincible weaponry. The structure of power relations in Rwandan society had fundamentally changed.[35]

World War I only made things worse. In 1916, Belgian troops invaded Rwanda from Belgian Congo, introducing more exactions to meet their need for supplies and porters. Once again, the royal court and the chiefs served as their agents. These events were closely followed in 1917 by an acute famine in the northwest of Rwanda.[36]

The Clash of Cultures and of Powers

From the arrival of the "white fathers" (missionaries) in 1900 to the time Mwami Musinga was deposed in 1931, cohesion within Rwandan society weakened with the disintegration of the unifying philosophy represented by the spiritually revered monarchy. After the colonial administration had proven its superior military might, Rwandans were unable to preserve their cultural unity, even after the colonial administration adopted the policy of indirect rule. Thirty years into colonialism, the internal discord within Rwandan society had provided the space for colonial administrators and the missionaries to redefine Rwandan identity in terms of distinct races.

The white fathers played a leading political role. Despite being initially ostracized by the royal court and the populace, they succeeded in receiving a sizable allocation of land, on which they built their missions. They essentially adopted the role of the patron in the Rwandan clientship framework. The catechists were people who had left the familiarity of the chiefs and the royal court to work for the church. One of Rwandans' major motivations for aligning themselves with the church was to avoid tributes and the traditional system of duties.[37]

The arrival of the Belgians in 1916 only strengthened the white fathers' position. The Belgians joined forces with those who had a good knowledge of the country and with whom they shared Catholicism and the French language. The white fathers in turn intervened in the internal politics of the royal court. In 1917, the mwami was forbidden from pronouncing a death sentence without the permission of the head of the Belgian administration, the resident. From 1922 on, he was assisted in the exercise of his judicial duties by a resident's representative. In 1923, he was additionally forbidden to make or revoke appointments of provincial chiefs, and the latter were forbidden to appoint or dismiss their juniors without prior consent from the resident's office.[38]

Upon seeing the mwami's power slip away, a group of aristocrats allied themselves with the Belgian administration and the white fathers. They received the nickname *inshongore*, which loosely translates as the "splendid ones." Since the 1920s, when the king had been forced to accept freedom of worship, the *inshongore* sent their children to catechism class. To preserve the essence of the monarchy, Musinga attempted to appease the Europeans while checking the spread of Christianity.[39] In 1925, the Belgian administration banished the lead ritualist Gashamura to Burundi and banned *ubwiru* (the sacred oral esoteric code that mystically regulated the functions of the monarchy) and the celebration of the harvest feast known as *umunganura*. The Catholic Church dealt this blow to the religious institutions at the foundation of the sacred kingdom as a way of implementing a tabula rasa. Musinga's resistance led to his deposition in 1931 at the request of Vicar Apostolic Léon Classe on grounds of "poor management, passive resistance, obscurantism, and dissoluteness in his private life."[40] Mwami Musinga had not understood that with a religion as strong as Christianity, the only hope for the monarchy resided in assimilating the religion just as it had done with the cult of Ryangombe.[41] He was replaced by his son Rudahigwa, who went by the dynastic name Mutara. The colonial administration and the vicar apostolic crowned him in a ceremony from which Rwandans were excluded from playing any role. Mutara Rudahigwa was thus perceived as the "mwami of the whites."[42] The demystification of the Rwandan monarchy emptied the institution of its cultural and political substance, which had up to then successfully maintained some measure of national unity.

The triumph of the Catholic Church was witnessed in the years that followed the deposition of Mwami Musinga. Rwandans, especially Tutsis, converted to Catholicism in the thousands, an event referred to as *La Tornade du Saint-Esprit* ("Tornado of the Holy Spirit").[43] Converts were required to renounce their cultural identity and zealously do away with pagan symbols.[44]

The Policy of Ethnic Exclusion

Until World War II, both the religious and administrative arms of colonial rule were profoundly influenced by the racist ideology Gobineau famously articulated in the mid-nineteenth century, which divided humanity into a hierarchy of distinct races. The application of the Hamitic hypothesis in Africa had a great impact on Rwanda, especially on Rwandans who attended colonial schools. According to this myth, Hamites were of "Caucasian" origin, were the agents of "civilization" in black Africa, and were lighter skinned.[45] In Rwanda, the colonialists identified Tutsis as the superior race, born to rule over the Hutu, who in turn were destined to be servants, whereas the Twa were relegated to the less than human.[46] In the middle of the 1920s, this ideological mind-set within the Catholic Church hierarchy combined well with the directives from Rome on the training of African elites to evangelize the natives.[47] After gaining the political support of the Tutsi elite, the next stage of establishing "ethnic" discrimination was founding schools that differentiated Hutu from Tutsi students by reserving for Tutsis the opportunities to advance in education (which included learning French). Initially, the mwami and the aristocracy declined to send their children to school, but they changed their minds when they saw that the graduates of these schools would be appointed to administrative positions. The schools run by Catholic missionaries therefore became an important instrument for actively disseminating the Hamitic myth within Rwandan society.[48] Earlier in 1919, the Belgians sought to appease Mwami Musinga by founding a public school in Nyanza for the sons of chiefs, to which Musinga sent his three eldest sons. The school was replaced in the early 1930s by the Groupe scolaire d'Astrida, whose role was to train clerks and technicians for the colonial administration. Until the 1959 revolution, the school's student body, and the administrative section in particular, were almost entirely Tutsi.[49]

The Restructuring of Rwandan Society

After 1919, the League of Nations granted Belgium the mandate over Rwanda and Burundi. The colonial administration undertook to make uniform the powers of the so-called customary chiefs. A number of provinces, such as Bukunzi and Busozo in the southwest and Ndorwa, Mulera, and Bushiru in the north had retained their autonomy, with Hutu chiefs in charge. Tutsi administrators from central Rwanda were subsequently appointed in their place.[50] The social impact of this move has been highlighted by Alison Des Forges:

> The people of Busozo and Bukunzi, like the Hutu in other areas, had idealized the mwami as their protector against the excessive greed of the notables and later against the centralizing zeal of the Europeans. With the destruction of the special status of Bukunzi and Busozo, the court's ability to protect the weak and those felt to be essential to the welfare of the kingdom suffered a serious blow.[51]

In 1926, Belgian authorities attacked the three-chief system, which consisted of the "chief of the land" in charge of agriculturalists, who was usually Hutu; the "chief of the pastures," who usually managed the pastures; and the "chief of warriors," who managed the cattle assigned to the army. The latter two posts were normally held by Tutsis, and both positions could be held by the same person. At the local level were a sizable number of people—Hutu, Tutsi, and Twa—who were the direct clients of the mwami. All of the leaders were constantly engaged in power struggles, giving the population some flexibility in playing the leaders against each other.[52]

Governor Charles Voisin's reform in 1926 replaced this tripartite system with a single chief and a limited number of subchiefs under him, which removed all Hutus from positions of authority. The reforms also reorganized all the territories so that 1,278 local notables, many of whom were Tutsi, were thereby required to work in the fields.[53] The position of chiefs and subchief were also made increasingly bureaucratic, with the accompanying regulation by strict rules and quantified performance targets. Schooling increasingly became a criterion for appointment.

A fraction of tributes were also converted into monetary payment. In 1927, the colonial administration transformed *uburetwa* into compulsory manual labor of every able-bodied adult male for one out of seven days. Rather than ease the burden of exactions, this modification actually greatly aggravated them because it transferred the *uburetwa* requirement from the household to the individual. In their haste to impose uniformity, the administration extended *uburetwa* to the rest of the country, including regions where until then, the original system was hardly known, if at all. To these customary levies was added unpaid forced labor for "public interest" (*akazi*), especially for road and terrace construction and maintenance.[54] There was also "work imposed by the European authority in the interest of the workers themselves,"[55] which consisted of compulsory cultivation of food crops such as cassava (to fight against famine) or of cash crops such as coffee. The peasantry was therefore under the pressure of various levies and tributes, both customary and colonial. *Akazi* was by far the heaviest burden by virtue of the difficult work and the number of days one would be away from one's of land, and as if things could get any worse, the official limit of sixty days of duty per year was often not upheld.[56]

Many men were forced to migrate in search of wage employment to pay the taxes they owed the state. After establishing a detailed comparison of the levies and compulsory manual labor before and after the reforms, Filip Reyntjens concurs with René Lemarchand, that he "rightly concludes that under the Belgian administration, the plight of the Hutu population was worse than ever before."[57] The forced migration of workers at the end of the 1920s to the Katanga mines in neighboring Congo, desperate for labor, would complete the Belgian colonial "employment policy" in Rwanda. To implement the policy, the capacity of the chiefs and subchiefs was boosted by hiring *capita* (foremen), police officers, and extra staff to join them at the bottom of the administrative ladder. These new employees frequently resorted to flogging and were nicknamed *abamotsi* ("barkers").[58] The Belgian government's "modernization" project was driven by its determination to make the country financially self-sufficient. The administration had access to labor investment, the only immediately and abundantly available resource, and overused it.[59] Forcing people to work compelled tens of thousands of Rwandans to migrate, either temporarily or permanently, to the British colonies of Uganda and Tanganyika in search of voluntary paid employment. At the end of the 1920s, about fifty thousand Rwandans, roughly one out of every six adult males, were emigrating every year.[60] Rwanda's involvement in the Allied war effort in the 1940s only worsened the situation.[61] Substantial amounts of foodstuffs and numbers of cattle were exacted from the population in Rwanda to feed mineworkers in Congo; the minerals fed the Allied war industry. In light of Rwanda's already precarious food situation and poor climatic conditions, this strain on the country's resources caused an unprecedented famine.

The colonial era in the first half of the twentieth century was divided into two distinct periods. The first period, between 1900 and 1925, was characterized by collaboration between the Tutsi elite and the Europeans, especially in the control of the country's remoter regions.[62] During the second period, from 1926 to 1952, the whole of Rwandan society, rulers and ruled alike, became politically, administratively, and religiously confined within the rigid colonial structure.

In theory, Belgium had decided since 1920 to govern Rwanda by indirect rule. In practice, however, and as Reyntjens notes, the Belgian colonial regime wielded absolute power.[63] The second period stood out as one of totalitarian colonial rule, in which the subordinate native authorities, who had become ex-

clusively Tutsi, were responsible for implementation of the colonial development policies the general population considered oppressive and pervasive.
This political and administrative structure, which entrenched ethnic discrimination within the native administration, colluded with the Catholic Church's
determination to wipe out the sociocultural practices that united Rwandans.
Finally, the missionary-run colonial schools disseminated the idea of the racial
superiority of the Tutsi over the Hutu.

After Mwami Musinga was deposed in 1931, the elites abandoned any
attempt at political and cultural resistance.[64] Nevertheless, the chiefs and subchiefs maintained some leverage within the system through their power to require forced labor from some people or exempt others from it.[65] This prerog-
ative became a tool of social and ethnic favoritism, and the colonial system
turned a blind eye to such abuses as long as the native authorities produced
results.

Changes Toward the Close of Colonial Rule (1945–1959)

At the end of World War II, the League of Nations was replaced by the UN.
The time had come for people to exercise self-determination and to challenge
colonial imperialism, and this wind of change had peculiar implications for
Ruanda-Urundi, which had come under "trusteeship." Political development
was expected to lead to mass participation in institutions of elective representation. This pressure from the newly instituted UN led Belgium to invest
heavily in helping its territories try to catch up with the neighboring colonies
in terms of development.[66]

The policies were reflected in the "Ten-Year Economic and Social Development Plan for Ruanda-Urundi, 1949–1959," which gave priority to the purchase of equipment, particularly for Usumbura, the colonial capital of Ruanda-
Urundi, allocating only 7 percent to agriculture and livestock. The main policy
for tackling the population explosion in its initial stages and the accompanying
increase in pressure on the land was to organize unused land into small hold-
ings in order to reduce congestion in the most densely populated regions.
Health, education, and social services experienced significant improvement.
The number of students attending primary school jumped from 30,000 in 1930
to 270,000 in 1960 out of the eligible 1.1 million.[67] Most of the students did
not attend school beyond the first or second year. Access to secondary school
education remained restricted and subject to systematic discrimination disfa-
voring the Hutu, which became one of the focal points of the most intense social conflict.

Even though Rwandan society had evolved in an environment of great
deprivation, it had also been modernized by 1950, thanks to the cash economy
introduced throughout the country, but the structures of ethnic discrimination
favoring the Tutsi begun in the 1920s persisted in new forms of discrimination,

especially in education and wage employment.[68] A key obstacle in the country's path to modernization was the discrimination against the Hutu within the school system, under the control of the Catholic Church and the colonial administration. The training of locals to become administrators, chiefs, subchiefs, medical or veterinary assistants, agriculturalists, and magistrates was offered only at the government-owned but church-run Groupe scolaire d'Astrida. Most of the students were Tutsi and formed a special elite regardless of their family background.[69] Even after they had graduated, "Astridian" alumni were expected to distinguish themselves.

Among the peasants, particularly Hutus, the best option for the most intelligent students was to study in the seminaries, where the humanist training did not prepare them for administrative posts, and so they would become teachers or lower-level workers. This social class, which was often found within the church, comprised ambitious and frustrated intellectuals known as *séminaristes*.[70] The *séminaristes* formed a social class that produced the Hutu counterelite.

The conflict at the close of the colonial era was essentially a struggle between the *évolués,* both Astridians and *séminaristes*, to gain access to the lucrative administrative posts within the colonial government and later access to power at independence. In their revolutionary quest, the *séminaristes* drew the support of the rural intelligentsia comprising primary school teachers, lower-level employees, artisans, and peasants who had often worked away from their home regions.[71] These people, who had managed to pull away from the grip of the subchiefs, were increasingly conscious of the injustice inherent in the forced-labor system.[72]

But for the general population there was little difference between Hutu and Tutsi. The great majority of Tutsi shared the same living conditions as their Hutu neighbors as shown by the results of the study conducted in Rwanda's rural areas in the mid-1950s. When excluding the tiny minority of those employed by the colonial state, Hutu and Tutsi families had almost the same level of average annual income, 4.439 Belgian francs for Tutsi and 4.249 for Hutu.[73]

Changes took place alongside the emergence of a new European workforce. From the 1940s onward, the former missionaries, mostly conservative, were replaced by younger Belgian priests who brought with them the socialist sensibilities of European leftist Catholics.[74] These new missionaries took up the cause of the "Hutu majority." The appointment in 1955 of the Swiss André Perraudin as head of the Catholic Church in Rwanda emboldened the Hutu cause.[75]

A comprehensive study by Ian Linden highlights two major events in the triangular relationship between the Europeans, the Tutsi elite, and the Hutu elite. At the beginning of the 1950s, the Rwandan elites formed a united front against the Europeans. A few years later, the Hutu intellectuals, disillusioned by their distant Tutsi peers, sought the support of the new missionaries, who were only too pleased with this interaction because it conformed to their socialist Catholicism.[76]

Faced with the nationalist cultural movement driven by Tutsi priests and seminarists promoting a social order that favored the Tutsi, members of the Hutu elite also saw their grievances from a "racial" angle.[77] However, Linden questions the motives of the Belgian clergy: Was this a subtle plot by the colonialist church to divide and break up a potentially powerful nationalist movement led by a Tutsi vanguard? Or was it the upwelling of Hutu political consciousness that for the first time saw through the mystification of Tutsi rule? "The young missionaries at the elbow of the counterelite were both in favor of drastic social reform and sympathetic toward independence movements, . . . but conservative Tutsi 'nationalism' disqualified itself by its elitist contempt for the mass population."[78]

In a dynamic well documented, there is little proof of missionaries' supposed sympathy toward African self-determination movements, particularly in Rwanda. Given the loyalties of the main Hutu protagonists to the missionaries up until 1959, one must conclude that the missionaries' support for reform was also nurtured by the desire for power and the desire to defend the status and privileges enjoyed by the Catholic Church in the country.

In retrospect, the 1950s emerge as a prerevolutionary period. Following two missions to Rwanda in 1948 and 1959, the UN Trusteeship Council condemned the slow pace of the country's political transition. The Belgians responded to this criticism with a decree on July 14, 1952, establishing representative councils at different levels of the administrative hierarchy, from the subchiefs and chiefs to the national level. These consultative structures were supposed to usher in democratization; however, the appointments to these representative councils at the first, subchieftaincy, level were made by the subchiefs, which made them the only real voters.[79] In the first "elections" held in 1953, Hutus won 58.38 percent of the seats at the lowes level, but only three Hutus were elected into the Country Supreme Council (CSP), constituting 9.4 percent of the seats. In the subsequent elections in 1956, in which members of the lowest-level electoral colleges were elected by adult male suffrage, the Hutus won 66.7 percent of the seats. However, their representation at the Supreme Council diminished because they garnered only 6 percent of the seats. Some observers have blamed this difference in Hutu representation in the electoral colleges and at the highest level of the Supreme Council on elections conducted by indirect vote and on the feudal mind-set of the Hutus, still mesmerized by the social prestige of the leaders, the "notables."[80]

One can therefore say that the elections of 1953 and 1956 had little impact on the integration of the Hutu into the local political and administrative hierarchy. These two failed attempts at democratization had raised the Hutu leaders' expectations but had also provoked the feeling that the beginning of the end of the traditional order was in sight.[81] Between 1953 and 1959, Mwami Rudahigwa and the Tutsi elite in the Supreme Council brought about social reforms within the limits of their consultative capacity. The most important of these changes was abolishing the pastoral clientship system of *ubuhake* in 1954 in favor of the equal sharing of cows between clients and patrons. But the preservation of *ibikingi* curtailed the reforms' potential for liberation.[82]

Meanwhile, environmental pressure from the growing population led to compromises made often with the approval of the chiefs and subchiefs. "The cow steps back, and the hoe moves forward," a 1959 report announced.[83] In 1958, Chief Prosper Bwanakweri mentioned the evolution taking place on the hills, where the transfer of portions of *ibikingi* to landless farmers appeared to have become common, which he considered irreversible and even desirable.[84] The CSP, controlled by young chiefs who had graduated from the Astrida school, at first demonstrated a commitment to limited reforms as they sought to retain the essence of the traditional hierarchical order. According to Lemarchand, these young people were deeply aware of the great qualities of their cultural heritage but were also conscious of the need to adapt their institutions to democratic demands, but few had an idea of how that could be carried out.[85]

Between 1956 and 1959, debates on injustices and ways to address them intensified. The debates were roughly guided by these questions: Was there a Hutu-Tutsi problem? Was the problem racial or social? To address these problems, should one begin with independence and have reforms later, or should it be democracy first and independence afterward? The profoundly diverging public positions taken prepared the ideological grounds for what was to become an open conflict.[86]

Rudahigwa's "Unexpected Move" in His Final Days

Following the appointment on April 16, 1959, of a Belgian parliamentary working group to study the political problem in Ruanda-Urundi, the mwami decided to take initiative by drawing up a strategy for the country's democratization before independence within the framework of internal self-rule. The context for this "unexpected move" is provided in a document stamped "strictly confidential," dated April 12, 1959, written by Lazarre Ndazaro, who appears to have been an informer for the colonial administration, and addressed to the resident of Rwanda and to the Ruanda-Urundi vice-governor general.[87] The document contains three main sections: the minutes of the twentieth session of the CSP held on April 11, 1959, the report on a secret meeting at the palace, and an overall conclusion. Ndazaro specifically reported, "A secret meeting had just taken place at the palace on the night of April 11 and 12," attended by the members of the mwami's think tank, such as the priests Janvier

Murenzi and Alexis Kagame as well as Claver Bagilishya, Pierre Mungarulire, Servilien Runuya, and other members of the political commission of the CSP, namely, Jean Chrysostome Rwangombwa, Anasthase Makuza, and Father Deogratias Mbandiwimfura.[88] Absent from the meeting was Michel Kayihura, president of the commission.

The objective of this overnight meeting was to draw up a broad outline of proposals the political commission would include in the report it would present to the Belgian parliamentary working group about to arrive. The main issues discussed were the inevitability of democracy, the establishment of internal self-rule, the formation of a government headed by the mwami, and the conversion of subchieftaincies into communes. In his general conclusion, Ndazaro provides analysis of the political situation prevailing in Nyanza, which in turn sheds light on the evolution in Mwami Rudahigwa's political thinking three months before his death. However, Ndazaro also paints a general picture of the different orientations that emerged from the CSP debate: conservatives clung to their positions under threat; progressive democrats made up about a third of the younger members close to the colonial administration; and finally opportunists formed the majority. The report's general conclusion merits closer attention because it reveals the complex situation on the eve of independence, often obscured by the reduction of issues to "ethnicity":

> The regime has been forced to retreat from open confrontation because of internal public disapproval. This option has given way to a practice of blackmail, even more widely spread among the évolués and gullible Batutsi than among the working classes. In this propagandistic blackmail the colonial administration, the church missions, and the Hutu elites are being accused of sowing discord among Rwandans by maintaining the public attention on the social and racial discrimination inherent in the feudal regime and supported by the former ruling class.
>
> This blackmail is coupled with a deliberate policy to rally all the smartest and well-educated Rwandans to support the crown. Those who stand to gain the most are the current members of the opposition, whose bold persistence has shown them to be more useful than the usual sycophants who will make an about-face at the slightest challenge.
>
> They have devised three ways to win over the antifeudalists: appeal to family influence, avoid contradicting what the antifeudalists stand for, avoid upsetting them in public or appearing less "sympathetic" than Europeans toward them, and dangling before them personal benefits to be gained from self-rule, such as high-profile and coveted positions, all on the condition that antifeudalists support and collaborate in achieving the monarchy's political objectives. The administration, bound by its respect for the law and "equal status," can never offer the same privileges.[89] The intended result is that the colonial administration will find itself isolated and will have no choice but to give in and recommend the end of the trusteeship. . . .
>
> This is the smartest ever political move from the native administration. It uses convincing arguments based on its apparent respect for freedom of expression, nationalist fervor, and immediate material gain. Under

normal circumstances, and as long as it is well implemented and does not meet an equally strong opposition, this approach cannot fail.*[90]

This document shows that Rudahigwa had abandoned his policy of confrontation with the leaders of the Hutu cause. His strategy seems to have consisted of winning over these leaders, and in so doing, isolating the colonial administration. We also witness here the dynamics of political scheming: the mwami was seeking to attract the Hutu leaders, and Ndazaro, the author of the document, was proposing that the colonial administration hit back by employing the carrot-and-stick approach with Tutsi "opportunists" within the CSP.

In April 1959, the CSP submitted to the Belgian working group a report proposing the democratization of the country before independence within the framework of self-rule. It envisioned the transformation of the subchieftaincies into communes and the election of commune councilors by direct universal suffrage as well as the election of the burgomaster by the commune council. At a higher level would be territories whose councils comprised two delegates per commune.[91] A new supreme council of the country would comprise a delegate from each commune, the presidents of the provincial councils, and a number of coopted members. By including a majority made up of delegates from the communes, the CSP in this new draft would allow more direct representation. During a meeting of the customary authorities held from April 20 to 24, 1959, the mwami managed to convince forty-three of the forty-four chiefs to accept the principle of a collective resignation.[92] The CSP seems to have pulled the rug out from under the feet of the mwami's critics.

At the end of three years of political debate from 1956 to 1959, distinct ideological trends had emerged. The first was that of the mwami and the CSP, who saw the protests of the Hutu counterelite as instigated by Western colonialism. The social reform of the CSP, cut short by the death of Mwami Rudahigwa, was accompanied for a long time by an obstinate blindness to the political reality based on overestimation of the historically central role played by the monarchy and the aristocracy. In reality, the monarchy's roots had already been profoundly undermined by colonial rule and the collaboration between the Rwandan nobility and the colonial administration in oppressing people. After the mwami and some of his chiefs had cut ties with Western colonialists, they adopted a confrontational approach, ignoring the unequal power relations and counting almost entirely on both the faraway UN to neutralize the Belgian trusteeship authority and on their influence on the population. These Tutsi neotraditional leaders had refused to recognize the symbolic power of the Hutu leaders for too long because they considered the latter as instruments of the colonial administration and the church. Mwami Rudahigwa's

---

*Quotes from sources originally in French are translated by Wandia Njoya.

action now was late.[93] At a broader level, Rwanda's underdeveloped modern political culture and its isolation from the rest of the world, both encouraged by the near monopoly of the education system under the white fathers as well as by the obscurantist Belgian tutelage, prevented more Rwandans from understanding sooner the extent to which the native political regime had lost touch with unfolding realities.[94]

However, even if the mwami seems to have realized belatedly the political danger facing the monarchy as well as the unity of Rwandans, he did want to act decisively. It is interesting to note that a few months before his death, some of his political adversaries thought him close to victory were it not for the decisive actions designed to oppose him.

The other remarkable feature of this period was an ideological division among the Hutu revolutionaries powerful enough to cause a schism within the Hutu Social Movement (Mouvement Social Muhutu) soon after the release of the Hutu manifesto.[95] One faction analyzed the political conflict in terms of race, whereas the other saw it more in terms of social class. The option of "racial" confrontation offered by the PARMEHUTU planted the seed that would tear Rwanda's social fabric apart.[96] The Catholic Church, under the leadership of Bishop Perraudin, gave moral support to the PARMEHUTU alternative and access to a wider audience through the control of the Kinyarwanda-language newspapers as well as to the entire network of Catholic orders and associations all around the country.[97]

The Path to Revolution (1959–1961)

The different stages in the social revolution are as follows.

The death of Mwami Rudahigwa. On July 25, 1959, Mwami Rudahigwa died in Bujumbura at the hands of his Belgian personal physician after having an allergic reaction to a shot of penicillin. The debate over whether his death was accidental or criminal persists given the absence of an autopsy and the king's agenda of political reform. According to a witness at the time, Rudahigwa's death left the impression that a threshold had now been breached: "Enemies and friends alike got the impression that from now on, anything—from the best to the worst—was possible in Rwanda."[98]

The crowning of Kigeri V Ndahindurwa. During Mwami Rudahigwa's funeral, the members of the king's court insisted that the mwami could not be buried before his successor was named. Ndahindurwa, Rudahigwa's young brother, was proclaimed mwami. Though taken by surprise, Resident-General Jean-Paul Harroy accepted the enthronement on the condition that the new king rule as a constitutional monarch. The traditionalists had won a first round.[99]

The creation of political parties. Three major Rwandan political parties were created in the months of September and October 1959 in addition to the Association for the Social Welfare of the Masses (APROSOMA), founded a few months earlier. The Rwandan National Union (UNAR) was formed on September 3, 1959, with objectives of immediate *independence* and the establishment of a constitutional monarchy. Among its officials were Kigali businessman François Rukeba, who served as president, and three prominent chiefs.[100] The party was also supported by the Swahili people living in the urban centers. In a confidential circular, Bishop Perraudin attacked the party's "'national socialism,' its anticlericalism, and its communist and Islamic tendencies."[101]

The Rwandan Democratic Union (RADER), created with the support of the Belgian administration and the Kabgayi Diocese, led by Father Arthur Dejemeppe, attempted to bring together progressive Tutsis (Astridians) and Hutus within a democratic party sympathetic to Belgian interests.[102] Made up of intellectually brilliant personalities such as its president, Chief Bwanakweri, RADER attracted mainly urban intellectuals and failed to build a support base among the grassroots.

On September 26, 1959, Grégoire Kayibanda transformed the Hutu Social Movement (MSM) into the PARMEHUTU with the blessing of Canon Eugene Ernotte and Father Réginald Endriatis. Its foundation was explicitly "racial"; it was fighting against the "hegemony of the invading Tutsi race." At a joint meeting with APROSOMA at Astrida, Kayibanda articulated his new party's ideology as follows:

> Our movement is targeted at the Hutu, who have been despised, humiliated, and regarded with contempt by the Tutsi. If we want to help the Hutu, let's not confuse them by playing with words. . . . Many wonder what APROSOMA means. They are told that APROSOMA are the "enemies of the mwami" and "monsters who want to devour the Batutsi." . . . We need to enlighten the people that we are here to restore the country to its real owners, as this is the country of the Bahutu. The small Mututsi came together with the noble ones. Who cleared the forest? There you have it![103]

The PARMEHUTU slogan was "democracy first, independence later." Kayibanda was the principal leader and was to become the future president of the republic. The party was organized into cells modeled on the Legion of Maria, a Catholic order, and had a propagandist on every hill. However, it was unequally spread and centered mainly in Gitarama and Ruhengeri Prefectures.

APROSOMA, formed in November 1957, broke away from the MSM of Kayibanda because Joseph Gitera opposed ethnic confrontation, advocating instead a sociopolitical critique. Later APROSOMA became a political party in February 1959. The party members were largely drawn from Hutus from

Astrida, such as its president, Gitera; its vice president, Aloys Munyangaju; and their close associates, Isidore Nzeyimana and Germain Gasingwa. Gitera's virulent opposition to the monarchy made him, at the beginning of the revolution, the principal enemy of the monarchy's supporters.[104]

The activities of the political parties, especially the mass rallies, created a confrontational environment bound to explode into violence. The conflict between UNAR and the Belgian administration became open starting September 12, 1959, when UNAR held its first rally. Among those who spoke were three UNAR chiefs who issued veiled criticisms against the Belgian administration, and others were more violent and unequivocal in their speeches. The Belgian trustee authority sanctioned the three chiefs through disciplinary transfers; instead the sanctioned chiefs tendered their resignations. The mwami openly took sides with UNAR and intervened on its behalf. Demonstrations were held in the areas under the chiefs' jurisdiction as well as in Kigali. Clashes between the police and the demonstrators left one person dead and four people injured. The tension had reached its peak, and every day UNAR published tracts attacking the trustee authorities, Bishop Perraudin, and RADER leaders Bwanakweri and Ndazaro. The trustee administration called in troop reinforcements from Congo.

The jacquerie *(rebellion) of 1959.* The "spark which ignited the powder keg"[105] was the slapping of Dominique Mbonyumutwa, a Hutu subchief and a key PARMEHUTU figure, by members of the UNAR youth wing in Gitarama. Soon after, a rumor spread that Mbonyumutwa had succumbed to injuries that he never had. On November 3, 1959, in the north in what was to become Gitarama Prefecture and in the Ndiza chiefdoms, where Mbonyumutwa's subchiefdom was located, a group of protestors who had come to express their anger grabbed Nkusi, a Tutsi subchief, and cut him down with machetes. Within one day, a revolt driven by complex motives swept across a large part of the country. The violence began in Ndiza and Bumbogo regions and spread to Ruhengeri and Gisenyi Prefectures, where traditional clan autonomy was strong and where communities grappled with acute land shortage, and then engulfed the rest of the country.[106] Lemarchand observes that people "burned and pillaged because they had been told to do so and because the operation did not seem to involve great risks and enabled them to seize the loot in the victim's hut."[107] Often, the peasant arsonists were told by PARMEHUTU activists they were acting on the orders of Kigeri, and during the mwami's subsequent peace tour of the country, some asked to be remunerated. The primary target of attack was the chiefs, subchiefs, and other Tutsi notables.[108]

On November 6, the monarchist circles organized a retaliatory attack targeted at the leaders of the APROSOMA and PARMEHUTU parties, reviving the traditional armies. Groups of Twa killers murdered several Hutu leaders in the Gitarama Prefecture and the surrounding areas of Nyanza. On November

13, in the face of a vigorous Tutsi counterattack, Kayibanda sent a telegram to the UN requesting the division of the country into separate Tutsi and Hutu zones,[109] and the telegram was read on the radio.[110] On November 10, the Belgian trustee administration had called in troops from Congo and declared a state of emergency that placed the country under the military command of Colonel Guy Logiest, appointed the "special resident" of Rwanda. The Belgian military intervention ended the repression by the monarchy threatening to have the upper hand in the revolt.[111] The events of November were essentially a peasant revolt against the leaders, hence the use of the term *"jacquerie"* in scholarship on these events.

Lemarchand underscores the importance of the Belgian role with regard to these conflicts: "The decisive factor was that the Belgian authorities reacted to these 'objective' conditions in such a way as to make the success of the revolution a foregone conclusion. After the Belgian administrators had decided on the spot that the peasant uprisings of November 1959 were a revolution (which they were obviously not), the real revolution could no longer be averted."[112]

At the end of November, there was a semblance of calm in the country also grappling with a massive exodus of Tutsi refugees who could no longer return to their hills. The visiting mission of the UN estimated the number of deaths as at least 200.[113] By the end of the revolt, 21 Tutsi chiefs and 332 subchiefs, constituting more than half of the officials, had lost their positions.[114] The extent of the violence and the support of the administration led to a radical change, a point of no return for the Hutu movement. The abolition of the monarchy, unimaginable up to this point, became the main agenda, and the liquidation of the Tutsi elite in particular became a legitimate goal. By transferring power to the Hutu, Colonel Logiest has been the most important architect of this revolution.

Appointment of interim authorities. Colonel Logiest replaced the Tutsi authorities ousted by the Hutu members or PARMEHUTU sympathizers. He also did everything within his power to get rid of chiefs and subchiefs not expelled by their respective populations.[115] The new interim authorities behaved like activists harassing the Tutsi, and the administration did not intervene to restrain these excesses.[116] This provoked a fresh wave of refugees, some of whom settled in the camps for the displaced at Nyamata. Others chose exile in the neighboring countries. The number of refugees leaped from 7,000 at the end of November 1959 to 22,000 by April 1960.[117] In 1960, the PARMEHUTU, now bearing the name MDR-PARMEHUTU, sent out the "Earnest Appeal from Ruanda to All the Anticolonialists of the World," in which it stated, "Tell the Tutsi who are in Dar es-Salaam [*sic*] that they can either continue their journey toward Abyssinia and resettle in the land of their ancestors or resolve to accept democracy and humbly return to Rwanda."[118]

The commune elections. The special resident organized communal elections for June 1960. UNAR, which had lost a large portion of its political base through the massive displacement of Tutsis and several Hutus faithful to the monarchy, decided to boycott the elections, leading to what Alexis Kagame called "political suicide."[119] The Belgian authorities banned all campaign material supporting the boycott. Colonel Logiest campaigned for the PARME-HUTU by cautioning the voters against UNAR.[120] The elections were marred by numerous incidents of violence committed by both sides. The most affected areas this time were the south and the west of the country, particularly in Gikongoro and Kibuye Prefectures.

About 80 percent of the population of voting age was registered to vote; 21.8 percent of them boycotted the elections in response to the call by UNAR, and the PARMEHUTU won 70 percent of the vote. But according to d'Herte-feld, the national average of those who did not vote had little significant impact. More interesting is a comparison between an A zone (158 communes; 330,506 registered voters; that is, 68.6 percent of the total registered voters) where abstention was at 5.2 percent, and a B zone (71 communes; 152,234 registered voters; that is, 31.5 percent of the registered voters) where abstention stood at 57.7 percent. This B zone was relatively homogeneous and stretched across all the east and part of the central and southern regions of the country as well as a strip in the extreme west.[121] One appreciates the magnitude of UNAR's political suicide when one considers that the party had rejected an opportunity to make itself a major actor in the new political arena.

In many regions, the new Hutu burgomasters found it difficult to find acceptance among the people. Some ambiguity in the framework establishing and regulating their positions, as well as the complicity of the Belgian authorities, enabled many burgomasters to use intimidation and clientism to rule their communes with a strong hand. No matter what abuses they committed, the burgomasters could count on the support of the Belgian administration.[122] They inevitably encountered the discontent and resistance of their constituents, most of them Hutu. The fear of mass dissatisfaction, the threat of incursions from across the border by Tutsi exiles, and the fear of the UN withdrawal of Belgium's trustee status prompted Hutu leaders to seek to complete the revolution.

The January 1961 coup of Gitarama. Having secured control at the local level, the revolutionaries set about to capture the central power. However, Hutu leaders feared that the program of national reconciliation (a conference bringing together all the political parties, a law of amnesty, and the repatriation of refugees), which the UN Trusteeship Council had set as a precondition for parliamentary elections, would provide a reprieve for UNAR that the latter would exploit to snatch back the reins of power.[123] The Hutu leaders therefore decided, with the complicity of Colonel Logiest, to present the UN and the vice-governor general a fait accompli. On January 28, 1961, 3,126 communal councilors and their burgomasters converged at Gitarama, where they proclaimed the dissolution of the monarchy, the establishment of the republic under President Mbonyumutwa, and the formation of a government led by Kayibanda as prime minister.[124] In its reaction to the coup, the UN Commission for Ruanda-Urundi observed, "A racial dictatorship of one party has been set up in Rwanda, and the developments of the last eighteen months have consisted in the transitions from one type of oppressive regime to another. Extremism is rewarded, and there is a danger that the [Tutsi] minority may find itself defenseless in the face of abuse."[125] Parliamentary elections and a referendum on the monarchy were finally set for September 25, and these essentially legalized the coup at Gitarama. For the PARMEHUTU burgomasters, the electoral campaign provided cover for the serious violence targeted not only at the political parties considered Tutsi, such as UNAR and RADER, but also at APROSOMA, which had broken ties with the PARMEHUTU. Colonel Logiest openly campaigned for the PARMEHUTU, and the movement won the elections with 77.7 percent of the vote. The monarchy was rejected by 75 percent of the voters.[126] On July 1, 1962, Rwanda gained independence.

Years later, the two main Belgian actors of this period would acknowledge the critical role played by the colonial administration in the revolutionary process. In his book published in 1984, the former resident-general, Harroy, talks of "an assisted revolution,"[127] and in Colonel Logiest's memoirs, he acknowledges his personal involvement and the integral role he and his Congolese troops played in the expulsion of the Tutsi aristocracy and the abolition of monarchy.[128]

The First Republic

The MDR-PARMEHUTU Dictatorship

A few months before Rwandan independence, the UN had instituted a number of measures toward reconciliation, contained in the New York accords signed on February 28, 1962. According to the agreement, UNAR would receive two ministerial posts, two posts of secretary of state, two prefect and subprefect posts, and one important post in the Refugee Commission. In the parliamentary elections, UNAR had won seven out of the forty-four seats in the national assembly. It also had an office in Kigali and published a periodical that relentlessly criticized the government.[129] These elements gave the impression that the new regime had genuinely accepted democratic practice, whereas in fact the opposite was true. In Butare Prefecture, Amandin Rugira, the PARMEHUTU regional secretary, systematically intimidated APROSOMA burgomasters and their constituents to the advantage of the PARMEHUTU to the extent that APROSOMA lost the Butare seat in the 1963 communal elections and practically ceased to exist.[130] The persecution of UNAR in 1962 and 1963 became more brutal: party members were subjected to permanent threats, arbitrary arrest, and violence. The PARMEHUTU imposed compulsory party membership. This oppression was followed by the execution of UNAR and RADER political representatives as part of the government's policy of terror following the attack by the *inyenzi* ("cockroaches," as the officials had nicknamed the rebels) in December 1963.

Refugees, Inyenzi, and Massacres

From November 1959 to September 1961, killings and insecurity forced tens of thousands of Tutsis, as well as a number of Hutus, to take refuge outside the country or to move into new settlement areas inside the country. During the proclamation of independence, the refugees numbered about 300,000. Of these, 120,000 were outside the country. After the 1963–1964 wave of violence, 300,000 refugees were registered with the UN High Commission for Refugees in Uganda, Burundi, Congo, and Tanzania.[131] Most of the refugees were peasants who had left their country with the hope of returning soon. Most of the UNAR leaders were wanted by the authorities and had fled the country from the start of "pacification." Abroad, and with the help of progressive governments, the refugees had organized a diplomatic offensive, especially at the UN headquarters, but their success was hampered by failure to enact the resolutions.

The most radical of these leaders joined the armed struggle and led refugees from the camps in neighboring countries in carrying out a number of attacks on Rwanda. Between March 1963 and November 1966, about a dozen significant attacks took place, with raids targeted at government officials and security personnel in the border regions. Each of the attacks acted as a signal for more or less widespread persecution of the Tutsi population within the country.

The December 1963 attack marked a turning point in the scale of repression, particularly with the genocidal massacres in Gikongoro.[132] On December 21, 1963, a few hundred *inyenzi* entered from Burundi armed with spears and arrows and some guns and managed to overrun the Gako military camp in Bugesera region. They proceeded to the internal refugee camp in Nyamata, where they increased their ranks to a thousand men and then headed for Kigali. They were stopped about twenty kilometers from the capital by the national guard, which was well armed and under the command of Belgian officers. The attackers suffered heavy losses, and the survivors returned to Burundi.[133] According to interviews Reyntjens carried out among Belgian and Rwandan security officers, they knew beforehand the site and time of attack, meaning the *inyenzi* had essentially walked into a trap.[134] One can therefore argue that President Kayibanda took advantage of the attack in order to unleash anti-Tutsi terror. About twenty UNAR and RADER leaders were arrested and executed. The president dispatched a minister to each of ten prefectures to supervise the organization of "self-defense" by the population, which led to a number of killings. The largest massacres took place in the Gikongoro prefecture and were supervised by Prefect André Nkeramugaba and Agriculture Minister Damien Nkezabera. The massacres began on December 23 before spreading to the other regions. The Hutu population, armed with machetes and spears, set about massacring Tutsis of the region, including women and children, in a systematic fashion. Lemarchand describes the situation as follows:

> In some places the prefects and the PARMEHUTU propagandists saw in the reprisals a golden opportunity to solidify their bases of support among the local Hutu populations. Realizing that a massive elimination of Tutsi would make their land "available" to Hutu, the politicians saw distinct political advantages in encouraging the liquidation of the local Tutsi population. Thus one can better understand why the prefect of Gikongoro, André Nkeramugaba, after he decided to present his candidacy to the National Assembly, in 1965, was elected by an overwhelming majority of votes in the prefecture of Gikongoro.[135]

In fact, Nkeramugaba's election slogan in 1965 was "If I am not elected, you may be prosecuted, but if I am elected, I will do my best to prevent any investigation." The prefecture had a large Tutsi population and was the heart of the political opposition to the regime. Conservative estimates put the number of deaths at around ten thousand. The news solicited strong reactions, but these were few given the suppression of information by the Rwandan and Belgian governments. Some newspapers talked of "genocide." Philosopher Bertrand Russell called the killings the "most horrible and systematic massacres we have witnessed since that of the Jews by the Nazis." Similar remarks came from Jean-Paul Sartre and Vatican Radio.[136] In response to these accusations, President Kayibanda made a "public address to the Rwandan emigrants or refugees abroad in the name of 'brotherly greetings'!" The statement read,

> The human lives that have been lost to terrorism despite our vigilance do not gain anything from the deafening noise of your lies. Who is acting genocidal? Ask yourselves this question honestly and answer it with your conscience. Are the Tutsis who have remained in the country and who live in fear of the popular anger provoked by your attacks, happy with your actions? . . . In the unlikely event that you capture Kigali, what will you say of the chaos of which you will be the primary victims? You say it among yourselves: "It would be the complete and rapid elimination of the Tutsi race." Who is for genocide?[137]

The Racist Anti-Tutsi Ideology

Until independence, the racist anti-Tutsi ideology the PARMEHUTU sought to popularize was primarily the work of party officials, leaders, and propagandists.[138] With independence, the PARMEHUTU widened the spectrum of those responsible for spreading its propaganda to include the state institutions, radio and print media, and schools. An intense and pervasive propaganda permeated leaders' speeches, radio waves, popular songs, and classrooms. According to the propaganda, the Tutsi was a foreigner who had conquered and oppressed the Hutu for four centuries, and the revolution and the republic were the expression of the Hutu majority's victory over the Tutsi minority. A troupe of professional singers had composed an entire repertoire of songs with these themes, and the songs were endlessly played on the radio, some becoming popular hits. A number of songs were in the form of a lament about the long servitude of the Hutu, and others were celebrations of the victory by the popular majority.[139]

However, the population also confronted the difficulties of everyday life. A commission of inquiry appointed by the Rwanda National Assembly in July 1968 noted,

> Unity, harmony, helping one another, trust, collaboration, and patriotism have lost their meaning and no longer exist. They have been replaced by denigration, hatred, selfishness, hostility, dishonesty, ill-feeling, and regionalism. The popular masses complain that the leaders misled them by telling them that their revolution of 1959 would liberate the people from injustice. The people now realize that it was a way for the leaders to carve out positions for themselves, which was followed by injustice worse than before. The people are not afraid to say that they long for the former system of rule through chiefs, as opposed to the current electoral system, because within the latter, those who deserve to be elected are alienated while those who do not deserve to be elected are picked as candidates.[140]

It is therefore important to understand the nuances of the popularity of the PARMEHUTU as well as the effects of its propaganda.

The Rise in Regionalism

After the political leaders of the Tutsi-dominated parties, UNAR and RADER, were eliminated at the beginning of 1964, the hegemony of the PARMEHUTU swallowed up APROSOMA and led to the establishment of a single-party state. In the absence of an external enemy or a political opponent to unite the regime, the PARMEHUTU splintered into different factions, rapidly weakening its social base. Now prominent party members from Butare were marginalized by members from Gitarama, the birthplace of President Kayibanda.[141]

The party was polarized between the leaders from Gitarama (in central Rwanda) and those from Ruhengeri (in the north). Within the group from the north, a conflict broke out following the National Assembly decision to redistribute the "feudal" landholdings. Many northern leaders hailed from Hutu *abakonde* families, that is, families of land patrons whose control had been usurped by Tutsi chiefs at the end of the nineteenth and the beginning of the twentieth centuries. The representatives of the former Hutu clients of the Tutsi chiefs also demanded the abolition of the client relationship with the ancient Hutu patrons and by extension the redistribution of the land. In the end, the *abakonde* prevailed, thereby posing a challenge to the ideals of the revolution, and no law on land distribution was passed.[142] This victory put the *abakonde* faction from the north in direct conflict with the Gitarama group. Through regionalist nepotism, the latter managed to marginalize and politically isolate its northern rivals.

Economic and Social Stagnation

July 1, 1962, marked the end of Belgian trusteeship, the elimination of the Tutsi aristocracy, and the political and later economic split of Ruanda-Urundi. The separation cost Rwanda dearly given that the capital of the former territory, the major infrastructure (international airport, port, major highways, telecommunications network), and the headquarters of major companies were located in Bujumbura. Rwanda had no capital city worthy of the name. The end of the trusteeship had brought with it a significant reduction in financial aid, and the elimination of the former aristocracy had also denied the country some of its administrative skills. The messy situation caused by political insecurity has increased the poverty of the country. Between 1964 and 1966, Rwandans on average received only 73 percent of the minimum required calories; globally only the people of Papua New Guinea were more hungry with 72 percent.[143]

By contrast, the peasants closest to the regime experienced, albeit temporarily, a significant improvement in their living conditions, a direct result of the revolutionary process. In 1966, the president issued a decree expropriating the land owned by Tutsis killed or in exile, and even in resettlement areas within the country. The decree only legalized a situation already in place and already exploited by PARMEHUTU supporters. In any case, many instances of "revolutionary" violence, such as the massacres in Gikongoro, were strongly motivated by taking the victims' land. The changes were further facilitated by the shift in priority from livestock to agriculture. The peasants embarked on seizing new land in less densely populated areas in the east as well as within the rural areas, draining the marshland previously reserved for pastures, and distributing the former *ibikingi* among themselves. These measures implemented from 1962 to 1969 increased cultivable land by 50 percent.[144]

In spite of this increase in land under cultivation, the output remained stagnant because of poor management and underinvestment in agriculture. The effects of this situation particularly were felt in the cash economy for crops such as coffee, the country's main foreign exchange earner, of which export volumes had increased only slightly. During this period, Rwanda never managed to attain its internationally set coffee quotas, a shortfall that meant a major loss of revenue for the state.

These difficult economic conditions at the beginning of the 1970s profoundly frustrated young intellectuals, mostly secondary and high school leavers, particularly those who were the lower-ranking employees, teachers, and students in high schools and the university.[145] These groups complained about their living conditions and the ceiling on their prospects of social advancement. The generation of the revolution had taken all the prestigious positions, and the economic stagnation offered no new opportunities. The young intellectuals thought of themselves as more qualified than the older generations and criticized the latter for their corrupt practices. The "Gitaramists" found themselves isolated at social and political levels as well as at the international level, where they remained confined to privileged relations within religious movements. Claudine Vidal, who was in Rwanda in 1973, paints a general picture of the situation prevailing at the time:

> Slowly the country turned into an island. The government feared its whole environment: it was horrified by the Congolese rebellions, reserved toward Tanzania, hostile to the Tutsi regime in Burundi, and dependent on the Ugandan roads for its imports. The inhabitants were inward looking and bore the country's slow shrinkage in silence. There were several forms of censorship: from a triumphant Catholic Church and from the government, which was afraid both of possible communist social movements and of the traditional manifestations that could be a reminder of the Tutsi imprint, which it considered with something like phobia. To the generalized lack of trust, rumor, secrecy, lack of breathing space: on top of material deprivation—the country was one of the poorest in the world and lacked almost everything—was added something like mental paralysis.[146]

The Events of 1973 and the Fall of the First Republic

Against the backdrop of the tension with neighboring Burundi, where the mainly Tutsi army had, in May and June 1972, conducted genocidal massacres against the Burundian Hutu, Kayibanda inspired a movement among high school and university students to reduce or eliminate the presence of Tutsis in the educational and private sectors. Tutsis had been criticized for being dominant in these two areas.[147] The relatively strong presence of Tutsis in secondary schools and universities was not only the legacy of the past discrimination in their favor but also the result of their determination to survive the hostile political and social environment. The private sector had also become a haven strongly sought by Tutsis given that quotas excluded them from the civil service. "Committees for public safety" emerged in schools and the university in order to beat and expel Tutsi teachers and students, who had become the scapegoat for social problems. Tens of thousands of Tutsis, this almost exclusively the youth, took the path of exile.

In the private sector, lists of Tutsi names were posted at the entrances of offices to turn Tutsis away. Foreign employers who wanted to defy the firing order were expelled on various pretexts. A month later the movement, initially dominant in the towns, began to spread to the rural areas, where it became a repeat of 1959: huts were burned down, Tutsi peasants were chased away, and many—possibly hundreds—were killed. The assailants also took the opportunity to settle scores not just with Tutsis but also with rich Hutus. Hutus originally from the north attacked Hutus from the central and the southern regions; in Kigali, names of government ministers appeared on the lists.

What was now happening went beyond the original plan of an ethnic conflict and was turning into an openly regional conflict between the north and the center-south. It would even seem that the political elite from the north secretly manipulated the crisis to destabilize the Kayibanda regime.[148] On March 22, 1973, after one month of watching the situation deteriorate, the Kayibanda government made a speech calling for pacification, and a ministerial commission toured the educational institutions to restore peace.[149] Intended to restore unity among Hutus behind Kayibanda's rule, the events had therefore achieved the opposite goal of isolating President Kayibanda further and rendering him more vulnerable. Within this context of tension and resumption of mistrust, two months later, on July 5, 1973, Major General Juvénal Habyarimana, minister of defense and army commander, seized power in the name of peace and reconciliation without meeting any resistance.[150]

Notes

1. See Young, ed., *Rising Tide of Cultural Pluralism*, 1993.
2. For a study of the missionary and colonial historiography, see Chrétien, "Hutu et Tutsi au Rwanda et au Burundi," 1985. One of the major thinkers of this school was Maquet, *Premises of Inequality in Rwanda*, 1961.
3. See Vansina, *Antecedents to Modern Rwanda*, 2004, pp. 31, 38.
4. Schoenbrun, *A Green Place, a Good Place*, 1998. Schoenbrun shows the ancient presence in the region including in present day Rwanda of Cushitic, Sudanic, Sahelian, and Bantu speaking communities ; Cox and Elliott, "Primary Adult Lactose Intolerance in the Kivu Lake Area," 1974; Sutton, "Antecedents of the Interlacustrine Kingdoms," 1993.
5. Schoenbrun, *A Green Place, a Good Place*, p. 230.
6. Ibid.; Reid, "Role of Cattle in the Later Iron Age Communities of Southern Uganda," 1991.
7. Vansina, *Antecedents to Modern Rwanda*, pp. 196–203.
8. Christian Thibon confirms this in a more systematic manner for precolonial Rwanda and Burundi. He also discusses the influence of this demographic pressure on the political and social evolution. Thibon, "Croissance et régimes démographiques," 1992.

9. Vansina, *Antecedents to Modern Rwanda*, p. 28.

10. Ibid., p. 40.

11. Ibid.

12. Ibid., p. 41.

13. Vansina insists on the fact that Ruganzu Ndori was Hima and not Tutsi. According to him, all the pastoralists in the subregion would have had to be Hima. In Rwanda, Burundi, Karagwe, and Buha, the label "Tutsi" designated the elite within the pastoralist community. In northern Rwanda, but above all in Tanzania and Uganda, the label "Tutsi" was unknown. Ibid., p. 46.

14. Ibid., 61–62.

15. Ibid., 65.

16. Mbonimana, "Les institutions traditionnelles constitutives de l'identité nationale," 2001, p. 29.

17. Berger, *Religion and Resistance,*1981, p. 81.

18. Republic of Rwanda, Office of the President, *Ubumwe*, 1998.

19. Nkurikiyimfura, *Le gros bétail et la société rwandaise,*1994, p. 88.

20. Ibid., p. 97.

21. Ibid., p. 96.

22. Vansina, *Antecedents to Modern Rwanda*, p.132.

23. Ibid., p. 134.

24. Ibid., p. 135.

25. Ibid., p. 136.

26. Ibid., pp. 138–139.

27. Ibid., p. 164.

28. Ntezimana, "Le Rwanda social, administratif, et politique à la fin du dix-neuvième siècle," 1990, p. 77.

29. Rumiya, *Le Rwanda sous le régime du mandat belge, 1916–1931,*1992, p.12; Newbury, *Cohesion of Oppression*, 1988, p. 60.

30. Vansina, *Antecedents to Modern Rwanda*, pp. 147–148.

31. Ntezimana, "Le Rwanda social," p. 78.

32. Des Forges, *Defeat Is the Only Bad News*, 2011, pp. 17–19; Rumiya, *Rwanda*, pp. 11–13.

33. Chrétien, "La révolte de Ndugutse, 1912," 1972.

34. Rumiya, *Rwanda*, p. 13.

35. For instance, Bukunzi, which had managed to remain autonomous, was subdued by a combined force of Tutsi notables and Belgian military forces (Newbury, *Cohesion of Oppression*, p. 63).

36. Ibid., 129.

37. Linden and Linden, *Church and Revolution in Rwanda*, 1977, pp. 59, 62.

38. De Lacger, quoted in Reyntjens, *Pouvoir et droit au Rwanda, droit public et evolution politique, 1916–1973*, 1985, p. 80.

39. Des Forges, *Defeat Is the Only Bad News*, pp. 183–193, 211, 214.

40. Reyntjens, *Pouvoir et droit au Rwanda*, p. 89.

41. Linden and Linden, *Church and Revolution*, p. 173.

42. Des Forges, *Defeat Is the Only Bad News*, p. 241.

43. Linden and Linden, *Church and Revolution*, p. 172.

44. Rutayisire, "Le remodelage de l'espace culturel rwandais par l'Église et la colonisation," 2001, p. 42.

45. Sanders, "Hamitic Hypothesis," 1969.

46. Chrétien, "Hutu et Tutsi au Rwanda et au Burundi," p. 39.

47. Linden and Linden, *Church and Revolution*, p. 162.

48. Ibid., 164–165.

49. Pierre Mungarulire, interview with author, June 25, 1998, Kigali.

50. Reyntjens, *Pouvoir et droit au Rwanda*, p. 98.

51. Des Forges, *Defeat Is the Only Bad News*, p. 203.

52. Newbury, *Cohesion of Oppression*, p. 45.

53. D'Hertefelt, in Reyntjens, *Pouvoir et droit au Rwanda*, p. 122.

54. Ibid., pp. 133, 138.

55. Guichaoua, *T. 1 de Destins paysanset politiques agraires en Afrique central*, 1989.

56. Reyntjens, *Pouvoiret droitau Rwanda*, p. 133.

57. Ibid., p. 142, referring to Lemarchand, "Coup in Rwanda," in Rotberg and Mazrui, eds., *Protest and Power in Black Africa*, 1970, p. 889.

58. Former chiefs testify that flogging with the *chicotte* was an integral part of the administrative policy at the time, whereas Newbury suggests that flogging in the 1940s was an abuse of power by colonial chiefs rather than a regular component of colonial administration. Republic of Rwanda, Office of the President, *Ubumwe*; Newbury, *Cohesion of Oppression*, p. 281, note 78. Rwandans saw these foremen as "barking dogs" (*aboyeur*s in French), but only the concept of barking was retained. The nickname almost became official, for even the administration referred to the foremen as *abamotsi*.

59. Gichaoua, *T. 1 de Destins paysans et politiques agraires en Afrique central*, p. 25.

60. Des Forges, *Defeat Is the Only Bad News*, p. 228. See also Chrétien, "Des sédentaires devenus migrants," 1978.

61. Gichaoua, *T. 1 de Destins paysans et politiques agraires en Afrique central*, p. 27.

62. We are using the term *colonization* to mean a tool of control and force in contrast to simple annexation.

63. Reyntjens, *Pouvoir et droit au Rwanda*, pp. 64, 167.

64. The population from the lower classes continued to practice traditional religion in secret. See Rutayisire, "Le remodelage de l'espace culturel rwandais par l'Église et la colonisation," p. 46.

65. Newbury, *Cohesion of Oppression*, p. 179.

66. Reyntjens, *Pouvoir et droit au Rwanda*, p. 210.

67. Guichaoua, *T. 1 de Destins paysans et politiques agraires en Afrique central*, pp. 28, 80.

68. Newbury, *Cohesion of Oppression*, p. 147.

69. Lemarchand, *Rwanda and Burundi*, 1970, p. 134.

70. Ibid., pp. 136, 140.

71. Ibid., p. 141.

72. Newbury, *Cohesion of Oppression*, p. 178.

73. Leurquin, *Le niveau de vie des populations rurales du Ruanda-Urundi*, p. 203.

74. Linden and Linden, *Church and Revolution*, p. 222.

75. Lemarchand, *Rwanda and Burundi*, p. 148.

76. Linden and Linden, *Church and Revolution*, p. 250.

77. Ibid., p. 91.

78. Ibid., pp. 250–251.

79. Reyntjens, *Pouvoir et droit au Rwanda*, pp. 186–188.

80. Maquet and d'Hertefelt, *Elections en société féodale*, 1959.

81. Lemarchand, *Rwanda and Burundi*, p. 149.

82. Reyntjens, *Pouvoiret droitau Rwanda*, p. 207; Lemarchand, *Rwanda and Burundi*, p. 130.

83. Belgian Ministry of the Colonies, *Rapport soumis par le Gouvernement belge à l'Assemblée générale des Nations unies au sujet de l'administration du Rwanda-Urundi pendant l'année 1959* (Brussels, 1960), p. 106.

84. Conseil supérieur du Pays (CSP), "Procès-verbal de la 15e session," in Nkurikiyimfura, *Le gros bétail et la société rwandaise*, p. 263.

85. Lemarchand, *Rwanda and Burundi*, p. 153. This was confirmed by Michel Kayihura, a former chief who was among the young Astridians. Kayihura, interview with author, May 27, 1998, Kigali.

86. Reyntjens, *Pouvoir et droit au Rwanda*, p. 236.

87. Ndazaro, "Situation politique à Nyanza," April 12, 1959, in *Rapport annuel 1959*, Archives africaines, RU 9 (11), Brussels.

88. Anastase Makuza was a Hutu coopted into the CSP, later to become one of the main leaders of Parmehutu.

89. "Equal status" (*statut unique*) was one of the political reforms made in Belgian territories on the path to independence. It offered equal pay and terms of service to both African and European civil servants.

90. Ndazaro, "Situation politique à Nyanza."

91. Nkundabagenzi, *Le Rwanda politique (1958–1960)*, 1961, pp.76–84.

92. Pierre Mungarulire, a former chief, interview with author, June 25, 1998, Kigali.

93. From this perspective, a comparison between his rule and that of his grandfather Rwabugiri is enlightening.

94. The white fathers were considered among the most retrogressive Catholic missionary orders.

95. At least this is the way René Lemarchand explains the split within the MSM. Lemarchand, *Rwanda and Burundi*, p. 151. Although the other leaders of APROSOMA were more consistent in their politically moderate position, Gitera, the head of the party, developed a radical rhetoric condemning the symbols of "Tutsi domination" such as the Kalinga drum. However, during the commune elections in 1960, Gitera caused a split within the party by creating, with a Tutsi called Rwubusisi, another party called APROSOMA-Rwanda-Union in order to distance himself from Hutu sectarianism. Reyntjens, *Pouvoir et droit au Rwanda*, p. 303, note 61.

96. Not all the members of the PARMEHUTU shared the same convictions about "race." For instance, Anastase Makuza, who came from Butare province, initially joined RADER and later asked to be a member of APROSOMA, a request turned down by Gitera because Makuza's wife was Tutsi. Reyntjens, *Pouvoir et droit au Rwanda*, p. 242, note 64.

97. Linden and Linden, *Church and Revolution*, p. 267.

98. Sebasoni, *Origines du Rwanda*, 2000, p. 135.

99. Reyntjens, *Pouvoir et droit au Rwanda*, pp. 156–157. The Belgian administration authorities held meetings attended by Bishop Perraudin, who came up with the idea of installing a regent (p. 248).

100. Both Hutus and Tutsis were among the most active members, including a cousin of Grégoire Kayibanda. Reyntjens, *Pouvoir et droi tau Rwanda*, p. 251.

101. Lemarchand, *Rwanda and Burundi*, p. 161.

102. Reyntjens, *Pouvoir et droit au Rwanda*, p. 252.

103. Musangamfura, "Le parti MDR-Parmehutu," 1987, p. 70.

104. Lemarchand, *Rwanda and Burundi*, p. 151.

105. Prunier, *Rwanda Crisis*, 1997, p. 48.

106. Linden and Linden, *Church and Revolution*, p. 267.

107. Lemarchand, *Rwanda and Burundi*, p. 163.

108. Ibid., p. 164.

109. "Télégramme envoyé à l'ONU par un leader hutu du Ruanda," telegram no. 426 from Ruanda-Urundi, November 13, 1959.

110. Sebasoni, *Origines du Rwanda*, p. 139.

111. Lemarchand, *Rwanda and Burundi*, p. 165.

112. Ibid., pp. 145–146.

113. Ibid., p. 147.

114. Linden and Linden, *Church and Revolution*, p. 269.

115. Reyntjens, *Pouvoir et droit au Rwanda*, p. 268.

116. Lemarchand, *Rwanda and Burundi*, pp. 173–177.

117. Ibid., p. 172.

118. Nkundabagenzi, *Le Rwanda politique*, pp. 247–248.

119. Kagame, *Un abrégé de l'histoire du Rwanda*, 1975, p. 187.

120. Reyntjens, *Pouvoir et droit au Rwanda*, p. 279.

121. d'Hertefelt, "Les élections communales," pp. 184, 427.

122. Lemarchand, *Rwanda and Burundi*, p. 184.

123. Ibid., p. 190.

124. Logiest, *Mission au Rwanda,*1988, p. 61; Lemarchand, *Rwanda and Burundi*, pp. 192–193.

125. *Interim report of the UN Commission for Ruanda-Urundi* (1961), cited by Lemarchand, *Rwanda and Burundi*, pp. 194–195.

126. Reyntjens, *Pouvoir et droit au Rwanda*, pp. 299, 303.

127. Harroy, *Rwanda: De la féodalité à la démocratie*, 1984.

128. Logiest, *Missionau Rwanda*.

129. Lemarchand, *Rwanda and Burundi*, p. 197.

130. Reyntjens, *Pouvoir et droit au Rwanda*, pp. 450–451.

131. Guichaoua, *Problem of the Rwandese Refugees and the Banyarwanda Populations in the Great Lakes Region,*1992, p. 16.

132. Lemarchand, *Rwanda and Burundi*, pp. 217–224.

133. Ibid., pp. 222–223.

134. Reyntjens, *Pouvoi ret droit au Rwanda*, p. 463.

135. Lemarchand, *Rwanda and Burundi*, p. 226.

136. Ibid., p. 224.

137. Erny, *Rwanda 1994*, 1994, p. 62.

138. "Propagandist" was an official position in the party and is the equivalent of party cadres within Marxist-Leninist organizational structures whose main focus is matters related to ideology.

139. Musangamfura, "Le parti MDR-PARMEHUTU."

140. Reyntjens, *Pouvoi ret droit au Rwanda*, p. 391.

141. Lemarchand, *Rwanda and Burundi*, p. 236.

142. Reyntjens, *Pouvoir et droit au Rwanda*, p. 493.

143. UNDP, *Human Development Report*, 1990.

144. Nzisabira, "Accumulation du peuplement," 1989, p. 39.

145. Lemarchand, *Rwanda and Burundi*, p. 238.

146. Vidal, *Sociologie des passions,* 1991, p. 171.

147. Reyntjens, *Pouvoir et droitau Rwanda*, p. 502.

148. Paternostre de la Mairieu, *"Toute ma vie pour VOUS mes frères!,"* 1994, p. 226; Chrétien, *Great Lakes of Africa*, p. 269.

149. Reyntjens, *Pouvoir et droit au Rwanda*, p. 503.

150. Ibid., pp. 506–508.

2

The Second Republic, 1973–1990

State-centered studies on this period have focused on the ethnic and regional discrimination policies, establishment of an authoritarian state, efforts to modernize the country, and finally, acute economic crisis.[1] However, a more complex perspective on the regime can be obtained by taking into account how both the common classes and the elite responded to different policies by the state. First, the central issue of the refugees, which preoccupied the regime from the beginning and throughout its reign, has often been overlooked or ignored in the analysis of President Juvénal Habyarimana's rule, yet, ultimately, it is this issue that will cause its downfall.[2] Second, despite the state-continuing marginalization of the Tutsi, Rwandan society did demonstrate some progress toward reconciliation and integration, to the extent that by the end of the 1980s, the Tutsi population was on the path to assimilation by the Hutu majority even though the assimilation was often an imposed survival tactic rather than a choice.

Finally, the rapid collapse of hegemonic control that President Habyarimana and his party exerted on society barely fifteen years after coming to power, before the democratic opening and the RPF war, demonstrates an unrecognized grassroots political strengh.

The Discourse of Reconciliation and the Continued Policy of Exclusion

A Regime of Contradictions (1973–1975)

On July 5, 1973, Major-General Habyarimana led the high command of the Rwandan National Guard in a coup that overthrew President Kayibanda and his government, dissolved parliament, and suspended political activities. A committee for peace and unity made up of army officials and directed by President Habyarimana governed the country. The coup was justified as a response to the "hatred, intrigues, injustice, and regionalism" and to President Kayibanda's attempts to assassinate army officials and influential politicians from the north.[3]

During his first meeting with newly appointed prefects on July 31, 1973, Lieutenant Colonel Alexis Kanyarengwe, the new regime's interior minister and second in command, explained: "Starting from the first few hours of the new orientation, the committee for peace and national unity and its president invite all citizens to cooperate in the spirit of hope for the development of the country at the national, rather than regional and ethnic, level."[4] The minister insisted: "In the efforts to reestablish peace and national unity, one must remember that bickering along religious, tribal, clan, ethnic, or regional lines is forbidden."[5] He then gave guidelines for action specific to each region to be carried out by respective prefects. The Gitarama prefect was to fight against intrigues and hatred among the residents. In Kibuye and Butare, the prefects were to keep a close eye on the Tutsi, especially those Kanyarengwe thought to be sowing division and seeking to impose "their feudal roles," and to pay close attention to the movements of refugees. In Kibuye and Byumba, the prefects had to fight against the massive return of refugees in accordance with the presidential decree of February 26, 1966, to which we shall return later. The interior minister asked the Gikongoro prefect to end the falsification of identity cards carried out by Tutsis.

Contradicting the change in public discourse and the official ban on ethnic hostility, the powerful minister of the interior ordered the leaders close to the new regime to continue the surveillance of Tutsis. He continuously employed terms related to the supposed feudal character in the Tutsi. The discussions of this important meeting therefore suggest that the policies of the Party of the Hutu Emancipation Movement (PARMEHUTU) era had not really changed. The anti-Tutsi discrimination policy was still in place even though the new government showed a different face in public.

The same observation can be made in relation to regional antogonisms. In the announcement of the July 5 coup, the army high command affirmed its great respect for Kayibanda. Subsequent speeches described the coup as a "moral revolution" that continued the "social revolution" of 1959. A year later, however, the new regime's approach to the PARMEHUTU changed. The members of the Gitarama political elite, to which president Kayibanda belonged, were physically eliminated. Throughout the 1970s, several top figures of the First Republic died in prison, and in 1976, President Kayibanda died, from neglect, alone in his home in Gitarama.[6]

The Refugee Problem

If there is any strong continuity in the policies of the two regimes, it is probably in how they handled the refugee issue. Praise for a humanitarian and practical approach was closely followed by hardened political positions. Contrary to the impression created by the memorandum "Position of the [National Revolutionary Movement for Development] MRND Central Committee on the Problem of Rwandan Refugees" of July 26, 1986, the Habyarimana regime since 1973 had paid significant attention to the refugee problem.

As we have seen, regarding the reintegration of refugees the interior minister cited the presidential decree of 1966 in his orders to the prefects on how to control the return of refugees who had just fled the country during the violence of February and March 1973. On October 25, 1973, a circular sent by the ministers of interior and justice to the burgomasters, deputy public prosecutors, and directors of ministries expounded on the decree, which regulated the modalities of return for refugees as well as the repossession of their property. A returning refugee had to report to the head of the prefecture in which he or she wanted to settle. The refugee then had to indicate the head of the homestead of his temporary residence and the hill on which he intended to settle permanently. The prefect could then give his consent but reserved the right to direct the refugee to settle elsewhere. Within the first year of arrival, the refugee had to present his provisional identity card to any state agent of the judicial police and obtain the burgomaster's prior approval to travel between communes. Finally, the refugee could not, under any circumstances, reclaim the land he had owned or cultivated if that land had already been possessed by the state.[7] In addition to these provisions of the 1966 decree, the 1973 circular now considered cattle "real estate" in the same category as land and invalidated any claims for payment of rent on vacant property seized by the commune. Finally, the circular strongly emphasized the fact that the presidential decree applied to refugees who left both before and during the 1973 crisis.[8] The provisions of the 1966 presidential degree were therefore lenient in comparison with the more restrictive instructions issued in July 1973 by the interior minister.

On May 22, 1975, Interior Minister Kanyarengwe sent a new circular marked urgent, in which prefects were ordered to definitively redistribute all "abandoned property" by the following July. In doing so, he went against the provisions of the previous circular outlining the provisional action to take regarding vacant properties. He cited another similar circular signed on October 18, 1974.[9] To understand the urgency of these new instructions, one must understand the refugee policy against the backdrop of the diplomatic development of the issue in 1974.

Kampala 1974: A Wasted Opportunity

Upon the advent of the new regime in Rwanda, Ugandan president Idi Amin Dada requested that the Rwandan government look for a definitive solution to the problem of Rwandan refugees living in Uganda.[10] From July 21 to 28, 1974, a five-person Rwandan delegation headed by Lieutenant Colonel Aloys

Nsekalije, minister of foreign affairs, including the minister of health and social affairs and the director of the president's office, Commandant Theoneste Lizinde, visited Kampala to discuss the refugee issue.[11] Nsekalije and Lizinde were prominent members of the new regime's ruling clique. A preliminary agreement between the Ugandan and Rwandan governments on the repatriation of refugees was drafted. The preconditions for its initiative were the desire for a permanent solution, an approach that was primarily humanitarian, and the "desire expressed by Rwandan refugees currently living in Uganda to return to their home country and live a normal and peaceful life in respect of the Constitution and the laws of the Rwandan republic." In principle, the Ugandan side stated that the "stay of the refugees in Uganda is only temporary and that it was ultimately up to their country of origin to create conditions favorable for the return of its nationals and to welcome the refugees when they express their intention to return." The Rwandan counterpart provided assurances that the conditions that had forced Rwandans to flee to Uganda no longer existed with the arrival of the Second Republic. The two sides agreed on a gradual timetable for repatriation.[12] The number of registered refugees in Uganda in the 1970s stood at about 70,000.[13]

The Rwandan government promised to do everything within its power for every refugee to recover property owned before fleeing the country "as long as that property has not become *res nullis* [unowned, or vacant]. In the event that it is impossible to recover the property, the Government shall do all it can to find any available means of resettlement."[14]

The repatriation program presented two points:

1. The Rwandan government agreed to welcome the following categories of refugees upon the signing of this accord:
   • Those who had property or a means of livelihood in Rwanda.
   • Those who had property in Rwanda as long as that property could be identified.[15]
   • Those who were professionals or skilled workers.
2. Other refugees would be repatriated within a period agreed upon by the joint commission.

Finally, the agreement provided an exemption clause by which the people concerned ceased to be considered refugees but would be able to live in Uganda as foreign residents. In this case, the Ugandan government would examine the possibility of naturalizing Rwandans who had lived for a long time in Uganda and expressed the desire to stay.

The program for repatriation was never implemented. Beyond this missed opportunity, the comments contained in the memorandum addressed to President Habyarimana by the Rwandan delegation, which included two of the most important figures of the regime, reveal the real government position on the refugee issue and the reasons for this failure. The Rwandan delegation appears to have been caught by surprise when it realized that the Ugandan government had already carried out a study in consultation with refugees and prepared a summary of their position.

In this document, the refugees expressed their gratitude to the two heads of state and articulated their willingness to collaborate, after which they presented six conditions for their return home: (1) complete security guaranteed by the Organization of African Unity (OAU); (2) the release of all political prisoners of the former regime; (3) the resettlement of all displaced persons with their assets and properties; (4) elimination of all forms of discrimination within the Constitution; (5) the equality of all Rwandans before the law as well as in all sectors of society, such as education, employment, commerce, religion, and public service; (6) organization and supervision of all these under the auspices of a committee with representation from the OAU, the Rwandan government, the refugees, international organizations devoted to refugee issues, and the countries hosting the refugees.[16]

In contrast to the humanitarian approach the Rwandan government claimed to favor, the refugees raised the political issue. In their memorandum to President Habyarimana, the members of the Rwandan delegation from the very beginning disregarded the refugees' demands so as to eventually deny the very legitimacy of this request for return:

> In view of the above [memorandum by the refugees] and deeply concerned about the successful implementation of this work, the Rwandan delegation considers itself to be sincere and realistic, and as such thinks that it would be advisable not to discuss the dangerous and categorical conditions presented in the above document.
>
> Beyond what we have previously stated, the six conditions not only do not take into account the current realities in Rwanda; they continue to misjudge the decisive and very important role that our two heads of state can play in resolving this problem. They seem to have placed their trust in the actions of the OAU and an executive committee. . . .
>
> Notwithstanding the interests of each side, which are of concern to the top leaders in charge of the destinies of the two brotherly peoples, it appears that for now, at least, Rwanda cannot and is not in a position to open up negotiations on such terms, which are, all things considered, suicidal for the Rwandan people.[17]

The memorandum continues with a long argument that emphasizes the country's overpopulation, poverty, and lack of resources as reasons to oppose the repatriation of the refugees. The last argument touched on the political dimension:

The Ugandan authorities are fully aware that the refugee question reflects not only the willingness and spirit of the Rwandan government team but also the absolute determination of the Rwandan people to choose freely the institutions that have guided their destinies since the social revolution of 1959, strengthened by the establishment of the Second Republic.

The Republic has been resolutely committed to reestablishing peace, unity, and national harmony—the hard-earned fruits of the social revolution of 1959—which the failing policies of the authorities of the First Republic had seriously compromised.

The Rwandan people, today at peace and reconciled with one another, could not allow some inopportune event to distract them and make them stray from the road they have paved to social and political emancipation. The people condemned and banished forever the monarchy and all its supporting institutions. It would go against the will of the people to impose on them again the burden of those whom they rejected from their hearts. Through the years following the independence and self-determination of the Rwandan people, these rejected people have ceaselessly attacked the Rwandan people from outside the country in the form of armed gangs, with the purpose of destroying the people and robbing them of their painfully earned freedom.

We are confident that the Ugandan authorities will understand that, having successfully guaranteed peace, unity, and national harmony within the country, the Rwandan authorities will not in any way guarantee the safety of the refugees, who in many ways might still have several scores to settle with the people who, deep inside, remain bitter about the unpunished crimes of the inyenzi terrorists.

We do not want to see any more bloodshed in our country. What the Second Republic has always sought to avoid is the resurgence of the hatred and division between Rwandans of different ethnic groups. Those who from the very beginning sought to fight reason with force, wisdom with contempt, caution with arrogance, and ethnic harmony with xenophobia have, at their own risk and peril, chosen the path they found most convenient. If in retrospect they had regretted their attitude as well as their serious wrongs against the security of the country, our diplomats accredited in our neighboring and friendly countries would already have recorded their grievances and submitted them for sympathetic consideration by the Rwandan people.

That is one of the ways that should have normalized the refugee question equitably. However, despite several calls for national reconciliation by the Rwandan authorities, the refugees have remained stunned, living in the delusion of the privileges they enjoyed in regimes long gone. . . .

We express our wish that the Ugandan authorities will readily understand the merit of the reasonable fears of the Rwandan government given the very precarious security situation the refugees would be wrong to underestimate regarding the Rwandan popular masses. We also wish the Ugandan authorities to do everything within their means to dissuade the refugees from such a hopeless venture for the sake of both the refugees and the entire Rwandan population.[18]

Here we see an outright dismissal that also serves as a stark warning. This unique document reveals the political and ideological motivations that underpinned the remarkably consistent policy of the regime toward refugees.

The 1976 Presidential Directives Regarding Refugees

In August 1976, the minister in the president's office sent presidential directives issued on June 22, 1976, to ministers whose portfolio touched on refugee issues. These directives became the defining document of the regime's policy and used the presidential decree of February 26, 1966, as their legal basis:

> [The president] asks for a systematic but discreet census of refugees living in neighboring countries as well as employees of international organizations. . . . The return of refugees must be strictly controlled and only encouraged when those applying to return are useful to the country. . . . [Ministers must] embark on a psychological campaign to persuade Rwandan nationals to remain in their host country. In this regard, the term "refugees" should increasingly give way to "Rwandan nationals." This term is better placed to persuade the persons concerned to remain in the country where they are currently living, since their massive return would conflict with the population explosion of which you are aware. Refugees who are willing and able to be naturalized should be encouraged to do so. In the meantime, a sensitization campaign should be carried out within the country in order to guide the people toward accepting this as a foundation of peace and harmony among all Rwandans. The requirements for returning to Rwanda should be flexible so that people remain at ease. Vagrants, those without steady employment, and undesirable elements should be prevented from entering the country. . . . The process should be fast and efficient so as not to discourage the applicants or call into doubt our goodwill.[19]

These instructions practically slammed the door on all those, especially peasants, whose survival and development depended on returning home. Unlike the 1966 decree, this document was silent regarding those who might still own property given that the interior minister had erased this category of people two years before by distributing these properties. The only ones allowed to return were a few elites who had fled recently and were considered politically and socially harmless and who were selected according to the authorities' discretion.

The July 1986 MRND's Humanitarian Policy

On July 26, 1986, the MRND central committee issued a statement entitled *Position du comité central du MRND face au problème des réfugiés rwandais* (MRND Central Committee Position on the Problem of Rwandan Refugees) in which in substance it denied the right of return to Rwandan refugees. Claiming that the country was overpopulated, MRND rejected the idea of a collective right of return for the refugees, but agreed to examine individual applications from those who were in a position to support themselves once back in the country. In its so-called humanitarian position, the MRND central committee showed that it preferred the refugees to settle abroad permanently.[20] The

MRND's statement simply brought out in the open the approach inherent in the 1976 presidential directives.

This official denial of the right of return to the refugees had a far-reaching impact on politically aware refugees outside the country for which it served as a rallying call. That the Habyarimana regime had made public its position on the refugees at that particular moment was no coincidence. During the early 1980s, a wide-ranging movement of cultural and political mobilization had started among the refugee communities, and the Kigali government must have been aware of it. But more importantly, the victory of Yoweri Museveni's National Resistance Movement (NRM)—six months before the publication of the MRND's position—in which thousands of combatant Rwandan refugees had participated, was highly disturbing for the regime.

In February 1989 the government established a special commission on the problem of Rwandan refugees tasked with the implementation of the 1986 "new" policy. In November 1989, the president of the special commission was able to present only 300 cases since 1986 of refugees returning home following individual arrangements.[21] In July 1990, the special commission proposed the implementation of new different practical measures. A census of those "entitled to refugee status" was planned but never carried out, and in October 1990, just when the Rwandan Patriotic Front (RPF) launched its attack, another plan was devised: "A committee of experts was to determine, upon consultation with the interested parties, those who desired to benefit, as soon as possible, from the right of return."[22]

However, the event that best exemplified the reality of the "humanitarian" approach to the refugee issue of the Second Republic occurred in October 1982, when Rwandan refugees and the Kinyarwanda-speaking population living in the south of Uganda were expelled by groups of youths associated with Milton Obote's Uganda People's Congress (UPC). The groups accused the Banyarwandas of taking part in the guerrilla war led by Yoweri Museveni, a Hima from the Nkoles, an ethnic group related to the Tutsis. At least 100 people died, 35,000 others sought refuge in the refugee camps where they were surrounded, and 40,000 others attempted to flee toward the Rwandan border. Those who succeeded in crossing the border were confined to camps on the Rwandan side of the border. The humanitarian aid was very slow to come, they suffered from hunger, and many died from diseases while groups of young people were taken away by the Rwandan military and never came back.[23] When Rwanda closed its border in November 1982,[24] a group of between 8,000 and 10,000 people were trapped on a slim stretch of no-man's land between the Rwandan soldiers on one side and UPC thugs on the other.[25] The newspaper *Le Monde* on December 23, 1982, reported that several elderly refugees preferred to take their own lives in the face of such humiliation.[26] The group stayed there for months wasting away, helped by the Red Cross but gradually dying from infectious diseases and despair.[27] To explain its denial of asylum to these expelled Kinyarwanda-speaking people, many of whom were refugees, the government in Kigali stated that under no circumstances would it welcome Kinyarwanda-speaking Ugandans.

The fact that the leaders of the Second Republic favored a military so-lution in the summer of 1990, when the attack by the RPF was looming, is a continuation of the 1974 revealing script, albeit with a different cast.[28] One therefore realizes that, contrary to widely held opinion, the Second Republic did not fail to address the refugee question in good time; rather, the refugee question had been a key component of its internal and international policies from the very beginning. "The regime's refusal to allow refugees to return was hardly driven by practical constraints as it claimed; rather, it was dic-tated by political considerations as well as ideological persuasion."[29]

Resistance to the Discourse of Ethnic Reconciliation

The shift in official discourse during the first years of the Second Republic has led Tutsi witnesses to describe them as a euphoric period of relief and excite-ment. This change, shortly after the dismissal of the PARMEHUTU regime, met with resistance among some Hutus but with joy among some Tutsis who mistook Habyarimana's call for reconciliation as his taking a stand in their favor. In a security report for the last trimester of 1974 he submitted to the president, the interior minister brought up the "behavior of some Tutsis who are going out of their way to irritate the masses by referring to the events of 1959."[30] Reports from the prefectures as well as exchanges of views between the president and the population during his tour around the country from April 16 to May 6, 1974, exposed the friction caused by the new discourse of recon-ciliation. During another tour to promote the newly created MRND, a single party founded on July 5, 1975, and to gauge public opinion, the president met with educated elites in the main towns of the prefectures.[31] The report of the talks held during the presidential tour mentions that the problem of the coex-istence of the three ethnic groups came up several times, whether it was related to the policy of ethnic balance, reconciliation, the need to reform the history programs in Rwanda, or the need to pay special attention to the Twa. The pres-ident's replies were summarized as follows:

> In democracy, the power must go to the majority without necessarily having to alienate minorities. Anything that is divisive, be it ethnicity or clan, must be rejected. It is important to be proud of one's ethnic group as long as it does not get in the way of the basic unity and peaceful coexistence. From now on, it is not necessary to remove references to one's ethnic group on the identity card because they will be emptied of whatever complexes they may contain.

In his response, the president went on to say that the policy of ethnic and regional balance was necessary to redress discriminatins that certain groups suffered from in the past. He also promised that the history taught in school would be adapted to the goal of reconciliation. Speaking at the close of his tour, the president responded to the challenging questions coming from certain Hutus by emphatically setting the record straight and reiterating his commitment to the ideology of the Republican Democratic Movement (MDR)–Party of the Hutu Emancipation Movement (PARMEHUTU) but with a caveat.[32]

He said,

> We know that for more than four hundred years, the Tutsi harshly oppressed the Hutu and did everything to deny the Twa confidence in their humanity. Our revolution of 1959 was the first to have overthrown Tutsi power through restoring self-respect and the power of the citizen majority [Abene-Gihugu benshi]. However, there was at some time a program to ignore the minority and even expel them from the country. Our movement must support and implement our commitment to abolish ethnic discrimination. The movement will give all Rwandans the opportunity to build their country in peace, unity, and integrity. When it comes to unity, we are taking this opportunity to warn all those who misinterpret this objective of our movement. Our movement does not seek to prevent a Hutu from being Hutu, a Twa from being Twa (or make him ashamed to be Twa), or a Tutsi from being Tutsi. Our movement wishes for everyone to feel truly Rwandan and to join hands with others to promote the progress of this country. The Tutsis should therefore stop provoking the Hutus by denying the achievements of the 1959 revolution. The Hutus also need to understand that Tutsis and Twas are truly Rwandan and that the MRND expects each and everyone to make constructive contributions to our country, Rwanda.[33]

In this speech, President Habyarimana gives assurances of his loyalty to the MDR-PARMEHUTU ideology allowing him to be critical of the discriminatory actions of the regime of the First Republic and to state his preference for more equal treatment for all ethnic groups. The delicate nature of this balancing act in the social context at the time is well rendered in the interior minister's report to the president for the second trimester of 1976:

> At the political level, it was brought to our attention that Tutsis were disrespectful toward the Hutu and that Hutus held a counterprotest, expressed in the tract of May 4 addressed to the head of state as well as in a letter from Joseph Gitera-Habyarimana on the ethnic reconciliation of the Hutu and Tutsi.[34]
>
> Regarding the behavior of the Tutsis, some of them have indeed been insolent and provocative toward the Hutu based on the illusion that the policy of coexistence among Rwandan ethnic groups means that the president of the republic supports only the Tutsi. There were rumors that the head of state was himself Tutsi because, it was alleged, he had Abagogwe facial features.[35] The consultations the president of the republic held with congress members from the prefectures, as well as the president's speech at the close of his tour, seem to have put an end to these incitements and rumors.[36]

Despite amending his speech on reconciliation by linking it to the continuation of PARMEHUTU ideology, it seemed to bring about subsequent relax-
ation of tension between the Hutus and Tutsis.

Limits to Reconciliation:
The Policy of Ethnic and Regional Balance

Alongside this talk of reconciliation, from the beginning, one of the most
important actions of the Habyarimana regime was to put in place a policy of
"ethnic and regional balance." Its justification was that Tutsis in general and
Hutus from the central and southern regions had been historically favored to
the disadvantage of people from the north. An ethnic and regional quota system for access to education and employment was put in place. As far as the
Tutsis were concerned, this policy had already been adopted under the First
Republic but had been applied sometimes loosely in educational institutions,
and the number of Tutsi in secondary schools went over the 10 percent quota
assigned to them. Because the violence of 1973 aimed at ridding schools of
Tutsis, the government of the Second Republic had decided to strictly implement the ethnic quota and to put in place regional ones as well. The quotas
were enforced in secondary and higher education at both public and private
institutions as well as in employment in the government and the private sector.

In the meticulously documented *The Life of Tutsis Under the First and
Second Republics*, Antoine Mugesera describes the manner in which Tutsis
were evicted from the schools and from public and private institutions in 1973.
His perspective is unique in that it attaches more significance to the 1973
events than other research on the subject. He reports that Canon Ernotte, an
important initial supporter of the PARMEHUTU and of President Kayibanda,
wrote to the president on February 21, 1973, denouncing the ongoing abuses
and calling them "ethnic cleansing" and "intellectual genocide." Mugesera
proves that the Habyarimana regime did not desist from these actions but instead implemented them more systematically. He explains that this campaign
of expelling Tutsis from secondary schools and formal employment in the
public sector had a long-lasting impact on the Tutsi in Rwanda, impoverishing
and instilling in them a deep sense of insecurity. Mugesera states that as a result, some Tutsi young men, even those who had managed to find some livelihood, were no longer getting married for fear of the future, and others sought
refuge in alcohol. Meanwhile, young women in vulnerable families either
married former members of the PARMEHUTU or settled for the status of mis-
tresses of the new men in power.[37]

However, the system was rapidly diverted, giving way to a system of arbitrary rule and corruption. In a security report of October 19, 1977, the inte-

rior minister reported, "The ordinary people say that in any case, priority in admission is enjoyed by the sons and daughters of the rich, namely of the highest civilian and military authorities, traders and entrepreneurs. They say that there is there is no need to talk of merit or equality because bribes and intervention are more important than anything else. It is the poorest who suffer most from this situation."[38] The system of ethnic and regional balancing fueled deep resentment toward the regime among Tutsis in general and Hutus from the central and southern parts of the country.

The Paradox of Ethnic Containment by the State and the Social Assimilation of the Tutsi

As it sought to enforce rigorously ethnic quotas, the state was confronted with the difficulties of identifying certain people. In addition to particular individual cases among the elites, records of the Interior Ministry show how official indications of ethnicity on identity cards and other official documents could prove problematic for whole family groups. There was a major influx in Tutsis who wanted to pass for Hutus, falsifying their ethnicity in official documents. The state's intention to entrench the indication of ethnicity was in reality going against the movement toward the assimilation—ambiguous, though real—of the Tutsis.

The interior minister carried out investigations of people who generally held positions of responsibility when doubts about their ethnicity had been expressed. The Central Intelligence Service also took part in these investigations.

In 1985, Tabaro (not his real name), director at the Ministry of Industry, was the subject of investigation. It appeared that his father had been "forced" to become Hutu by the native authorities during the 1949–1950 census because he had no livestock and thus could not belong to the pastoralist class. The Interior Ministry wrote to the prefect of Gitarama on December 3, 1985, with instructions that the burgomaster of Tabaro's home commune was not to change the director's Hutu ethnic identity.[39] However, on February 11, 1987, the president's office ordered the interior minister to reinstate the "real" identity of the director.[40] The interior minister then wrote to the prefect of Gitarama, ordering him to confiscate the documents of all descendants of Tabaro's grandfather and to issue them others that indicated their "true" Tutsi identity.[41]

This intervention from the president provoked the interior minister to demand that his Department of Research and Evaluation, charged with investigating falsification of identity, prepare a comprehensive report on the issue. The investigation was completed in 1989, synthesized in a memo in which the department director starts by recalling the laws against falsification of identity.

These were Article 206 of the penal code, which imposed a penalty of three months to two years in prison and/or a fine of 10,000 francs, and Article 207, which imposed on the public official involved a prison sentence of one to five years and/or a fine of 50,000 francs.[42]

The note goes on to distinguish two periods in the ethnic identity falsification trends—before and after the revolution. The director explains that traditionally, a Hutu servant might come to be considered Tutsi. During the 1949–1950 census, a number of Hutus received Tutsi identity cards in this way, and that is how some Hutu families were divided into two groups of different ethnicities. In this case, the director of research and evaluation proposed that such individuals retain their Tutsi identity because they had freely made that choice out of opportunism. Another case is that of Tutsi families that had become too poor, had no cattle, and were therefore classified as Hutu during that census. Then there was the falsification of identity during and after the 1959 revolution, almost all by Tutsis who wanted to pass for Hutu. The director proposed that they be forced to adopt their initial ethnic identity and in addition be prosecuted in court, especially those who falsified their documents during "peacetime."[43]

To illustrate, the director presented the case of two former university professors. One, Rusagara (not his real name), a doctor of medicine, admitted that he was in fact of Tutsi descent, but he was one of the "little Tutsis" who became Hutu during colonial time. As he pursued his studies as a nurse's assistant, he had earned some money to live on, working from 1949 to 1952 in Congo, and had subsequently returned to the country and lived as a "good patriot." The second, Gasana (not his real name), produced the identity booklets of his grandfather and his father, dated 1936 and 1960, respectively, both of which had no deletions and that identified them as Hutu, but the Central Intelligence Service established that Gasana's father may have falsified his identity between 1964 and 1970. The director conveyed the opinion of the burgomaster of Gasan's home commune that this was a case of "little Tutsis" trying to change their ethnicity. He noted that in Gasan's village, there were conflicting opinions on his family ethnic identity.[44]

These difficulties reflect, in certain cases, the dynamic nature of ethnosocial identification, susceptible to change with the passage of time when there is a prolonged change in socioeconomic conditions. The rigidity of the colonial practices of ethnic marking became problematic when it came to establishing the ethnicity of a group undergoing a social mutation, specifically in the periphery of the country where ethnic identity was less salient for a long time. One may assume that in a society as poor as Rwanda, which had suffered recurrent famines and cattle disease during the transition from the precolonial to the colonial period, a number of Tutsis fell between the two identities when identity booklets indicating one's ethnicity were first issued in 1936 as well as during the 1949 census.[45] These were the people most likely to choose the ethnic identity most suitable in the political context because it was difficult to assign them a definite ethnic identity objectively. By choosing not to systematically respect the official ethnic notation in the identity documents issued before and during the revolution and not to consider the opinion of the local communities, for a section of society, the Second Republic had opened a real Pandora's box.

Moreover, the efforts of the Second Republic to make citizens return to their "real" ethnic identity went against the social current of ongoing assimilation of Tutsis evident in their somewhat decreasing significance to the people. The Division of Census and Statistics of the Interior Ministry observed in 1987,

> Another equally significant problem is the decreasing proportion of the Tutsi population because of the falsification of ethnicity and of mixed marriages. It has been noted that some Tutsis betray a certain complex and change their ethnicity in order to better protect their interests. On the other hand, the mixed marriages, almost always between Hutu men and Tutsi girls, contribute significantly to decreasing proportion of the Tutsi population.[46]

This observation is corroborated by many testimonies, especially from the rural areas in the south and the center of the country, affirming that the consciousness of difference in Hutu-Tutsi social relations was beginning to diminish toward the end of the 1980s.

Loyalty to the Revolutionary Narrative and Persistent Fear Among the Tutsis

The 1978 population census exposed the persistent fear of the Tutsis five years after President Habyarimana seized power and of his speeches declaring reconciliation. The announcement that ethnicity would feature as a criterion fed this fear because a number of Tutsis thought it might presage their elimination. Some Hutus spread false rumors to scare the Tutsi into fleeing so that they could seize the property left behind. For example, one of the propagators of such rumors was the former director of OVAPAM, a large livestock project located on the eastern plains bordering Uganda, who hoped to seize the livestock belonging to the region's cattle owners. He incited the local Tutsi and Hima pastoralists to flee by making them believe a massacre had been planned for the nights of August 15 and 16, 1978, when the census was to take place.[47] Agence France-Presse reported that 300 Tutsi families crossed the border with 3,000 head of cattle. In a speech on July 5, 1978, Habyarimana made an effort to reassure the public, and most of the escapees returned home.[48]

The constitutional referendum of December 24, 1978, was yet another occasion that exposed how some rural and urban populations still held onto the memory of the 1959 revolution. In particular, the use of black ballot boxes to indicate a "no" vote was criticized because the black color of the ballot boxes for the 1961 referendum, referred to as Kamarampaka, meant the rejection of the monarchy. According to an Interior Ministry report, the common people believed that "burying the color black was burying the Hutu." This symbolism would have had repercussions on the vote in the rural regions, whereas among the "intellectuals," it was said that the use of the color black was nothing less than a "challenge" to history.[49]

The following year, ethnic tension resurged, fomented by former associates of President Habyarimana and led by Major Lizinde and Colonel Kanyarengwe, who sought to destabilize the president. The last incident of heightening ethnic tension before 1990 was in 1988 during the massacres at Ntega and Marangara Communes in Burundi, close to the border with Rwanda. On the Rwandan side bodies were retrieved, and a state procession from Kigali to the south was organized to give them a dignified burial.[50]

At a glance, therefore, the ethnic politics of the Second Republic appear contradictory. However, even amid this ambivalence, it is possible to make out major lines of action. To better identify them, one may need to analyze the continuities and breaks in the relation to the legacy of the previous MDR-PARMEHUTU regime. The breaks are located within the method of action, especially with regard to the manner the First Republic used the dramatization of ethnic animosity to legitimize its policy of violent ethnic exclusion. Although the Habyarimana regime's leaders preferred to talk in a more sober tone, they were making substantial use of a policy legitimacy already established. The regime of the Second Republic added to ethnicity regional origin as criteria for exclusion and instituted an elaborate, graduated quota system of access to the state and its resources that in effect led to arbitrariness and grabbing of public resources by Hutu social and political groups from the north.

The Attempt to Create a Rural, Totalitarian State

Besides the institutionalization of exclusion, the second important thread in the political and social action of the Second Republic was the attempt to build a rural totalitarian state.

The Creation of the MRND

On May 20, 1975, as he marked the end of his tour of the prefectures, President Habyarimana announced his intention to create a "revolutionary movement that united all Rwandans and was founded on development."[51] The MRND was created on July 5, 1975. In the documents establishing the movement, the MRND refused to be considered a political party. According to the interior minister, it was a movement with two objectives: "To rally the Rwandan people as a whole toward a better political organization" and "to unite, stimulate, and intensify the efforts of the Rwandan people with the goal of achieving their development in peace and unity according to the plan defined in the movement's manifestos."[52]

Every Rwandan was a member of the movement from birth. There was, therefore, no particular party membership process, and permanent participation was required of all citizens. The MRND boldly declared its totalitarian ambition: "The movement intends to be popular and expects unreserved support. In other words, the action of the people, of the whole society, is modeled on one sole pattern, producing unity of purpose, harmony, and cohesion from the cells at the base of the movement up to the top of the pyramid—in other words, the entire nation. No individual or group of individuals can escape the total social control at work here."[53]

The MRND invested heavily in achieving its goal of total control of Rwandan society through an elaborate structure of which effects were felt even in the remotest hills. It was in 1976 that the organs of what was to become a party-state were put in place. In the MRND statutes of 1976, there was an almost complete merger between the state and the party. Both the National Council for Development—that is, the legislative assembly—and the government were official party organs. However, in the 1981 statutes they were withdrawn from the party structure, so the merged party-state only remained at the local level. The consultative bodies of communes, the congress, and committee were MRND organs whereas the executive branch was not. At the lower sector and cell levels the state administrative structures and the party formed a single body.[54]

There was resistance to the new political structure from intellectual circles as well as from the general public. A few months after the president's second tour of the prefectures and the subsequent establishment of MRND structures, the interior minister recorded some of the criticisms: "With regard to the functioning of institutions, it should be noted that the definition of the MRND still raises concern among the people in that the insistence that the MRND is not a political party is not accepted by everybody. For some, the political movement everyone is obligated to join is more than an ordinary party; it is a totalitarian one."[55]

This criticism obviously came from the intellectuals. From 1976 onward, the leaders of the different bodies within the MRND were elected, but it was only on December 17, 1978, that the political structure of the MRND was subjected to mass approval through a constitutional referendum. Against the background of close monitoring and the pressure for unanimity, "Yes" carried the day with 89.09 percent of the vote from 100 percent of the registered voters, because voting was compulsory in Rwanda.[56] According to the standards the Rwandan electoral consultations had to adopt, the 10 percent total of

"No" votes was a sign of defiance. The presidential elections held a week later on December 24, 1978, voted in Habyarimana with 98.99 percent of the vote.[57] The constitutional referendum, on the contrary, showed some important deviations in voting behaviors in the different prefectures: in three prefectures, more than 10 percent voted "No," namely, Butare (11.9 percent), Gikongoro (38 percent), and Kibuye (29.3 percent).[58] This significant number of "No" votes was not surprising, at least for Gikongoro and Butare because these southern regions were politically defiant toward the regime compared with their counterparts in the north. More surprising were the voting patterns in Kibuye. Socioeconomic factors also played an important role: Gikongoro and Kibuye were the poorest prefectures in the country. The other surprise from the electorate was the smaller size of the "No" vote in the Gitarama Prefecture (7.8 percent) given that reports from the Interior Ministry in the first few years after the coup 1973 had pointed out that practically only Gitarama showed resistance to the new regime, an attitude to be expected because this prefecture was the home of the deposed regime.[59] My impression that significant pressure must have been put on voters in Gitarama is reinforced by the fact that, a week later, the president was voted in by 98.99 percent of the vote and that 99.3 percent of the voters in Gikongoro voted for the president.[60] The regime was doubtless taken by surprise in these particular prefectures, but from then on, in elections where the political prestige of the president was at stake, the rule was a unanimous vote.

Umuganda: The Return of Forced Communal Labor

After the 1959 revolution, a movement opposed to the stifling rural structure inherited from the colonial period had emerged among the peasants, who uprooted coffee trees, abandoned the fight against soil erosion, and neglected certain farming practices. At the same time, the positions left vacant by European technicians allowed the agricultural officers to rise in the ranks and create a Ministry of Agriculture, which until then did not exist. In the context of widespread poverty and weak external cash flow, the authorities of the Second Republic had decided to put their energies into reviving developmental activities. Given the financial challenges, the authorities chose to use the abundant labor available and "put the people to work again."[61] *Umuganda*, the practice of compulsory communal labor, was imposed in February 1974: the whole population was compelled to participate once a week, on Saturday morning, in community work generally devoted to road maintenance, combating soil erosion, reforestation, and construction of public buildings.[62] In addition to its utilitarian aspect, the spirit behind this practice was one of the key components of rural totalitarianism the regime tried to establish. The Interior Ministry, which oversaw its implementation, explained the project's objectives as follows:

The intended political goal of umuganda is the revalorization of manual work. Umuganda thus aims for extensive mobilization of the population for development. This policy should take prominence in the urban areas, above all, given that the revalorization of manual work by the civil servants and other paid workers is one of the factors that will push the rural areas to follow.[63]

The analogy with colonial forced labor was inevitably evoked. In the summary report of the discussions President Habyarimana held with the prefecture congresses of the MRND in April and May 1976, it was noted, "Umuganda communal work is still not well understood. It is still seen by some as forced labor—*akazi k'uburetwa*."[64]

Lastly, the other key element of MRND social control was "animation" (performances), sessions of song and dance in which key phrases on development from the president of the republic were recited. Each year, he selected a theme intended to orient the people toward national activities.[65] The goal of animation was to mobilize the population through compulsory celebrations. The performances were also occasions to sing the praises of the MRND president and generally took place on Wednesday afternoons.

These were the claims to unanimity and total political control that compelled some analysts to think the system was the principal agent for mobilizing the population to commit genocide.[66] This analysis fails to consider the people's responses to the system, which mitigate the idea of complete domination by the state. We have seen that each of the state initiatives had regularly provoked sharp criticism from intellectual circles. Later we shall see the fast-changing people's response to state indoctrination when the socioeconomic situation started unraveling.

A Brief and Fragile Economic Recovery (1974–1986)

External Factors Responsible for Growth

As the regime vigorously implemented social and political control, it made development its ideological pillar. Every year, a theme for the national campaign permeated every official speech. Each news bulletin on national radio began with a brief segment read by the head of state to sensitize "militant people" on a certain issue of development. President Habyarimana loved to have himself photographed on Saturday afternoons, sweating as he took part in *umuganda*. This speech, the disciplined character of the country, and its benevolent conservatism impressed foreign donors.

From 1974 to 1981, the country witnessed a growth rate of 5.4 percent per year.[67] Three reasons are given for this growth: favorable weather, better terms of trade for Rwanda's main agricultural exports, and above all significant growth in international aid. In comparison with the previous period, 1969–1974, aid as a percentage of the gross domestic product (GDP) had increased sixfold. In 1978, foreign assistance equaled 15 percent of the GDP, 122.1 percent of exports, and 93 percent of imports. In 1979, this aid reached $34 per inhabitant (almost double what was received by other African countries) and corresponded to 80 percent of investment. During the period 1974–1981, 75 percent of this aid was in grants and the remaining 25 percent was in soft loans. Finally, the Rwandan authorities succeeded in keeping a balanced budget throughout this period.[68]

The Habyarimana administration used this relatively thriving period for the Rwandan economy, which continued until 1986, to erect an actual state apparatus and make significant efforts to provide amenities, especially in the development of Kigali into a proper city albeit a very small one. One of the best networks of roads in the region was built as well as efficient postal and telecommunications services, water distribution systems, and an electricity network. The commercial and service sectors also experienced major growth. The plethora of development projects and the large number of expatriates encouraged the growth of employment and a real estate market. Thanks to the country's stability and the strength of the Rwandan franc compared with other currencies in countries in the region plagued by instability (Burundi), chaos (Zaire), or war (Uganda), Rwanda tapped into the coffee and bean production of its neighbors for a long time. Indeed all these advancements were modest, the country remained extremely poor and underdeveloped, only comparing favorably with neighboring quasi-failed states. External factors that had caused major growth factors reversed from 1984 onward. Aid continued to be important, but its increase began to slow down. Meanwhile, coffee and tea prices on the international market collapsed. Finally, situational and internal structural factors worsened the economic situation of the country.

The Economic Crisis

Table 2.1 shows not only the change in the economic situation in the mid-1980s but also the harshness of that change.

The sharp decline in growth in 1984 and 1989 corresponded to periods of drought that brought about food shortages and even a famine in Gikongoro Prefecture in 1989. Finally, 1986 corresponded with the collapse of coffee prices on the international market, and the price of tea—the country's second largest export—had already begun to drop in 1984.[69] When one compares the GDP with the population growth rate, the economic situation appears even worse. The annual growth in GDP between 1980 and 1990 was 1 percent, but during the same period, the population grew by 3.07 percent.[70]

Table 2.1 Growth of Gross Domestic Product, 1981–1991

Year	Real Annual Growth (%)
1981	2.8
1982	4.1
1983	6.2
1984	−5.0
1985	4.6
1986	5.1
1987	−0.6
1988	0.5
1989	−6.0
1990	−0.1
1991	−3.3
Average 1981–1991	0.8

Source: Stefaan Marysse, Tom De Herdt, and Elie Ndayambaje, *Rwanda: Appauvrissement et ajustement structurel* (Paris and Brussels: L'Harmattan and CEDAF, 1994) p. 31.

Between 1970 and 1980, Rwanda was a model of international cooperation because, in contrast to most African countries, development achieved relatively gratifying results. During the 1980s, the country greatly benefited from the favor of different bilateral and multilateral aid agencies. Alain Hanssen has shown the geographical omnipresence of development projects managed by expatriates. Rwanda had the greatest concentration of foreign experts per square kilometer in Africa, and as Peter Uvin writes, in almost every corner of the country, one saw four-by-four vehicles driven by technical assistants.[71] Hanssen shows the glaring gap between this world of technical assistants and Rwandan citizens. The numerous projects, a source of considerable pride to their promoters, were actually islands of relative efficiency, the impact of which declined after the expatriates had left and their investments dried up. Hanssen also notes that all these projects fueled the comforting ideology of development, functioning "in a closed circuit between foreign development agents and their compatriot investors on the one hand and the local ruling class on the other."[72]

The prescribed model of rural development at the grassroots had as its prime horizon the improvement of subsistence agriculture, supposedly reflecting the values of modesty of the Hutu peasantry. However, in the end it had compromised the interests of those it wanted to promote, as suggested by the World Bank in 1991: "Rwanda is clearly at a crossroads in that the old strategy is no longer viable: the vision of a nation of self-sufficient peasants meeting through their labor alone their needs for food and shelter, leading tranquil and meaningful lives centered on the local community, unbeholden to the world without, that vision is no longer sustainable."[73]

Table 2.2 Global Rankings from the Bottom for Selected Social Indicators

Rank from Bottom	Annual Population Growth Rate (1960–1988)	Percentage of Population in Rural Areas (1988)	Percentage of Rural Population in Poverty (1977–1987)	Percentage of Population with Access to Health Care (1985–1987)	Calories per Capita per Day (1984–1987)	Percentage of Required Calories (1984–1986)	Percentage of Children in Secondary School
1	Cote d'Ivoire (4.1)	Bhutan (95)	Central African Rep. (91)	Mali (15)	Mozambique (1,600)	Mozambique (69)	Malawi (5)
2	Kenya (3.7)	Burundi (93)	**Rwanda (90)**	Benin (18)	Chad (1,720)	Chad (69)	Burundi (6)
3	Uganda (3.5)	**Rwanda (93)**		Zaire (26)	Ethiopia (1,750)	Ethiopia (71)	Mozambique (7)
4	**Rwanda (3.3)**			Somalia (27)	Guinea (1,780)	Guinea (77)	Bhutan (7)
5				**Rwanda (27)**	**Rwanda (1,830)**	**Rwanda (81)**	**Rwanda (7)**

Source: UN Development Programme, *Human Development Report*, 1990.

On a number of vital social indicator rankings, Rwanda was at the end of the 1980s and before the civil war in 1990 slightly ahead of the worse-off, "failed states" and countries at war at the time, countries at the bottom of the least-developed countries (see Table 2.2).

The level of nutrition was particularly alarming: with 1,830 calories per person per day, the Rwandan average was well below the minimum required by international standards of 2,100 calories. However, this average hid deep regional differences: whereas some communes located mainly in the less-populated eastern part of the country reached 2,086 calories per head, others as in Gikongoro Prefecture—epicenter of all the violence since 1963—reached only 657 calories.

The severity of the economic and social crises, the acuteness of hunger, the violence and hopelessness related in the testimonies and reports of local government at the time are aptly reflected in the life expectancy curve (see Figure 2.1).

In 1960, Rwanda had a life expectancy at birth of 42.2 years, which grew to a peak of 49.9 years in 1984. From this year, the life expectancy dropped sharply to 32.6 years in 1990.[73] It was the shortest recorded life expectancy in Africa from 1960 to 1990, to the exception of Sierra Leone between 1960 and 1968, shorter than any country at war or failed state.[74] Between 1984 and 1990, life expectancy in Rwanda fell more than seventeen years (see Table 2.3).

Usually sudden falls in life expectancy are the result of a resurgence of infant mortality. In Rwanda that was not the case because, on the contrary, it

Figure 2.1 Life Expectancy in Rwanda, 1980–2012

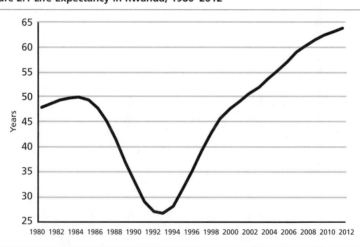

Source: World Bank, *World Development Indicators*, 2014.

Table 2.3 Annual Change in Life Expectancy, 1984–1994

Category	1984	1985	1986	1987	1988	1989	1990	1991	1992	1993	1994
Life Expectancy at Birth (years)	49.9	49.3	47.6	44.9	41.2	36.9	32.6	29.1	27	26.7	28.2
Annual Change in Life Expectancy		−0.6	−1.7	−2.7	−3.7	−4.3	−4.3	−3.5	−2.1	−0.3	+1.5

Source: World Bank, *World Development Indicators*, 2015.

passed from 99.4 per thousand in 1984 to 92.2 in 1990, below the sub-Saharan average of 107 per 1,000.

In Rwanda for the period 1984–1990, the adult mortality rate increased dramatically. In 1960 it was estimated at 397.1 for women and 458 for men per 1,000; it decreased steadily until 1982, when it reached its lowest point at 337.2 for women and 401.4 for men per 1,000. In 1990 the rate started to increase to 558.1 for women and 625.8 for men per 1,000. Again, a rapid change occurred between 1982 and 1990 on the order of 65 percent and 56 percent for women and for men, respectively. In 1990, Rwanda had a prevalence rate of AIDS of 5.3 percent, alone insufficient to explain the sharp increase in adult-mortality.[74]

These extremely rapid changes in life expectancy and adult mortality rates were caused by several factors, including hunger, disease, and AIDS but also the widespread deadly physical violence. Thus, in the mid-1980s and early 1990s, Rwanda experienced a silent humanitarian and security catastrophe that profoundly undermined the survival capabilities of the population.

A Catastrophe for the Peasants

The foundation of this crisis was very rapid population growth. In 1949, the Rwanda population was 1,830,000 inhabitants; in 1990, it was 6,750,000 inhabitants. In other words, the population doubled every twenty years. This population occupied a small area of 26,000 square kilometers, thus creating high population density. In the middle of the 1980s, an average of 250 people lived in every square kilometer, but the density varied according to region. In some rural regions population density was more than 500 people per square kilometer.[75]

Increased population density in agricultural areas forced the people to make adjustments using two strategies: condensed occupation of space and intensified use of seasonal weather conditions. After the 1959 revolution, which removed a number of barriers to settlement, Rwandan peasants set out to occupy all available land. On the one hand, they moved to the hills and valleys; on the other hand, they colonized land in less densely populated regions often unfavorable for agriculture. This involved the cultivation of steep slopes, which dramatically increased soil erosion. The intensified use of seasonal weather conditions consisted of diversifying the crops cultivated on the same piece of land by using different growth cycles so as to have several harvests within the same year. This land exploitation strategy did not translate into increased productivity because it exhausted the soil. The decrease in available space also led to a decline in cattle rearing, which in turn meant a decrease in organic manure; meanwhile, fallow land all but disappeared.[76]

Despite significant efforts, this type of agriculture remained extensive. As a result of the constant depletion of the soil, the output in cereals and legumes (beans, peas, and sorghum) consistently diminished and was taken over by cultivation of tuber crops (cassava and sweet potatoes), which expanded rapidly at the end of the 1980s following a disease affecting beans in 1988 and the drought of 1989.[77] As a result, the slight increase in produce per person as well as the lower nutritional value of these crops eventually brought about malnutrition. The drought of 1984, which caused a serious food shortage; excessive heavy rains in 1987 that destroyed the maize, potatoes, and bean crops; and the bean disease that hit the southwest were followed by the drought of 1989, which caused a food shortage in the southwest, the center, and the east and famine in Gikongoro Prefecture.[78] The structural problems in agriculture had led to a chronic food deficit: a real famine of regional proportions occurred by 1989, and by 1990 only one prefecture out of ten, that of Kibungo, was spared. Hunger killed more than 1,000 people, and nearly 34,000 migrated to other regions and neighboring countries.[79] Apart from this episode, unlike the examples of spectacular famine in Ethiopia in 1984 and in Rwanda in the late 1980s and early 1990s, in much of the country hunger was acute but insidious; it was almost constant but didn't kill immediately.

This crisis for the peasantry was aggravated by their unequal access to land in the newly populated areas, which generally favored the elite in government and business sectors. In 1984, 16 percent of the farming lands were larger than 2 hectares (ha), constituting 42.9 percent of the total land surface, and 56 percent of farms consisted of 1 ha or less and made up 25.3 percent of the total land under cultivation.[80] Even in the most densely populated areas, distress sales benefited wage earners and business people taking over these lands.[81]

Another important consequence of the crisis was that rural households needed to find supplementary income outside their homes, which led to migration and delinquency.[82] Land shortage created acute underemployment, particularly among the youth. Men either looked for employment nearby or defied the laws against rural exodus and traveled to towns—or even the neighboring countries of Tanzania, Zaire, and Burundi—to serve as migrant laborers over weeks or years. Agriculture was therefore taken over by women.

Young adults formed the most disadvantaged group in the hills. Faced with the prospect of inheriting a nonviable plot of land, many of them saw no future in agriculture. The alternative of going to school was blocked. The most the majority of peasant children could hope for was to finish primary school because entry into secondary school was extremely difficult. Under school reforms, primary school was extended by two years in order to offer rural trade education within the framework of the integrated rural and vocational training schools (CERAI). However, the professional skills offered were vague, and the rural vocations for which these youth were trained ran into obstacles such as lack of equipment and a financially solvent market in the hills.[83] The other alternative for the youth was migration, usually for a longer period than for their elders. These youth with an uncertain future no longer believed in official announcements and often engaged in defiant behavior.[84] Peasant society had lost confidence in its way of life and sank into deep despair.[85]

Insubordination, Social Violence, and Despair

Several observers who have taken seriously the claims about political unanimity and complete social control by the MRND party-state and the collaboration of the elites long sheltered from the crises[86] have explained these with the supposed submissive national character of Rwandans and the legacy of the country's ancient social structure.[87] The reality was almost exactly the opposite. The Rwandan peasantry adopted subtle and indirect behaviors of insubordination despite the claims of total control by the MRND party-state. This behavior is no different from that of their African counterparts who, faced with theocratic one-party states, often expressed their "disobedience" using religion or crime.[88]

On June 7, 14, and 21, 1986, an interministerial coordination committee (CIC) held its first meetings. The committee was a think tank responsible for advising the government on issues deemed a priority. In the first three meetings, which brought together five ministers and nine high-level officials, only two issues were on the agenda: the behavior of members of banned sects and the explosion of crime. On the first issue, the CIC condemned the conduct of the Jehovah's Witnesses, who considered, among other things, saluting the flag blasphemy and carrying a pin with the picture of the president an act of adoration and who did not participate in "patriotic" parades, national holidays, *umuganda*, or taxes. For the committee, this conduct constituted "religious fanaticism that made it possible for them to set up a state within a state," and it grouped the Jehovah's Witnesses with other bodies such as the Abarokore, Abantu b'Imana, and East African Revival, who adopted similar behaviors. Members of these religious groups went from house to house preaching, and their movements rapidly grew. Faced with this proselytism, the CIC recommended swift repression. On the matter of crime, the CIC noted an "explosion in wanton, blatant, and spectacular crimes":

> Murders in cold blood are committed with no fear of admitting guilt; theft is committed in the public view. The collective assassinations in recent times and other isolated but deliberately planned cases, such as the assassination of the burgomaster of Rusumo Commune on February 6, 1983, demonstrate the transformation of certain individuals into real human beasts. The wave of crime is reported throughout the country and is not the monopoly of any single region. It is spreading to all the prefectures in the country and infecting both the countryside and urban centers.[89]

The members of the CIC wondered if they were witnessing "crimes aimed at emulating the events that preceded the moral coup d'état of July 5, 1973, and the events of April 1980" to destabilize the authorities. After reviewing the social and economic causes of these criminal behaviors, the CIC declined to dismiss that possibility.[90] These phenomena brought to the minds of these leaders the possibility of foreign subversion. They did not consider this insubordination to be the expression of an authentic popular political position. The criminal behaviors described by the CIC seemed to contain a measure of defiance to the established order, an element to which the CIC was particularly sensitive.

At the end of the 1980s, with the rapid deterioration of living conditions, this defiance of authority could only spread, particularly among the young rural people. Guichaoua noted that in the hills, the youth were "most susceptible to turning a deaf ear to 'rural values,'" and as a collective, they were harder and harder to mobilize. He also observed in the peasants' words the "profound bewilderment of the elders and of the authorities in the hills," who helplessly watched the young people slip out of their control.[91]

The crisis caused hardening of social relations, which in turn caused an increase in conflicts between neighbors and especially increasing violence within families, leading to intergenerational conflicts, murders by poisoning, machete attacks, and in the regions with more sophisticated social interactions such as Butare, hired hitmen.

Researchers Catherine André and Jean-Philippe Platteau did a survey in a small village in the north inhabited exclusively by Hutus except for one Tutsi woman. This village had 87 families and about 460 people. During the period from January 1993 to January 1994, they recorded 158 aggravated conflicts.[92] Anthropologist Danielle de Lame reports similar violence, this time in the northern hills of Kibuye, between 1988 and the summer of 1990:

> In the hills, without violence being more frequent than in our [European] cities, it was more visible, and everyone knew killers or more moderate attackers who had been freed, and their victims. In addition, constantly hovering was the fear of less open violence, such as the use of "poison" and the various charges of physical attacks from some neighbors during a brawl. The violence seemed to constitute, with alcohol, one of the few remedies to the boredom of rural life. Cases were numerous enough to be part of the normal memory in the hills mingled with the very practical souvenir of the actions of some people at the time of the revolution, actions from which only they benefited.[93]

A Red Cross document mentions the feeling of impending doom that prevailed at the time: "Food production was slowing as dramatically as the population was increasing. . . . In the late 1980s Rwanda's foreign residents were speculating on a catastrophe before the end of the century. Would it be famine, which struck the Rwandan southwest in 1989, or AIDS with a 33 percent infection rate in urban areas in 1990? Bloody conflict arrived first."[94]

The political history of the Habyarimana regime, just like that of the First Republic, can be interpreted as a process of continuous political exclusion of increasingly larger sections of society. Barely in power, the regime of the Second Republic had restored the policy of a ban on refugees and had institutionalized the policy of ethnic and regional balancing, which established the political marginalization and social quotas, in greatly varying degrees, of Tutsis and Hutus of the center and south. Ruhengeri, Gisenyi, and Byumba Prefectures, in the north, were assigned the larger slice of the national pie. In 1980, a coup attempt allowed President Habyarimana to alienate his political allies from the Ruhengeri Prefecture and the Bugoyi Region within the Gisenyi Prefecture.[95]

During the 1980s, power was concentrated in the hands of people originally from the small Bushiru region (Gisenyi Prefecture) and more particularly in the hands of the president's wife's family. Rwandans called this group *akazu*, meaning "small hut," in reference to the *mwami*'s inner circle. This group and its allies, through corruption and close connections within the ruling political and military class, held a concentration of power that resulted in a stranglehold on the country's resources.[96] At the time of the presidential and parliamentary elections in 1988, the regime was betraying signs that it was running out of steam: "Strong dissensions within the ruling organs of the party and increasingly open popular disinterest in the politics characterized by lies, double-speak, corruption, nepotism, ethnocentrism, and regionalism were publicly exposed during electoral campaigns that resembled more of a circus."[97]

The economic and social crisis shrank the political base of the regime, with the majority of the peasants increasingly asserting their move away from the MRND. The party had banked too heavily on general mass support and neglected to create a real political base, albeit smaller, but at least more expansive throughout the country.[98] At the end of the 1980s, the signs of the "last days of a dying regime" multiplied.[99]

The early 1990s deepened the severe crisis experienced in the country since the late 1980s. A new element was the structural adjustment program (SAP) initiated by the World Bank in 1991 with the promise of financing of $90 million.[100] Rwanda devalued its currency by 40 percent in 1990 and 15 percent in 1992. However, Rwanda did not experience a rise in exports, one of the major objectives of the SAP.[101] The SAP dramatically affected urban populations because of the high inflation and spending cuts by the government, contributing to the reinforcement of a "formidable anxiety across the Rwandan social fabric at the beginning of the 1990s."[102]

In the following chapter, we will see how the social groups excluded by Habyarimana would, in the last four years of the regime, join forces against him before the revival of the ideological hostility toward the Tutsi inherited from the First Republic. This division of those excluded from the Second Republic would allow the regime to make a last-ditch effort that would end in a terrifying bloodbath.

Notes

1. Prunier, *Rwanda Crisis*, 1997, pp. 74–90; Reyntjens, *L'Afrique des Grands Lacs en crise*, 1994, pp. 31–36; Uvin, *Aiding Violence*, 1998, pp. 19–160.

2. Guichaoua, *The Problem of the Rwandese Refugees and the Banyarwanda Populations in the Great Lakes Region*, 1992.

3. République rwandaise, Ministère de l'Intérieur et des Affaires judiciares, *Procès-verbal de la réunion des préfets tenue à Kigali le 31 Juillet 1973 sous la présidence de monsieur le Lieutenant-Colonel Kanyarwenge Alexis*.

4. Ibid.

5. Ibid.

6. Reyntjens, *L'Afrique des Grands Lacs en crise*, p. 30.

7. Presidential Decree No. 25/01, February 26, 1966.

8. Republic of Rwanda, Ministry of Interior, Ministry of Justice, *Circular No. 2420/A.90/ in Relation to the Presidential Decree No. 25/01 of February 26, 1966, Providing Procedures for the Reintegration of Refugees and Various Other Claims*, October 25, 1973.

9. Republic of Rwanda, Ministry of Interior and Public Service, *Lettre circulaire du Ministre aux Préfets portant sur la destination des biens abandonnés par les réfugiés*, May 22, 1975.

10. In its memo, the Rwandan delegation to Kampala indicates that the initiative came from the Ugandans. Republic of Rwanda, Ministry of Foreign Affairs and Cooperation, *Mémorandum sur les réfugiés rwandais en Ouganda de la délégation rwandaise partie en mission à Kampala du 21 au 28 juillet 1974*, n.d.

11. Republic of Rwanda, Ministry of Foreign Affairs and Cooperation, *Lettre du Ministre au Président de la République du 31/07/74 faisant rapport de la mission à Kampala et transmettant différents documents y afférents*.

12. Republic of Rwanda, Ministry of Foreign Affairs and Cooperation, *Avant-projet d'accord entre le gouvernement ougandais et le gouvernement rwandais sur le rapatriement des réfugiés rwandais*, July 1974, Kampala.

13. Guichaoua, *Problem of the Rwandese Refugees*, p. 18.

14. Ibid.

15. On October 18, 1974, four months after the Kampala meeting, the interior minister sent his first circular to the prefects asking that all vacant property abandoned by refugees be definitively reallocated.

16. Republic of Rwanda, Ministry of Foreign Affairs and Cooperation, *Mémorandum des réfugiés rwandais en Ouganda* ,July 1974, Kampala.

17. Republic of Rwanda, Ministry of Foreign Affairs and Cooperation, *Mémorandum sur les réfugiés rwandais en Ouganda*.

18. Ibid.

19. Republic of Rwanda, Office of the President, *Instructions présidentielles relatives aux réfugies*, June 22, 1976.

20. République rwandaise, MRND, *Position du comité central du MRND face au problème des réfugiés rwandais*, 26/07/1986.

21. Guichaoua, *Problem of the Rwandese Refugees*, p. 26.
22. Ibid.
23. Refugees, interviews with author.
24. Watson, *Exile from Rwanda*, 1991, p. 10.
25. Prunier, *Rwanda Crisis*, pp. 69–70.
26. *Le Monde*, December 23, 1982.
27. Prunier, *Rwanda Crisis*, p. 70.
28. Most, if not all, members of the delegation who had drafted this memorandum were no longer at the center of the decision made in 1990.
29. Guichaoua, *Problem of the Rwandese Refugees*, p. 26.
30. Republic of Rwanda, Minister of the Interior, *Rapport de sécurité du Ministre au Président de la République pour le troisième trimestre 1974.*
31. République rwandaise, Ministère de l'Intérieur, *Dialogue entre le Président-Fondateur de la République et les congressistes préfectoraux lors de la tournée présidentielle du 16 avril au 6 mai 1976.*
32. Ibid.
33. République rwandaise, Présidence de la République, *Allocution du Président de la République, Président-fondateur du MRND clôturant sa tournée du 16 avril au 6 mai dans les préfectures.*
34. This tract addressed to the head of state stated, "The coexistence and collaboration of Hutus with Tutsis require a realistic approach, especially when it comes to equality in employment and in schools; it also implies that some positions (officers, prefects, and burgomasters) must be exclusively reserved for the Hutus."
35. The Abagogwe is a Tutsi subgroup that lives in the northern region of the country.
36. République rwandaise, Ministère de l'Intérieur, *Rapport sur la situation du pays du Ministre au Président de la République pour le 2e trimestre 1976.*
37. Antoine Mugesera, *Imiberero y'Abatutsikuri republika yambere n'iyakabiri (1959–1990)*, pp. 263–270.
38. République rwandaise, Ministère de l'Intérieur, *Rapport sur la situation du pays du Ministre au Président de la République du 19 octobre 1977.*
39. République rwandaise, Ministère de l'Intérieur, Direction Études et Évaluation, *Note au Ministre: Ethnie de monsieur Tabaro (pseudonyme) directeur au Minimart*, March 1, 1987.
40. République rwandaise, Présidence de la République, Ministère de la Présidence, *Lettre du Ministre au Ministre de l'Intérieur portant sur l'ethnie de monsieur Tabaro* (pseudonym), February 11, 1987.
41. République rwandaise, Ministère de l'Intérieur, *Lettre du Ministre au préfet de Gitarama portant sur l'ethnie de monsieur Tabaro* (pseudonyme), n.d.
42. République rwandaise, Ministère de l'Intérieur, Direction Études et Évaluation, *Réflexion sur le problème de la falsification des identités*, December 7, 1987.
43. Ibid.
44. République rwandaise, Ministère de l'Intérieur, Direction Etudes and Evaluation, *Falsification des identités: cas du Dr. Rusagara Philipe et Gasana Jean* (pseudonyms), February 13, 1989.
45. Toward the close of precolonial Rwanda and in the first years of the colonial period, determination of ethnic identity for certain people and family groups in social transition interacted with a complex network of social, economic, and cultural criteria. See Newbury, *Cohesion of Oppression*, 1998, p. 51.
46. République rwandaise, Ministère de l'Intérieur, Division Recensement et Statistiques, *Recensement administratif de la population rwandaise durant la période de 1960–1987*, October 1987, p. 10.

47. The Hima is a traditionally pastoralist people related to the Tutsi, whose area of settlement was Uganda and Tanzania and extended into northeastern Rwanda.

48. République rwandaise, Ministère de l'Intérieur, *Rapport du Ministre au Président de la République sur la situation du pays au troisième trimestre 1978*; République rwandaise, Ministère de l'Intérieur, *Rapport du Ministre au Président de la République sur la situation du pays au troisième trimestre,* November 3, 1978.

49. République rwandaise, Ministère de l'Intérieur, *Rapport du Ministre au Président de la République sur la situation du pays,* February 2, 1979.

50. From testimonies. For more on the events in Ntega and Maranagara, see Chrétien, Guichaoua, and Le Jeune, *La crise d'août 1988 au Burundi,* 1989; Reyntjens, *L'Afrique des Grands Lacs en crise,* pp. 55–61.

51. République rwandaise, Ministère de l'Intérieur, *Bilan des 25 ans d'indépendance du Rwanda: 1962–1987,* 1987, p. 148.

52. Ibid., p. 144.

53. Mouvement Révolutionnaire national pour le développement, manifesto, cited in *Traits d'Union Rwanda,* 1996, p. 10.

54. République rwandaise, Ministère de l'Intérieur, *Bilan des 25 ans d'indépendance du Rwanda,* pp. 143–148.

55. République rwandaise, Ministère de l'Intérieur, *Rapport sur la situation du pays du Ministre au Président de la République pour le quatrième trimestre 1974.*

56. République rwandaise, Ministère de l'Intérieur, *Résultats du référendum constitutionnel du 17 décembre 1978.*

57. République rwandaise, Ministère de l'Intérieur, *Résultats des élections présidentielles du 24 décembre 1978.*

58. République rwandaise, Ministère de l'Intérieur, *Résultats du référendum constitutionnel du 17 décembre 1978.*

59. République rwandaise, Ministère de l'Intérieur, *Rapport sur la situation du pays du Ministre au Président de la République sur la situation du pays pour le quatrième trimestre 1974*; République rwandaise, Ministère de l'Intérieur, *Rapport sur la situation du pays du Ministre au Président de la République pour le premier trimestre 1975.*

60. République rwandaise, Ministère de l'Intérieur, *Résultats des élections présidentielles du 24 décembre 1978.*

61. Guichaoua, "L'ordre paysan des hautes terres centrales du Burundi et du Rwanda," 1989, p. 144.

62. République rwandaise, Ministère de l'Intérieur, *Bilan des 25 ans d'indépendance du Rwanda,* pp. 187–190.

63. Ibid., pp. 189–190.

64. République rwandaise, Ministère de l'Intérieur, *Dialogue entre le Président-fondateur du MRND, Président de la République et les congressistes préfectoraux lors de la tournée présidentielle du 16 avril au 16 mai 1976.*

65. République rwandaise, Ministère de l'Intérieur, *Bilan des 25 ans d'indépendance du Rwanda,* p. 190.

66. Here, one may cite Gérard Prunier, who expresses an opinion held by many analysts of the Rwandan political situation: "The genocide happened not because the state was weak but on the contrary because it was so totalitarian and strong that it had the capacity to make its subjects obey absolutely any order, including one of mass slaughter." Prunier, *Rwanda Crisis,* pp. 353–354.

67. World Bank, *Rwanda: Economic Memorandum* (Washington, DC: World Bank, 1983), p. 32.

68. Ibid., 60.

69. Marysse, De Herdt, and Ndayambaje, *Rwanda: Appauvrissement et ajustement structurel*, 1994, p. 29.

70. Ibid., p. 30.

71. Hanssen, *Le désenchantement de la coopération*, 1989, p. 10; Uvin, *Aiding Violence*, pp. 41–42.

72. Ibid., p. 33.

73. World Bank, *World Development Indicators*, 2014.

74. Ibid.

75. Willame, *Aux sources de l'hécatombe rwandaise*, 1995, p. 21.

76. Bart, *Montagnes d'Afrique, terres paysannes,* 1993, p. 215.

77. Willame, *Aux sources de l'hécatombe*, p. 35; Marysse, De Herdt, and Ndayambaje, *Rwanda,* pp. 43, 51.

78. Willame, *Aux sources de l'hécatombe*, p. 133.

79. Nkulilyingoma, "Iyi nzara itututse he, iragana he?" *Imbaga* 1 (1990): 8–9.

80. Guichaoua, "L'ordre paysan des hautes terres centrales du Burundi et du Rwanda," p. 59.

81. See ibid., pp. 1–28; De Lame, *A Hill Among a Thousand*, 2004.

82. Guichaoua, "L'ordre paysan des hautes terres centrales du Burundi et du Rwanda," pp. 128–130. Although aptly demonstrating the loss of authority of rural social structures and the increasing rise in popular insubordination, Guichaoua minimizes the important rise in violence in the countryside.

83. Ibid., p. 176.

84. Ibid., pp. 128–130.

85. Willame, *Aux sources de l'hécatombe,* p. 155.

86. From 1980 to 1992, the share of the agricultural sector in the revenue had slightly diminished, whereas, during the same period, revenues for civil servants had doubled. See Maton, *Développement économique et social au Rwanda entre 1980 et 1993,* 1994, annexe B5.

87. Prunier, *Rwanda Crisis*, pp. 141, 248; Gourevitch, *We Wish to Inform You,* 1998, p. 23; Willame, *Aux sources de l'hécatombe*, p. 105.

88. See especially Bayart, Mbembe, and Toulabor, *Le politique par le bas en Afrique noire*, 1992; Azarya and Chazan, "Disengagement from the State in Africa," 1987.

89. République rwandaise, Ministère de l'Intérieur et du Développement communal, Comité interministériel de Coordination, *Lettre du ministre et président du CIC au Président de la République faisant rapport des réunions du CIC*, August 29, 1986.

90. Ibid.

91. Guichaoua, "L'ordre paysan," pp. 128–134.

92. See André and Platteau, "Land Tenure Under Unbearable Stress," 1998.

93. De Lame, A *Hill Among a Thousand,* p. 309.

94. International Federation of Red Cross and Red Crescent Societies, "Under the Volcanoes: Special Focus on the Rwandan Refugee Crisis," in *World Disasters Report*, 1994 cited by Uvin, *Aiding Violence*, p. 181.

95. Prunier, *Rwanda Crisis*, p. 85.

96. Reyntjens, *L'Afrique des Grands Lacs en crise*, pp. 32–33.

97. Nsengiyaremye, "La transition démocratique au Rwanda," p. 239.

98. The popular disengagement from the regime emerges more clearly in the focus on regional and local studies in subsequent chapters.

99. Marie-France Cros, "Atmosphère de fin de règne à Kigali," *La Libre Belgique* (October 31–November 1, 1989).

100. Uvin, *Aiding Violence*, p. 58.
101. Marysse, De Herdt, and Ndayambaje, *Rwanda,* p. 57.
102. Willame, *Aux sources de l'hécatombe*, p. 155.

3

The Winds of Change

Against the background of the devastating socioeconomic crisis
Rwanda experienced in the late 1980s described in Chapter 2, in this chapter
I seek to explain the circumstances that led to the 1994 genocide. In one aspect, the genocide was a desperate attempt by the National Revolutionary
Movement for Development (MRND) political and military elites to retain
power in the face of the challenge posed by both the Rwandan Patriotic Front
(RPF) war beginning in 1990 and the internal Hutu political opposition. In another more fundamental way, it was an attempt by a wide range of people and
groups to defend the Hutu political identity of the Rwandan state inherited
from the 1959 revolution. Accordingly, those in power would not have been
able to conceive the scale and depth of the genocide, or carry it out, without
the contribution of its second most important agent, the Hutu-power ideological coalition centered in the former opposition party, the Republican Democratic Movement (MDR). In its confrontation with the RPF and the Hutu democratic opposition, the MRND elite was firstly preoccupied with retaining its
power and privileges, whereas the MDR–Hutu-power coalition motivation
was of a more ideological nature.

In the first part of this chapter, I recall the sequence of events between October 1990 and April 1994, focusing on the actions of the MRND political and
military elites up to the genocide. In the second part, I focus on the evolution
of the political opposition to the MRND, from its united front in 1991, when
political pluralism was established, to its split and the subsequent formation of
the Hutu-power coalition. I analyze the ideological path that led to the genocide along with the associated violent political culture in Rwanda at the time,
in which the "democratic" political opposition often proved as abusive as the
former party-state it confronted.

The MRND Party-State Resistance to Change

The War of October 1990

On October 1, 1990, the army of the RPF infiltrated the northeast of the country from Uganda, setting off a war against the regime. The movement was made up of Rwandan refugees living in Uganda as well as those scattered in neighboring countries and elsewhere around the world. The RPF demanded the rule of law, the abolition of ethnic and regional discrimination policies, and the right of return for refugees. The political-military movement was led by Rwandans who had been top ranking officers in the Ugandan Army and had made a major contribution to the victory of President Museveni's guerrilla army four years earlier.[1] According to Gérard Prunier, the RPF leaders moved up the start date of the war because of the decadence of the Habyarimana regime, the official process to select refugees eligible for repatriation (negotiated in July 1990 with Uganda),[2] and the pressures on the Kigali regime to democratize. According to him, the Habyarimana regime was aware of the RPF preparations for attack but did not respond, hoping that an armed conflict would give it the opportunity to settle scores with opponents within the country.[3] Developments within Uganda also had an effect because Rwandan military commanders were being sidelined, threatening their access to military resources they intended to steal to launch their attack in Rwanda.

The Rwandan government denounced the close political and military relations between the Ugandan Army and the Rwandan Patriotic Army (RPA), the armed wing of the RPF, from the first days of the war and also refused to respond to the political issues raised by the war. With decisive military help from France, the government stopped the advance of the RPA, and on October 30, 1990, the regime celebrated the "end of the October war."[4] The RPA then opted for guerrilla warfare and permanently occupied the northern strip of the country.

From October 4, 1990, on, the regime's reaction was to imprison between 6,000 and 7,000 people it accused of collaboration with the enemy. Among them were a large number of important Tutsi figures and Tutsi professionals, some Hutus targeted for score-settling as well as "opponents" who hailed from regions resistant to the regime, such as Gitarama Prefecture. Following strong international pressure, these political prisoners were released in April 1991.[5] The other reaction by the authorities was the massacre, in that very month of October 1990, of hundreds of Tutsis in the peripheral zones, in the Kibilira Commune in the northwest of the country, and in the areas around the military operations where Hima pastoralists lived.[6]

The Democratization Process

In the face of the rise in peasant disobedience in rural areas, the pervasive mood of political fragility, and the winds of change blowing across the rest of the world and particularly Africa, President Juvénal Habyarimana announced on July 5, 1990, the creation of a national synthesis committee whose mandate was to begin dialogue with all the active forces in the country in order to renew the country's political structures. The initiative was to remain under the auspices of the MRND. On September 1, a group of thirty-three intellectuals published a document in which they strongly demanded political pluralism. In December, the commission released a preliminary draft of a national political charter and a law on political parties. In the meantime, political groups were forming in a clandestine manner. The first party to come out in the open, in March 1991, was the MDR, which adopted part of the name of the former MDR–Party of the Hutu Emancipation Movement (PARMEHUTU). The new MDR laid claim to the heritage of President Kayibanda's social revolution but without adopting the acronym *PARMEHUTU* given its current goal of ethnic reconciliation.[7]

Other parties soon followed suit: the Social Democratic Party (PSD), considered the party that drew intellectuals and many Hutus as well as Tutsis from the south; the Liberal Party (PL), made up of business people, the party with which the Tutsis identified; and the Christian Democratic Party (PDC), whose influence was very limited.[8] There were a great many other tiny parties we will not discuss here. On June 10, 1991, President Habyarimana promulgated the new constitution and, one week later, the law on political parties. In July 1991, the parties were officially registered. In the following six months, the new parties worked feverishly to compel the regime to hold a national conference and form a coalition government that included them.

On October 13, 1991, President Habyarimana appointed Sylvestre Nsanzimana, a personality from the MRND known for his integrity, to form in December a government whose members almost all came from his party. The opposition saw this as direct provocation and organized a protest campaign aimed at destabilizing the regime.[9] In the towns, the main parties formed a cartel, the Steering Committee of Democratic Political Parties, to defend their demands in a united platform. The committee organized a protest campaign that culminated in huge demonstrations on January 7, 8, and 11, 1992, in Gitarama, Kigali, and Butare Prefectures, respectively.[10] The demonstration in Kigali was designed to make a huge impression: according to some sources, between 30,000 and 100,000 people took to the streets. On January 11, 15,000 people marched through the streets of Butare. The government, shaken, resumed negotiations with the opposition.[11] This period of democratic openness was accompanied by freedom of speech and a sudden wave of numerous newspapers denouncing the misdeeds of the regime, real or imagined, with some also launching hate propaganda.[12] The demonstrations exposed the political isolation of the MRND, which from then on faced double opposition: internal from the political parties and external from the political and military RPF. This political development resulted in an unspoken alliance between the internal and external opponents of the MRND and the MRND response of building a strategy of bloody resistance to change.

On April 2, 1992, the president appointed, on the recommendation of the opposition cartel, Dismas Nsengiyaremye, an MDR figure, to form a government that included the MRND and other major political parties. The MRND kept nine ministries, including the Defense and Interior Ministries, and opposition parties received eleven portfolios, among them the Ministries of Primary and Secondary Education, Information, Finance, and Justice as well as the crucial Ministry of Foreign Affairs, which pursued negotiations with the RPF.[13] The government's action plan, signed by the MRND and the opposition, included seven items: negotiate peace with the RPF, ensure internal security, streamline administrative operations to enhance efficiency and neutrality, revive the economy through structural adjustment, organize a national debate on the opportunity for a national conference, resolve the refugee problem, and organize general elections.[14]

Right from its formation, the transition government scored some points, including the abolition of the ethnic and regional quota system in April 1992 by Agathe Uwilingiyimana, the minister for primary and secondary education. This major move had earned her great popularity but also provoked the anger of the MRND bosses, who would not accept that one of the most important tools of the political and social domination by the north be ended by a woman from the south. On May 8, 1992, she was attacked at her home by unknown people suspected to be MRND members. Over the next few days, around 3,000 women from the opposition and 10,000 students from schools in Kigali marched in the streets to demonstrate their support for the minister. Security services were shared between two different ministries. The managing director of the Rwanda Office for Information (ORINFOR), Ferdinand Nahimana, future cofounder of the hate station Radio Télévision Libre des Mille Collines (RTLM), was fired for having called for ethnic hatred on national radio. The prefects accused of being linked to massacres in the countryside were also fired and replaced with members of the opposition. At the top, justice exhibited signs of independence as the Constitutional Court overturned laws passed by the still-majority-MRND parliament, and even presidential decrees, as unconstitutional.[15]

The Arusha Peace Process

The landmark event for the transitional government was definitely the launch of the negotiation process that led to the Arusha, Tanzania, peace accords. Between March 29, 1991, the date of the initial cease-fire agreement, and July 31, 1992, several cease-fire agreements were violated by one side or the other. The first interactions between the RPF and a delegation of three opposition parties—MDR, PSD, and PL—took place in Brussels between May 29 and June 3, 1992, to clear the way for negotiations with the government to begin in Paris a few days later. The final communiqué on this meeting affirmed their convergence in the fight against a dictatorial regime.[16] This meeting was extremely contentious for members of the internal opposition and marked the beginning of an ideological divorce. Meanwhile, a psychological threshold had been crossed, and it opened the way for the negotiations sought by the Nsengiyaremye transitional government.

On August 18, 1992, the protocol of agreement on the rule of law was signed in Arusha. On October 30, 1992, and January 9, 1993, the first protocols of agreement on power-sharing within a broad-based transitional government (GTBE) were signed. On June 9, 1993, the protocol on the repatriation of refugees and the resettlement of displaced persons was signed, and protocols on the integration of the armies of both parties as well as on final arrangements were signed on August 3, 1993.[17] On the day after the signing of the first protocol, the political climate radically changed, and after that every period surrounding the conclusion or signing of an accord was characterized by significant political tension and massacres of Tutsis as the Habyarimana regime pursued its strategy of sabotaging the peace process.

The president of the republic and the MRND were the greatest losers in the peace accords. In sum, the president was stripped of almost all his powers and retained only a ceremonial role. The real power landed in the GTBE, made up of the MRND, members of the political parties led by the MDR and the RPF. Six parties were to form a government in which the RPF and MRND had six ministers each; the MDR would have five ministers and retain the prime minister portfolio. Finally, the integration of the RPF and the government army was planned to comprise 60 percent from the government army and 40 percent from the RPF, whereas the two sides equally shared the positions at the top of the military hierarchy. The institutions for transition were to be put in place thirty-seven days before the final signing of the accord—that is, on September 10, 1993—and a UN observation force was to oversee the proper implementation of the accord. This political transition was to take twenty-two months, with only one extension allowed.[18] From August 1993 until his death on April 6, 1994, President Habyarimana increased delay tactics to slow down the establishment of transitional institutions, including the government itself; the divisions among the opposition political parties only aided him.

The MRND accused the Nsengiyaremye transitional government and the opposition in general of treason. As part of its strategy, the president's party had helped create in March 1992 an openly racist party, the Coalition for the Defense of the Republic (CDR), a relatively limited but extremely violent political organization. The CDR aimed for the creation of a common Hutu front to fight all the Tutsis as well as the Hutus who sided with the Tutsis. The other institution that carried out the work of the MRND was the Interahamwe ("those who attack together") militia, the MRND's youth wing, which also became very powerful beginning in March 1992.[19] Last but not least, extremist newspapers constituted the third civilian pillar of radicalization of the regime.[20]

The most striking element of this resistance strategy consisted of provoking massacres of Tutsis in order to ethnicize the conflict to the maximum, destabilize the transition government, and breach the objective alliance between the country's internal opposition parties and the RPF. This was particularly evident in an attack on November 7 and 8, 1991, in the Murambi Commune east of Kigali that left one person dead, dozens injured, and hundreds displaced.[21] The burgomaster and the deputy prefect of the region, both MRND hard-liners, were directly implicated in the violence. This moment corresponded with the beginning of a tug of war between the opposition parties and the MRND-dominated transition government following the appointment of Nsanzimana as prime minister on October 13, 1991. On the nights of March 4 and 5, 1992, during the period of bitter negotiations between the president and the opposition, several communes in the Bugesera Region in the south of Kigali were the scenes of massacres of several hundred Tutsis and Hutu members of the opposition. From August 20 to 22, 1992, the violence was perpetrated against Tutsis in the Gishyita and Rwamatamu Communes in the Kibuye Prefecture; dozens of people were killed, hundreds injured, and thousands displaced.[22] The violence took place two days before the signing of the first protocol of the peace agreement on the rule of law. From January 21 to 25, 1993, hundreds of Tutsis were massacred in the south in the Gisenyi Prefecture and in an adjacent commune in Kibuye Prefecture. The killing occurred twelve days after the protocol of accord on power-sharing, which gave the Interior Ministry to the RPF, and in so doing caused an uproar within the president's party.[23]

The formation of Dismas Nsengiyaremye's government in April 1992 marked the beginning of a struggle between the MRND and the MDR along with the opposition in general for political supremacy in the countryside outside the MRND strongholds in the north. The struggle affirmed the supremacy of the MDR and the opposition parties in a large section of the country. However, faced with the magnitude of the massacres, the RPF on February 8, 1993, broke the cease-fire for the first time since the Arusha peace process and advanced to within fifty kilometers of Kigali. The "February war" marked a turning point in the conflict and provoked political realignments that only gave President Habyarimana more room to maneuver, even as the confrontation with the opposition January 19–20, 1993, marked a temporary isolation of his party.

In addition to these incidents of violence perpetrated by the MRND and the CDR, they began to set up more machinery for mass murder toward the end of 1992. In October 1992, the Habyarimana Defense Ministry placed a huge order for the purchase of light arms and grenades that exceeded the needs of the Rwandan Army.[24] At the end of September and beginning of October 1992, the army chief of staff sent a command to all military units and camps to draw up lists of all RPF accomplices.[25] Between January 1993 and March 1994, 581 tons of machetes were imported into Rwanda; these were just a fraction of the 3,385 tons of metallic products, clubs, picks, and hooks imported within this period. Estimating the weight of a machete as one kilogram, Human Rights Watch (HRW) calculated that would translate into 581,000 machetes imported, that is, one machete for every three adult Hutus, doubling the machetes imported in previous years. These weapons were imported by businessman Félicien Kabuga, a close friend of President Habyarimana.[26] On January 20, 1993, a group of military officers, the Alliance of Soldiers Provoked by the Age-Old Deceitful Acts of the Unarists (AMASASU), wrote an open letter to the president of the republic signed by "Commandant Mike" in the name of the Supreme Council.[27] Commandant Mike recommended the creation of a battalion of robust young men from every commune ready to join a popular army that would lend strong support to the regular army. HRW suggests Commandant Mike was Colonel Theoneste Bagosora, head of the administration at the Defense Ministry, later accused of being the main architect of the genocide.[28]

By late 1992 and early 1993, a pattern of actions both political and practical, suggested the Habyarimana regime's will to prepare for a mass killing of Tutsis, and the conditions for the implementation of genocide began to coalesce. However, having opted to use the masses for this purpose, the groups planning the genocide still lacked one crucial element: sufficiently broad political support. The year in which that support would emerge was 1993, when the president's inner circle succeeded in breaking out of its political isolation with its theme of a "race" war.

The Consequences of the RPF Attack of February 8, 1993

The February 8 RPF offensive displaced nearly 860,000 people, who deserted the war zones and fled south.[29] The huge mass of people camping not far from Kigali offered a concrete image of the military power of the RPF. The considerable psychological impact of the assault and the accusations of exactions and summary executions against the RPF made a good number of Hutus from the opposition doubt the real RPF intentions. They wondered if, after all, the propaganda of the president's party was not correct in portraying the RPF as a Tutsi instrument to take over power.[30] Politically, the February offensive widened the ideological gap within the most important opposition party, the MDR, placing Habyarimana back in control. This opportunity appeared shortly after the president's party, the MRND, had lost to the MDR in most of the country[31] and just after the International Commission of Inquiry into the Violation of

Human Rights in Rwanda released its report that implicated Habyarimana's regime in the massacres occurring within the country since 1990.[32]

The Hutu-Power Movement

Three developments contributed to the rise of the Hutu-power movement: first, psychological shock caused by the February 8 offensive that would lead in particular to the split within the MDR in July 1993 and coincide with the replacement of Nsengiyaramye, whose mandate as prime minister had officially ended;[33] conclusion of the Arusha accords and signing of the protocol on the integration of the armed forces on August 3, 1993, which had become controversial since the February RPF offensive;[34] and political exploitation of the assassination of the first elected Hutu president of Burundi, Melchior Ndadaye, on October 21, 1993, by Burundian Tutsi army officers.[35] The impact of these events and their exploitation by politicians gave rise to the Hutu-power movement that, at the end of 1993, brought together the MRND, the CDR, the majority of the MDR, and a significant faction of the PL. Among the opposition parties, only the PSD stood its ground, and only a marginal minority joined the Hutu-power movement.[36]

The rise of the Hutu-power movement symbolized alignment of a large segment of the opposition with the MRND and CDR theory of fighting total "racial" war and the concurrent elimination of Hutu RPF "accomplices." The movement crowned the success of President Habyarimana's strategy to ethnicize the conflict right from the beginning in 1990. Led by Frodauld Karamira of the MDR, Hutu-power leaders revived the CDR criticism of Habyarimana for his concessions to the RPF. They defiantly asked President Habyarimana if he was ready to lead the Hutu-power movement, confront the RPF, and liquidate its "accomplices" within the country, Tutsis as well as Hutus who continued to defend the Arusha accords.[37]

The Assassination of President Habyarimana

The end of 1993 and the beginning of 1994 were characterized by the development of urban terrorism in Kigali, street violence, and political assassinations such as that of principal PSD leader Félicien Gatabazi.[38] President Habyarimana deployed a whole series of strategies to block the implementation of the Arusha accords. The accords called first for the establishment of the GTBE including the RPF. At the end of March 1994, the president had exhausted his stock of maneuvers, and pressure from the European Union, the UN, the neighboring countries, and the entire international community had intensified.[39] Filip Reyntjens cites two conflicting testimonies, one of which stated that the president, a few days before he traveled to Dar es Salaam, was not ready to yield to this provision of the accords. The other, from his chief of cabinet, Enoch Ruhigira, affirmed that before the president's departure, he had asked Ruhigira to prepare a communiqué announcing that the institutions would be established on April 8.[40] On April 6, 1994, President Habyarimana headed for Dar es Salaam to participate in a regional summit for heads of state. The situation in Burundi was the main item on the agenda, but for most of the meeting practically all of the heads of state admonished their Rwandan counterpart to end his intransigence.[41] As he returned, two missile shots brought down his presidential plane.

The identity of the culprits and those who ordered the attack has been the subject of heated debate for years. The most tangible indication eventually came in February 2012 from a ballistics report commissioned by French judges Trevidic and Proux that established that the missiles were fired from the area of Habyarimana's presidential guard barracks, implying that the main suspects were members of the slain president's own guard.[42]

Although responsibility for the death of the president is an important issue, HRW raises the question of whether this event caused the genocide:

> Responsibility for killing Habyarimana is a serious issue, but it is a different issue from responsibility for the genocide. We know little about who assassinated Habyarimana. We know more about who used the assassination as the pretext to begin a slaughter that had been planned for months. Hutu-power leaders expected that killing Tutsis would draw the RPF back into combat and give them a new chance for victory or at least for negotiations that might allow them to win back some of the concessions made at Arusha.[43]

The Eruption of the Genocide

In its comprehensive report on the genocide, HRW presents a long chronology from November 1993 to April 4, 1994, proving that in the months preceding Habyarimana's death, there was overwhelming evidence of preparations of a large-scale massacre targeting members of the opposition and Tutsis in general. The regime established arms caches, distributed weapons to militias, trained militias, set up a rapid communication network between the commanders of the militias, and drew up lists of RPF sympathizers designated as the first to kill. These developments were confirmed with revelations made at different times by a member of the conspiracy.[44] In the face of all this, General Romeo Dallaire, head of the military contingent of the UN Assistance Mission in Rwanda (UNAMIR) serving as a peacekeeping force, repeatedly asked for authorization to intervene, particularly to seize the arms caches as a warning to those preparing the massacres. However, the UN office in New York turned down the request each time, arguing that the peacekeeping mandate of the UNAMIR did not allow him to intervene.[45] In UN meetings, the United States, still smarting from the Somali experience, categorically refused to reinforce the mandate of the UNAMIR, thwarting the efforts of Belgium, which since February 1994 had detected the risk of genocide.[46] On its part, France defied the odds and continued to support the Habyarimana regime.[47] The passiveness of the UNAMIR and the assurance of French support emboldened the planners of the genocide.[48]

On the day following the death of the president, in the wee hours of April 7, 1994, the killing machine—made up at the beginning of contingents of the elite presidential guard, the para-commando and reconnaissance battalions, and the Interahamwe militia, all coordinated by Colonel Bagosora and other top military officers from the north—went into action and targeted Tutsi notables and opponents as well as Hutu members of government opposed to the Hutu-power movement.[49] That was the beginning of the resumption of the war against the RPF, the genocide against the Tutsis, and the massacre of opposition leaders that would last for three months, causing the extermination of about 75 percent of the Tutsi population living in Rwanda and the deaths of thousands of Hutus.[50]

There is sufficient evidence to support the theory of state control of the genocide in Rwanda, but on its own, the theory offers a partial and reductionist framework of interpretation. A different reading of the events that focuses on the role of the political opposition and civil society from 1991 onward, and that above all takes into account the political developments outside the capital and other urban centers, leads us to a noticeably different interpretation of the process as the genocide unfolded. It also better illuminates the sociology of the mass participation in the genocide.

The Political Opposition at the Root of the Genocide

Most of the analyses of the genocide focus mainly on the role played by the state and the former state-party the MRND and its propaganda machinery in the initiation of the genocide. In this section I will elaborate on the role played by the civil and nonstate political society in the implementation of the genocide. I seek to show the vital role played by the MDR, which between 1991 and 1994 constituted the center of gravity of the opposition in the country. The party incrementally over time, rather than abruptly in the summer of 1993, offered the president's clique the political resources necessary to accomplish the genocide project throughout the country, especially in the regions with significant Tutsi populations. I also trace the way a significant number of MDR members entered into the genocide because this faction, far from having "renewed" itself, owes its participation in the extermination to its commitment to the PARMEHUTU ideology.

Ambiguities in the MDR Ideology

Jordane Bertrand's study on the complexity of the ideological debate at the heart of the MDR is a good starting point. According to Bertrand, the MDR was reactivated when the democratic space opened up for different reasons. On the one hand, a real ideological attachment to the party from former prominent PARMEHUTU figures or their sons and daughters and other sections of society still existed; on the other, the desire of some in the center of the country for revenge against the northerners persisted. Finally, there was a general feeling that for these reasons, the relaunching of President Kayibanda's party would rapidly mobilize a large number of people. The calculation proved correct: at least 237 people initially signed up to relaunch the MDR. However, in 1991, unmitigated appeals to President Kayibanda's party, the MDR-PARMEHUTU, were controversial because of its history of violence and persecution against Tutsis. During the period of political mobilization in 1991 and up to the appointment of Nsengiyaremye as prime minister, party speeches constantly oscillated between idealizing the Kayibanda regime and emphasizing the need to strive for national reconciliation:

> The discussions on the choice of the party initials already revealed a problem. Faustin Twagiramungu, who participated in articulating the call, proposed to preserve the acronym because of its mobilizing power but change its content. His proposed "Mouvement Démocratique Rwandais" [Rwandan Democratic Movement, or MDR] was rejected, although it made it possible to avoid referring to the republic, which, as we will see, remained ambiguous. Discussions were even more heated on whether to preserve the mention of "PARMEHUTU" after the MDR. The term was finally abandoned in the call to relaunch the new party. It would also not be in the program manifesto and the party statutes, which started being broadcast in May 1991. It openly reappeared in 1993, at the moment of crisis. This discussion of the mention of ethnicity revealed a double problem: it was necessary to avoid reviving the demons of the past and the image of the PARMEHUTU as the defender of the power of the Hutu majority and as the instigator of the anti-Tutsi pogroms of 1959, 1963, and 1973. What needed to be shown was that the problem in Rwanda was not ethnic but social. But ambiguities remained, revealed by the decision of some to relaunch the MDR-PARMEHUTU newspaper *Urumuri rwa Demokrasi*. The paper reappeared in June 1991 and, symbolically, its issue number was the one following the last issue released when the magazine ceased publication eighteen years before! There was no greater proof of continuity, be it declared, assumed, or affirmed.[51]

The goal for the initiators of the renovated party was to promote continuity and change. Therefore, party ideologues were using social terms to interpret and defend the democratic achievements of the 1959 revolution and to accuse the MRND of suspending those gains. The "ethnic Hutu" was replaced by the "social Hutu." As in 1959, it was a question of fighting the "oppressor," but in 1991 it was clear that the oppressor could be Hutu or Tutsi. The goals were still the same, but the enemy had changed. In 1991, the enemy was Hutu, which should prove that the new MDR had refused to be an ethnic party. It wanted to be the party that defended the "little guy," the ordinary person, and fought for the freedom of the masses. The MDR framed its loyalty to the 1957 Bahutu manifesto in exclusively social terms, but that text had presented social and ethnic issues as a seamless whole.[52] Bertrand raises the important question of how much difference these new subtleties made in the minds of people exposed over a long time to the PARMEHUTU ethnic propaganda:

> But who can tell what remains of these speeches in the minds of people after thirty years of this kind of propaganda? Is the distinction between the ethnic and the social clear enough to dispel fears of any confusion? The glorification of Grégoire Kayibanda's regime did not allow one to clarify the issues cited during that time; the party merged the two problems by defining the social as ethnic. . . . Several testimonies report MDR leaders and militants reviving a good portion of the PARMEHUTU discourse. The red and black colors of the new MDR flag were the PARMEHUTU colors. The songs of the 1959 Revolution were reinstated to their former prestige. The *imparamba* dances of the revolutionary period were revived at meetings. We are therefore witnessing the recreation of a whole atmosphere that can only encourage confusion.[53]

My study of the content of speeches given by the national and regional MDR leaders in 1991 at a meeting in Butare, the country's third largest city, corroborates this opinion. The MDR made a deliberate effort to link the audience to an uncritically glorified PARMEHUTU past.[54] As we shall see later on, in the minds of peasants in Gitesi and Kigembe Communes, the MDR meant the MDR-PARMEHUTU.[55] This correspondence in two remote and contrasting communes supports Bertrand's thesis, suggesting that this "confusion" in the countryside between the historical MDR-PARMEHUTU and the MDR revived in 1991 was the result not only of their differences being too complicated but also of a deliberate MDR policy to cause "confusion." The ideological attachment to the PARMEHUTU ethnocentrism and the concern for political efficiency worked simultaneously. The reformists' criticism of this heritage did not go far enough, but more importantly, they limited their criticism to urban and intellectual circles, leaving the party free to promote the PARMEHUTU memory in rural communities.[56] This complicity of reformists and MDR conservatives in the rural areas worked in the end to the advantage of the conservatives and led to defeat for the reformists.

For a long time, this confusion between the historical MDR-PARMEHUTU and the new MDR rendered the party's position in the opposition coalition ambiguous, especially on the ethnic question. The problematic heritage of the PARMEHUTU was strongly felt among the younger generation in leaders such as Twagiramungu, who adopted a critical outlook on the issue. In an interview with a Rwandan publication in June 1991, Twagiramungu expressed his vision of a stabilizing multiple-party period that was "not liberating," thus distancing himself from the MDR-PARMEHUTU propaganda of the 1960s:

> Others within the party remained cautious and avoided adopting a position that was too critical. On the other hand, some did not deny this legacy, among whom were leaders of the older generation such as [Donat] Murego and François Xavier Gasimba. It is important to understand that it is primarily this relationship to Rwandan political history that generated, from the beginning, different tendencies within the new and revived MDR.[57]

The reaction of the different leaders to the crisis following the RPF military and political offensives followed the divide defined by the more or less strong support for the PARMEHUTU ideology. These differences, muzzled during the political mobilization against the MRND, were publicly heard the day after the RPF February 8, 1993, offensive.[58] From February 25 to March 2, five opposition parties including the MDR and the RPF met in Bujumbura; this meeting was an initiative of the opposition's search for ways to renew dialogue and revive the peace process. The final communiqué from the meeting called for, among other things, a lasting cease-fire and the resumption of the Arusha accord negotiations. On the closing day of the Bujumbura meeting, in Kigali President Habyarimana obtained his first success in building a Hutu common front. He had called a "national conference" attended not only by the MRND and the CDR but also by representatives of the four parties in government, namely, the MDR, PSD, PL, and PDC. The Kigali meeting resolutions, supported by the Rwandan armed forces, opposed the Bujumbura communiqué practically point by point, with a belligerent tone against the RPF, which supposedly sought to take power by force.[59]

Although the official leaders of the four opposition parties that participated in President Habyarimana's "national conference" released a communiqué disowning their fellow party members at the conference, the fruit was already rotting from within. The schism within the PL, the PDC, and above all the MDR became more pronounced and accelerated during subsequent political crises. Only the PSD stood its ground behind the leadership of Frederic Nzamurambaho, Félicien Gatabazi, and Theoneste Gafaranga in its choice to engage with the RPF against the Habyarimana regime. Within the other opposition parties, the dividing line would henceforth separate those who thought a rapprochement with RPF should be pursued and those who thought the RPF was the enemy even if ultimately Habyarimana will have to be ousted. The factionalism that affected the PL, the PDC, and especially the MDR led to constantly changing and complex political configurations with different motivations: differences in ideology and personality, political rivalries, and even the most trivial corruption. However, beyond this political fluidity, especially in late 1993, Bertrand observes that the common thread running through these divisions was the ideology that would lead to ethnic "clarification."[60]

One of the most significant initiatives in that direction came from the revival of the "Peace and Democracy" discussion "club" by its founder, Emmanuel Gapyisi. Gapyisi was an intellectual in the MDR, but he recruited members from each opposition party to create a large movement, rallying the various Hutu political forces to fight for the "Hutu people majority" against the RPF and President Habyarimana. With his fellow party members Murego and Frodauld Karamira, he contributed to the organization of the PARME-HUTU faction within the MDR. Stanislas Mbonampeka brought with him the support of the PL and Gaspard Ruhumuliza, a part of the PDC. From the PSD, only individuals with no major influence joined the group. The Peace and Democracy club became popular, with Gapyisi's reputation giving a touch of respectability to the ordinarily extremist politics of the CDR, better known for its violence and excesses. On May 18, 1993, Gapyisi was assassinated by unknown assailants.[61] Murego and Karamira then led the PARMEHUTU faction within the MDR. The definitive split from the MDR of the openly extremist faction that adopted the acronym PARMEHUTU exploded during the fight to appoint a replacement for outgoing Prime Minister Nsengiyaremye and appoint the prime minister proposed by the MDR to lead the future GTBE.[62] The two prime minister posts went to the MDR. Twagiramungu, then MDR president, proposed Uwilingiyimana as Nsengiyaremye's replacement without notifying the party *bureau politique*. This move alone caused major tensions within the party, but Twagiramungu's opponents focused their attention on the future prime minister of the GTBE. With Nsengiyaremye having withdrawn his candidacy, three-quarters of the members of the party *bureau politique* supported Jean Kambanda,[63] a little-known and dull personality who was president of the party finance commission and vice president of the Butare section of the MDR. On July 20, 1993, the party *bureau politique* made his candidacy official, and the following day Twagiramungu wrote to President Habyarimana presenting his own candidacy. Uwiligiyimana's and Twagiramungu's candidacies were accepted although presented in violation of MDR statutes. An agreement between Habyarimana and Twagiramungu was definitely suspected; the latter defended his personal political interests and the president finally succeeded in dividing the MDR that had caused him much political anxiety.[64]

On July 23 and 24, the MDR met at an extraordinary congress that confirmed the decisions of the *bureau politique*: it expelled Twagiramungu and Uwilingiyimana from the party as well as all those who had agreed to be part of Uwilingiyimana's government, and it cancelled Twagiramungu's self-nomination and confirmed the candidacy of Kambanda, who was close to the PARMEHUTU faction. The congress of the MDR, the most powerful opposition party, handed victory to the extremist faction with more than 70 percent of party representatives present and accepted the decisions by an overwhelming majority of more than 90 percent.[65] The MDR was split between a politically moderate minority known as the MDR-Twagiramungu and the MDR-PARMEHUTU majority, which progressed in the direction of extremism to become the epicenter of the Hutu-power movement. The split in the MDR was essentially a result of ideological disagreements that had divided the leaders from the beginning. That is what the Benelux section of the MDR suggested, saying that the crisis within the party was "linked primarily to the revisionism of the party's history, theories defended by Twagiramungu and his cronies."[66] A similar phenomenon, foreshadowed by the participation in the Peace and Democracy club, appeared in the PL and the PDC and to a lesser extent in the PSD. Near the end of October 1993, following the assassination of the newly elected Burundian Hutu president Ndadaye, the Hutu-power movement became official. This was the movement that would rely on the small group of military officers and politicians within the president's inner circle who would decide to launch the genocide.

MDR *bureau politique* had supported the PARMEHUTU faction by a majority. Afterward, the congress, largely made up of delegates from the prefectures, amplified the victory of the PARMEHUTU faction. To better grasp the political influence and ways of operating of the MDR in the country, one must see the party in action at the grassroots, in Kigali and in the rural areas. Without going into great detail, I give here an overview of the geographical distribution of the influence of MDR in the country and its recurring modes of action.

An important clarification must be mentioned here. Even if since the revival of the MDR in 1991 there was an important continuity between loyalty to PARMEHUTU ideology and later on to involvement in the genocide, that does not necessarily mean that all members of the MDR with this predisposition followed the same path to the Hutu-power coalition and then participated in the genocide. Within the party there were people who, although defending the Hutus' right to dominate the Rwandan state because they were the majority, did not cross the line into genocide.

The Parties at the Grassroots

Political parties had four principal public activities: rallies, demonstrations, press conferences, and publication of communiqués. The political parties intensely solicited the population through numerous rallies in the cities or in the main centers of the prefectures, the communes, and even the administrative sectors. These activities took place in a spirit of fierce competition. The populations responded positively to the call by political parties and enrolled in large numbers, participated in rallies, and formed dance troupes and choirs similar to the MRND *groupes d'animation* (entertainment groups) of the past. These groups were responsible for warming up the audience before the rallies began and for giving the parties maximum visibility. Performances to publicize the meetings began the previous evening with the partisan groups singing, dancing, and beating drums, often late into the night. The more noise a party made, the more it was perceived as powerful. In this society, which lived on so little, the parties distributed caps in the party colors, scarves, and even shirt uniforms. Another site of partisan activity was the cabarets, the small bars in both the town and the countryside where endless political discussions took place. The parties put great effort into respecting Rwandan tradition in which the big man offers drinks to the ordinary folk, one of the most important recruitment strategies. Finally, political parties quickly carried out much-disputed internal party elections, even in the most remote hills.

Shortly, the ground for activism was occupied by party youth wings with evocative names. The MRND had the Interahamwe; the MDR had the Inkuba, meaning "lightning," or Youth for a Democratic Republic (JDR); the PSD had the Abakombozi, from the Kiswahili word for "liberators"; and the CDR had the dreaded Impuzamugambi, or "those who have the same goal." In the face of competition among the political parties, the party youth wings supporting the regime transformed themselves into true militias. These militias began to receive military training at the beginning of 1992. In 1992 and 1993, 200 people had been killed in sectarian violence by the Interahamwe and other groups.[67]

Political parties in Kigali. In Kigali, in the poor neighborhoods, members of different parties, especially of the youth wings, lived together in an often violent atmosphere, especially after the installment of the Dismas Nsengiyaremye coalition government in April 1992. Violent incidents were most intense during demonstrations and meetings, such as during a march organized by the Interahamwe on May 28, 1992, against the youth wings of the other parties at the same time the PSD was holding a rally in a different neighborhood. The street battles that took place that day left forty people seriously injured.[68] The gravity of these violent incidents was not necessarily in proportion to the size of the demonstration. On August 4, 1992, the CDR organized a demonstration in Kacyiru, Kigali's administrative district, in order to demand the release of its party members from prison, and in clashes with police, two CDR members and a police officer were killed.[69]

Another incident of extreme political violence in Kigali took place in the period following the signing of the Arusha protocols on October 30, 1992, and

January 9, 1993. On November 15, 1992, in a speech in Ruhengeri, President Habyarimana disowned the peace negotiations led by the government and called the Arusha accords "scraps of paper."[70] On November 17, 1992, Prime Minister Nsengiyaremye wrote to the president, criticizing among other things his double-speak concerning the peace negotiations and his call to the Interahamwe to build up a strike force for his "election tours."[71] Two days later, the MDR, PSD, PL, and PDC organized an aggressive demonstration in support of the government and the Arusha accords. The demonstrations, in which members of different parties exchanged blows, left eighty people seriously injured and eighty houses and twenty-eight vehicles destroyed. The young social democrats, the Abakombozi of the PSD, proved just as violent as their counterparts in the MDR, MRND, and CDR. The violence provided an opportunity for other acts such as looting of stores, extortion, unpaid bar bills, petty theft, and mugging pedestrians.[72]

During creation of the Hutu-power coalition, the change in the political climate at the grassroots manifested itself for the first time through ethnic violence in the streets of Kigali. On the day after they organized the October 23 rally at the Nyamirambo Regional Stadium, in honor of the birth of their coalition, the MDR-PARMEHUTU, MRND, and CDR hunted down only Tutsis, looted their shops, and raped a number of them.[73] These events were the opportunity to settle personal scores.[74]

However, Kigali had the worst incidents of violence on February 23 and 24, 1993. This was in response to the lynching the day before in Butare of the CDR president by PSD partisans seeking to avenge the assassination in Kigali of their leader, Gatabazi. The violence led by the CDR and Interahamwe in the streets of Kigali left 35 people dead and 150 people injured.[75] After the establishment of the Hutu-power movement in October 1993, which attenuated the rivalry between the militias of the opposition and those of the president's camp, street violence became increasingly ethnic. With the military training of the Interahamwe and the Impuzamugambi militias in 1993, the capital was controlled by the militias.

MRND- and CDR-dominated zones. In March 1992, the Interahamwe participated for the first time in a massacre of Tutsis in Bugesera. In late 1992 and early 1993, the youth militia was again implicated in massacres that took place in the northwest.[76] It was no coincidence that the most violent acts took place in these areas.

Similarly, there were several Interahamwe militias in the north and northwest, namely, in Gisenyi, Ruhengeri, and Byumba Prefectures but also in the east and southeast in Bugesera and Kibungo Prefectures. For a long time, these regions were underpopulated in comparison with the rest of the country, and they had welcomed many immigrants from the Gisenyi and Ruhengeri Prefectures, mostly daily-wage agricultural workers. Finally, many members of the northern political and economic elite had acquired "large" parcels of land for livestock and farming in the east. Northerners mobilized in favor of the MRND and the CDR in these regions, often using violence because a significant portion of the local elite were opposed to these parties. After the February 1993 offensive by the RPF, the Interahamwe recruited extensively among those displaced by the war in the Byumba Region.[77]

Kubohoza, [78] *the hegemonic violence of the MDR.* The methods of action used by the MDR in the rural areas under its control received little scrutiny, yet the MDR, the principal actor in the opposition, often used physical intimidation to control entire communes, sectors, and even cells, generally situated in the remotest areas.[79]

The following is a chronology of the main events that began in August 1991 and intensified after the installation of the Nsengiyaremye government:[80]

*Gitarama Prefecture.*This is the prefecture where the practice of *kubohoza* [to "liberate" the communes from the grip of the MRND] began. From the establishment of political pluralism until the end of 1992, clashes between the MDR and MRND supporters were practically permanent, especially in the Ndiza and Gacurabwenge Regions, in the north of the prefecture, composed mainly of Nyakabanda, Nyabikenke, Rutobwe, Kayenzi, Taba, and Runda Communes.[81]

Nyakabanda Commune. This is the commune where everything began, when in mid-1992 MDR partisans blocked the roads, preventing the burgomaster, Straton Sibomana, and other employees of the commune from getting to work. Faced with harassment from the MDR members, the burgomaster preferred to tender his resignation. On the nights of July 5 and 6, 1992, in the Kibimba Sector, three MRND supporters attacked and seriously injured a member of the MDR. Almost immediately, a rumor spread that MRND supporters had killed a member of the MDR. The head of the MDR in the commune gathered a small troop of supporters who attacked the attackers, the councilor of Kibimba sector, and other MRND sympathizers. Hundreds of victims of this revenge attack sought refuge at the commune headquarters.[82]

Nyabikenke Commune. After the expulsion of the burgomaster of Nyakabanda, the action continued in neighboring Nyabikenke Commune. MDR supporters rejected the newly appointed burgomaster, Mathias Bishokaninikindi, accusing him of being an MRND stooge and of professional incompetence.[83] Several incidents provoked confrontations of MDR and MRND supporters from the commune throughout 1992, but the most violent ones took place outside a rally organized on November 1, 1992, by the MRND. A certain Renzaho, a member of the MRND, lost his life on that day when he and his friends fell into an ambush of MDR supporters. The next morning, as a certain Habumuremyi was returning from the prosecutor's office, where he had gone to report the circumstances of Renzaho's death, he was intercepted by JDR members who beat him to death.[84]

Taba Commune. On April 26, 1992, a certain Claver Kamana, a well-known MRND partisan who was arranging medical emergency transport to the Remera-Rukoma Hospital, was forced to abandon his vehicle and flee after MDR partisans punctured his tires. On May 1, 1992, MDR members accused the burgomaster, who was attending community work *umuganda* organized by the MRND, of having taken sides and banned him from setting foot in the commune headquarters. This political tension was transformed into violence against MRND sympathizers, many of whom were forced to flee their homes at night, leaving the houses at the mercy of looters. Several houses as well as the MRND office were destroyed. On May 4, 1992, a demonstration by opposition parties headed for the commune office to demand the release of their colleagues imprisoned for the attack against Kamana on April 26. The presence of gendarmes and of the assistant prefect did not deter the demonstrators. A certain Eugène Haguminshuti was shot dead by a gendarme, and two other people were injured.[85]

Masango Commune. In this commune situated in the south of the prefecture, MDR partisans attempted to carry out *kubohoza* on the burgomaster, Esdras Mpamo. The operation failed because of opposition from a section of the population.[86]

Butare Prefecture. Here, we will simply mention that the Kigembe and Nyakizu Communes were the scenes of extremely violent *kubohoza* operations, and the chaos spread into the Nyaruhengeri Commune. The sectors of the Muganza, Muyaga, and Ntyazo Communes were also affected. The PSD and PL did the same thing in the Nyabisindu Commune. More details on Butare will come in the following chapters.[87]

Gikongoro Prefecture. In August 1991, there were repeated acts of arson in the forests, especially in the communes of the Munini Subprefecture. The damage was significant: several hectares of eucalyptus and pine trees were burned, and beehives and cassava plantations were destroyed. The Mount Uwagahunga side of Nyungwe Forest was equally affected.[88] In mid-1992, after having forced the burgomasters of Nshili and Kivu communes to resign, MDR supporters seized fields granted to groups of landless cultivators; burned down the communal forests; and gave themselves the right to impose taxes, imprison people, and convene the population. The prefect and subprefect of Gikongoro were taken hostage as they tried to restore calm.[89] In the Kinyamakara Commune, MDR supporters forced the burgomaster to carry MDR emblems at a rally.[90]

Kibuye Prefecture. This prefecture, which we shall discuss in detail later, did not experience major incidences of *kubohoza* except in the Nyamarebe Cell of Burunga Sector, Gitesi Commune. In August 1991, state-owned forests were set on fire in almost all the communes. The majority of these acts took place after MDR rallies.[91] From August 20 to 22, 1992, violence was committed against the Tutsis of Gishyita and Rwamatamu, as we have already seen. These acts of violence were financed by supporters of the president's inner circle, but because it was a region in which MRND had lost most of its influence, they hired MDR supporters to carry out the violence.

Cyangugu Prefecture. In August 1991, in Kagano, Gatare, and Gafunzo Communes, MDR supporters incited people to destroy equipment used to prevent soil erosion and to invade state-owned land.[92]

Nyakabuye Commune (May to November 1992). From the month of May onward, serious conflicts erupted between supporters of the MDR and the MRND. On November 7, 1992, in the Kaboza Sector, MDR supporters attacked those of the MRND and looted their property, forcing the latter to flee. On November 8, the burgomaster, accompanied by police officers, attempted to intervene, and there was a commotion. The officers shot and killed three protestors. In response, the MDR supporters looted and burned twenty-three homes and ten stores. MRND sympathizers and their families sought refuge in the commune office and the Kibirizi Parish.[93]

Kagano Commune (July 1992). On July 10, 1992, MDR supporters, with the help of their friends from Kagano and Gatare Communes, put up roadblocks and shattered the windows of stationery vehicles, but the gendarmes quickly intervened and quashed the attack.[94]

Kirambo Commune (July 1992). On July 8, 1992, MDR supporters, with the help of their friends from the Kagano and Gatare Communes, attempted to overthrow the burgomaster by attacking the commune headquarters, but several residents of the commune opposed the move and protested, and the attack failed.[95]

Gatare Commune (July 1992). On July 13, 1992, MDR supporters in the commune, with the help of their friends from the Kagano and Birambo Communes, attempted to throw out the burgomaster of the commune by attacking the commune office. The assailants managed to hold the burgomaster and three police officers hostage. The coup was cut short after the gendarmes intervened.[96]

In regions favorable to the opposition and particularly to the MDR, these provocations were a demonstration of strength by their party. In general, *kubohoza* unfolded in several communes that formed homogeneous subregional blocks, far from the main centers of the prefecture. In at least two of the prefectures, these operations were located in the zones that were the scenes of major violence perpetrated by the MDR-PARMEHUTU during the revolution. In the north of Gitarama Prefecture, *kubohoza* started in the Ndiza and Gacurabwenge Regions, where the 1959 *jacquerie* also started. The violence affected the southwest of Butare, the initial home of MDR-PARMEHUTU influence in the region and the scene of the 1961 violence.

However, it is important to go beyond kubohoza and come back to the question of political control of the population to try to determine which regions were under the influence of which parties. In the absence of a genuine electoral process throughout the country at the time, the study of a particularly high-conflict episode between the president's party and the opposition should be sufficient for us to attempt an answer.[97]

Demonstrations and Counterdemonstrations of January 1993

The demonstrations organized by the MRND and the CDR and the counter-demonstrations by the opposition were the turning point of the major confrontation between the Nsengiyaremye government and the president's camp. The cause of this confrontation was the signing, in Arusha on October 30, 1992, and January 9, 1993, of the protocols on power-sharing within a broad-based government that included the RPF. As we have already noted, on November 15, 1992, Habyarimana had called the accords "scraps of paper" and Prime Minister Nsengiyaremye had reacted. We have also seen that on November 19, 1992, the MDR, PSD, PL, and PDC had organized a huge demonstration in Kigali. On November 22, Léon Mugesera, then vice president of the MRND in Gisenyi Prefecture, gave a speech that created a sensation, in which he asked that members of the opposition who were traitors to the Hutu cause be "judged and executed" and that Tutsis be sent back to Ethiopia via the Nyaborongo River, implying as dead bodies.[98]

On January 20, 1993, the MRND and the CDR began to demonstrate again in different parts of the country. On the evening of January 19, Nsengiyaremye, in a speech broadcast on national radio, called upon opposition supporters to mobilize for self-defense.[99] Demonstrations and counterdemonstrations followed, and the president's clique, faced with the militant hostility of the opposition throughout the country, organized massacres of Tutsis in the heart of the regime, the Ngororero Subprefecture, located south of the Gisenyi Prefecture. Nsengiyaremye himself analyzed the facts as he defined the zones of influence of both the president's circle and the opposition:

> As a protest against the protocol of agreement, the MRND and its satellite parties under the umbrella of the Alliance for Democracy in Rwanda (ADERWA) have decided to oppose, by force if necessary, the acceptance of the protocols of agreement already signed and the pursuit of negotiations. . . .
>
> With the support of the local authorities, the MRND has organized violent demonstrations throughout the country from January 20 to 22, 1993, and announces its intention to paralyze all activities. The opposition parties refused to be intimidated and have organized counterdemonstrations that neutralized the activities of the MRND and its affiliates in Byumba, Kibungo, Kigali-town, Kigali-rural, Gitarama, Butare, Gikongoro, Cyangugu, and

Kibuye Prefectures (except the Rutsiro Commune). In Gisenyi, Ruhengeri, Kigali-rural (Bumbogo and Buliza Zones), Byumba (Tumba Commune), and Kibuye (Rutsiro) Commune, the demonstrations rapidly turned into riots and the so-called demonstrators took to killing Tutsis and members of the opposition. Four hundred people died and 20,000 people were displaced.

These so-called demonstrations are in fact a cover for a major operation aimed at provoking a general civil war in line with the plan Léon Mugesera made public.[100]

Nsengiyaremye's somewhat understated reference to the "neutralization of the activities of the MRND and its affiliates" through counterdemonstrations by the opposition in fact referred to a real confrontation, often in the form of street battles that caused many deaths and injuries as well as significant property damage.[101] We need to understand the nuances of the geographic distribution of the zones where the president's clique had successfully organized demonstrations, and where the opposition had successfully neutralized the clique's influence, as presented by the prime minister. I have established three categories of prefectures:

1. The prefectures in which the MRND and its allies had successfully organized important demonstrations and in which their political dominance on the ground was unquestionable.
2. The prefectures in which opposition parties were entrenched and in which they had either succeeded in neutralizing the MRND demonstrations or persuaded them against any activity.
3. The prefectures in which the two forces shared influence and in which one or the other had organized demonstrations.

To a large extent, Gisenyi, Ruhengeri, and Byumba Prefectures belonged to the first category.

In the second category were Gitarama Prefecture, where the MRND held no demonstrations; Butare Prefecture, where the MRND had made a feeble attempt at a demonstration; Kibuye Prefecture, where the MRND had successfully organized a major demonstration in the Rutsiro Commune but had also met with resistance from the remote communes such as Bwakira and Gisovu and had not organized anything in the remaining six communes; Gikongoro Prefecture, where the MRND was only able to organize a weak demonstration; and Kigali-town, dominated by the opposition parties.

Finally, in the third group were Cyangugu Prefecture, where in the four communes along the border with Zaire the MRND and its allies successfully organized demonstrations but where nothing changed in the interior and in the north; Kibungo Prefecture, where the president's people had successfully organized major demonstrations that spread throughout the prefecture but where the opposition organized counterdemonstrations; and Kigali-rural Prefecture.[102]

This confrontation between the two camps was a real political test and clearly defined each side's sphere of influence. In a large part of the country—Gitarama, Butare, Gikongoro, Kibuye (almost all), Cyangugu (a large part), and Kigali-town(in part)—the president's camp, which essentially controlled the state's coercive forces (the army and the police), was not able to mobilize a large enough section of the population to organize demonstrations of such magnitude. This reveals the extent to which the president's party had lost control of the population. The geographical distribution of the political influence of different parties was confirmed two months later by the brief election experience reported by Reyntjens.[103] In March 1993, the government replaced thirty-eight burgomasters for inefficiency. A great number of them, at least in the center and south of the country, were compelled by the kubohoza activities to resign, or their mandate was so disputed that they could not carry out their duties effectively. Their replacement effectively led to a restricted electoral process, a kind of "preselection" by an electoral college that included the heads of the sectors, members of the commune's development council, heads of development projects, and representatives of parties and churches in the communes.[104] Reyntjens explains:

> Even if the action was limited and the electoral college was controlled, the "preselection" of March 23, 1993, nevertheless provided some indication of the relative strength of the different parties. Here are the first-place winners, as follows: sixteen MDR, fifteen MRND, four PSD, two PL, and one CDR. More significantly, from a regional point of view, one notes that the MRND won all the top positions [except in the Ramba Commune in Gisenyi, which went to the CDR, at the time allied with the MRND] in the Prefectures of Gisenyi, Ruhengeri, Byumba, and Kibungo, whereas MDR took them in the Gitarama Prefecture. Elsewhere, the scenario is less monolithic; the greatest diversity is in Butare (three PSD, two PL, one MDR, and one MRND). One can therefore confirm their impression that MRND has kept control of the north, MDR monopolizes the center but maintains a respectable presence in other areas, and the PSD had only a limited regional presence in the south (Butare and Gikongoro).[105]

Thus we can observe that, at least until March 1993, there was a clearly defined geography of the spheres of political influence between the president's party and the opposition. In the opposition-controlled zones, one notes an overall and complete dominance of the MDR in Gitarama Prefecture; a section of Gikongoro Prefecture; and a major part of Butare, Kibuye, and Cyangugu Prefectures (see Map 3.1).

Earlier, I attempted to demonstrate that the question of MDR reform was predominantly debated in urban areas, most of all in the capital, Kigali, and

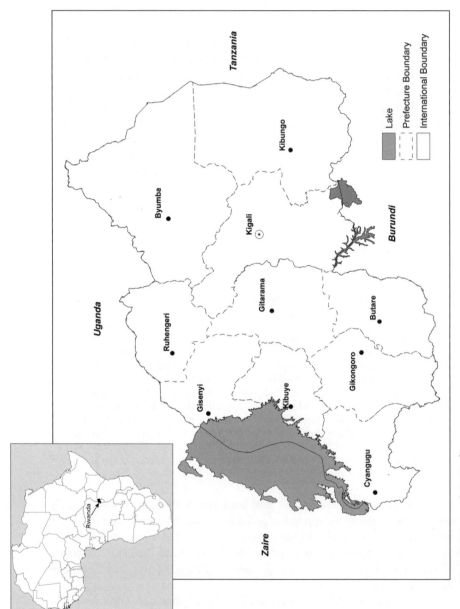

Map 3.1 Rwanda's Prefectures

that in the prefectures and the regions the continued connection with the MDR-PARMEHUTU had already been cultivated since August 1991. This awareness emerged during the extraordinary party congress of July 23 and 24, 1993, with the rising military power of the RPF in the background. On that basis, I advanced the theory that the core MDR membership in the prefectures and the regions easily embraced the Hutu-power ideology because of its pre-existing ideological affinities and because the revival of the PARMEHUTU legacy encouraged the expectation of predatory campaigns at the grassroots.

A second observation can be made at this point: although the core of the MDR had joined with the president's circle at the end of 1993 in favor of total war against the RPF, the Tutsi, and the remaining opposition, the MDR and MRND, the two main political forces constituting the Hutu-power movement, still kept the political control they exercised separately in their respective backyards. This means that at the time of the genocide, mostly carried out through mobilization of the people, the collaboration of the MDR—and even more broadly of the Hutu-power factions of the former opposition parties— was indispensable for spreading the genocide to the regions they controlled; otherwise the MRND-controlled state would not have been able to obtain compliance.

The detailed HRW chronology of the political developments in the polit-ical center of the country, Kigali, on the day following the death of Habyari-mana and the beginning of the genocide seems to support this last hypothesis. Its investigation indeed identified the main organizers of the genocide, such as Colonel Bagosora and other top-ranking military officers from the north, sup-ported by the elite armed forces, the police, and the Interahamwe. The report showed that an overwhelming majority of the first victims of the massacres were Tutsi but also Hutu politicians in government and other decisionmaking bodies and more generally Hutu members of political parties still opposed to the Hutu-power coalition. HRW explained that from April 6 to 11, 1994, around 20,000 people had already been killed, most of them Tutsis, in Kigali and to a small extent all over the country, although not in a consistent fashion. Several members of former opposition parties, including Hutu-power sympa-thizers, feared a political manhunt targeted at opposition parties. Around the country, Hutus had united with Tutsis to push back groups of killers. On April 8, Colonel Bagosora formed an interim government exclusively made up of Hutu-power members with a president from the MRND, Théodore Sindikuwabo, as president and an MDR-power leader, Jean Kambanda, as prime minister, both originally from Butare.

However, it was only on April 11, 1994, that a real effort to expand the political and social base of the genocide machine began, with a meeting of pre-fects convened in Kigali during which the interim government made it clear the killings had to continue. The expansion of the political base in support of the genocide was accomplished by coopting Hutu members of political groups other than the MRND and people originally from the center and south of the country, but above all by specifying the target of the massacre campaign, that is, explaining clearly that the enemy to kill was the Tutsis exclusively. This campaign, which aimed at forming an alliance against the Tutsis that transcended political and regional divisions, began on April 11, 1994 after having completed the elimination, of Hutu and Tutsi political leaders who might have resisted the genocidal political coup:

> The next day, both political and governmental leaders began mobilizing popular support for genocide. By inciting the people against Tutsis, they clarified the indirect message delivered the previous day to the administrators. Speaking on Radio Rwanda early on the morning of April 12, MDR-power leader Frodauld Karamira told his listeners that the war was "everyone's responsibility," an idea that would be frequently repeated over the next few weeks. He called on the people to "not fight among themselves" but rather to "assist the armed forces to finish their work." This was a directive to MDR-power supporters to forget their differences with the MRND and the CDR and to collaborate with them in tracking Tutsis. Without this collaboration, advocated by Karamira since his "Hutu-power" speech the previous October, the genocide would have remained limited to strongholds of the MRND and the CDR.[106]

If one follows the HRW interpretation, the collaboration offered by the Hutu-power factions of the former opposition parties facilitated the genocide project of the MRND, CDR, and MRND-dominated state to reach the Tutsis living in the regions they controlled almost completely—that is, Gitarama, Butare, Kibuye, and Gikongoro Prefectures, which corroborates my analysis. The 1991 census put the number of Tutsis living in these four prefectures at 56.8 percent of the country's entire Tutsi population. To this number one has to add the Tutsis living in regions partially controlled by the former opposition, namely, Cyangugu, Kigali-rural, Kigali-town, and Kibungo Prefectures (37.1 percent of the country's Tutsi population), where without the collaboration of the former opposition the extermination would have been more complicated. By contrast, the 36,240 Tutsis living in 1991 in Gisenyi, Ruhengeri, and Byumba Prefectures, or 6.1 percent of the total Tutsi population, would also have been doomed. This theory, using the projected numbers, serves only to illustrate the importance of the collaboration of the Hutu-power factions of the former opposition parties in the successful implementation of the genocide in April–July 1994.

Notes

1. Prunier, *Rwanda Crisis*, 1997, pp. 89–116.
2. The act of calling the refugees "immigrants" shows the spirit in which the special commission expected to establish its repatriation project, that is, by evading the po-

litical dimension of the refugee question. Another limitation was the fact that the refugees were not involved in the repatriation plan.

3. Consequently, in the summer of 1990, delegates of the special commission on the problems of Rwandan immigrants who wanted to launch the repatriation project were asked not to rush the process. Prunier, *Rwanda Crisis*, p. 99.

4. Reyntjens, *L'Afrique des Grands Lacs en crise*, 1994, p. 93.

5. Ibid., pp. 94–98.

6. Prunier, *Rwanda Crisis*, pp. 109–110.

7. Reyntjens, *L'Afrique des Grands Lacs en crise*, pp. 104–106.

8. Ibid., pp. 106–107.

9. Bertrand, *Rwanda,* 2000, pp. 136–139; Reyntjens, *L'Afrique des Grands Lacs en crise*, pp. 109–110.

10. Reyntjens, *L'Afrique des Grands Lacs en crise*, pp. 108, 111.

11. Ibid., p. 111; Bertrand, *Rwanda*, pp. 139–145.

12. Chrétien et al., *Rwanda*, 1995.

13. Bertrand, *Rwanda*, pp. 174–175.

14. Reyntjens, *L'Afrique des Grands Lacs en crise*, pp. 111–112.

15. Ibid., pp. 115–116.

16. Bertrand, *Rwanda*, pp. 115–116.

17. Reyntjens, *L'Afrique des Grands Lacs en crise*, pp. 248–249.

18. Ibid., pp. 248–251.

19. Des Forges, *Leave None to Tell the Story*, 1999, p. 101.

20. Chrétien et al., *Rwanda*.

21. Reyntjens, *L'Afrique des Grands Lacs en crise*, p. 184.

22. Prunier, *Rwanda Crisis*, p. 162.

23. République rwandaise, Ministère de l'Intérieur, "Note sur les manifestations des partis MRND et CDR les 19, 20 et 21 janvier 1993," n.d.

24. Des Forges, *Leave None to Tell the Story*, p. 97.

25. Ibid., p. 99.

26. Ibid., p. 127.

27. *Amasasu* means "bullets" in Kinyarwanda.

28. Human Rights Watch establishes a parallel between the notes of "Commandant Mike" and the speech by Léon Mugesera of January 1993 announcing that the militants would implement their own form of justice on the accomplices—the Tutsi and members of opposition parties—if the competent authorities failed to act. He called for civilian self-defense on the principle that "he who wishes for peace prepares for war." Des Forges, *Leave None to Tell the Story*, p. 84.

29. Ibid., p. 87.

30. Ibid.

31. Nsengiyaremye, "La transition démocratique au Rwanda, 1989–1993," 1995, pp. 255–256.

32. International Federation of Human Rights et al., *Report of the International Commission of Investigation on the Violations of Human Rights in Rwanda Since October 1, 1990*, March 1993.

33. Reyntjens, *L'Afrique des Grands Lacs en crise,* pp. 122–124; Bertrand, *Rwanda*, pp. 231–236.

34. Des Forges, *Leave None to Tell the Story*, p. 126.

35. This event, which in itself definitely caused a rise in ethnic tension, was exploited to the end by the RTLM, which then began a real campaign of propagating hate with amazing efficiency. Chrétien et al., *Rwanda*, p. 69.

36. Prunier, *Rwanda Crisis*, p. 188.

37. Des Forges, *Leave None to Tell the Story*, p. 139.

38. Reyntjens, *Rwanda*, 1995, p. 61.

39. Prunier, *Rwanda Crisis*, p. 209.

40. Reyntjens, *Rwanda*, p. 23.

41. Ibid., p. 211.

42. Cour d'Appel de Paris, Tribunal de grande instance, "Destruction en vol du Falcon 50 Kigali (Rwanda)," *Rapport d'expertise*, January 5, 2012; Maria Malagardis, "Les dix-huit ans d'intoxication d'une enquête en sens unique," *Libération*, January 12, 2012.

43. Des Forges, *Leave None to Tell the Story*, p. 185.

44. Ibid., pp. 143–172.

45. Ibid., pp. 172–175.

46. Ibid., pp. 131–132, 175–177.

47. France maintained its collaboration with the interim government while the latter carried out the genocide in full view of the world.

48. Prunier, *Rwanda Crisis*, pp. 228, 352–353.

49. Reyntjens, *Rwanda*, pp. 56–58; Des Forges, *Leave None to Tell the Story*, pp. 182–185, 223..

50. Des Forges, *Leave None to Tell the Story*, pp. 15–16.

51. Bertrand, *Rwanda*, p. 88.

52. Ibid., pp. 91–92.

53. Ibid., p. 92.

54. Stratégie, n.d. (an unsigned campaign strategy document that was not on letterhead). The interior minister, who distributed it to the prefects, attributed it to the MDR. The content reflecting the desire to revive the past credibly implicates the MDR as its author, for instance in Subsection 11, which advises, "in the search for political representation, seriously considering the natural regions of each prefecture (the former chieftaincies of the colonial era)." Ibid. Also, at the Butare meeting, Dismas Nsengiyaremye used only the ancient names of the historical regions in his overview of the spread of the MDR in the country. Butare Prefecture, *Minutes of the MDR Meeting at Huye Stadium, February 16, 1992.*

55. Straton Nyarwaya, interview with author, May 26, 2001, Kigembe Commune. Nyarwaya was an accountant of the Kigembe Commune for more than ten years. Augustin Karara, interview with author, June 1, 2001, Kibuye Prison. Karara was burgomaster of Gitesi from 1990 to September 1994.

56. Bertrand, *Rwanda*, pp. 259–260.

57. Ibid., pp. 94–95.

58. It was only relatively muzzled because of the tendency MDR-PARMEHUTU had started to radicalize in mid-1992, during the rapprochement of the MDR with the RPF. Ibid., p. 224.

59. Prunier, *Rwanda Crisis*, p. 179.

60. Bertrand, *Rwanda*, pp. 252, 257.

61. Prunier, *Rwanda Crisis*, pp. 182–185.

62. The GTBE was the government organ set up in the Arusha accords; its role was to guide the transition process.

63. Reyntjens, *L'Afrique des Grands Lacs en crise*, p. 124.

64. Bertrand, *Rwanda*, pp. 223–224.

65. Reyntjens, *L'Afrique des Grands Lacs en crise*, p. 124.

66. Ibid., p. 122.

67. Des Forges, *Leave None to Tell the Story*, p. 56.

68. Préfecture de Kigali, *Note au Ministre de l'Intérieur de la part du préfet de Ki-*

gali portant sur les violences du 28/05/1992, May 28, 1992.

69. République rwandaise, Ministère de l'Intérieur, *Situation de sécurité dans le pays suite au discours du Premier ministre du 28 août 1992*, n.d.

70. Prunier, *Rwanda Crisis*; Bertrand, *Rwanda*, pp. 170, 198.

71. Dismas Nsengiyaremye, cited by Bertrand, *Rwanda*, p. 199.

72. République rwandaise, Ministère de l'Intérieur, "La manifestation des membres des partis MDR, PSD, PL et PDC du 19 novembre 1992," May 25, 1992. The members of these youth wings were politically unpredictable and switched parties as soon as a party offered better pay and opportunities for looting. Charles Karemano, interview with author, April 8, 2002, in Namur.

73. République rwandaise, Ministère de l'Intérieur, "Lumière sur les actes de violences qui seraient dirigés contre les Tutsis suite à la tentative de coup d'Etat au Burundi dans la nuit du 20 au 21 octobre 1993," November 17, 1992.

74. In fact, after May 1992, clashes between the Interahamwe and JDR in the area of Karambo—of the Murambi cell, Gikongo sector—were also a fight between Muvunyi of the MRND and Nzirorera of the JDR, two prominent personalities in the neighborhood who mobilized these youth to engage in personal combat by proxy. Finally, the Interahamwe got the upper hand, forcing about forty JDR members to seek refuge at the Burundian Embassy. République rwandaise, Ministère de l'Intérieur, "Rapport sur l'affaire d'une quarantaine de Rwandais qui se sont réfugiés dans l'ambassade de Burundi en date du 26 novembre 1992," November 27, 1993.

75. Prunier, *Rwanda Crisis*, p. 206.

76. Des Forges, *Leave None to Tell the Story*, p. 89.

77. Testimonies.

78. *Kubohoza* means "to liberate" in Kinyarwanda. The MDR partisans who carried out the violence against the local administrators considered loyal to the MRND claimed they were "liberating" the inhabitants from the yoke of the MRND.

79. Two examples of studies are Des Forges, *Leave None to Tell the Story*, pp. 54–57; Wagner, "All the Bourgmestre's Men," 1998, p. 32.

80. The *kubohoza* campaign, said to be an MDR strategy adopted after the installation of the government of Nsengiyaremye, was intended to enhance his power by giving him a territorial base.

81. République rwandaise, Ministère de l'Intérieur, "Les actes de violences et les opérations du *kubohoza* dans différentes parties du pays," n.d.

82. Ibid.

83. République rwandaise, Ministère de l'Intérieur, "Les conflits entre les partis politiques," November 1992.

84. Ibid.

85. Ibid.

86. Ibid.

87. This was the only commune besides Kigali where these parties initiated the *kubohoza*.

88. The interior minister's report accuses "political parties," without specifying which ones, of being behind the arson.

89. République rwandaise, Ministère de l'Intérieur, "Situation de sécurité dans le pays suite au discours du Premier ministre du 28 août 1992," n.d.

90. Ibid.

91. République rwandaise, Ministère de l'Intérieur, "Rapport sur la sécurité au mois d'août 1991."

92. République rwandaise, Ministère de l'Intérieur, "Les conflits entre les partis politiques," November 1992.

93. Ibid.

94. République rwandaise, Ministère de l'Intérieur, "Les actes de violences et les opérations du *kubohoza* dans différentes parties du pays," n.d.

95. Ibid.

96. Ibid.

97. Even the by-elections for burgomasters in May 1993 allow us to elaborate on an answer.

98. This was the metaphor reflected in the images of bodies of Tutsis floating in the Nyabarongo River during the massacres of the 1960s. Recording of Léon Mugesera's speech at Kabaya on November 22, 1992; transcript of Mugesera trial by the Canadian government in Montreal in 1995 and 1996 for, in particular, incitement to genocide.

99. République rwandaise, Ministère de l'Intérieur et du Développement communal, "Rapport de mission sur les troubles qui se sont perpétrés dans certaines communes des préfectures Gisenyi et Kibuye fin décembre et en janvier 1993," February 1, 1993.

100. Nsengiyaremye, "La transition démocratique," p. 256.

101. République rwandaise, Ministère de l'Intérieur et du Développement communal, "Rapport de mission sur les troubles qui se sont perpétrés dans certaines communes des préfectures Gisenyi et Kibuye fin décembre et en janvier 1993"; République rwandaise, Ministère de l'Intérieur et du Développement communal, "Note sur les manifestations de partis MRND et CDR les 19, 20 et 21 janvier 1993"; République rwandaise, Ministère de l'Intérieur et du Développement communal, "Sécurité dans les préfectures," January 1993.

102. République rwandaise, Ministère de l'Intérieur et du Développement communal, "Sécurité dans les préfectures," January 1993.

103. Reyntjens, *L'Afrique des Grands Lacs en crise*, p. 226; Des Forges, *Leave None to Tell the Story*, p. 112.

104. Ministerial Directive no. 46.04.09.01, March 11, 1993 (regarding the preselection of candidates for burgomaster).

105. Reyntjens, *L'Afrique des Grands Lacs en crise*, p. 226.

106. Des Forges, *Leave None to Tell the Story*, p. 202. Prime Minister Agathe Uwilingiyimana attempted such an act of resistance before she was assassinated.

4

Butare:
The Politically
Moderate Prefecture

Butare stood out as the prefecture that remained calm while the genocide had become the order of the day in the rest of the country, only to plunge into the genocide twelve days later under heavy external pressure. During these twelve days, different Hutu communities displayed a large spectrum of attitudes and actions from outright armed resistance to zealous, early participation in the genocide. The turning point was the visit of Théodore Sindikuwabo, president of the interim government, during which he rebuked the locals for their apathy. The president was accompanied by members of the presidential guard and militias coming from outside the prefecture to better incite the residents of Butare to join in the massacres. Indeed, Butare Prefecture was relatively removed from the conflict zones of the war between the RPA and the FAR that was now in its fourth year. Other prefectures such as Kibuye, Cyangugu, and Gikongoro were even more removed, yet that did not prevent them from plunging into the genocide on April 7, 1994. To be fair, parts of Gikongoro, Gitarama, and Kibuye delayed for a couple of days their involvement in the genocide, but did not resist it as neatly as many communities in Butare. The inhabitants of Butare were known for their long-standing political and ethnic moderation, for their defiance to the National Revolutionary Movement for Development (MRND) regime, and before to the MDR-PARMEHUTU. Kibuye, subject in later chapters, like Butare had a large Tutsi population, was remote from the war zone, was very poor, and was reticent about the MRND yet people in the prefecture participated rapidly and intensively in the genocide. The comparison of the attitudes toward the genocide of the two prefectures with similar social and political settings will prove very informative.

In order to better grasp the political moderation of the Butare population, I sought first to retrace the prefecture's political and social history between the late colonial period and the end of the political monopoly of the MRND party-state in the early 1990s. The first part of this chapter examines the period of the 1959 revolution in the Astrida area, which would become Butare in 1963.

We shall see that the area was distinctive in its development of a politically moderate culture, thanks to the action of APROSOMA, headquartered there, and the presence of the kingdom capital in its northen outskirts. The second part of the chapter retraces the social and political evolution of the prefecture under the Second Republic. We will see how deteriorating living conditions, reinforced by the looming threat of famine, significantly increased social disorder expressed through delinquency and serious crime. This social unrest, characterized by a high level of violence and mass unruliness, had taken on an aspect of generalized political dissent, although it did not turn into ethnic animosity until 1994.

Historical Context

The Northern Core of the Kingdom and the Southern Periphery

The north and northeast of Butare Prefecture, including the Nyanza Region, were part of the cultural and political central region, hub of the kingdom known as Nduga after the founding of the kingdom by Mwami Ruganzu Ndori in the seventeenth century.[1] The Nyanza Region, an important home to the monarchy from the nineteenth century on, became the permanent royal residence and the kingdom's capital from the beginning of colonial rule. In 1772, Mwami Cyilima Rugugira launched a war against Burundi that ended in the conquest of the whole southern region of Butare up to the Akanyaru River, which to this day remains the boundary between the two countries. Rugugira established two military companies, turning this region into the launchpad for his military assault on Burundi. Up to the 1959 revolution, these regions south of Butare had kept the names of the armies that were established in the area, such as Nyaruguru, Bashumba-Nyakare, and Mvejuru. These military zones, densely populated with Tutsis, corresponded to present-day Runyinya, Gishamvu, Nyakizu, Kigembe (in part), Nyaruhengeri, Ndora, and Muganza Communes (see Map 4.1 and Table 4.1).[2]

The concentration of Tutsis in these communes was very high, higher than the average in the prefecture, which in turn was higher than the national average. After the political chaos of the time and particularly the massacres of Tutsis in 1961, proximity to the border favored the escape of a good segment of this Tutsi population.[3] However, the area with the important Tutsi population did not quite reach the border marked by the Akanyaru River. On the southern side of the prefecture, a riverfront strip of about ten to twenty kilometers in the communes bordering Burundi was almost entirely populated by the Hutu. The level of political integration of precolonial southern Butare into the center of monarchical power is subject to debate. Jean-François Saucier carried out a study on traditional social relations in the southwest of the prefecture in Nyakizu and Gishamvu Commune and defends the integrated character of this re-

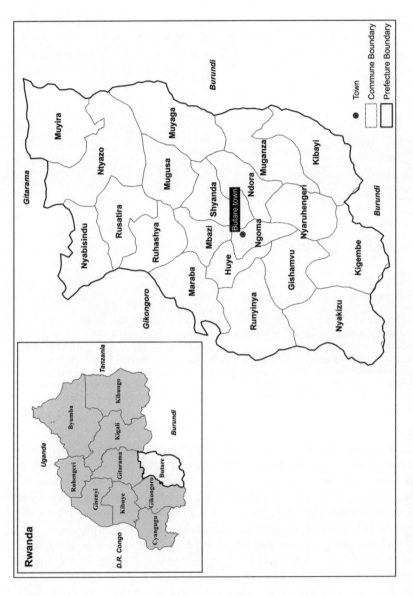

Map 4.1 The Prefecture of Butare

Table 4.1 **Ethnic Distribution of the Population
by Commune in Butare Prefecture, 1987**

Commune	Tutsi	Hutu	Twa
Nyabisindu	18.9	79.7	1.4
Ntyazo	15.7	83.6	0.7
Muyira	13.5	84.2	2.3
Rusatira	11.9	87.2	0.9
Ruhashya	13.1	86.4	0.5
Mugusa	22.7	76.3	1.0
Muyaga	11.6	87.0	1.4
Maraba	10.6	88.6	0.8
Mbazi	12.0	87.8	0.2
Shyanda	2.6	97.3	0.1
Huye	24.7	74.8	0.5
Ngoma	27.8	72.0	0.2
Kibayi	5.8	94.0	0.2
Runinya	42.3	56.7	1.0
Gishamvu	27.6	71.8	0.6
Nyakizu	18.4	80.7	0.9
Nyaruhengeri	25.6	59.4	5.0
Kigembe	7.7	92.0	0.3
Ndora	31.7	67.6	0.7
Muganza	35.8	63.5	0.7
Butare Prefecture	**18.7**	**80.3**	**1.0**
Rwanda	**10.94**	**88.53**	**0.53**

Source: République rwandaise, Ministère de l'Intérieur et du Développement communal, *Recensement administratif de la population rwandaise durant la période de 1960–1987*, 1987, p. 42.
Note: Table 4.1 presents the ethnic distribution in 1987. Although the Tutsi population in the entire country had diminished following the ethnic cleansing of 1959 and the massacres in the Gikongoro region, the proportional distribution of Tutsis by commune in Butare Prefecture was not profoundly altered; hence, the 1987 figures reflect the proportion of the Tutsi population before 1959.

gion with central Rwanda. Marcel d'Hertefelt, in contrast, uses its specific traditional military administration to define it as socially peripheral and distinctive from the political center. For example, the *ubuhake* pastoral clientship relations linking lineages with outside pastoral and political patrons appeared late in precolonial history. Families with warrior lineages in this region were more prone to have the more equal *umuheto* clientship with army chiefs.[4]

In 1900, during the colonial period, the first Catholic mission in the Save Region (today's Shyanda Commune) was established in what is now Butare Prefecture. Before 1930, two other missions were built in Astrida (today's Butare Town) and Kansi (today's Nyaruhengeri Commune). From the colonial period on, Astrida was the largest town in the country and home to several educational institutions, such as the elite school of Groupe scolaire d'Astrida and the Grand séminaire de Nyakibanda. However, the distinctive role played by Butare really began during the revolutionary period of 1959 to 1961.

In 1963, in the administrative restructuring that led to the creation of prefectures, the former Astrida Region became Butare Prefecture. The region lost some areas in the west that were transferred to Gikongoro Prefecture, but it gained some of the southern part of what was Nyanza, corresponding to today's Nyabisindu Commune, including the seat of the former royal capital and Ntyazo and Muyira Communes, that is, part of the Mayaga Chiefdom, a strongly pastoralist area tightly connected to the monarchy.

APROSOMA

During the political and social upheavals of the 1959 revolution, many Hutus from Astrida, although committed to the revolution, were original in their preference for interpreting conflict with the Tutsi aristocracy in terms of politics and social class rather than in terms of race, the dominant line at the time. The APROSOMA Party provided an option that avoided turning the political and social conflict into one entirely about ethnic identity. The success of APROSOMA was limited because the party did not receive support from the two main institutions of power, the colonial administration and the Catholic church. The erratic behavior of its main leader, Joseph Gitera, may also have made the party's situation even worse. A minority of the Hutu in the prefecture who supported the revolution opted for the PARMEHUTU, as almost all of the country had done since the commune elections of June 1960.

After the publication of the Hutu manifesto in 1957, Grégoire Kayibanda created the Hutu Social Movement (MSM), of which the goals were to renew the demands of the Hutu manifesto and to gather its signatories.[5] This became the first formal, politically oriented organization in the country. It brought together the leaders of the Hutu cause from across different cultures, regions, temperaments, and viewpoints. In his 1959 pamphlet, "The Politics of Rwanda," one of these men, Aloys Munyangaju, revealed that the fundamental difference among them was "determining whether the campaign should be led against all the Tutsis indiscriminately, against the top Tutsi aristocracy, or against the abuses committed by some members of the Hamitic race."[6] The leaders from today's Butare Prefecture disagreed with their counterparts from the center and north of the country by arguing against an ethnic blanket approach, favoring a campaign based on politics and social class differences. For this particular reason, in November 1957, Gitera created APROSOMA, which, although advocating a radical struggle against the Tutsi monarchy, was no less open to all people regardless of their ethnicity.[7] APROSOMA became a political party in February 1959. Right from the beginning, Gitera stood out for his extremely violent criticism of the Tutsi and of the social-political system in place at the time.[8] APROSOMA brought together mainly Astridian Hutus, such as its president Gitera, its vice president, Munyangaju, and their close allies Isidore Nzeyimana and Germain Gasingwa. Gitera's vitriol against the monarchy made him the main enemy to defeat for the defenders of the monarchy. In the *jacquerie* of 1959, in which many APROSOMA militants participated, supporters of the monarchy killed party members trying to suppress the revolt. The secretary-general of APROSOMA, Joseph Kanyaruka who had sought refuge in Burundi and his host, Elias Renzaho, were murdered by Chief Hormisdas Mbanda's warriors.[9] On the same day, a raid comprised of armed monarchists set off for Save, where Gitera lived, but were dispersed by the police.[10] Gitera's unstable behavior damaged APROSOMA influence to the extent that it limited the party's impact in Astrida and seriously weakened its representation in Shangugu, the only branch outside of Astrida.[11]

The November 1959 *jacquerie* had relatively little impact on the Astrida territory and part of Nyanza Province, which correspond to today's Butare Prefecture few of the local traditional authorities were unseated. The commune elections set for June 1960 changed this situation. In April 1960 in Mvejuru and Buhanga-Ngara Chiefdoms, located in the south and southeast of Astrida Region, incidents of violence marred the preparation for the June–July elections. Several hundred huts belonging to Tutsis were burned or destroyed, but according to official estimates by the Belgian military resident, only a few people were injured. On April 22, 1960, 2,100 out of 3,000 refugees were reintegrated.[12] These were the first instances of mass violence witnessed in Astrida, and it is important to note that they took place in the south of the prefecture.

The June 1960 commune elections. During these elections, APROSOMA on its own obtained 7.4 percent of the national vote, essentially from the Astrida territory and to a negligible degree from Nyanza Province.[13] In Shangugu territory, APROSOMA had formed an alliance with the PARME-HUTU and garnered 6 percent of the vote.[14] Out of 537 seats for commune councilors in Astrida, APROSOMA won 223, the PARMEHUTU 237, and RADER 28; 49 went to other parties. But the abstention advocated by the monarchist Rwanda National Union (UNAR) was also quite important.[15] The results of the commune elections clearly demonstrate the political inclinations in what was to become Butare Prefecture because they came from a relatively transparent election during which different political orientations could be expressed quite openly. In subsequent elections the heavy hand of the Belgian administration and the PARMEHUTU distorted the democratic process.

During the elections boycotted by UNAR, abstention implied voting for it.[16] According to D'Hertefelt a large majority—more than 80 percent—of eligible adults were registered as voters.[17] On Map 4.2, one can identify a strip covering the whole north of present-day Butare Prefecture, formerly south of most of Nyanza Province, where more than 50 percent of registered voters abstained. This area mainly covered Muyira, Ntyazo, Nyabisindu, and Rusatira

Communes in 1994, part of Nyanza now attached to the Butare Prefecture. Farther south, the rate of abstention in this strip was briefly interrupted, and then resumed substantially to the south inside the 1994 Gikongoro Prefecture, to the west of the 1994 Butare Prefecture. A small section of this second strip where abstention increased again crosses over the western border of Runyinya Commune inside Butare Prefecture. The rest of the territory of the Butare Prefecture of 1994, where participation in the elections was high or very high, strongly supported the revolutionary parties of the APROSOMA and the PARMEHUTU.[18] Within this vast zone, two areas participated in the elections in relative moderation, with 50 percent to 80 percent turnout, one situated in the southwest and the other in the east (see Map 4.2).

Using the ethnic distribution as a factor to explain instances of high abstention, I have distinguished two zones. The first comprises the four communes in present-day Butare that at the time were located in Nyanza Province. Because I don't have the percentage of the Tutsi population in these areas in 1960, I use numbers from 1980. On average, in 1980, Tutsis represented 15 percent of the population of these four communes: Nyabisindu (18.9 percent), Ntyazo (15.7 percent), Muyira (13.5 percent), and Rusatira (11.9 percent).[19] This area generally corresponded to Busanza, Kabagali (part), and Mayaga (part) Chiefdoms, which then consisted of the former communes of Gacu (voter turnout 30.9 percent), Rwesero (13 percent), Maza (35 percent), Runyinya (7.3 percent), Muyira (10.4 percent), and Ntyazo (54.8 percent).[20] On average, these six communes had a voter participation rate of 25 percent.[21] On Map 4.2 rates of participation in the June 1960 commune elections have been geolocalized and projected into the map of Butare prefecture and communes as it stood in April 1994. Even if one factors in the losses from the Tutsi population leaving the area following the events of the 1960s, it did not greatly affect the region; the Tutsis living in these communes formed a small minority. These numbers indicate that in this region, the 75 percent rate of abstention in the commune elections came overwhelmingly from Hutu voters. Thus, in this region the Hutus heeded the UNAR call for boycott, demonstrating political solidarity with the Tutsis. Thirty-four years later, in April 1994, this Hutu-Tutsi solidarity emerged again. It is the only part of Butare where a real, armed, organized resistance united Hutus and Tutsis for several days after the prefecture went up in flames. Nyanza Region was the headquarters of the kingdom and the royal capital. There the ties between Hutus and Tutsis were ancient and strong.

The second zone with a high rate of abstention, at 59.5 percent, in the commune elections of June 1960 corresponds to Nyaruguru Chiefdom.[22] In the other parts of Butare Prefecture, abstention fluctuated between zero and fifty percent. Nyaruguru was located halfway between the current Gikongoro and Butare Prefectures; in Butare it covered mainly Runyinya and Gishamvu Communes. In the part that stretched into Gikongoro Prefecture, abstention was strongest, as well as along the western border of Runyinya

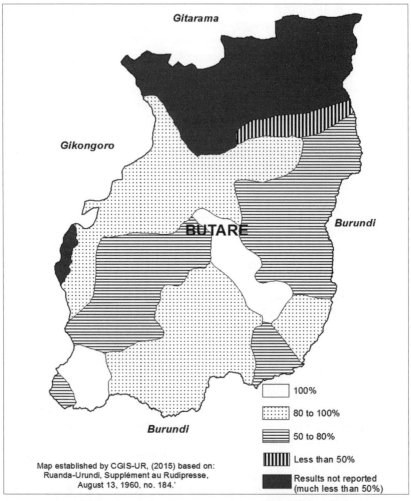

Map 4.2 Geolocalization of the Results of the June 1960 Commune Elections in 1994 Butare Prefecture and Communes

Commune. In these localities, the Tutsi population formed more than 60 per-cent of the population. In Nyaruguru Chiefdom as a whole, as d'Hertefelt notes, more than half the population at the time was Tutsi, suggesting that the high abstention rate in the region was because of the large number of Tutsis that boycotted the polls.[23] If one accepts this argument—and there is no reason not to—one can conclude that for the most part only the Tutsis from Nyaruguru boycotted the vote, and therefore the voting patterns of the

Hutus and Tutsis of this region were strongly polarized. This polarization is reinforced by the fact that PARMEHUTU won forty seats out of seventy-five in the former chiefdom.

Within the vast zone of high participation in the elections, one has to differentiate motives of more moderate participation in the southwest and the east. In the eastern part of Runyinya, the western part of Gishamvu, and part of Ngoma and Huye Communes, the relatively moderate turnout for the election can be explained by the relatively high numbers of the Tutsi population, lower than in Nyaruguru Chiefdom but still relatively high. On the eastern side of the prefecture, around Muyaga, part of Shyanda, Ndora, and Muganza Communes, moderate participation can best be explained by the political culture of this subregion. Similar to the northern part of the prefecture but to a lesser extent, this region traditionally called Mayaga, although mostly populated by Hutus, was dedicated to cattle herding, and there, ties between Tutsis and Hutus were also traditionally strong.

The geographical distribution of the vote between the two revolutionary parties, the APROSOMA and the PARMEHUTU, projected into Butare Prefecture in 1994, is also crucial to understanding the later actions of the different communes of Butare during the genocide. Excluding the northern communes, with a high level of abstention following the UNAR appeal for a boycott, the PARMEHUTU won most of the seats in the whole western side of the 1994 prefecture, including Ruhashya, Maraba, Runyinya, Gishamvu, and Nyakizu Communes. In June 1960 APROSOMA won what would become the Kigembe Commune of 1994, but its influence was to change dramatically with the violence of the September 1961 legislative elections, which put the area firmly under PARMEHUTU control. APROSOMA won the elections in the center, the east, and the southeast of the prefecture. This would correspond to Mugusa, Muyaga, Mbazi, Ngoma, Ndora, Muganza, Nyaruhengeri, and Kibayi Communes in 1994 (see Map 4.2 and Table 4.2).

The PARMEHUTU, with a number of seats in the commune councils (178 out of 464 available seats) relatively lower than APROSOMA (222 seats), was well represented right from the beginning of pluralism in what was to become Butare Prefecture.[24]

This representation was important in terms of a mandate but not in terms of local social influence because the PARMEHUTU gained its strongest support in the regions where the abstention was highest, where the majority of Hutus either abstained (as was the case in the north) or voted for the PARMEHUTU even though they were the minority compared with Tutsis in terms of population (as was the case in the communes of the southwest). In these regions, the PARMEHUTU systematically outpaced APROSOMA.[25] APROSOMA for its part fully dominated the center, the east, and the southeast of the 1994 prefecture, whereas the north showed strong loyalty to UNAR.

Table 4.2 Distribution of Votes Between PARMEHUTU and APROSOMA in the June 1960 Commune Elections in the Parts of Nyanza and Astrida Provinces that Became Butare Prefecture

	Participation	Number of Seats	PARMEHUTU	APROSOMA	Other
Nyanza Zone (Nyabisindu, Rusatira, Ntyazo, and Muyira Communes)	25%	70	46	7	10
South Busanza Chiefdom (Ruhashya and Maraba Communes)	86.2%	68	56	7	5
Nyaruguru Chiefdom (Runyinya, Gishamvu, and part of Nyakizu Communes)	40.5%	75	40	14	21
Mvejuru, Bashumba-Nyakare,[a] Buhanga-Ndara Chiefdoms (Mugusa, Muyaga, Mbazi, Ngoma, Ndora, Muganza, Nyaruhengeri, and Kibayi Communes)	83%	234	25	178	34
Nyagisozi Commune (major part of Nyakizu Commune)	100%	17	11	6	0

Source: Ruanda-Urundi, *Supplément au Rudipresse*, August 13, 1960, no. 184.
Note: a. Not including the Nyagisozi Commune. Votes from parts of Nyanza and Astrida Provinces, now Butare Prefecture.

The June 1960 commune elections, the first and the last relatively free and fair elections the country would experience prior to 1994, the political nature of the future Butare Prefecture. We shall see that despite the coming PARME-HUTU hegemony, which led to the extinction of UNAR influence and eventual dismissal of APROSOMA from its bastion, Butare for a long time stood out for its political openness and moderation in interethnic relations and, at the earliest opportunity, brought back this distinction.

Between August and November 1960, a radical shift occurred following the commune elections. Mass dissatisfaction with PARMEHUTU abuses quickly emerged, and the party sought to further consolidate its power. In November, APROSOMA and two other so-called Tutsi parties, RADER and

UNAR, formed a united front against the PARMEHUTU dominance. The front defined the PARMEHUTU as "racist, racial, and antidemocratic . . . aimed at using corruption and intimidation to deliberately crush other parties."[26]

The September 1961 legislative elections. Legislative elections were finally slated for September 1961. They were to include a referendum on the monarchy and on the person of Mwami Kigeli V Ndahindurwa. Serious violence perpetrated primarily by the PARMEHUTU but also by UNAR occurred in scattered areas during the preelection period. Whereas UNAR violence was politically targeted and repressed by Belgian colonial authorities, the PARMEHUTU violence, covered up by the colonial administration, was more extensive and targeted the Tutsi population along with political parties including APROSOMA supporters.[27] According to a *Sunday Times* journalist, between August and September 1961, 150 people were killed, mostly Tutsi, 3,000 huts burned, and 22,000 people made refugees in Astrida alone. This time, the violence seems to have begun in the Astrida territory and subsequently spread to Nyanza, Kigali, and Kibungo Prefectures.[28] During this violence, some communes in the south of Butare shifted their support to the PARMEHUTU.

On the eve of the legislative elections, Joseph Gitera caused a split within his party by seeking to rename the party the APROSOMA-Rwanda Union. His goal was to reinforce the orientation of the party and to affirm the unity of the three ethnic groups within the party.[29] The other APROSOMA leaders, Gasingwa and Munyangaju, opposed changing the name just before elections because it would only cause confusion among voters. Gitera presented his list of the APROSOMA-Rwanda Union with a Tutsi called Rwubusisi, while Munyangaju and Gasingwa led a campaign under the name APROSOMA. The party, whose seats were already restricted to Astrida Prefecture, emerged severely weakened.[30] APROSOMA won 3.5 percent of the vote and two seats at the legislative assembly. The party led by Gitera, as well as other small parties, garnered 1.7 percent of the vote and won no seat.[31] On October 2, 1961, the parliament was installed. Munyangaju of APROSOMA was elected vice president of the assembly, and Amandin Rugira, who hailed from Butare but belonged to the PARMEHUTU, was elected president. APROSOMA obtained two ministerial posts in the government: Sindikuwabo became minister of public works and Gasingwa minister of health.[32]

APROSOMA was weakened not only by Gitera's inconsistencies but also by the deliberate PARMEHUTU efforts to wipe out other parties, particularly UNAR.

Rugira, the PARMEHUTU regional secretary of Butare, took upon himself the task at the end of the 1960s. APROSOMA had virtually identical results as the PARMEHUTU in the commune elections in the prefecture: the PARMEHUTU won 237 seats and APROSOMA 223, which gave APROSOMA 4 out of 8 seats from Butare in the parliament established in Gitarama on January 28, 1961. The party controlled a considerable number of communes in Butare. Rugira began by infiltrating APROSOMA beginning with its burgomasters because he knew that, in a country where authority still had great influence, the people of the commune would follow the defection of the burgomaster. He convinced the burgomasters that APROSOMA had no future as a national party, that the struggle among Hutus should be avoided because it worked to the advantage of UNAR, and it was therefore time to close ranks with the PARMEHUTU. This argument was persuasive, and after joining the PARMEHUTU, the burgomaster explained to a public gathering the general reasons for switching parties. Naturally all the people followed and immediately signed up as members of the PARMEHUTU. This kind of activity took place from 1961 to 1963. At the end of 1963, APROSOMA was practically nonexistent as a political party. Although the party was never dissolved, its members generally became PARMEHUTU.[33]

After the failure of his APROSOMA–Rwanda Union in the parliamentary elections, Gitera quit active politics for a few years. In August 1962 he was imprisoned for six months for "posing a threat to national security"[34] at the instigation of the prefect of Butare, Jean-Baptiste Habyarimana, a former member of APROSOMA. In 1965, Gitera attempted to present himself for elective post in the parliamentary elections in Butare but finished thirteenth and did not capture a seat.[35] In 1967, the PARMEHUTU won over Gitera's loyalty, and in 1969 he was elected as the PARMEHUTU member of parliament from Butare.[36]

Class rather than race. The other important APROSOMA figure, Munyangaju, also distinguished himself through the positions he had taken, removed from the prevailing ethnocentrism. In a 1959 article, "The Current Politics of Rwanda," Munyangaju demonstrated that Tutsi domination of the society of the time had not been achieved by the Tutsis as a whole but was in fact exercised by a few families within a small number of clans and lineages.[37] In the article, Munyangaju highlighted the social dimension of the political problem then facing the society, portraying it not as a divide separating Hutus and Tutsis but also as a divide within the Tutsis between the aristocracy and the ordinary people. He emphasized the futility of resolving the sociopolitical problem by simply transferring class privileges from one ethnic group to the other without democratizing society and the government: "We will not have solved the problem by giving Hutus the class privileges now reserved for the top Tutsi aristocracy. That would be replacing one evil with another, redressing one injustice to create another."[38] In the same publication, Munyangaju talked of a "social-democrate party being formed."[39] In 1962, he published "The Moderates' Manifesto," addressed to the UN Commission for Ruanda-Urundi, asking for the union between the two countries.[40] Following its publication, he was forced to resign from his position as vice president of parliament and was replaced by a PARMEHUTU legislator.[41] During his tenure as a member of parliament (1961–1965), Munyangaju distinguished himself by his active and rigorous respect for legal and democratic principles.[42] He and Gasingwa, his fellow party member, remained APROSOMA legislators until 1965. They then joined the PARMEHUTU but eventually quit active politics.[43] With the fall of APROSOMA during the parliamentary elections of 1965, the PARMEHUTU became the de facto single party. According to Reyntjens, APROSOMA, with political support already reduced to Butare Prefecture and to a smaller extent Cyangugu Prefecture, was a victim of internal divisions and of the predatory politics of the PARMEHUTU. Despite the existence, through APROSOMA, of a revolutionary Hutu alternative that rejected ethnic identity policies, the weakness and eventual death of this alternative left a political monopoly for violent and discriminatory PARMEHUTU extremism.

Catharine Newbury argues that the different options offered by PARMEHUTU and APROSOMA leaders were undoubtedly linked to the respective leaders' regions of origin. Main APROSOMA leaders Gitera and Munyangaju came from Astrida, whereas Kayibanda and Balthazar Bicamumpaka of PARMEHUTU hailed from the central and northern regions, respectively.[44] Lemarchand adds to this regionalist divide the issue of the difference in education, professional outlook, and opportunities to which the leaders from each group were exposed:

> The conflict goes back to the period immediately preceding independence, when PARMEHUTU desperately tried to rally to its cause those Hutu already affiliated to RADER and APROSOMA. Behind this cleavage between "moderates" and "activists" lay a more fundamental rift, centered upon two different categories of intellectuals—the ex-séminaristes and the "Astridiens." The most important source of disharmony lay in the widely different career opportunities to which each group could aspire by virtue of education and training. Unlike the ex-séminaristes, who lacked the necessary qualifications to hold administrative posts, the Astridiens knew that they would be the first to reap the benefits of constitutional and administrative reforms. Their reformist, gradualist outlook, the logical consequence of their professional training, gave them an overwhelming inclination to join APROSOMA. The ex-séminaristes, on the other hand, stood little chance of making their mark in life because the Centre Scolaire d'Astrida remained the only channel for recruitment to government posts. Faced with denial of career opportunities, they were naturally predisposed to reject political reforms. Nothing short of a revolution of the kind advocated by the PARMEHUTU would enable them to satisfy their aspirations to leadership.
>
> Thus, when independence became a reality, the first step taken by PARMEHUTU diehards to achieve republican unanimity was to weed out or neutralize their moderate opponents, most of whom belonged to APROSOMA.[45]

The overwhelming PARMEHUTU victory was inevitable, particularly in light of the Catholic Church support for Kayibanda and his project before and after the *jacquerie* of 1959 and the unconditional public support directed by Colonel Guy Logiest, the military resident in charge of Rwanda during the state of emergency.

The following extract by Reyntjens shows the political bias of the Belgian administration toward the PARMEHUTU. During the parliamentary election campaigns, violence by promonarchy UNAR was vigorously suppressed by the Belgian military administration, whereas the PARMEHUTU benefited from the support of Logiest:

> By contrast, the threats and violence perpetrated by the PARMEHUTU pro-pagandists, who were often burgomasters or commune councilors, were left unpunished and even covered up by the administration. It is here, without a doubt, that the Belgian resident took a step too far in evolving into a PARMEHUTU propagandist, with the obvious goal of making it a single party. For Colonel Logiest, this was the logical outcome of his long-standing support for the party, in accordance with his conviction that in a revolution there can only be a single revolutionary party. By supporting the revolution, the resident necessarily supported the PARMEHUTU.[46]

Within such a context, APROSOMA and its ideas stood no chance, leaving the country to the PARMEHUTU political and ideological monopoly and all the consequences.

Political Marginalization of Butare Under the First Republic

In the absence of a political platform beyond Hutu supremacy, the bonds cementing the PARMEHUTU hierarchy crumbled after Hutu leaders had seized power.[47] This vacuum exposed the party to all manner of rivalries based on personal, ideological, regional, and clan differences.[48] After the political demise of APROSOMA, the second split within the party occurred between leaders originally from Butare and those originally from Gitarama.

The regional secretariat of the PARMEHUTU party in Butare carried out the political elimination of APROSOMA, particularly through the efforts of its chief, Rugira.[49] However, it was not long before Rugira found himself in the camp of his former opponents in APROSOMA against the group from Gitarama. The conflict erupted during the commune elections of August 1963. For these elections, the party secretariat had decided that none of the legislators would run for an office in the commune. Rugira, then the president of parliament and the regional secretary of Butare, decided to issue a different directive.[50] Having all but wiped out APROSOMA, Rugira had decided to take Nyabisindu Commune for the PARMEHUTU. The commune had been the headquarters of the former Nyanza Kingdom, and therefore the influence of UNAR there was strong. Thus Rugira endorsed the candidacy of Jean-Baptiste Utumabahutu, a legislator, former assistant interim chief, and commissioner for refugees, a well-respected public figure.[51] But the UNAR candidate won the election and was appointed burgomaster. Out of ten seats of commune councilor, six went to UNAR and four to the PARMEHUTU. Nyanza thus became the only commune in the country that escaped PARMEHUTU control in the 1963 elections.[52]

During these elections, another incident took place, in Butare Prefecture, in Ndora Commune, where election irregularities were observed.[53] The Rwandan Supreme Court nullified the election result and ordered that elections be reorganized. Victory had been denied to a protégé of Calliope Mulindahabi, minister of defense and longtime stalwart of both President Kayibanda and PARMEHUTU executive secretary Maximilien Niyonzima, a blow to the Gitarama political elite. The defeat was blamed on Chief Justice Isodore Nzeyimana, one of the leaders of APROSOMA before he joined the PARMEHUTU in 1960. Nzeyimana and Rugira, who both hailed from Butare, were poorly regarded by the party leaders originally from Gitarama. The dismissal of Nzeyimana as chief justice required the consent of the government and of parliament; the speaker was none other than Rugira. Rugira was suspended from the party for six months for having disregarded the directive on the nonparticipation of PARMEHUTU members of parliament as candidates in commune elections. Feeling isolated, he resigned as speaker. Two days later, on September 11, 1963, during a meeting of the government and parliament, President Kayibanda announced a disagreement between the government and the Supreme Court, and the solution had been the dismissal of Nzeyimana as chief justice. Members of parliament from the opposition—such as Michel Rwagasana from UNAR and other "Butarians" such as Munyangaju and Gasingwa, both from APROSOMA—attempted to initiate a debate on the merits of the action, but the PARMEHUTU members of parliament blocked the move and united to support the motion of dismissal. The APROSOMA representatives from Butare attempted to come to the aid of their fellow colleagues from Butare and formerly staunchest PARMEHUTU political enemies. The regional PARMEHUTU leadership was removed and replaced with lower-profile political figures, which indicated the end of the important political role played by Butare. Butare was simply the first victim of the regionalist politics that sealed the political isolation of the PARMEHUTU elite from Gitarama and eventually swept them away.[54]

The fact that the Butare politicians and elite eventually shared the same fate despite their different political affiliations is probably what reinforced their regionalist orientation.

Butare Under the Second Republic

Ambiguities and Contradictions of the New Regime's Ethnic Politics

The anti-Tutsi violence of February–March 1973, which precipitated the end of the PARMEHUTU and of the First Republic, was particularly intense in Butare Prefecture. The mayhem that accompanied the expulsion of Tutsis from different institutions was concentrated in the area of education. Consequently, Butare was particularly affected because a large number of secondary schools and practically all higher education institutions, the national university and grand seminary of Nyakibanda heading the list, were located in the prefecture. Several institutions closed their doors following the violence. One of the goals of the violence, orchestrated from above, was to reduce the number of Tutsis in learning institutions.[55] The Catholic Church, which ran the majority of the country's secondary schools, completely collaborated in the enterprise of getting rid of Tutsis not only in the public schools it managed but also in its own private schools, such as the seminaries. The violent expulsion of Tutsi students by their Hutu fellow students was followed with arbitrary administrative expulsions. In his letter to Prefect Palatin Kabalisa of Butare dated December 1973, announcing the reopening of the Petit séminaire de Butare, Bishop Jean-Baptiste Gahamanyi of Butare explained the measures taken following the violence that rocked the seminary. With regard to the elimination of students, the bishop explained that the attackers, most probably Hutus, were retained, whereas the victims of the expulsions, most probably Tutsis, were eliminated under the pretext of respecting the ethnic quota rule.[56]

In Butare Prefecture, the February–March 1973 violence did not spread much to the rural areas, but it did spark an exodus of refugees, mostly Tutsi students, civil servants, and salaried employees in the private sector.[57] After President Habyarimana took power on July 5, 1973, the new government, claiming its desire to fight against discrimination as part of its policy of "Peace and National Unity," sought to apply a quota for Tutsis. On July 31, 1973, the minister of the interior and justice, Alexis Kanyarengwe, held his first meeting with the newly appointed prefects, in which he ordered the prefect of Butare to fight against the fraudulent "change of ethnic identity," to abolish any "feudal practices," and to ensure that the "authorities committed all their energy to monitoring and fighting against . . . Tutsi maneuvers aimed at maintaining an atmosphere of disunity and dissension among the people."[58]

Two years later, the top state hierarchy sought to discourage as much as possible the refugees from returning by putting pressure on the burgomasters who seemed not to have quite understood what was expected of them and those who showed defiance. In April 1975, the prefect of Butare responded to a confidential letter from the minister of the interior and the public service, reporting on the refugee situation in his prefecture:

Essentially, the refugees have always sought ways to enter through unpatrolled routes, especially in the Nyakizu, Kigembe, Muyira, and Ntyazo Communes. At numerous times I have issued both verbal and written instructions that the refugees should be driven back. Moreover, during the conference of prefectures on April 7, 1975, I spoke again to the burgomasters about this problem. I asked them to be very strict and diligent. With regard to the refugees' protests, there was a time that their former properties were not definitively redistributed by the commune authorities. It seems to me that the commune authority was placed in an awkward position by Circular No. 2420/A.09, regarding Presidential Decree No. 25/01 of February 26, 1966, on measures for reintegrating refugees and various claims, on point C, page 5: precautionary measures concerning unoccupied property. It is obvious that one commune authority or the other, instead of definitively distributing the unoccupied property to the ordinary citizens, settled for renting them out, so that the refugee who returned and found that his property was still available wasted no time in reclaiming the property through intimidation. However, I have just requested of all the burgomasters that the commune council meet and study the situation of all property left vacant by the refugees and give the property once and for all to ordinary citizens. On the other hand, I have noted that the local courts accepted that refugees take ordinary citizens to court for holding their property. From this perspective, the magistrates, especially the newly recruited ones, do not have a consistent line of conduct with respect to the requests and complaints brought forward by the refugees.[59]

This letter clearly shows the gap between, on the one hand, the empathy to refugees from at least some of the commune authorities and local judiciary and on the other the desire of the central government to keep the refugees outside the country.

One month later, Interior Minister Kanyarengwe, obviously reacting to similar reports on refugees from prefects, wrote an urgent letter to the prefects asking them to dispose of the property belonging to refugees by selling or giving it away, reminding them that he had already sent them similar instructions in October 1974. This time, the minister demanded that by July 1975, every "abandoned" property should have been conclusively reallocated and that the prefects send him a detailed report.[60]

Lastly, in his July–September 1975 trimester report, the Butare prefect stated that in Gishamvu, Nyaruhengeri, Nyakizu, Runyinya, Kibayi, Mugusa, Muyira, Mbazi, Ruhashya, Ngoma, Huye, Kigembe, and Nyabisindu Communes, all properties abandoned by refugees were distributed to needy people for free, but that the redistribution operation had experienced some problems in Runyinya and Gishamvu Communes, where people attempted to resist, arguing that their inheritance was being distributed.[61]

Five years after the events of 1973 and the subsequent implementation of the policy for keeping the refugees outside the country, pressure from the refugees to return continued. In his April–June 1978 trimester report, Prefect Kabalisa of Butare attached a circular he distributed to all prefecture offices in which he expressed concern about the refugee issue. He denounced the UN High Commission for Refugees (UNHRC) in Bujumbura for giving Rwandan refugees "request for repatriation" documents without these documents being forwarded by the Rwandan Embassy there, the only place designated to authorize repatriation after verifying that a candidate met all the requirements. The prefect's circular ordered the immediate rejection of all refugees provided with "request for repatriation" documents not issued by the Rwandan Embassy.[62]

The fact that most senior state officials considered it necessary to make a great deal of effort for refugees to remain outside the country shows there was pressure from refugees to return and that this pressure would not have existed if the local social climate had been favorable.

In April 1975, an event Prefect Kabalisa considered highly subversive once again demonstrates the politically sensitive character of Butare residents and their penchant to weave interethnic alliances. Soon before President Habyarimana visited Butare Prefecture; the prefect sought to bring to the interior minister's attention the troubling political situation there.[63] He accused a group of people from Butare, apparently inspired by the former leader of APROSOMA, Gitera, of sowing seeds of subversion with the aim of creating conditions favorable for the establishment of a political party just when President Habyarimana was about to form the MRND.[64] According to the prefect, the group was inspired by Gitera but incited by a certain Jean Berchmans, a Tutsi "cultivator" from Gitarama who had "changed his ethnicity."[65] The main group was made up of ten people, among them a teacher; former burgomaster; six farmers, two of whom had been councilors of the commune; a tailor; a former police constable of the commune; and a local court magistrate. The group was divided into two subgroups on an ethnic basis. According to the prefect, the group planned to foster agitation among students between June and October 1975. This group of subversives had apparently been in contact with a band of thugs organized in the Cyangugu Prefecture whose headquarters were in Runyinya Commune (Butare Prefecture) and Rwamiko Commune (Gikongoro Prefecture). These thugs engaged in robbery and pointless destruction, including burning teaching materials in Butare primary schools. Two of the main instigators of this sabotage had been arrested, but Gitera was not one of them. The situation was considered serious enough for the prefect to call a closed-door meeting of burgomasters to declare a curfew in the communes from 8 p.m. to dawn.[66] This attempt at organized political subversion evolved into a wider movement of disobedience reaching Butare Town and certain communes. In his July–August 1975 report, the prefect directed attention toward continued resistance to authorities in the Nyaruguru Region, in Runyinya and Rwamiko Communes. Again Nyaruguru Region had apparently experienced the "effects of the feudal mentality" created by intrigues, lies, and false rumors.[67] Tracts circulating there targeted the burgomaster of Runyinya and the prefect of Butare. A group of army reservists in the commune accused the prefect of ostracizing them, but according to the prefect's investigations, these reservists belonged to the "wave of banditry" linked to the Gitera group whose actions hid their politically subversive goals.[68]

While groups of subversives demonstrated interethnic cooparation, the state policy continued to promote the political marginalization of the Tutsis. On December 21, 1975, the first elections of MRND cell committees were organized throughout the communes. A cell was the basic political subdivision of the new single party, but the state administrative structures and the party formed a single body at the cell and sector levels.[69] The 621 cells in the prefecture had 940 inhabitants each on average, and the vote was compulsory for the entire population of voting age.[70] Whereas Tutsis formed about 18 percent of population of the prefecture at the time, after the elections they formed 15.66 percent of members of cell committees. However, at the leadership level of the 621 cell committees, only two Tutsis were elected as cell leaders in the entire prefecture.[71] The same marginalization of Tutsis was at play at the next administrative and political level. In the elections held on January 20, 1980, for commune councilors in charge of the sectors, only 3 out of 206 commune councilors elected in Butare Prefecture were Tutsi.[72] The candidates for the commune council elections were chosen by the commune congress of the MRND. The councilors held considerable power over the daily life of the people, which meant that despite party-state local hierarchy control, these elections were relatively disputed. For example, in Muganza Commune, the councilors received an average of 60 percent of votes, and it was not rare, across the entire prefecture, for councilors to be elected by less than 40 percent of the votes cast.[73] The bulk of the lively competition of local elections took place exclusively among the Hutus within the single party.

At this time Gitera's uniqueness came forward again. During President Habyarimana's nationwide tour from April 16 to May 6, 1976, Gitera had a verbal exchange with him in Butare.[74] Gitera asked the president how he expected to reconcile Rwandans. The president responded by asking Gitera what divided the Hutus and the Tutsis. Gitera replied, "We have been opposed to each other and will continue being opposed to each other because of the government in power."[75] Sometime later, on May 7, 1976, Gitera published in Butare a semipoetic, semipolitical analysis of the Hutu-Tutsi conflict. In this short document, Gitera advocated complete rejection of ethnic identification and granting the same rights to all Rwandans so that the new Rwanda would have no other *ubwoko* (social identity) than that of Rwandan.[76] By so doing he took the complete opposite of the MRND position by appearing to hold steadfast to his old political and ideological leanings.

In April 1980, Colonel Théoneste Lizinde, national security chief, fomented a coup attempt.[77] Ethnic tensions were to be used to destabilize the Habyarimana regime, and Butare was expected to play an important role. The meeting of the Butare Prefecture security committee on June 10 was called specifically to discuss three pamphlets published by the National Salvation Committee.[78] The security committee was alarmed by the content of the pamphlets, especially Pamphlet 5, which was virulent and aimed at provoking ethnic violence. The leaflets were addressed to the students of the National University and the National Institute of Education. The security committee made a distinction in the impact of the leaflets on the rural and urban areas of Butare, suggesting that the ethnically polarized atmosphere in the town had not reached the communes and worrying about the potential for that eventuality because of the "unstable behavior of the Butare population."[79] According to the security committee, the subversive groups wanted to concentrate their efforts in Butare in order to use students to spread ethnic tension throughout the country.

A large number of leaflets were distributed by mail posted from Kigali. The security committee also noted that the main instigators of subversion did not hail from Butare. Lastly, the security committee noted that the upsurge in banditry had a political dimension and was aimed at proving the government's inability to maintain order.[80]

The prefecture authorities decided to crack down on "some Tutsis who want to form groups and in so doing risk frustrating even Hutus who would like to support peaceful coexistence between ethnic groups."[81] Consequently, the prefecture security committee decided to demand that the exclusively Tutsi cultural group called Abagizumwe, famous for "its arrogance and defamation of the Hutu ethnic group" and "of the governing authorities," change its attitude.[82] In late June 1980, the office of the president of the republic reacted to the minutes of this meeting in Butare and wrote to the minister of justice informing him of the president's order to dissolve the Abagizumwe.[83]

After this incident official documents never mention again the occurrence of interethnic tension in Butare prefecture until the early 1990s. However, one cannot avoid noting, during this incident, the receptiveness of the elite to ethnic manipulation, even in Butare.

In the second half of the 1980s, occurrences of Tutsis falsifying their identities increased. A meeting of the Butare Prefecture security committee on February 26, 1986, drew attention to the problem of complacent burgomasters who easily granted new identity cards on the basis of information from the applicants, without making the effort to verify it through the commune census records, which indicated citizens' ethnicity.[84] The security committee implied that the burgomasters did so knowing that many people were taking advantage of the opportunity of renewing identity cards to make false claims and "change their ethnicity." The other strategy cited was that of Tutsis moving to other communes. The burgomaster would issue them a transfer form with a list of elements for official identification, including ethnicity, which the person had to submit to the new burgomaster. Some Tutsis, without hesitation, struck out the original ethnicity listed. The importance of the phenomenon of changing identity suggests some friendly or corrupt complacency on the part of the burgomasters.

Criminality and Unruliness (1973–1983)

After a lull in 1973 and 1974, a resurgence of delinquency and petty crime in Butura occurred in 1975. These activities corresponded with a severe food shortage that made the distribution of emergency food aid necessary throughout the prefecture. From July to September 1975, 865 tons of beans, sorghum, and flour were distributed to the population. Most seriously affected were Shyanda, Mbazi, Gishamvu, Maraba, and Runyinya Communes,[85] whereas the least affected were Muyira, Ntyazo, and Muyaga Communes, located in the northeast of the prefecture, the least populated and most fertile. Although this northeastern region needed the least emergency food aid, it was the region in which the first meeting of the subprefecture security committee was called because of an alarming surge in petty crime.[86] Eight years later, the security committee, which met on September 21, 1983, stated again that the Muyira and Ntyazo Communes had some of the highest levels of crime in the prefecture.[87]

Butare Town also experienced significant criminal activity by thugs bold enough to attack patients at the university hospital in wards and individual rooms.[88] These petty thieves had adopted the behavior of hiding in unexpected places such as churches, reforested areas, and official building annexes.[89]

On October 25, 1975, Prefect Charles Nkurunziza organized a meeting of the prefecture council security committee that brought together officials responsible for maintaining order: the police and army as well as all of the burgomasters and all of the heads of the cantonal prisons of the prefecture.[90] The committee identified the main security problems in the prefecture as begging, vagrancy, prostitution, and robbery. The committee described robbers as those who made a living through extortion, theft, and intimidation and committed physical attacks and even murder as opposed to thieves who carried out their crimes while staying out of sight. The meeting participants highlighted the causes of these crimes as hunger, shortage of land for cultivation, and the resulting idleness that leads people to loiter in the streets and around the bars.[91] The food shortage that ravaged the country in late 1976 caused numerous suicides and destabilized families, with men abandoning their wives and children and families deciding to leave the area or the country permanently and settle in Burundi or Tanzania.[92]

According to the participants of the security committee meeting, the material motives behind delinquency and hard-core crime nevertheless did not sufficiently account for this criminal behavior. A meeting of the Nyanza security subcommittee held on August 18, 1980, highlighted acts they defined as "defiance that was relatively provocative."[93] In Nyanza Town, in Mugozi and

Gakenyeli sectors, robbers stole by throwing the "Gatalina" stone.[94] Also in Nyanza, the same week, robbers attacked the home of the president of the state council and injured his night guard.[95]

On the night of August 15, 1980, robbers attacked the office of Ntyazo Commune and seriously injured the police officer on duty before getting away in a jeep. The criminals then went to rob the home of a certain Robert Dessy and while leaving, decided to pass by the home of the assistant prosecutor, where they left an old hat without stealing anything. The same gang then went to the home of the head of intelligence in Nyanza and looted the kitchen. The burgomaster of Nyabisindu Commune also drew participants' attention to the habits of people who forced local authorities to give them land to cultivate, by cultivating, in mass and by force, the commune's marshy lands.[96] The Butare Prefecture security committee, which met on May 7, 1982, warned of a new technique used by local criminals that consisted of attacking in a group, isolating the target, and denying the latter any chance of being rescued by intimidating the neighborhood night watch team. "The striking thing about these thugs, who attack in groups of twenty and more, is that they target individuals with modest incomes, so that one cannot say that they are going after the most profitable prey. One is therefore inclined to think that these acts are more about settling scores than about getting rich through violence."[97]

The significant degree of crime and delinquency created overcrowded prisons, to which the state responded by regularly decreeing amnesties and the massive release of prisoners, who most often resumed their criminal activities.[98] In the early 1980s, incarceration seemed to have become a banal social phenomenon because of the large number of people who experienced it. During a meeting of the security committee on July 16, 1982, the subject of the causes of delinquency and crime, at the time on the upsurge, was raised once again. The participants considered the causes social, economic, and cultural, including the "large concentration of people around Butare Town and the lack of employment opportunities to occupy the youth who do not always have enough land to cultivate."[99] The meeting also noted that imprisonment no longer seemed a deterrent and that the fate of prisoners raised mixed feelings within the population.

> A certain group of people no longer fears prison, and some youth even prefer to live in prison than rot in misery on their hills. Every now and then we hear such opinions expressed by the population. The people go as far as to say that the thugs are being maintained by the state. The latter leave prison stronger, having put on weight, ready to dive back into their work with more vigor. This situation is only worsened by almost widespread sympathy for the individual prisoner. As a result, the prisoner feels more or less supported in his wrongdoing.[100]

In the face of difficult living conditions and unoccupied youth with no land, crime became socialized, and its suppression provoked in the ordinary people mixed feelings toward the state. On the one hand, they considered the state lax in its duties, and on the other they had feelings of sympathy for the criminals, perhaps because people in the rural areas identified with the conditions that forced them to act.

In December 1983, presidential and parliamentary elections were held. Fearing trouble, the burgomasters of Maraba, Mbazi, Nyakizu, Muganza, and Shyanda Communes requested troop reinforcements so that there would be a significant military presence in the communes during the elections. The Butare Prefecture security committee noted that the state of the roads did not allow military trucks to reach the sectors, so "their presence was likely to be limited to the big centers and would not reach the sectors, yet the real problems were to be found in the remotest corners and in the polling stations."[101] To compensate, the security committee decided that each polling supervisor should have a vehicle at his disposal and would be accompanied by a few military officers. The security committee also lamented that in Kibayi, Nyakizu, and Nyabisindu Communes, photographs of some parliamentary candidates had been vandalized.

In this period, from 1973 to the early 1980s, the following factors stand out: first, the significant delinquency in the prefecture; second, the prevalence of delinquency in urban Ngoma Commune and surrounding Shyanda, Mbazi, Huye, Gishamvu, Nyaruhengeri, and Ndora Communes on the one hand, and rural Nyabisindu, Ntyazo, and Muyira Communes on the other.[102] It is obvious that overpopulation, shortage of land to cultivate, and the resulting low level of agricultural production played a central role in the crime rates in the communes. However, the fact that Ntyazo and Muyira were among the communes with the highest crime rates, yet the richest and most fertile communes with the largest amount of available land, indicates that other factors must come into play, perhaps linked to the less recent history of the Mayaga Region. The ambiguous nature of this delinquency and crime seemed at times to express defiance and infrapolitical protest, which some burgomasters strongly sensed at the time.[103]

The population of Butare was unruly through other, more direct methods, especially when local factions openly challenged the authority of the burgomasters. In 1975, the burgomaster of Runyinya had to confront a protest organized by army reservists.[104] Two reservists had mounted a clandestine campaign against the burgomaster, writing letters to different authorities containing all manner of accusations. They had also tried to rally the public. The Butare Prefecture security committee, which met on November 25, 1975, gave the burgomaster its support and decided to find employment for the two reservists to tone down their frustration.[105]

In the Saga and Nyagahuru Sectors of Kibayi Commune, a group of men mobilized the people against the burgomaster.[106] In July 1976, about a dozen houses were torched in these sectors. On August 2, 1976, when the burgomaster and his police officers went to the scene, they were seriously beaten by a group of armed people. In 1974 six houses had been burned in the same area. According to the Butare Prefecture security committee, this protest was the work of a group of judges whose sights were on the burgomaster's position as well as of former burgomasters under the First Republic who were turning the population against the burgomaster.[107]

In 1977, a personal conflict between Burgomaster Nshimiryayo of Nyakizu Commune and a businessman called Rugwizangoga evolved into a political conflict that split the council of the commune, with nine councilors supporting the businessman and five councilors maintaining their support for the burgomaster.[108] The nine councilors wrote to the prefect a letter of protest against the burgomaster. The prefecture committee declared its support for the burgomaster, and the prefect headed for Nyakizu Commune to call the protestors to order. Incidents of protests against the burgomasters disappear from the prefectures' official reports from 1977 on. It would seem this was a case of nostalgia for the First Republic, when the factionalism rife within the PARME-HUTU allowed local actors to play factions and politicians against each other to the detriment of the authorities of the central state, such as the burgomasters. With the centralized MRND and the efficiency of its structures of local control, these open power games were no longer possible and eventually stopped, at least for a time.

Explosion in Local Crime and Infrapolitical Violence (1984–1989)

The trends observed during the decade from 1973 to 1983, especially in docility, significantly increased.[109] From the mid-1980s, this disobedience eventually became a generalized movement of mass dissent, at times violent and explicitly political, and led local state representatives to start fearing the population. As we have seen in Chapter 2, the years from 1984 to 1989 coincided with a severe nationwide economic and social crisis based on situational and structural factors. The situational causes were particularly severe in Butare, including the 1984 drought and the resulting serious food shortage in some regions; the heavy rains of 1987; and plant diseases, especially that of beans in 1988.[110] The 1984 food shortage seems to have hastened the effects of the social crisis, given that after that year, social tension intensified and became harsher. The social chronology of the second half of the 1980s in Butare prefecture essentially reads like a long litany of various incidents of violence and acts of subversion against the established order. I propose here an overview of this list by presenting a slice of life stemming from reports of the local administration, commune by commune, covering only two months, May and June 1985.[111]

Rusatira Commune. In Maza Sector, a certain Gahima attacked Gapeli's home on the night of May 20, armed with a spear. Some unidentified people had stolen forty kilograms of coffee a few days earlier from Gahima.

On April 29 in Kinazi Sector, a certain Niyibizi and a certain Karonkano got into a fight and were seriously injured after cows belonging to Niyibizi damaged the cassava crop of Karonkano.

In the same sector on the same day, Nkulikiyinfura threw a stone at Munyampundu, who owed him RF1,000, and injured the latter in the head.

In Kabona Sector, Rusatira, Nsabimana, Sehene, Nshimiyimana, and Nahayo attacked, beat, and seriously injured Kalinda Modest on May 5.

In Buremera Sector on May 5, thugs broke down the door of Rusatira's home in broad daylight and stole forty kilograms of coffee.

In the same sector on May 20, in Nyarugunga Cell, Kamazi injured his younger brother with a machete.

In Gahana Sector, Habimana injured his young brother in the neck with a machete.

In Kato Sector, the house of Ndibwami was torched by unidentified persons.

Nyakizu Commune. In Maraba Sector, François Njangwe was killed on April 1, 1985, at his home and his body thrown into a river.

In Ngobyi Cell in Rutobwe Sector, Baraserura, Kayitankore, and Sebalinda were attacked with knives by Habib on April 6.

Shyanda Commune. In Kinteko Sector on June 2, 1985, the commune councilor, accompanied by a police officer called Twagiramungu, was attacked by an unidentified person who called them worthless, beat up the officer, and tore his uniform.

In Bwiyambo Sector, a house was burned down by unidentified persons.

In Gatoke Sector, Ngiruwigize was injured by Ndyisenga with a machete.

In Kamudahunga Sector, Kimonyo injured Liberate Kuradusenge with a machete.

In Gatoke Sector, Lakwene and his wife, Mukamurenzi, were killed at night by a group of robbers.

In an unnamed sector, Déo Shirampaka was injured by his younger brother.

In Munanira Sector, Sebitenga, the head of the cell, was injured in the neck as he patrolled the bars.

Ngoma Commune. In Cyimana Sector, Kakarehe Cell, unidentified individuals attacked and injured Mbanjeneza with knives.

In the same sector, Seyoba was stabbed by robbers Nzeyimana, Bacamuwango, and Ndayisenga.

In the town sector, robbers attacked and injured Ruharirwashema with a knife.

Nyabisindu Commune. In Kibinja Sector, Nagatwa fought with a pregnant young woman and caused her to miscarry.

In Rwabicuma Sector, Aline Mushiyimana buried her newborn baby alive in a field.

Kibayi Commune. Ndizihiwe, Nyilindekwe, and Kamageli attacked and injured Badakengerwa at his home.

Gishamvu Commune. In Mubumbano Sector, Rushingabigwi was suspected of selling cannabis and of hiding a stash at his mother's home.

In Sheke Sector, theft of plants from the cultivating fields was reported.

In Gikunzi and Nyakibanda Sectors, neighbors fought over pastureland.

Nyaruhengeri Commune. Thugs entered Ndamusoneye's home and forcefully took his bean harvest.

In Bimba Sector, the cell committee no longer obeyed Councilor Rucyahana and refused to mobilize the people as requested by him.

In Mukande Sector, a certain Ndihoreye beat up the head of Kidwange Cell.

In the same sector, illegitimate wives were the source of serious conflicts in households.

In Kinyereli Sector, leaflets against the members of Ntamunoza, Mugemana, and Nahimana Cells were circulating.

In Gisagara Sector, Godelive Nyirakaje poisoned Bunyundo's child, who subsequently died.

In the same sector, Mbuguje of Kabuye Cell insulted the leaders of the cells and even tried to strike one of the cell committee members.

In Mugueter Cell, Thérèse Habitable was killed by unidentified people; Ndihoreye, Nteziryayo, Nyabyenda, and Uwizeyimana are suspects.

Ntyazo Commune. In Kimvuzo Sector, Nkusi and Mubiligi attacked with a knife people heading for *umuganda.*

Kigembe Commune. Kigembe Commune witnessed several disturbances during this period that I will analyze in the following chapters.

Among other incidents of social disorder, there were reports of infanticide and child abandonment in Nyabisindu Subprefecture as well as the "problem of fools and beggars wandering around and in the commercial neighborhood of Nyanza in particular."[112]

The list reveals four types of acts: theft of produce from the farms and homes; resorting to violence to settle minor disputes; the tendency to use violence against local authorities, members or heads of cell committees, and even commune councilors; and increasingly violent professional crime. Generally, from records of the local administration, one notices a hardening of social relations increasingly affected by violence. While keeping in mind that these events took place during less than two months, the question of measuring the frequency and severity of these incidents with a view to determine the extent of their impact on the daily social life in the prefecture should be raised. One way of determining the importance of these incidents is to call on the understanding the actors have of them and to attempt to document the consequences. The effect of these criminal tendencies was highlighted in several reports of the meetings of the Butare Prefecture security committee. In November 1984, the committee drew attention to the rise of deadly violence, noting that the "recent acts of crime reported in the region are characterized by an exceptional degree of violence. Several people were injured or killed."[113] One of the causes of the deadly violence would be "family disagreements. Sometimes family members are in court over land, and they hire people from far away to kill the opposing party."[114] The security committee also noted a problem of insubordination against local authorities: "We have effectively learned from here and there that the councilors and cell committee members are getting beaten up by the people as they organize patrols. If these authorities would behave in a dignified manner, they would enjoy a certain amount of respect. This way, the people they get to accompany them on the patrols would not hesitate to protect them."[115]

Here, the security committee gives a narrow interpretation of the cause of violence against the local authorities was fear among them, at the time still mostly at cell and sector levels and rarely at commune level.[116] In October 1984, the Butare Prefecture security committee considered the resignation of Christian Ndahimana, burgomaster of Mbazi Commune, citing among other things his premonition of a dangerous attack from people he had penalized in the course of his duties, given that the house in which he lived had no bars.[117] One and a half years later, the security committee expressed similar worries for its law enforcement officers living in towns: "It has been noted that state agents, especially the law enforcement officers, are very poorly housed in Butare and Nyabisindu. The prefect highlighted the difficulties of housing, and particularly the condition of the old houses with no protection bars."[118]

Another consequence of the rise in crime was the radical reaction from people who would not hesitate to pursue justice. Thus at Shyanda, in cases of assault, the criminal was not only killed when caught but his family was also wiped out. When investigations were carried out, the local authorities and those involved retreated into silence.[119]

The acts of insubordination within the local branch of the MRND party-state multiplied in the second half of the 1980s. Also, in Ruhashya Commune, Jehovah's Witnesses refused to pay for compulsory MRND membership. A search was carried out at the home of their leader, and documents as well as payrolls were discovered, which caused the Butare Prefecture security committee meeting on October 31, 1985, to conclude that there was a foreign connection to the movement.[120] Two months later, six Jehovah's Witnesses were arrested in Nyabisindu Commune "for preaching in public messages aimed at disobeying the rules and ideals of the MRND." Six members of a different sect known as the "temperates" were also arrested in Nyabisindu.[121] An unknown number of other Jehovah's Witnesses were jailed at Karubanda Prison in Butare Town. In October 1989 the dissidence of Jehovah's Witnesses continued, and Prefect Frédéric Karangwa wrote to the burgomasters asking them to inform him of the locations in which the movement operated.[122]

The Butare Prefecture security committee meeting of February 28, 1986, also drew attention to the case of a young woman, Chantal Uwimana, who claimed to have had night visitations.[123] The young woman was staying in Ndora Commune, and from there she would "often disturb the peace at Ngoma [a popular district in Butare] with her false visions, which attracted a good number of criminals."[124] The security committee ordered her arrest "for lack of a residency permit and insubordination and ordered sanctions against those who hosted the young woman in their homes."[125]

During the Butare Prefecture security committee meeting held on June 28, 1985, Prefect Emmanuel Ruzindana expressed in a letter to the minister of health his indignation at the activities of the secretariat for national family welfare.[126] According to him, the "Catholic clergy of Butare were trying to provoke a real confrontation by undermining primary health care," specifically information on birth control methods distributed by the National Office for Population (ONAPO).[127] A woman named Antoinette Mukamusoni roamed the hills to spread her message, distributing a variety of documents, notably a circular from the Rwandan bishops on sale in the parish secretariats. The woman had toured two communes where she held sensitization sessions against the methods of spacing childbirth promoted in health centers. She had attracted a "significant audience of catechists, mothers, and engaged couples to carry out this campaign."[128]

The period preceding the war and the democratic transition ended in a serious food shortage that affected the whole prefecture but especially Maraba, Runyinya, and Nyakizu Communes. Families began to relocate to escape the hunger, others headed for Mayaga Region in the northeast of the prefecture, and others even emigrated to Tanzania. The prefect requested emergency food aid for the families worst affected.

As the prefecture went through different waves of social disorder, the party-state continued its mass mobilization activities. On October 18, 1988, President Habyarimana visited Butare Prefecture as part of his tour of the country in preparation for the presidential elections to be held two months later. In readiness for this visit, the prefect asked the burgomasters to "reenergize the entertainment troupes," whose songs were supposed to capture the themes of the presidential and parliamentary elections "while making clear the unconditional support of the people of Butare for President Habyarimana."[129] In 1989, on July 5, like every other year, the Butare population was invited to a memorial march in support of the head of state. In the thirteen communes that sent a report on the celebrations, 84,000 people marched in the sectors, that is, 6,500 people per commune. This kind of mass mobilization led some observers to think that the MRND party-state exercised almost total control over the population and to ignore the unfolding "simulacra of power" that tied the party-state to the peasantry.[130] The peasants seemed to obey during occasions bearing high political pressure in order to avoid open confrontation with the state, but in daily life they often took a different route when confronted by lesser authorities.

It is on this fertile ground that the democratic opening will sow the seeds of ethnic discord (with difficulty) and partisan predations. The bandits, the violent, and the desperate will rise in rank by forming the shock troops of the political parties.

Notes

1. Vansina, *Antecedents to Modern Rwanda*, p. 49.
2. Table 4.1 shows the population ethnic breakdown in 1980 in Butare prefecture. Although the Tutsi population has significantly decreased in the order of 15 to 30 percent following the violence of 1959–1962 and the massacres of 1963 in Gikongoro and elsewhere, the northen region of Butare was less affected by revolutionary violence, suggesting these 1980 figures reflect fairly accurately the orders of magnitude of the Tutsi population in 1960.
3. Marcel d'Hertefelt explains that in 1960 Tutsis formed the majority in the Nyaruguru region, which is currently split between Butare and Gikongoro Prefectures; in Butare, this area covers Runyinya, Maraba (part), Nyakizu (part), and Gishamvu (part) Communes. D'Hertefelt, "Les élections communales et le consensus politique au Rwanda," p. 435, note 36.
4. Saucier, "Patron-Client Relationship in Traditional and Contemporary Southern Rwanda," p. 60. D'Hertefelt, personal communication to Reyntjens, quoted in Reyntjens, *Pouvoir et droit au Rwanda,* p. 199.
5. Lemarchand, *Rwanda and Burundi*, p. 151.
6. Munyangaju, *L'actualité politique au Ruanda*, p. 24.
7. Lemarchand, *Rwanda and Burundi*, p. 151.
8. Reyntjens, *Pouvoir et droit au Rwanda*, p. 253.
9. Lemarchand, *Rwanda and Burundi*, p. 166.
10. Ibid.
11. Reyntjens, *Pouvoiret droit au Rwanda*, p. 253.
12. Belgique, Ministère des Colonies, *Rapport soumis par le gouvernement belge à l'Assemblée générale des Nations Unis au sujet de l'administration du Ruanda-Urundi pendant l'année 1959* (Brussels: Van Muysewinkel, 1960), p. 27.
13. In the Shangugu region, the APROSOMA formed an alliance with the PARMEHUTU.
14. Reyntjens, *Pouvoir et droit au Rwanda*, p. 283.
15. Ibid.
16. d'Hertefelt, "Les élections communales et le consensus politique au Rwanda," pp. 424–428.
17. Ibid., p. 422.

18. Ibid., p. 426.

19. The figures in parentheses correspond with the Tutsi percentage of the population in each of the communes. République rwandaise, Ministère de l'Intérieur et du Développement communal, *Recensement administratif de la population rwandaise durant la période de 1960–1987*, 1987, p. 42.

20. The configuration and names of communes and provinces changed in 1963. The territory of Astrida, which became Butare Prefecture, previously consisted of forty-two communes but only twenty communes were left in 1994. I geolocalized the 1960 communes into the 1994 Butare Prefecture and communes. The figures in parentheses correspond to the percentage of participation by commune. Ruanda-Urundi, *Supplément au Rudipresse*, August 13, 1960, no. 184.

21. Exactly 25.2 percent of the participation rate. Ibid.

22. d'Hertefelt, "Les élections communales et le consensus politique au Rwanda," p. 427; Ruanda-Urundi, *Supplémentau Rudipresse*

23. Not all Tutsi boycotted the elections in Nyaruguru; out of the seventy-five seats in the chiefdom, the RADER, a small, mainly Tutsi party, won fourteen. d'Hertefelt, "Les élections communales et le consensus politique au Rwanda," p. 427.

24. These numbers are different than those for Astrida territory.

25. Ruanda-Urundi, *Supplément au Rudipresse*. Later, I will examine what was at stake in the historically important representation of the PARMEHUTU in Nyakizu Commune and the whole southwestern region of Butare Prefecture.

26. Lemarchand, *Rwanda and Burundi*, p. 189.

27. Reyntjens, *Pouvoir et droit au Rwanda*, p. 299.

28. Lemarchand, *Rwanda and Burundi*, p. 195.

29. Reyntjens, *Rwanda*, p. 303.

30. Ibid.

31. Ibid.

32. This is the same Sindikuwabo who would, thirty-three years later, become president of the interim government during the genocide and whose forceful personal intervention plunged Butare Prefecture into the genocide. Reyntjens, *Pouvoir et droit au Rwanda*, p. 304.

33. Ibid., p. 450.

34. Ibid.

35. Ibid., p. 367.

36. Ibid., p. 448.

37. Munyangaju showed that all forty-five chiefs in office in 1958 were Tutsi, but hailed from only six out of the eighteen clans. The aristocratic lineages within the two clans of Abanyiginya and Abega shared 80 percent of the chief positions between them, and the royal lineage of Abahindiro occupied 30 percent of leadership positions. Munyangaju, *L'actualité politique*, pp. 20–21.

38. Ibid., p. 43.

39. Ibid., p. 28.

40. Reyntjens, *Pouvoir et droit au Rwanda*, p. 450.

41. Ibid.

42. Ibid.

43. Ibid.

44. Newbury, *Cohesion of Oppression*, p. 193.

45. Lemarchand, *Rwanda and Burundi*, pp. 233–235.

46. Reyntjens, *Pouvoir et droit au Rwanda*, p. 299.

47. Lemarchand, *Rwanda and Burundi*, p. 229.

48. Reyntjens, *Pouvoir et droit au Rwanda*, p. 473.

49. Ibid., p. 482; Lemarchand, *Rwanda and Burundi*, p. 235.

50. Lemarchand, *Rwanda and Burundi*, p. 235; Reyntjens, *Pouvoiret droit au Rwanda*, p. 482.

51. Reyntjens, *Pouvoir et droit au Rwanda*, p. 482; Lemarchand, *Rwanda and Burundi*, p. 235.

52. Lemarchand, *Rwanda and Burundi*, p. 236; Reyntjens, *Pouvoir et droit au Rwanda*, p. 482. In March 1993, the town of Nyabisindu repeated this achievement when it voted in a Parti Liberal burgomaster, the only Tutsi burgomaster in the entire country.

53. Reyntjens, *Pouvoir et droit au Rwanda*, 482, Lemarchand, *Rwanda and Burundi*, p. 235.

54. Reyntjens, *Pouvoir et droit au Rwanda*, pp. 482–483.

55. Reyntjens illustrates this explanation using the following examples: in 1972, there were 120 Tutsis (46 percent of the total 260 students) at the Groupe Scolaire de Butare, and 200 Tutsis (40 percent of the total 500 students) at the Université nationale. Reyntjens, *Pouvoir et droit au Rwanda*, p. 502.

56. Diocese of Butare, *Lettre de l'Evêque Gahamanyi au Préfet de Butare du 20/12/73*.

57. Reyntjens, *Pouvoir et droit au Rwanda*, p. 501.

58. République rwandaise, Ministère de l'Intérieur et des Affaires judiciaries, *Procès-verbal de la réunion des Préfets tenue à Kigali le 31 juillet 1973 sous la présidence de Lieutenant-colonel Alexis Kanyarengwe*.

59. Préfecture de Butare, *Lettre du Préfet au Ministre de l'Intérieur et de la Fonction publique portant sur la situation des réfugiés et celle des milieux religieux de Butare du 09/04/75*.

60. République rwandaise, Ministre de l'Intérieur et de la Fonction publique, *Lettre circulaire du ministre aux préfets portant sur la destination des biens abandonnés par les réfugiés du 22/05/75*.

61. Préfecture de Butare, *Rapport trimestriel des mois de juillet, août et septembre 1975*.

62. Préfecture de Butare, *Rapport trimestriel des mois d'avril, mai et juin 1978*.

63. Préfecture de Butare, *Lettre du Préfet au Ministre de l'Intérieur et de la Fonction publique portant sur la situation politique dans la préfecture de Butare du 24/04/02*.

64. Ibid.

65. Ibid.

66. Ibid.

67. Préfecture de Butare, *Rapport trimestriel des mois de juillet, août et septembre 1975*.

68. Ibid.

69. République rwandaise, Ministère de l'Intérieur, *Bilan des 25 ans d'indépendance du Rwanda: 1962–1987*, 1987, pp. 143–148.

70. According to the 1975 administrative census, the prefecture had 585,000 inhabitants in the 621 cells. République rwandaise, Ministère de l'Intérieur et du Développement communal, *Recensement administratif de la population rwandaise durant la période de 1960–1987*, 1987, p. 24.

71. Préfecture de Butare, *Rapport trimestriel des mois d'octobre, novembre et décembre 1975*. Both Tutsis elected as the heads of cell committees both came from Ndora Commune.

72. The sector was an administrative and political constituency above the cell and

directly below the commune. In 1980, the 206 sectors of Butare Prefecture contained an average of 3,088 inhabitants. République rwandaise, Ministère de l'Intérieur et du Développement communal, *Recensement administratif de la population rwandaise durant la période de 1960–1987*, p. 36; Préfecture de Butare, *Résultats des élections communales du 20 janvier 1980*.

73. Ibid.

74. République rwandaise, Ministère de l'Intérieur, *Dialogue entre le Président-fondateur de MRND, Président de la République et les congressistes préfectoraux lors de la tournée présidentielle de 16 avril au 6 mai 1976*.

75. Ibid.

76. Joseph Habyarimana Gitera, *Protocole de la réconciliation nationale entre les Rwandais, Butare, le 7 mai 1976*.

77. Prunier, *Rwanda Crisis*, p. 84.

78. The security committee comprised the heads of the military camps and police stations, the prefecture head of intelligence, the assistant prefects, and the prefect. Préfecture de Butare, *Procès-verbal du la réunion du comité de sécurité du 1er juin 1980*.

79. Ibid.

80. Ibid.

81. Ibid.

82. Ibid.

83. République rwandaise, Cabinet du Président, *Lettre du Ministre à la Présidence au Ministre de la Justice du 30 juin 1980 portant sur le compte rendu de la réunion du comité de sécurité de Butare du 10 juin 1980*.

84. Préfecture de Butare, *Procès-verbal de la réunion du comité préfectoral de sécurité tenue le 28/02/86*.

85. Préfecture de Butare, *Rapport trimestriel des mois de juillet, août, septembre 1975*.

86. Ministère de l'Intérieur et de la Fonction publique, *Lettre circulaire du Ministre aux Préfets du 07/03/75 portant sur la recrudescence du banditisme*.

87. Préfecture de Butare, *Procès-verbal de la réunion du comité préfectoral de sécurité tenue le 21/09/83*.

88. Préfecture de Butare, *Procès-verbal de la réunion du comité préfectoral de sécurité du 15 avril 1975*.

89. Ibid.

90. Préfecture de Butare, *Procès-verbal de la réunion du comité préfectoral de sécurité tenue le 25 octobre 1976*.

91. Ibid.

92. Préfecture de Butare, *Compte rendu de la réunion de sécurité du 16/12/76*.

93. Préfecture de Butare, *Procès-verbal de la réunion de la sous-commission de sécurit de Nyanza du 18/08/80*.

94. At the time, in Rwanda and also in Burundi, organized gangs of thugs attacked a home by throwing a huge rock they called Gatalina, against the door they wanted to break down while shouting Gatalina so as to instill fear among the neighbors.

95. Préfecture de Butare, *Procès-verbal de la réunion de la sous-commission de sécurité de Nyanza du 18/08/80*.

96. Ibid.

97. Préfecture de Butare, *Procès-verbal de la réunion du comité préfectoral de sécurité tenue le 7 mai 1982*.

98. Ibid.; Préfecture de Butare, *Rapport trimestriel d'avril, mai et juin 1977*.

99. Préfecture de Butare, *Procès-verbal de la réunion du comité préfectoral de sécurité du 19/07/82.*

100. Ibid.

101. Préfecture de Butare, *Procès-verbal de la réunion du comité préfectoral de sécurité tenue le 16/12/83.*

102. In 1978, Ngoma, Shyanda, Mbazi, Huye, Gishamvu, Nyaruhengeri, Ndora, and Nyabisindu Communes had between 400 and 500 or more inhabitants per square kilometer, whereas Ntyazo and Muyira Communes had between 200 and 300 inhabitants per square kilometer. Nzisaabira, "Accumulation," pp. 39, 46.

103. To better grasp the ambiguous links between crime and political protest, see Crummey, ed., *Banditry, Rebellion, and Social Protest in Africa.*

104. Préfecture de Butare, *Procès-verbal de la réunion du comité préfectoral de sécurité tenue le 25/11/75.*

105. Ibid.

106. Préfecture de Butare, *Procès-verbal de la réunion du comité préfectoral de sécurité tenue le 10/08/76.*

107. Ibid.

108. Préfecture de Butare, *Rapport trimestriel d'avril, mai et juin 1977.*

109. We are limiting this period to 1989 because of the upheavals experienced in the country during the second half of 1990, which mark a break with the previous period.

110. Willame, *Aux sources de l'hécatombe*, p. 133.

111. Préfecture de Butare, *Tableau récapitulatif de l'état de la situation de la sécurité dans la préfecture de Butare entre le 17/05/85 et le 27/06/85.*

112. Préfecture de Butare, *Procès-verbal de la réunion du comité de sécurité de la sous-préfecture de Butare tenue le 02/01/85.*

113. Préfecture de Butare, *Procès-verbal de la réunion du comité préfectoral de Butare tenue le 02/11/84.*

114. Ibid.

115. Ibid.

116. On February 18, 1986, for example, the burgomaster of Rusatira Commune and the commune police officers were attacked, and that would not be the first time. Préfecture de Butare, *Tableau récapitulatif de l'état de la situation de la sécurité dans la prefecture de Butare entre le 17/05/85 et le 27/06/85.*

117. Préfecture de Butare, *Procès-verbal de la réunion du comité préfectoral de sécurité tenue le 05/10/84.*

118. Préfecture de Butare, *Procès-verbal de la réunion du comité préfectoral de sécurité tenue le 28/06/85.*

119. Ibid.

120. Préfecture de Butare, *Procès-verbal de la réunion du comité préfectoral de sécurité tenue le 31/10/85.*

121. Préfecture de Butare, *Procès-verbal de la réunion du comité préfectoral de sécurité tenue le 29/11/85.*

122. Préfecture de Butare, *Lettre circulaire du Préfet aux Bourgmestres portant sur les activités des Témoins de Jéhovah dans les communes du 24/10/89.*

123. Préfecture de Butare, *Procès-verbal de la réunion du comité préfectoral de sécurité tenue le 28/06/85.*

124. Ibid.

125. Ibid.

126. Ibid.

127. Ibid.

128. Ibid.

129. Préfecture de Butare, *Lettre circulaire du Préfet aux Bourgmestres portant sur la préparation de la visite du Président de la République.*

130. Mbembe, "Provisional Notes on the Postcolony."

5

From Tolerance to Genocide in Butare

This chapter examines the actions and reactions of the population of Butare Prefecture in the three defining events of the 1990–1994 Rwanda crisis: the Rwandan Patriotic Front (RPF) attack on October 1, 1990, and the ensuing war, the establishment of political pluralism in July 1991, and finally, the genocide in April 1994. I retrace the political and social history immediately preceding the outbreak of the genocide and give a synthesis of the dynamics of genocide across the communes of Butare. Through this record of the regional history, I focus on the processes of mobilization of the people for participation in the genocide at an intermediate level, prefecture and communes, rather than on the dynamics of the mass participation in the genocide at the grassroots, which I will outline in the next few chapters.

I will show how, during the multiparty period, people of Butare's political behavior passed from acts of disobedience against the National Revolutionary Movement for Development (MRND) party-state to radical rejection of the regime. Strikingly, the inhabitants of Butare communes participated in the genocide along political and ideological lines inherited from the 1960s, revived by the re-establishment of political pluralism in 1991, making the genocide in Butare appear the culmination of a process begun in 1959.

The October 1990 War

The launching of the war by the RPF did not have significant repercussions at the grassroots level. In Butare Prefecture, there were two reactions to the war: some ethnic tension among the educated and salaried elite in Butare and Nyabisindu Towns and almost total calm among the residents in the rural communes.

Even though Butare Prefecture was far from the combat zones, the outbreak of hostilities pushed the prefecture authorities to take some measures such as a ban on travel between communes without a travel permit. The community patrols for carrying out checks on pedestrians and vehicles in the communes were systematically reinstituted, and roadblocks were erected on various road networks and paths. In urban Butare and Nyabisindu, like elsewhere in the country the day after the sham fighting in Kigali on October 4, 1990, prominent Tutsis and other people considered lukewarm to the regime were arrested: 256 were arrested in Butare and 41 in Nyabisindu, in addition to the 315 people arrested in Kigali but incarcerated in Karubanda Prison in Butare.[1] Discipline in carrying out security measures slackened rather rapidly, with councilors taking down roadblocks without authorization from the prefecture and burgomasters sending security reports explaining that their communes were peaceful.[2] From late 1990 on, sporadic acts of crime and crop theft increased both in homes and farms, evidence of a difficult food situation, especially in urban Ngoma Commune (in Butare Town).[3]

In general, no ethnic tension in the prefecture is recorded in official documents of the period following the outbreak of the war; it appears in such documents only after February 1991, following the RPF surprise attack on Ruhengeri Town on January 23, 1991. The security report for February 1991 notes the formation in Butare Town of small ethnically homogeneous groups likely aimed at provoking tension, rumors of ethnic tension in a sector of urban Ngoma Commune, and an ethnically charged incident at the National University.[4] In Nyabisindu, Tutsis formed groups in bars and walked home together given the rumors circulating of ethnic massacres planned for specific nights. In the secondary schools, ethnically motivated student riots were instigated by staff members and aided by latent tension within the faculty. The Groupe scolaire for boys at Save, the School of Economics and Social Science in Kansi, and the Groupe scolaire of Nyanza all carried out preventive expulsion of the students considered ringleaders.[5]

The Butare Prefecture security report warns of "movements of people leaving . . . probably to join enemy ranks. . . . In Muyira, Kibayi, and Nyakizu Communes, Rwandans were arrested attempting to leave the country secretly." The surge in petty crime "despite the rounds and military patrols" during this period of war led the prefect security council to ask itself whether it was dealing with an RPF strategy, a scheme of destabilization, or simply crime.[6]

The council also took note of a food shortage in the prefecture. The prefecture administration listed 15,000 families totaling 60,000 people, or 10 percent of the prefecture population, as suffering from hunger and in need of emergency food aid. According to the security committee, "Each of the needy families owns less than 20 ares." To remedy this precarious situation, it was suggested that the more densely populated areas of Mbazi and Shyanda Communes be decongested in the direction of the rice-growing areas in the southeast of Butare. Finally, the report gives an update on the release of people detained on suspicion of collaboration with the RPF a day after the mock attack of October 4, 1990. Of the 612 people detained in the prefectures, the majority of them Tutsis, 133 still remained in the prefecture prisons in March 1991. Prefect Justin Temahagali congratulated himself that in his prefecture, prisoner releases had not caused the tensions witnessed in other parts of the country.[7]

According to the prefecture's security report of January 3, 1992, the war with the RPF in almost all the communes seemed not to concern the local people, who felt that the war was far removed from them. By contrast, in the communes bordering Burundi, the residents were anxious about the political situation in that country and feared an attack from Burundi.[8]

As I note in the next chapter, on February 5, 1991, panic seized the inhabitants of Kigembe Commune and the neighboring Kibayi Commune, who believed the RPF was attacking from Burundi. At the end of 1991, the prefecture took a small informal opinion poll on different subjects among the population, including the war with the RPF. Here are some of the responses by commune:

Mbazi Commune

The peasants' perception of the war was that the *inyenzi* ("cockroaches," or rebels) had taken over a part of the country because the peasants could not imagine why people would leave their homes and let them become overgrown wastelands unless those people were fleeing someone. The peasants wondered why it was said that a solution to the war existed, but no one applied it, just as it was with the cease-fire agreements signed but never respected. However, the residents were not worried about the war; they were more worried about the situation in Burundi.

Gishamvu Commune

The peasants had the impression that the war at the borders was far away. They were more worried about what was happening in Burundi.

Muyaga Commune

The peasants did not support the continuation of the war. They were angry that the leaders did not agree on a way to end it and angry at the manner the motive of the attack was presented, as if there was no justification of this attack coming from Uganda.

Mugusa Commune

There was no sign of tension caused by the war, except for four people who secretly left the commune. After that, nobody secretly left or returned to the commune any more.

Ntyazo Commune

People were not worried about the war; they were more worried about a possible attack from Burundi.

Nyaruhengeri Commune

The people were not worried by the war; rather, they were afraid of the war that might have come from Burundi.

Kigembe Commune

The people remembered the war only when it was discussed on the radio.

Runyinya Commune

The people remembered the war only when it was discussed on the radio.

Muyira Commune

Regarding the war, the peasants of Muyira were worried about the one that might have come from Burundi, and they remembered the war being waged at the border in Byumba and Ruhengeri only when it was discussed on the radio.[9]

The events in Burundi referred to in the report were the beginning of military clashes in Bujumbura and in Cibitoke and Bubanza Provinces on November 23 and 24, 1991, massacres by the Palipehutu followed by others committed by the Burundian Army, claiming several thousand victims.[10]

The peasants' worries were fueled by the influx of refugees created by the turmoil in Burundi.

Multiple Parties in Butare

Contrary to a popular notion among analysts, Rwandan peasants responded favorably to the appeals by dissident social elites and engaged in political activism.[11] In Butare, the emergence of political parties followed defined ideological divisions reviving a political situation almost identical to that of the commune elections in June 1960. The atmosphere of liberalism and tolerance that reigned in Butare Town and a large part of the prefecture sharply contrasts with the violence and intimidation prevailing in the Republican Democratic Movement (MDR)–dominated southwestern communes of the prefecture.

Ideological and Territorial Fidelities

In late July 1991, the country's main political parties formed regional sections at the prefecture level in Butare. The National Revolutionary Movement for Development (MRND), Republican Democratic Movement (MDR), Social Democratic Party (PSD), Liberal Party (PL), and Christian Democratic Party (PDC) established branches by providing lists of signatories to the statutes of their parties' sections in Butare. The MRND had ninety signatories, the MDR twenty-seven, the PSD nine, the PDC two, and the PL two.[12] The MRND of Butare was the only one whose regional godfathers were well-known political personalities, such as Minister of Commerce and Consumer Affairs François Nzabahimana, Speaker of Parliament Théodore Sindikubwabo, Member of Parliament Amandin Rugira, Advisor to the President Runyinya-Barabwiriza, National University president Maurice Ntahobari, and member of the MRND political bureau Professor Jean Rumiya. The regional signatories of the other political parties were mostly low- or middle-level government officials, with a few exceptions such as Félicien Gatabazi, former minister and signatory supporting the PSD. The ninety MRND signatories were evenly distributed in all the prefecture's twenty communes. The distribution of MDR signatories by communes is striking: of its twenty-seven signatories, twelve came from the four communes in the southwest of the prefecture, two times higher than the result of an even distribution would have been for the commune. Of these twelve, four came from Kigembe, three from Nyaruhengeri, three from Gishamvu, and two from Nyakizu. The case of Kigembe is also interesting: out of the four signatories from this commune, two were peasants, one a state administration officer, and the other a doctor. These peasants were the only members of their social and professional status among the signatories of all parties, as if to indicate that Kigembe would be the base of the MDR popular support. The list of MDR signatories shows that, from its beginnings, this party was essentially rooted in the southwest of the prefecture.

Political Rallies

Political rallies, soon to become the primary political activity in the communes, began on August 15, 1991, with an MDR rally in Gishamvu Commune. In these first rallies organized by the MDR, prefecture officials noted that the MRND and all top authorities of the country were targets of harsh criticism. After less than two weeks of legal political activity by various parties, the people were no longer properly paying taxes or participating in obligatory development activities such as *umuganda*, anti-soil-erosion efforts, family planning, or reforestation. Some commune councilors as well as members of cell committees began to support opposition parties. After less than two weeks of these public activities, an inspection tour of the communes by Prefect

Temahagali noted that MRND supporters had become the minority in almost all the communes.[13] In these first days of demonstrative political activity, the ambiguous MDR position on the ethnic question became evident in its recruitment policy. In Runyinya Commune, where half the population was Tutsi, the MDR invited Hutus to join whereas "Tutsis joined on their own initiative."[14] The civil disobedience campaign launched by opposition parties was accompanied by a wave of invasions of the sector's public pastures, which compelled the prefect to send a circular to all burgomasters asking them to prevent the people from invading and cultivating land for grazing without authorization.[15]

The following record by the prefecture administration of PSD and MDR meetings provides an overview of the messages disseminated among the Butare population by these two opposition parties.[16]

The PSD rally at Huye Stadium (Butare Town) December 15, 1991. Those who participated in this huge rally at the prefecture level included top PSD leaders, such as President Frederic Nzamurambaho from Gikongoro Prefecture, Secretary-General Félicien Gatabazi from Butare Prefecture (Shyanda Commune), Vice President Félicien Ngango from Kibungo Prefecture, and Vice President Théoneste Gafaranga from Gitarama Prefecture. These national figures were accompanied by party officials at the prefecture level and certain representatives of the PSD committees from the communes. From the detailed account by the prefecture officials, I highlight four major facts:

1. The PSD focused its communication with the people of Butare almost exclusively on local political problems, beginning with criticism of the MRND, and made almost no mention of the war.
2. In their Butare stronghold, the PSD leaders emphasized party entrenchment in the region.
3. PSD leaders took a clear position against ethnocentrism both historically, in their criticism of the founding fathers of the republic, and with respect to the present period.
4. These leaders proposed compulsory birth control, certainly asserting the elitism and the dedication of their party, which could risk offending the rural, still strongly profamily audience.[17]

The year 1991 ended with a difficult food situation, brought up in the Butare Prefecture security council meeting on January 3, 1992. The minutes noted the usual social problems, especially those linked to land shortage: family tensions in Mbazi Commune, "illegitimate" children mistreating their biological fathers; youth forcefully seizing land belonging to their parents in Nyaruhengeri Commune; young men invading and cultivating public grazing land in Muyaga Commune; and, in Huye and Mugusa Communes, robbers in gangs of fifty attacking and injuring merchants.[18]

During the same period, tensions between the Hutu and Tutsis were reported. In late 1991, when Hutus were signing up to join the MDR, there were rumors that lists had been drawn up of Tutsi to be killed. This tension originating from Gishamvu Commune had reached the neighboring Runyinya Commune. This is the first time in many years official documents mentioned ethnic tension among the population in the rural communes of Butare Prefecture. This tension, expressed mostly in the form of death threats, appeared in the communes southwest of Butare as a consequence of political mobilization by the MDR. The political parties continued their campaigns to recruit supporters. Despite the violent speeches at MDR rallies, the security committee meeting reported no violence resulting from political party activities. By contrast, the political parties' flags hoisted at their offices indicate that the MDR and the PSD were probably the two most popular parties in the prefecture, with the MRND in decline almost everywhere.[19]

On January 11, 1992, the MDR, PSD, and PL organized a large demonstration in Butare Town.[20] The demonstration was part of the opposition cartel's national protest against the formation of Prime Minister Sylvestre Nsanzimana's government on December 30, 1991. Nsanzimana had been appointed by the president of the republic after the collapse of negotiations on the conditions for participation of the opposition in the government.[21] On January 28, 1992, the MDR organized rallies in all the communes to commemorate the "coup d'état of Gitarama" of January 28, 1961, which had proclaimed the republic and put into place republican institutions.[22]

The MDR rally at Huye Stadium February 16, 1992. This huge rally of great significance in the prefecture records the participation of members of the national MDR political bureau such as Dismas Nsengiyaremye, Jean Kambanda, and Eliézer Niyitegeka as well as MDR representatives from nine of the country's ten prefectures, including Agathe Uwilingiyimana, representative of Butare Prefecture. From the prefecture's minutes of the meeting, four elements stand out:

1. The populist nature of the message delivered at this rally by the national and regional MDR leaders, who focused their speeches on criticizing the MRND and the symbolic significance of the colors of the flags. The war against the RPF figured only minimally, and its importance was played down.

2. Repeated references to the MDR-PARMEHUTU and in general terms to the past, either by mentioning the Rwanda National Union (UNAR), using the regional historical names no longer in use, or by evoking *ubuhake*. Among the three speakers who referred to the MDR-PARMEHUTU, only Nsengiyaremye touched on the subject of the rejuvenation of the MDR without addressing further the reasons for this new orientation of the party, whereas Kambanda asked for a minute of silence for the "hero" Grégoire

Kayibanda. MDR leaders at this rally placed the actions of the reformed party in the context of continuity with the MDR-PARMEHUTU without much elaboration on the question of the party's revival.

3. Justifications for the party use of violence by regional and national leaders, particularly carrying out *kubohoza* operations, and for the forced dismissal of local authorities.

4. Finally, the speakers at the rally who hailed from Butare Prefecture, either leaders of the Butare branch of the party or Butare members of the national *bureau politique,* such as Kambanda and Uwilingiyimana, all originally came from the southwest of the prefecture (Gishamvu, Nyakizu, Kigembe, and Nyaruhengeri Communes); this fact proves once more the entrenchment of the party in this part of Butare.[23]

After this rally, the first incidents of political violence occurred in Butare, particularly in the southwest communes and almost always at the hands of MDR supporters.

Key events in Butare Prefecture from March 1992 to February 1994 demonstrate a significant rise in violence: political violence by MDR supporters in the communes in the south, mob justice resulting from mass exasperation with thieves, and political violence originating from outside the prefecture in the form of exploding landmines, with thieves using military weapons.

At the same time, from June 1992, when Tutsi member of the PL party Jean-Baptiste Habyarimana was appointed as prefect, to August 1993, when the Butare MDR branch suspended its president, Uwilingiyimana, one observes a convergent effort of the leaders of opposition political parties, Butare prefect, and its highest-ranking military officers to maintain a climate of tolerance and moderation within the prefecture. In late 1993 and early 1994, the political climate became polarized. On the one hand, ethnic animosity was instilled in the prefecture and, on the other, the PSD, the main political party in Butare, radicalized its opposition to the MRND and its allies and managed to prevent the Hutu-power factions from expressing themselves in Butare and Nyanza Towns.

Political Violence in MDR-Dominated Communes and Sectors

The political violence that began in March 1992 corresponds with a particular political set of circumstances at the national level. The MDR, which had joined the government and obtained the prime minister position following a wave of huge demonstrations led by the opposition—and by the MDR in particular—wanted to build on its advantage. The party sought to establish a local base throughout the country, and it is from this perspective that we should understand MDR burgomasters' and councilors' incitement of the public to participate in *kubohoza*. This wave of political violence incited at political rallies was accompanied by anti-Tutsi speeches by leaders who sought to revive the ideological discourse inherited from the PARMEHUTU.

Nyakizu Commune. On March 1, 1992, the MDR began in Nyakizu Commune its fight to expel the MRND from the southwestern communes of the prefecture, which it considered its preserve. The Butare Prefecture security council traced the violence in the commune to the rejection of the MDR application for a permit to hold a rally because the MRND had applied before the MDR. Upon arriving at the venue, MRND supporters found a soccer match by MDR supporters in progress. The MRND supporters had to relocate their rally. As the rally went on, MDR supporters approached and began to create a racket by drumming buckets, beating drums, and blowing whistles. MRND supporters started to sing and succeeded in drowning out the noise. Peace returned, and the rally ended without incident. On their way back, MRND supporters arrived at the small urban center of Gasasa, and there the MDR supporters threw stones at them, breaking the windows of the car transporting the MRND supporters. Some MRND members, including the party flag bearer, were stabbed and seriously injured. Police officers who arrived to restore calm also had stones thrown at them, and one officer was injured. Two commune leaders of MDR were arrested.[24]

MDR supporters from Nyakizu Commune then decided to organize demonstrations and even made an unsuccessful attempt at holding the burgomaster hostage to exchange his release with that of their imprisoned comrades. They used tree trunks to block the roads in the commune. To help out their friends, MDR sympathizers from other communes decided to demonstrate in both the town center and other communes of Butare. After this incident, some students were beaten in Kigembe Commune because of their parents' party affiliations. These acts of intimidation in Kigembe were committed by the commune's MDR supporters, who threatened to repeat what their comrades in Nyakizu had done.[25]

In Nyakizu, on the night of June 4–5, 1992, the local MDR committee, led by its president, Ladislas Ntaganzwa, finally expelled the burgomaster from the commune.

A flurry of events began in June 1992 in Nyakizu following a series of attacks against MRND members to force them to get MDR membership cards, public acts of defiance against the authorities, and vandalism of commune head offices.[26] One night, a police officer named Ntezirembo knocked at the door of a widow called Cecile. Minani, Cecile's uncle, called out to the officer in order to identify him. Taken by surprise, the officer shot Minani in the chest. Public opinion in the commune considered the incident a murder sponsored by Burgomaster Jean-Baptiste Gasana to harass the opposition. Opposition party members were up in arms and called for sacking the burgomaster. Several accusations of alleged mistakes and embezzlement were leveled against him. MDR members erected barriers and obstructed the roads to the commune headquarters with tree trunks then prevented the law enforcement officers and prefecture officials from intervening. On the night of June 4 to 5, MDR supporters led by Ntaganzwa, armed with stones, clubs, machetes, and axes, smashed down the doors and windows of the burgomaster's home. Out of fear, the burgomaster fired at the crowd, injuring a young man named Charles Nyandwi. He managed to break free and rescue his family and subsequently sought refuge in Butare Town.[27]

Just as in some other communes where the incumbent burgomaster was rejected by his constituency, the elections for the burgomaster's successor took place on March 23, 1993, and gave rise to new violence by the MDR. The PSD and MDR candidates in Nyakizu each garnered seventeen votes. On the day before the second round of elections was to take place, MDR supporters feared that PSD members would bribe the voters of the "preselection committee."[28] They put up roadblocks on the road leading to the commune head office, where they held the PSD supporters hostage and released them the following day, which was Election Day. Before the actual election began, MDR supporters threatened not to accept the results if their candidate did not win. Ntaganzwa, the MDR candidate, the president of the party's commune branch and the main instigator of the campaign of violence, finally won with twenty votes. PSD supporters protested, denouncing MDR use of intimidation.[29]

Kigembe Commune. The situation in Kigembe will be studied in greater detail in the next two chapters. In general, the commune also witnessed major violence pitting the MDR against the MRND that ended in a *kubohoza* operation against the MRND burgomaster of the commune, forcing the latter to escape. One man died and dozens of homes were burned as a result of this confrontation.

The spread of MDR violence and tension in other southern communes. A few days before the violence in Kigembe Commune on June 3, 1992, there was a huge MDR rally in Busoro Subprefecture in the neighboring Gishamvu Commune, "during which the speakers lashed out at MRND party members, making threats against the Interahamwe, raising awareness and deliberately inciting Hutus against the Tutsi."[30]

The wave of violence in Nyakizu and Kigembe Communes in the southwest of Butare Prefecture between the end of May and beginning of June 1992 spread to the southeast of the prefecture—to Muganza, Nyaruhengeri, and Kibayi Communes—where MDR supporters also carried out attacks.[31] In Nyaruhengeri Commune, MDR supporters in Bimba Sector ransacked and destroyed homes of MRND members. A few people were molested, but intervention from the subprefect and the burgomaster successfully stopped the violence.[32] Still in Nyaruhengeri Commune, in Bimba and Gikore Sectors, MDR supporters seized pastureland to farm it.[33]

During a meeting of the prefecture committee on July 24, 1992, the burgomasters of Runyinya, Muyira, Nyaruhengeri, and Gishamvu Communes asked that those responsible for the violence in Kigembe and Nyakizu Communes be arrested; otherwise, those with similar intentions in their own communes would be encouraged. In the same meeting, the public prosecutor in Butare explained that the individuals arrested during the violence in Nyakizu and Kigembe Communes were released because of a procedural defect in their arrest. However, those who had witnessed and experienced the events firsthand said that MDR supporters were released upon the intervention of Uwilingiyimana, then MDR minister of education.[34] Unable to control his commune, the Kigembe burgomaster was retired, and the Nyakizu burgomaster himself said that he no longer wanted to carry on as burgomaster in a commune where he could no longer set foot.[35] During the meeting, Major Tharcisse Muvunyi, commandant at the Gikongoro-Butare Army Base, expressed concern that in several of the communes of Butare and Gikongoro on the border with Burundi, the people were at loggerheads with its leaders and eventually expelled them.[36]

The reign of MDR violence in the southwest communes of the prefecture was accompanied by the instillation of ethnic animosity. In late 1992, tracts circulating in Gishamvu, Nyakizu, and Kigembe Communes stated that Minister Lando Ndasingwa, a Tutsi high-ranking PL official, was planning to stir up trouble to provoke a war between Burundi and Rwanda.[37] The three communes in question were MDR strongholds.

MDR Violence in the Rest of the Prefecture

In the communes out of its stronghold of the southwest of Butare Prefecture, where MDR was not strong enough to control the commune, *kubohoza* operations and other acts of violence could target lower administrative circumscriptions, sectors, or even cells.

On April 25, 1992, the prefect asked the burgomaster of Ntyazo Commune to charge a group of MDR supporters with attacking MRND supporters returning from a rally in Gatonde Sector on April 22.[38]

On June 26, 1992, in Muganza Commune, MDR supporters attacked MRND sympathizers returning from a rally in Bwisha.[39] On April 17, 1992, MDR supporters terrorized and struck inhabitants of Mugusa Sector of Mugusa Commune.[40] In Muyaga Commune, the burgomaster was relentlessly confronted by MDR, PSD, and PL opposition members who wanted to demonstrate against him and pressure him to resign.[41]

In July 1992, in Muganza Commune, MDR supporters unsuccessfully attempted to dismiss by force (*kubohoza*) the councilor of Gishubi Sector. They then invaded collective land assigned to groups of cultivators and farmed them, destroying the crops they found growing there. When the officers of the commune police sought to intervene, the troublemakers blocked the roads with tree trunks and promised to attack the commune head office directly.[42]

On August 5 and 6, 1992, in Ntyazo Commune, thirty MDR supporters seized land that belonged to the councilor of Ntyazo sector. Everyone who participated was to receive a payment of RF100.[43]

In Muyaga Commune, a group of MDR supporters locked up the councilor of Nyiranzi Sector in his office and assaulted him. He was freed the next day after the police intervened. On August 14 and 18, 1992, forests in Ntyazo Sector were burned.[44]

Throughout September 1992, MDR and MRND supporters in Ntyazo Commune fought with knives.[45]

Lastly, villagers fed up with the spate of robberies united to form community patrols and killed thieves they apprehended. These organized, nonpolitical killings were committed in communes and sectors where the MDR was powerful.

In mid-April 1992, in Kabusanza Sector of Maraba Commune, inhabitants fed up by the spate of robbers chased after thieves who had just stolen a sheep and were slaughtering it in the bush. The animal's owners chased the culprits, one of whom they caught and killed.[46]

On August 7, 1992, in Nyaruhengeri Commune, residents beat eleven robbers to death. They first caught and beat up two of the robbers in order to force the robbers to denounce their accomplices. The robbers had recently attacked the residents more than ten times. In Gishamvu and Muganza Communes two robbers were killed in each under similar circumstances.[47]

PSD and PL Kubohoza *Against the Burgomaster of Nyabisindu*

The PSD and PL mostly did not use politically motivated violence in the prefectures and rural areas.[48] In Butare Prefecture, members of these parties sometimes participated in the *kubohoza* operations but mostly as individuals rather than as implementers of party policy. Politically motivated violence by these two parties was rare in Butare and was concentrated in Nyabisindu Town and Commune, thought to be provoked by the burgomaster and the subprefect, both fervent MRND members in a region dominated by the PSD and the PL.

The weakening of public order allowed landless people to grab public and sometimes private land. Often, such people acted in their capacity as party members. On May 17, 1992, in Nyabisindu Commune (formerly Nyanza Province), a group of cultivators from across ethnic groups and persuasions forcibly cleared the marshy areas given to people whom they considered wealthy.[49] This cooperative action between Tutsis and Hutus in the former

Nyanza Province could be explained by the fact that the PSD and the PL were powerful in the commune.

On May 17, 1992, the PSD held a political rally in Nyabisindu Town led by secretary-general and main figure Gatabazi, who declared that the search for peace with the RPF could not be achieved as long as President Habyarimana remained in power. In reference to a local demand, he affirmed that the Nyanza market could not be built as long as Vincent Ngiruwonsanga remained burgomaster because he wanted to grant the construction of the market to a person from the president's clan. Gatabazi asked that the Nyabisindu burgomaster and subprefect go exercise their dictatorship elsewhere. Finally, he accused the police of planting mines. During the same meeting, four councilors considered former MRND members by default publicly joined the PSD.[50] Gatabazi seems to have thus launched a public appeal for the overthrow of the Nyabisindu burgomaster.

On July 17, 1992, a large number of PSD and PL supporters, led by two PSD and PL commune councilors, wanted to carry out *kubohoza* against the burgomaster of Nyabisindu Town. Nyabisindu inhabitants were invited to participate, but commune authorities and national police eventually managed to protect the burgomaster. No damages were reported. According to the Nyabisindu deputy prefect, on the previous day as they left a meeting at the stadium to prepare for the event the next day, PSD supporters attacked the manager of the Nyabisindu creamery, the director of the electric company, a legal advisor to the court of appeals, and the director of the jail.[51]

This was one of the rare times when a *kubohoza* operation was attempted by PSD and PL supporters.

Rising Insecurity in the Prefecture

On March 17, 1992, in order to resolve the flag war between the parties, Prefect Temahagali asked burgomasters to organize the hoisting of the flags only in front of the offices of party heads at the sector, commune, and prefecture offices.[52]

On May 6, 1992, a mine exploded at Falcon Hotel in Butare without causing any injuries or fatalities. Investigators were not able to identify the culprit. Public opinion accused gendarmes of acting on behalf of the president's party, which was losing ground in Butare.[53]

On May 29, 1992, Prefect Temahagali enforced a curfew declared by the government from midnight to 5 a.m. to mitigate against insecurity.[54]

On July 26, 1992, in Mbazi Sector of Mbazi Commune, six men armed with machetes and firearms, some dressed in military uniform, attacked Joseph Kanyamibwa's home. They fired six bullets, but no one was injured. They took a bicycle.[55]

Building an Opposition Coalition Around the New Prefect

In July 1992 Jean-Baptiste Habyarimana, then a professor at the National University of Rwanda, was appointed the new prefect of Butare. Habyarimana, a Tutsi, was a PL member from Runyinya Commune. He had studied in the United States, where he obtained his PhD in engineering.[56]

In contrast to what was happening in the communes of the southwest, opposition political parties in Butare Town mainly respected a policy of mutual tolerance and managed to preserve a certain amount of peace in the town. The new prefect quickly developed a political consensus around him, aimed at countering the attempt at destabilization by political groups of the president's inner circle. In so doing, he managed to contain MRND representatives of Butare.

On August 25, 1992, the Butare branches of the MDR, PL, and PSD wrote to the prefect in reaction to an announcement of the first rally to be held by the extremist, anti-Tutsi, and anti-opposition CDR party. Stigmatizing the party's incitement to violence and vandalism as well as its extremist anti-Tutsi rhetoric, the party branches threatened the CDR with violence from "their people."[57]

On August 18, 1992, Prefect Habyarimana set up a political party consultation committee comprising members of MDR, PL, and PSD. MRND boycotted the meeting.[58]

Confronted with rising violence and insecurity in the prefecture, Habyarimana called for a special security meeting for August 19, 1992, that would bring together prominent personalities regardless of party affiliation, originally from Butare or currently working in the prefecture, from ministers all the way to burgomasters of communes. The meeting questioned the MDR on its *kubohoza* policy. Uwilingiyimana, the president of the MDR Butare branch and minister of education, defended *kubohoza* as not wrong in principle and stated that only acts of violence were to be condemned. At the end of the meeting, it was agreed that police patrols be increased in the communes. The meeting participants also asked that the communes that no longer had burgomasters receive new officials and that the power-sharing between the opposition and the MRND also apply at the commune level in order to bring the new burgomasters up to speed with the political sensibilities of the majority of those under their jurisdiction.[59]

On September 11, 1992, following the decision made at the August 19 meeting, the prefect invited party representatives to participate in a conference and debate with the people of Butare at Huye Stadium. On the agenda for discussion were the actions of multiparty government from its creation until April 16, 1992.[60] Thus, the prefect backed the opposition parties as his way of giving visibility to the accomplishments of the multiparty government despised by members of the president's inner circle.

In late August 1992, MDR, PSD, and PL supporters from Nyanza Town organized a huge public rally to call for an end to the MRND and CDR presence there. The mobilization had been provoked by a rumor about the arrival of MRND Interahamwe militias in town.[61]

The more restricted Butare Prefecture security committee meeting of September 26, 1992, noted the resurgence of young people, certainly Tutsis, crossing the Burundi border to join the RPF. The meeting participants decided to ask the burgomasters and councilors to be more vigilant as they issued the documents required for obtaining passports.[62]

A few days earlier, tension had risen in Muganza Commune following the departure of six young people passing through Burundi supposedly to enlist with the RPF. The residents pointed fingers at the families of the young men, and the parents explained in turn that they had no way of detaining their sons. The tension died down thanks to meetings organized by Burgomaster Elie Ndayambaje, who wondered in a letter for how long he could keep the people reassured.[63]

In late 1992, the Butare branches of the MDR, PSD, and PL issued a communiqué calling for vigilance from Butare residents because the "killers" were coming into the prefecture.[64]

Claiming to face a worsening security situation, the youth wing of the PSD, the Abakombozi, of Cyarwa-Sumo Sector of urban Ngoma Commune in Butare Town decided to enforce security parallel to the sector administration, contrary to the Ngoma burgomaster's wishes.[65]

Solidarity of civilian and military leaders against the MRND and CDR in Butare. On December 31, 1992, a grenade exploded in the popular Hotel Ibis in Butare. The culprits were not identified. Participants at a prefecture security committee meeting held on January 2, 1993, suggested that the grenade attack was the work of those seeking to scuttle the Arusha peace talks with the RPF. They also expressed support for the negotiations and hoped talks would be successful as soon as possible.[66]

On January 19, 1993, the prefecture security committee deliberated on the plan by MRND and CDR supporters to organize demonstrations to start on January 20 and last until these political parties' demands were fulfilled. The security committee decided to ban the planned demonstrations on grounds that it wanted to prevent the violence in Ruhengeri and Kigali from spreading.[67] These demonstrations were planned as part of the national reaction against the Arusha agreement protocol on power-sharing. In the end, the MRND and the CDR organized a small demonstration in Butare Town that did not lead to any violence.[68]

On February 13, 1993, the burgomaster of urban Ngoma Commune (in Butare Town) wrote a letter to the prefect informing him of the presence of several foreigners in the town and requesting authorization to reintroduce the residence permit system.[69]

The special meeting of the Butare Prefecture security council held on February 11, 1993, attended by 150 people, including all parties' prefecture and commune representatives, burgomasters, and a large number of prominent personalities of the prefecture, expressed its unwavering support for the Rwandan Armed Forces (FAR) in the resumption of the war with the RPF. The participants deplored the conflicting positions held by the president of the republic (MRND) and the prime minister (MDR) on holding political rallies after February 8, 1993, when the RPF violated the cease-fire.[70] The president had imposed a ban on political rallies everywhere in the country because of resumption of the war, whereas Prime Minister Nsengiyaremye had decreed the end of rallies only in the combat zones. The stakes were high because mass political rallies were an effective tool for opposition parties to put pressure on the MRND.

The Butare Prefecture security council meeting of February 15, 1993, included representatives of political parties, and the advisability of suspending political rallies in the prefecture was considered.[71] The prefect suggested a compromise solution: suspending the rallies but proposing that political parties give speeches at the numerous public meetings organized by the prefect and the burgomasters as well as the sector councilors. The MRND representative said he was satisfied with the compromise, whereas the MDR representative vehemently protested. The decision was endorsed at the next meeting.[72]

In the next meeting, held on February 25, 1993, the prefect decided to suspend political rallies and decided that the administration would call for nonpolitical public meetings to discuss the issue of maintaining security.[73]

On March 15, 1993, despite the presidential ban, the ministerial decree, and the position of the Butare Prefecture security council, the MDR organized a rally in Busoro Subprefecture, of which the administrative center was in Gishamvu Commune. According to the Butare head of intelligence of the Interior Ministry, the rally had received the prefect's verbal endorsement. Speakers at the rally had apparently told the people to disregard pronouncements by the president of the republic.[74]

On March 23, 1993, all over the country, because of the new political contestation, a number of burgomasters could not perform their duties anymore, and a limited electoral exercise called *preselection* was organized to replace them. It was in fact an election by an electoral college made up of a specific number of commune notables. The electoral college was made up of sector heads, the members of the commune development council, the heads of ongoing commune projects, and representatives of parties and churches in the commune. Generally the outcome of these elections reflected fairly the leaning of the political majority in the communes.

In Butare Prefecture, preselection of seven replacement burgomasters was organized. The following were elected as burgomasters:

- Nyabisindu Commune: Alexendre Munyemana (PL)
- Nyazo Commune: Narcisse Nyagasaza (PL)
- Rusatira Commune: Vincent Rukeribuga (PSD)
- Shyanda Commune: Théophile Shyrambere (PSD)
- Muganza Commune: Chrysologue Bimenyimana (MRND)
- Nyakizu Commune: Ladislas Ntaganzwa (MDR)
- Kigembe Commune: Sephorien Karekezi (PSD)[75]

One may observe that Nyabisindu and Ntyazo Communes, which correspond to the former Nyanza Region, were the only communes in the whole country to have elected burgomasters from the PL, both Tutsis. Although, due to voting irregularities, Munyemana was replaced by Jean-Marie Vianney Gisagara. In Muganza Commune, Bimenyimana from the MRND was first beaten by his competitor from the PSD, but his protector, the still-powerful outgoing burgomaster, Ndayambaje, managed to arrange a second vote marred by corruption. Bimenyimana won by eighteen votes against thirteen for the PSD and two for the MDR.

Destabilization maneuvers in the prefecture. On February 25, 1993, two mines exploded in Nyabisindu Town. On April 19, 1993, a mine exploded in urban Ngoma Commune (in Butare Town). Fifteen people were injured, two of them seriously. The perpetrators of the attack were not identified.

In mid-April 1993 a gang of five robbers armed with grenades were arrested in Nyabisindu Commune. They had a list of business people from Mbazi Commune to attack. Members of the group, none of whom hailed from Butare, had come from Kigali specifically for this purpose and had carried out attacks on several places in the prefecture. The individuals had attacked the home of university professor and MDR member Fidèle Nkundabagenzi, injured his daughter by shooting her four times, and carried away several items. The gang had also attacked and seriously injured a gendarme. During the same period in Ntyazo Commune, three people were molested by unknown assailants and their houses destroyed by stones thrown by unknown criminals. In Shyanda Commune, a grenade was planted by an unidentified person at the home of a driver employed at the university. It exploded on the evening of April 19, 1993, destroying virtually the whole house.[76]

In mid-May 1993, three thugs attacked and robbed the deputy public prosecutor at his home after terrorizing people by brandishing grenades. As the thugs left, one of them wanted to attack another house, not knowing that it was the residence of the head of the military contingent in Butare. The soldiers on guard took him by surprise and overpowered him before he threw his grenade. The culprit gave the names of his two accomplices and admitted that they were on a mission in Butare to steal and kill. All three came from Ruhengeri Prefecture.[77]

On May 27, 1993, Prefect Habyarimana organized a large public consultation meeting at Huye Stadium of which the agenda was to find solutions to the deteriorating security in the prefecture. His opening address highlighted the crisis in the prefecture by referring to the different mine explosions, grenade attacks, and robberies committed by people armed with military weapons. He explained that such acts were on a sharp rise and emphasized that after they were arrested, the criminals systematically turned out to be people from prefectures other than Butare. The prefect said that all leads pointed to an outside attack targeting Butare Prefecture, and that there were people whose goal was to destabilize the prefecture in order to introduce there disorder similar to that happening in other prefectures. He appealed to the population of Butare to block these attacks.[78]

After a long debate, the meeting yielded some resolutions, such as the establishment of a fund of personal voluntary contributions from the community for maintaining security. An award of RF10,000 was set up for people who contributed to the arrest of people who had thrown grenades or used military weapons to steal. Meeting participants also planned to set up a network of informers run by the Butare Prefecture security committee.[79]

The May 24, 1993, meeting of the Butare Prefecture security council examined the conflict between two rival student associations at the National University of Rwanda. The General Association of Students of the National University of Rwanda (AGEUNR) was the traditional university association and close to opposition parties. The AGEUNR accused a new association of students from the north, the League of Students of Rwanda (LIDER), of having formed by those who had not accepted the election results for the AGEUNR executive for 1992–1993. LIDER was also accused of being composed of MRND and CDR sympathizers, of sowing division among students, and of using intimidation. The Butare Prefecture security council decided to suspend LIDER's activities until it was officially registered.[80]

The MDR Butare Branch Alignment with the National MDR-PARMEHUTU Faction

After the suspension of some of the MDR political bureau members, including Uwilingiyimana (see Chapter 3), by the MDR extraordinary congress on July 23 and 24, 1993, in Kigali, the MDR Butare section met on August 7, 1993, and replaced Uwilingiyimana with her rival, Kambanda.

In a letter to the prefect dated September 14, 1993, Uwilingiyimana informed him that the MDR Butare section was still led by the same group. She asked the prefect not to allow rallies at the prefecture and subprefecture levels of the MDR unless the requests were signed by the current president of the MDR of Butare and not to consider applications she had not signed. On their part, Uwilingiyimana's opponents wrote several letters to the prefect asking him to no longer respect the letters written by her on behalf of the MDR because she had been expelled from the party.

The prefect asked the Butare Prefecture security council for help in resolving the dispute. Because Uwilingiyimana had given instructions to the prefect in the name of the party and not in her capacity as prime minister, and considering the fact that the disagreement within the MDR had repercussions for some communes in Butare, the council decided to suspend all MDR rallies at the prefecture, subprefecture, and commune levels until the minister of the interior had given instructions on who was to be the MDR prefecture representative. The confirmation of Uwilingiyimana's expulsion by the MDR Butare congress reveals the minority status of the moderate MDR faction in Butare to which Uwilingiyimana belonged.

Attempts were also made in Butare Prefecture to split political parties and establish a Hutu-power coalition. In late 1993, the PL followed the MDR into becoming fragmented. In a letter to the Mbazi Commune burgomaster, the commune PL president denounced the maneuvers of some PL party members to replace elected commune party leaders with "members of the Interahamwe."[81]

The end of 1993 was characterized by a significant rise in ethnic tension in different communes of the prefecture, even in areas such as Nyabisindu Subprefecture, where this tension had been less expected. On December 3, 1993, the Nyabisindu security committee held a special meeting focused on the issue of ethnic tension.[82]

The Radicalization of the PSD and the Low Profile of the Hutu-Power Coalition in Butare

The rise in tension and political violence at the national level gave way to greater violence by the PSD in Butare. Following the murder of Secretary-General Gatabazi of the party on February 21, 1994, in Kigali by a group of unknown people, PSD supporters lynched the CDR president, Martin Bucyana. In the late morning of February 22, Bucyana was driving from his home in Cyangugu Prefecture. The road from Cyangugu to Kigali passes through Gikongoro Town and along the edge of Butare Town, where the PSD had a strong presence. As Bucyana reached Gikongoro, some PSD members followed his vehicle to Butare, where other PSD members took up the chase. They caught him in Mbazi Commune near Butare Town and lynched him. Of the two people accompanying him in a different car, one was also killed and the other was severely beaten.[83]

After lynching Bucyana, the youth members of the PSD in Butare Town and some communes carried out a campaign of intimidating Hutu-power supporters and people from the north in general. The two CDR leaders in the popular neighborhood of Tumba in Butare Town, Lauren Baravuga and Simon Remere, decided to take temporary refuge at the police station.[84]

February 22 and 23 were dominated by demonstrations organized by the PSD. On February 24, a requiem mass at Huye Stadium preceded the burial of Gatabazi.[85] President Habyarimana's supporters were banned from attending the funeral.[86]

On February 26, 1994, the PSD released a communiqué addressed to citizens in Butare, asking them to be on the lookout because the *akazu* had planned another assassination after Gatabazi's to be carried out by Captain Iledephonse Nizeyimana from the school for noncommissioned officers (ESO), which also served as the headquarters of the army in Butare Prefecture.[87] Less than two months later, the same Captain Nzeyimana would become one of the main organizers of the genocide in Butare.[88] In contrast to the MDR and the PL, both of which had split, with their majority factions becoming part of the Hutu-power coalition, the PSD was radicalized by Gatabazi's death against the Hutu-power movement and the presidential clique one and a half months before the genocide. Just before his death, Gatabazi had started to distance himself from the RPF. A small group of PSD militants, while claiming PSD membership, aligned themselves with Hutu-power positions. However, it was not until the start of the genocide and the assassination of the top leaders of the party that these middle-ranking militants proclaimed themselves the leaders of the PSD.

A Political Map of the Prefecture

Based on the information presented above and on discussions with two key witnesses on separate occasions, I have been able to draw a political map of Butare Prefecture during the democratization period, according to the party that seemed most popular (sometimes thanks to a fairly high level of intimidation such as in Nyakizu and Kigembe Communes) as well as the burgomaster's political affiliation.[89]

• *Ngoma Commune (Butare Town)*: All of the different political sensibilities were represented, with the PSD being strongest, so the ever-ambivalent burgomaster, Joseph Kanyabashi, joined the PSD.
• *Nyabisindu Commune*: The PL was the strongest party, followed by the PSD; the former MRND burgomaster was overthrown and replaced by a newly elected PL burgomaster. The PSD contested the regularity of his election, and in turn he was replaced by a PSD elected official, Jean-Marie Vianney Gisagara.
• *Muyira Commune*: The PL and the PSD were the most popular parties, but the MRND managed to impose itself on local officials. The first MRND burgomaster had resigned and was replaced by another MRND member.
• *Ntyazo Commune*: The PL was strongest; a new PL burgomaster was elected.

- *Rusatira Commune*: The PSD was strongest; a new PSD burgomaster was elected.
- *Mugusa Commune*: The PSD was strongest, but the burgomaster remained MRND.
- *Muyaga Commune*: The PSD was strongest, but the burgomaster remained MRND.
- *Ruhashya Commune*: The MDR was strongest, the burgomaster was MDR.
- *Maraba Commune*: The MDR was strongest.
- *Mbazi Commune*: The MRND was strongest; the burgomaster was neutral.
- *Huye Commune*: The PSD was strongest; the burgomaster joined PSD and then returned to the MRND.
- *Shyanda Commune*: The PSD was strongest; a new PSD burgomaster was elected.
- *Ndora Commune*: The MRND was strongest, and the burgomaster remained MRND.
- *Muganza Commune*: The MRND was strongest; an MRND burgomaster was elected.
- *Kibayi Commune*: The PSD was strongest, but the PL had a strong political presence, and the burgomaster remained MRND.
- *Runyinya Commune*: The PL was strongest; the former MRND burgomaster remained but became politically neutral.
- *Nyakizu Commune*: The MDR was strongest; the burgomaster was overthrown and replaced by a member of the MDR.
- *Kigembe Commune*: The MDR was strongest; the burgomaster was overthrown and replaced by a member of the PSD.
- *Gishamvu Commune*: The MDR was strongest; the burgomaster, a Tutsi who had "changed his ethnicity," belonged to the MDR, and was close to Kambanda.
- *Nyaruhengeri Commune*: The MDR was strongest; the burgomaster remained in place and was affiliated with the MRND.

This information is presented in Map 5.1.

The changing political relations between the commune inhabitants and their burgomasters were strongly evident in that the burgomasters who by default belonged to MRND before the transition to democracy had to adapt to the dominant political leaning in their communes, most often characterized by hostility to the MRND. The burgomasters did so by changing parties, or if they remained in the MRND, they downplayed their party allegiance. In communes generally hostile to the MRND, burgomasters who maintained a formal affiliation with the MRND or downplayed it and continued to carry out their duties could only be found in communes dominated by the PSD or

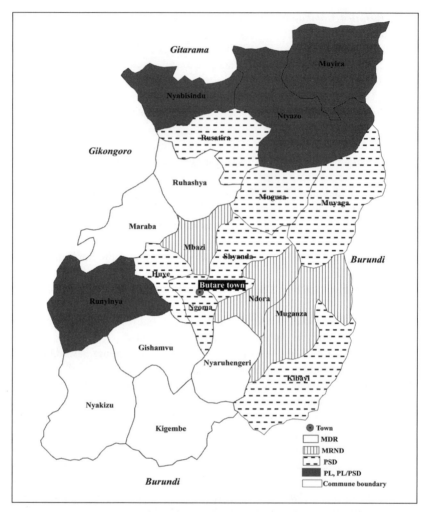

Map 5.1 Distribution of Party Influence in the Communes of Butare, March 1994

the PL. The fact that out of twenty communes, seven still had a formally MRND burgomaster after March 1993 does not reflect the true political influence of the former party state. Thus, all communes with a higher percentage of Tutsis than the prefecture average of 18.7 percent kept their MRND burgomaster. The most important reason is certainly because Tutsi communities, even when they could influence their communes' political balance, preferred to remain conservative and keep nonactivist MRND burgomasters because they felt they could not impose a burgomaster of their choice, most likely PL. Also, the other likely choice would have been a member of MDR. This was the case in Runyinya(42 percent Tutsi); Muganza (34 percent), Ndora (30 percent), Ngoma (26 percent), Gishamvu (26 percent), Nyaruhengeri (25 percent), Huye (23 percent), and Mugusa (20 percent) Communes.

The violent MDR hegemony did not allow MRND burgomasters to keep their posts. Generally, in places where the MDR was stronger, the burgomaster became MDR, by force if necessary. Here also, one finds the exception of Kigembe Commune, where the dominant MDR did not manage to take the burgomaster's post because of the acts of excessive violence it had previously committed. The other exception was Nyaruhengeri Commune, where the MDR was the strongest party but not the dominant one because of the relatively large Tutsi population. The burgomaster who remained MRND had a Tutsi wife.

The prefecture's main political scene. At the central level, in Butare Town, the prefecture's evolution between August 1991 and March 1994 was generally marked by a climate of tolerance and moderation, certainly a result of the PSD dominance and the noticeable presence of the PL in Butare politics. Beneath this general trend, one may also note three political periods:

1. From the beginning of pluralism until the departure of Prefect Temahagali of the MRND in June 1992, despite the rapid destabilization of the MRND, the party continued to enjoy a significant influence in Butare Town, and the opposition parties did not have any influence in running the prefecture despite their control of the streets.

2. After the arrival of Prefect Habyarimana, the MRND was isolated. With the cooperation of the military leaders stationed in the prefecture, the new prefect governed through consultation with opposition political parties and involved them in the political management of the prefecture.

3. With attempts at destabilization coming from outside the prefecture, the PSD asserted itself politically even more, and its youth wing made its presence felt more as a militia that monitored rather than attacked people. The PSD political strength in the town contributed to limiting the spread of the Hutu-power movement in the prefecture. Less than two months before the start of the genocide, during the events surrounding the death of Gatabazi, the PSD became radicalized, paralyzing the Hutu-power coalition. Butari's resistance effort to the genocide should be situated in this convergence between the prefect, the Butare military authorities, and the PSD political dominance of the prefecture. The momentum from the MDR-controlled communes in the southwest caused the first cracks in this resistance. One must also emphasize the

contrast between the MDR actions in Butare Town and in the communes in the southwest. At the prefecture level, the MDR cooperated with the prefect and the PSD in maintaining civilian peace in Butare, whereas in the southwest, the MDR engaged in violence and intolerance. This difference may be explained by the stronger influence of the moderate faction of the head of prefecture branch of the party, Uwilingiyimana, while the communes were dominated by the MDR-PARMEHUTU faction. Uwilingiyimana's suspension from the Butare MDR signified the failure of MDR reformers who became a minority in their party in Butare, as they did in Kigali and the rest of the country.

At the commune level. The PSD took the lion's share of political support at the commune level. It was the most popular party in seven communes, including the Butare Prefecture capital, and was also the second strongest party in almost all of the other communes. In the PSD-dominated communes, few political incidents were reported. The PL was also well represented; it was the dominant political force in about four communes. Meanwhile, the MRND quickly lost its political influence, and only managed to maintain it in certain areas because of political patronage of the local elites rather than its actual popularity. For example, in Ndora Commune, Deputy Prefect Gisagara was the foundation of MRND political strength, whereas in Muganza Commune, the director of the large, public, rice-producing company called the shots. Finally, the MDR influence was split between two other zones, the southwest where the party had a strong influence, and Maraba-Ruhashya, in center-west along Gikongoro prefecture where its presence was less pronounced. In the political life of the communes and sectors where the MDR was influential, the party often used violence and intimidation to impose its hegemony. Its hegemonic ways, violence, and anti-Tutsi ideology were largely the product of its identification with the historical MDR-PARMEHUTU, cultivated by leaders of the "renovated" MDR of the 1990s.

Historical Roots of the Ideological and Political Divisions During the Second Interlude of Pluralism

Some analysts of MDR's violence in Nyakizu Commune during the multiparty era of the 1990s and the genocide failed to see its ideological dimension, spread within the region, and historical roots.[90] Yet the political map of Butare Prefecture during democratization corresponds almost exactly to the political and ideological divisions resulting from the commune elections of June 1960.

Similarly, the PL imposed itself in the zones where there was a large electoral boycott ordered by the UNAR, that is, in Runyinya Commune (at the heart of the former Nyaruguru Province), and in Nyabisindi and Ntyazo Communes (formerly part of Nyanza and Mayaga Provinces).[91]

The central and eastern sections of the prefecture, where the PSD was well represented (part of Rusatira, Mugusa, Muyaga, Shyanda, Huye, Butare-town, and Kibayi Communes), corresponded to all the regions dominated by the APROSOMA in June 1960. Only in Kigembe, Nyaruhengeri, and part of Gishamvu Communes did the PSD not get the level of political influence as in June 1960. The bloody attacks against Tutsis during the parliamentary election campaigns in August 1961 in this subregion contributed to radicalizing of these communes and bringing them completely into the PARMEHUTU fold.[92]

The new MDR found itself in the two big zones where the PARMEHUTU was entrenched in June 1960, specifically the Maraba and Ruhashya Communes on the one hand, and the zone covering Nyakizu Commune and the surrounding areas on the other hand. Unlike APROSOMA losses, the PARME-HUTU in 1961 and subsequently the new MDR in 1992 won influence in part of Gishamvu, Kigembe, and Nyaruhengeri Communes compared with the results of the June 1960 communal elections.[93] We have seen the affinity in ideology and political method between the MDR of the 1990s and the MDR-PARMEHUTU of the 1960s. It is important to point out the similar ideological continuity between APROSOMA and the PSD, both of which defined themselves as against the PARMEHUTU and the MDR, respectively, and their shared Hutu supremacism. Despite the willingness of the leaders to make the PSD a modern party breaking away from the past, its local supporters clearly associated it with the old APROSOMA.[94] Political demarcations that emerged during the opening of democratic space in the early 1990s in Butare re-created, almost identically, the political and ideological fault lines established during the 1959 revolutionary period.

Genocide in the Prefecture

My proposed synthesis of the genocide in Butare Prefecture essentially focuses on the dynamics of mass mobilization.

Here we will largely depend on the chronology of the genocide in the prefecture as presented in the study published by Human Rights Watch (HRW), and edited by Alison Des Forges, *Leave None to Tell the Story*.

The main objective of the HRW report is largely, but not totally, limited to documenting the genocide within the framework of defending human rights, that is, focusing its investigation on the responsibility of individuals with civic and military authority. As a result, even though the report's regional analysis of the genocide in Butare may provide an overview of the sociopolitical mechanisms of mass mobilization, it does not do so systematically. Its specific mission inevitably renders its examination of the genocide in Butare essentially descriptive and rather ahistorical. My study, in contrast, aims to shed light on the issue of mass mobilization by cross-checking HRW findings with the main variables stemming from the social and political history and more recent evolution of the prefecture presented in the previous chapter and this one.

We examine only the beginning of the genocide, when there was an important variation in the process of mass mobilization, because later, as we shall see, the state reasserted its political domination through its regional and local officials. Let us recall succinctly the major aspects of the genocide in Butare. At the beginning of 1994, officially, around 128,145 Tutsis—17 percent of the prefecture population and 21.6 percent of the entire Tutsi population in Rwanda—lived in Butare.[95] The bulk of this Tutsi population lived in the center and southwest of the prefecture: in Runyinya, Huye, Ngoma, and Ndora Communes in the west-central area and in Nyakizu, Gishamvu, Nyaruhengeri, and Muganza Communes in the southwest. This huge area with a significant Tutsi population, the largest Tutsi concentration in the country, did not reach the border with Burundi. In Nyakizu, Kigembe, and Kibayi Prefectures, a strip of land on the shore of the Akanyaru River made up the border with Burundi, a few kilometers where there were practically no Tutsis. Within Nyakizu and Kigembe Communes, the distance between the southern border of the highly concentrated Tutsi population and the Akanyaru River was less than twenty kilometers. The Butare Prefecture had a long border with Burundi, and according to survivors' testimonies, fleeing toward Burundi was their best chance of survival.[96]

With fewer than 500 soldiers and police stationed in Butare during the genocide,[97] along with the fact that the prefecture had not experienced the development of political party militias,[98] the physical control and subsequent extermination of the large majority of this Tutsi population were essentially the work of civilians. One must also consider here the important role played by Burundian refugees in the genocide in the communes along the border. The Hutu-power phenomenon in the prefecture had been contained by the generally unfavorable political environment and its interethnic relations, generally good until the eve of the genocide. In many communes, both Hutus and Tutsis together staffed surveillance patrols even a few days after the death of President Habyarimana. There are three stages of the prefecture's political evolution, from the civilian and military authorities' resistance to the genocide to their incitement and coercion of the people to participate in the genocide. The rather quick chronological succession of these stages in no way diminishes the importance of their difference in character and political, social, and moral significance.

From April 6 to 17 the administration, military, and police actively[99] worked to preserve civil peace,[100] thanks to the resolve of Prefect Habyarimana and the cooperation of Lieutenant-Colonel Muvunyi, the military commander for Butare and Gikongoro Prefectures, and Major Cyriaque Habyarabatuma, the Butare commandant of the gendarmes until the evening of April 17, when it was announced on radio that the prefect had been sacked.[101]

Between the evening of April 17 and April 19, when the interim president, Sindikubwabo, and a high-profile government delegation that included the interim prime minister, Kambanda, arrived to drum up support for the new prefect, the political forces in the communes had understood that the resistance to the genocide had ended.[102]

Then, on April 19, during the ceremony to install the new prefect in Butare Town, Sindikubwabo gave a speech broadcast on the radio in which he took the people of Butare to task for preferring to watch on the sidelines while others "were working."[103] The speech, together with orders by other prominent people such as Kambanda, clearly instructed burgomasters, deputy prefects, army officers stationed in Butare, and other administrative officials to adopt the policy of massacres, even if they were never called that. The departure on the same day of Habyarabatuma for Kigali, where he had been transferred, reinforced the change in the political climate of the prefecture.[104] On April 20 the new prefect, Sylvain Nsabimana, chaired a meeting of the Butare Prefecture council security committee, which issued measures to carry out the massacres couched in euphemisms. Only Burgomaster Gisagara of Nyabisindu Commune publicly protested against the massacre program, explaining that the people under his jurisdiction were opposed to the sacking of Prefect Habyarimana and that they were thinking of building a base for resisting the genocide.[105] HRW suggests that the plan of attack seems to have been created during this meeting: "On the last line of the entry for this meeting, the note-taker wrote 'Ndora-Rusatira,' and then instead of continuing the list of names of communes, he struck it out and wrote simply, 'All on Friday except Mbazi.' There were attacks in most of the previously untouched communes on Friday, April 22, except for Mbazi, which was targeted the following Monday, April 25."[106] During the three stages I have identified, different subregions of Butare adopted contrasting attitudes that may be divided into three groups:

Group 1: In the southwest and the southeast, such as in Maraba, Runyinya, Nyakizu, Gishamvu, Kigembe, Muganza, Nyaruhengeri, Huye, and Muyira (in a limited manner) Communes, the sieges and massacres of Tutsis at places they gathered, such as churches and administration buildings, had begun before April 18:

> After meeting with the Gikongoro prefect on Saturday, Habyarimana spent the weekend dealing with one crisis after another. The violence had spread from its first major center along the western frontier in Maraba, Runyinya, and Nyakizu Communes further to the east and south into adjacent Huye, Gishamvu, Kigembe, Muganza, and Nyaruhengeri Communes. Another center of violence established in the northeast by raids from Kigali and Gitarama Prefectures was expanding southwest through Muyira Commune. The attacks were no longer the work of outsiders alone: people from Butare

Prefecture were taking up their machetes to join killers from Gikongoro and the other prefectures.[107]

Group 2: In the central part of Butare Prefecture, Mbazi, Ngoma, Ruhashya, Mugusa, Shyanda, Ndora, and Kibayi Communes were almost completely peaceful until April 19 and began the massacres only after Wednesday, April 20, under pressure from national authorities: "Although many had already moved to violence on or before April 18, the first day when people became generally aware of Habyarimana's dismissal, Ngoma Commune and others forming a protective shield to its north—Mbazi, Ruhashya, Mugusa, Shyanda, and Ndora Communes—were largely, if not completely, quiet."[108]

Group 3: In the northeast of Butare Prefecture, Nyabisindu, Ntyazo, and Muyira Communes, Hutus and Tutsis were in solidarity in organized resistance against the massacres *beyond* April 20. "Of all the communes, the three northernmost, Nyabisindu, Muyira, and Ntyazo Communes seem to have offered the most concerted resistance to the genocide. Perhaps this reflected the history of the area, the heart of the old kingdom, where bonds between Tutsis and Hutus were multiple, long-standing, and strong, disposing the Hutus to defend the Tutsis more vigorously."[109]

In the communes, mass mobilization for (in the case of Group 1) and against (in the case of Group 3) the massacres mostly emerged from the internal dynamics of each commune, particularly from loyalty and obedience to local political party leaders as distinct from the line of command of the administration and the state. In the communes of these two groups, the burgomaster may or may not have been one of the political leaders promoting or resisting the massacres. In Group 2, mobilization for the massacres emanated from dynamics outside the commune, which included submission to the state, often through the burgomaster and his administration. Map 5.2 shows how and when the communes of Butare entered into the genocide.

The HRW descriptions of events suggest that behavioral differences between communes could be attributed to the spread of violence against Tutsis from Gikongoro Prefecture, where the massacres had begun on April 7.[110] Only for the northern region of the prefecture, the communes in Group 3, does HRW give sociohistorical reasons for resistance. Although I recognize some truth in the theory about the spread of violence, the historical approach should be applied to the two other modes of entering into the genocide. As we shall see later, however, these two explanations can be considered consistent. I propose that the different types of behavior at the beginning of the genocide were determined above all by the political dynamics in these different communes before the genocide that took shape during the multiparty period.

One can widen the scope by comparing these three behavioral trends with the different variables of Butare Prefecture's social and political history pre-

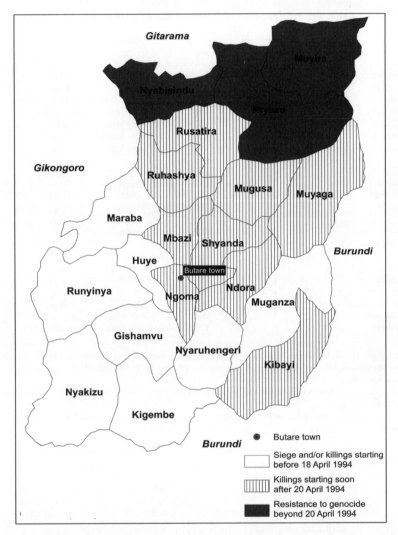

Map 5.2 Butare Communes' Mode and Timing for Carrying Out Genocide

sented in Chapter 4 and this chapter, and in particular with the level of crime and the dominant political party in the area. To these two variables, one may add a third: the population density that, for many, determined the extent to which people's needs for sufficient food were met (see Table 5.1).

In Table 5.1, one first notes a strong relation between the population density and the crime rates. All the communes with a high population density also have a high crime rate; they are those surrounding Butare Town as well as

Table 5.1 Behaviors in Communes of Butare at the Beginning of the Genocide

Commune	Type of Behavior[a]	Dominant Party[b]	Level of Crime[c]	Population Density (1978)
Nyabisindu	3	PL/PSD	High	High
Ntyazo	3	PL	High	Low
Muyira	3,1	PL/PSD	High	Low
Rusatira	2	PSD	Fairly high	Average
Ruhashya	2	MDR	Fairly high	Average
Mugusa	2	PSD	Fairly high	Average
Muyaga	2	PSD	Fairly high	Low
Maraba	1	MDR	Fairly high	Average
Mbazi	2	MRND	High	High
Shyanda	2	PSD	High	High
Huye	1	PSD	High	High
Ngoma	2	PSD	High	High
Ndora	2	MRND	High	High
Muganza	1	MRND	Fairly high	Average
Runyinya	1	PL	Fairly high	Low
Gishamvu	1	MDR	High	Average
Nyakizu	1	MDR	Fairly high	Average
Nyaruhengeri	1	MDR	High	Average
Kigembe	1	MDR	Fairly high	Average
Kibayi	2	PSD	Fairly high	Average

Source: G. Delpierre, *Tableau de répartition et de densité de la population rwandaise par secteur communal et région agricole, situation au 15 août 1978*, Ministère de l'Agriculture et de l'Elevage.

Notes: a. Groups classifying the behavior of each commune of Butare during the genocide, as defined in text.

b. The dominant party in each commune during the multiparty era. Information derived from different sources, including Charles Karemano, interview with author, April 8, 2002, in Namur.

c. The level of crime in each commune at the end of the 1980s, according to the official documents compiled in Chapter 4.

Nyabisindu Commune. Ntyazo and Muyira Communes have both a lower population density and a high crime rate, which is difficult to explain.

Thus, among the communes with high crime rates, one was dominated by the PL, two by the MDR, three by the MRND, and four by the PSD, the latter also controlled the largest number of communes. One of the surprises in Table 5.1 is the absence of a strong relation between the rate of crime and the timing of commune participation in the genocide, whether relatively early or later. Similarly, among the ten communes with a high crime rate, three belong to Group 1, four to Group 2, and three to Group 3. Also, the three communes in which Hutus and Tutsis jointly resisted the massacres (Group 3) even after April 19 were among those with a high crime rate. This observation challenges the thesis of material gratification as the trigger of mass participation,

especially given that the massacres were almost always accompanied by looting. Thus, the level of poverty and crime had no direct impact on the *initial*
impulse of the people to participate in the genocide.

The link between the dominant party in the commune and the type of behavior at the beginning of the genocide is indeed very strong. Out of the nine
communes first to plunge into the genocide (Group 1), five were dominated by
the MDR, one by the MRND, one by the PSD, and one was dominated by the
both the PSD and the PL. Out of the communes that succumbed to orders from
the authorities soon after April 20 (Group 2), four were dominated by the PSD,
two by the MRND, and one by the MDR. Out of the three communes that resisted beyond April 20 (Group 3), one was dominated by the PL and two by
both the PL and the PSD. Muyira Commune is in both Group 1 and Group 3,
reflecting its peculiar political situation. The burgomaster was from the
MRND, and relatively limited killings took place at the commune office at the
initiative of the burgomaster, who had to bring in killers from neighboring Gitarama Prefecture before April 18. However, the majority of the commune
leaned more toward the PSD/PL as in the two others of the north, Ntyazo and
Nyabisindu Communes, where most people resisted the killings beyond April
20. "In Muyira Commune, authorities had been obliged to bring in militia
from neighboring areas to get the genocide started, and the aggressors encountered stiff resistance."[111]

Similarly, the MDR was dominant in five communes in Group 1, one
commune in Group 2, and none of the communes in Group 3. Meanwhile, the
PSD was relatively strong in the communes in Group 1, very strong in those
in Group 2, and relatively strong in the ones in Group 3. The relation of these
factors therefore reveals that the incitement and political control were critical
for the rapid mass participation in the genocide. In addition, in Butare Prefecture, the incitement and political control were carried out by local political
party leaders and members whose ideological orientation determined the quick
or delayed entry of the communes into the genocide.

Here we should remember that in almost all the Butare communes, the
meso-level of political control, the dominant party in the commune, was determined largely by genuine popular support as I have shown in my description of how political parties took hold of the communes during the democratic multiparty period. In communes dominated by the PSD, national and
prefectural political coercion had to be applied on local leaders for them to
adopt the order of the day and commit genocide upon a section of their constituencies. PL-dominated communes eventually caved in as well but after
having initially resisted. Burgomasters of Nyabisindu and Ntyazo Communes led the resistance, whereas in Muyira Commune the population itself
did. In communes dominated by the MDR, the impulse to start the genocide
after it was the order of the day nationally came from within the communes,
in defiance against the prevailing calm in the prefecture.

Table 5.1 identifies the MDR as the main internal political agent of the early killings, given the decisive momentum with which the massacres began in the communes it dominated, before the movement received support from the prefecture administration and the core state security forces based in the prefecture. The autonomy of this local action leads one to conclude that to achieve it, the MDR essentially depended on the mobilization and participation of the local population, including that of Burundian refugees.

Three distinct political regions in the prefecture stand out: the south and southwest, dominated by the MDR, which took part in the killings before receiving orders from the state representatives in the prefecture; and the eastern-central section of the prefecture, dominated by the PSD, which resolved to start killing only after external political pressure and actions by institutions of the central government and the prefecture; and finally, the northeast, dominated by the PL and PSD, which in large part resisted for quite a while the massacres.

The entrenchment of MDR dominance in the southwest of the prefecture had significant consequences given that this was the region with one of the greatest concentrations of the country's Tutsi population, and it was also where the largest massacres at the national level took place. As we will see in the study of Kigembe Commune in Chapters 6 and 7, the tight political control that MDR hegemony successfully achieved during the multiparty period allowed the party to achieve mass participation during the genocide, leaving already-trapped Tutsis little chance of reaching Burundi, so close by.

We have just seen that the different courses of action of Butare communes at the beginning of the genocide were determined by the political parties that dominated the communes. Yet, in the previous section, we saw also that the party support in the communes of Butare was largely determined by political and ideological demarcations in the late 1950s and early 1960s. Thus, the reasons for the different ways in which the communes behaved at the beginning of the genocide should be ultimately traced to the first multiparty period (1959–1961) as the origin of political and ideological splits of the second multiparty period (1991–1994). For instance, in the north of the prefecture, resistance by Group 3—Nyabisindu, Ntyazo, and Muyira Communes—corresponded with the former communes that largely boycotted the 1960 commune elections in Nyanza and Mayaga Provinces. The Group 2 communes, largely dominated by the PSD, which plunged into the genocide only after the interim government intervened and the prefect and the military commander were replaced, largely correspond with the center-east where, in June 1960, APROSOMA won the majority of votes, and participation in the 1960 commune elections was either strong or moderately strong.

The communes in Group 1, of the south and southwest of Butare Prefecture, were all politically dominated by the MDR-PARMEHUTU in 1960 and 1961. In the west, Maraba, one of the communes in Group 1 that had begun the sieges and massacres of Tutsis before Prefect Habyarimana's removal, largely corresponds with the Busanza-south Chiefdom, which had massively voted for the PARMEHUTU in the 1960 elections. In the southwest, the area corresponding with Runyinya, Nyakizu, and part of Gishamvu Communes in 1994 was part of the Nyaruguru Chiefdom, the second zone in which the election boycott of 1960 was strong (because of the large Tutsi population) and the majority of votes cast were for the PARMEHUTU. In part of Kigembe, Gishamvu, Nyaruhengeri, and Muganza Communes, roughly corresponding with the former Bashumba-Nyakare and Mvejuru Chiefdoms, the majority had voted for APROSOMA in 1960 but shifted political allegiance to MDR-PARMEHUTU after the violent campaign for the August 1961 legislative elections.[112]

The transitive nature of the causal relations between the 1960–1961 Butare political map and the one that emerges in 1991–1993 during the democratization process and the early or delayed participation in the genocide leads us to affirm that the behavior of the communes at the start of the genocide was strongly determined by the ideological and political cleavages inherited from the first multiparty era of 1960–1961. The best evidence for this is the extensive overlap seen in Maps 4.1, 5.1, and 5.2. At least for Butare, this puts into perspective theories explaining mass participation in the genocide by ethnic hatred; fear of the RPF, which had resumed military hostilities; or anger in response to President Habyarimana's plane being shot down.

The huge majority of the population in the communes that plunged into the genocide only upon pressure from the state and in communes that resisted the genocide were Hutus. This leads me to assert that in Butare Prefecture, ethnicity was not the determining factor of how people behaved at the beginning of the genocide; rather, it was the ideological divisions inherited from the 1959 revolution revived by the democratic opening. The peace maintained in the prefecture for ten days was crucial; it allowed the communes of Butare to choose their path into the genocide; it shielded them temporarily before the national order of the day prevailed.

Two alternative explanations are related to the role played by Burundian refugees and the spread of the violence from Gikongoro Prefecture. The camps with Burundian refugees were located on the edge of the border with Burundi. I have discussed some communes belonging to Group 1—Maraba, Runyinya, and Gishamvu Communes—that plunged into the massacres at an early stage, were dominated by the MDR, and experienced major massacres, but where Burundian refugees had little or no role. By contrast, in Nyaruhengeri, Muganza, Kigembe, and Nyakizu Communes, Burundian refugees played an important role along with the Rwandans, but always under the direction of the Rwandan MDR political leaders. Burundian refugees' participation in the massacres and the Rwandan people's emulation of it stemmed from the same local political dynamics.

The spread of the massacres from Gikongoro Prefecture toward the southwest of Butare Prefecture definitely played an important role in the launch of the massacres in this subregion. One must also keep in mind, however, that the political dynamics on both sides of the border in the southern part of the two prefectures were very similar. In this region, communes on both sides of the prefectural border came to be dominated by the MDR during the democratization era of the 1990s. Moreover, the majority of the southeastern population of Gikongoro Prefecture, just like its counterpart in Butare Prefecture, had also voted for the PARMEHUTU in the June 1960 elections. In other words, the political and ideological continuity driven by the MDR in southwest Butare during the two periods of political pluralism was also at work in the neighboring population of Gikongoro Prefecture. Both sides of the prefectural border were part of the same sociopolitical entity, notably corresponding with the former Nyaruguru Chiefdom.

The same can be said of the three northern communes of Butare that resisted the genocide, Nyabisindu, Ntyazo, and Muyira Communes. In 1960, the regional boycott of the commune elections stretched on both sides of the 1994 border between Butare and Gitarama Prefectures in what used to be the Nyanza Chiefdom. Likewise, on the Gitarama Prefecture side of the border, in the Mayaga region, participation in the genocide was also delayed.

Lastly, one must emphasize that the extermination of Tutsis eventually took place all over Butare Prefecture and ended up being one of the most radical in the country.

Notes

1. Préfecture de Butare, *Compte rendu de la réunion du comité préfectoral de sécurité de Butare tenue ce 09/03/91 au palais du MRND.*

2. Préfecture de Butare, *Lettre du Préfet au conseiller du secteur Nyarugenge commune Mugusa portant sur les barrières du 31/12/90*; Commune Ruhasya, *Rapport de sécurité*, 16/11/90; Commune Maraba, *Rapport de sécurité*, 15/11/90.

3. Commune Ngoma, *Rapport portant sur les vols dans les secteurs du 23/11/90.*

4. Préfecture de Butare, *Compte rendu de la réunion du comité préfectoral de sécurité de Butare tenue ce 09/03/91 au palais du MRND.*

5. Ibid.

6. Ibid.

7. Ibid.

8. Préfecture de Butare, *Compte rendu de la réunion du comité préfectoral de sécurité de Butare qui s'est tenue le 03/031/92 au palais du MRND.*

9. Ibid.

10. Reyntjens, *L'Afrique des Grands Lacs en crise*, 1994, p. 307.

11. Ibid.,pp.220–224; Uvin, *Aiding Violence*, 1998, p. 61.

11. Préfecture de Butare, *Liste des signataires des statuts régissant le parti MDR dans la Préfecture de Butare*, n.d.; Préfecture de Butare, *Liste des signataires des statuts régissant le parti MRND dans la Préfecture de Butare*, n.d.; Préfecture de Butare,

Liste des signataires des statuts régissant le parti PSD dans la Préfecture de Butare, n.d.; Préfecture de Butare, *Liste des signataires des statuts régissant le parti PL dans la Préfecture de Butare,* n.d.; Préfecture de Butare, *Liste des signataires des statuts régissant le parti PDC dans la Préfecture de Butare,* n.d.

13. Préfecture de Butare, *Compte rendu de la réunion du comité préfectoral de sécurité de Butare tenue le 30/08/91.*

14. Ibid.

15. Préfecture de Butare, *Lettre circulaire du Préfet aux Bourgmestres portant sur le problème des pâturages publics du 22/10/91.*

16. This information on the two political rallies is derived from prefecture reports.

17. Préfecture de Butare, *Rapport portant sur le meeting politique du PSD tenu le 15 décembre 1991 au stade Huye.*

18. Préfecture de Butare, *Compte rendu de la réunion du comité préfectoral de sécurité de Butare tenue le 03/031/92.* The problem of children mistreating their fathers generally had to do with sons of unmarried women who harassed and threatened their biological fathers to obtain land to cultivate. For a more detailed study on the tension caused by land pressures, see André and Platteau, "Land Tenure Under Unbearable Stress."

19. Préfecture de Butare, *Compte rendu de la réunion du comité préfectoral de sécurité de Butare tenue le 03/031/92.*

20. Préfecture de Butare, *Lettre du Préfet d'autorisation de manifestation du 08/01/92.*

21. See Reyntjens, *L'Afrique des Grands Lacs en crise,* pp. 110–111.

22. Préfecture de Butare, *Lettre circulaire du Préfet aux bourgmestres portant sur les meetings populaires du MDR à l'occasion de la Fête du 28 janvier 1992.*

23. Préfecture de Butare, *Compte rendu du meeting politique du MDR organisé le 16 février 1992 au stade Huye.*

24. Préfecture de Butare, *Compte rendu de la réunion du comité préfectoral de sécurité tenue le 11/03/1992.*

25. Ibid.

26. Wagner, "All the Bourgmestre's Men," p. 32.

27. République rwandaise, Ministère de l'Intérieur et du Développement communal, *Note sur les conflits entre les partis politiques,* Novembre 1992.

28. Replacement of burgomasters was carried out through "preselection" by an electoral college comprising the sector heads, the members of the commune development council, the heads of ongoing commune projects, and representatives of parties and churches in the commune. *Instruction ministérielle n° 46/04.09.01 du 11 mars 1993 relative à la présélection des candidats au poste de bourgmestre.*

29. République rwandaise, Ministère de l'Intérieur et du Développement communal, *Note sur les conflits entre les partis politiques,* Novembre 1992.

30. République rwandaise, Ministère de l'Intérieur et du Développement communal, *Rapport portant sur la situation de sécurité dans le pays du mois de juin 1992.*

31. Préfecture de Butare, *Compte rendu de la réunion du comité préfectoral de sécurité tenue le 20/06/92.*

32. République rwandaise, Ministère de l'Intérieur et du Développement communal, *Note sur les conflits entre les partis politiques,* Novembre 1992.

33. Préfecture de Butare, *Lettre du Préfet au bourgmestre de la commune de Nyaruhengeri portant sur la sécurité du 24/06/92.*

34. Sephorien Karekezi, interview with author, May 3, 2001, in Butare; Straton Nyarwaya, interview with author, May 26, 2001, in Kigembe.

35. Préfecture de Butare, *Compte rendu de la réunion du comité préfectoral de sécurité tenue le 24/07/92*.

36. Ibid.

37. Préfecture de Butare, *Compte rendu de la réunion du comité préfectoral de sécurité tenue le 02/01/93*.

38. Préfecture de Butare, *Lettre du Préfet au Bourgmestre de Ntyazo du 25/04/92*.

39. Préfecture de Butare, *Lettre du Préfet au Bourgmestre de la commune Muganza portant sur le comportement violent de Venant Nzabamwita du 26/06/92*.

40. Commune de Mugusa, *Lettre du Bourgmestre au Président du MDR dans la commune du 21/05/92*.

41. Commune de Muyaga, *Lettre du Bourgmestre au sous-préfet de Gisagara du 16/05/92*.

42. Sous-préfecture de Gisagara, *Lettre du Sous-Préfet au Préfet de Butare portant sur la sécurité du 15/07/92*.

43. République rwandaise, Ministère de l'Intérieur et du Développement communal, *La situation de sécurité après le discours du Premier ministre du 28/07/92*.

44. Commune de Muyaga, Lettre du Bourgmestre au Sous-Préfet de Gisagara portant sur la sécurité dans la commune du 18/08/92.

45. Préfecture de Butare, *Compte rendu de la réunion du comité préfectoral de sécurité tenue le 18/09/92*.

46. Commune de Maraba, *Lettre du Bourgmestre au Préfet du 19/04/92*.

47. Préfecture de Butare, *Compte rendu de la réunion du comité préfectoral de sécurité tenue 10/08/92*.

48. This was in contrast to what was happening in Kigali, where the Abakombozi (PSD youth militias) were fighting with the Interhamwe. Charles Karemano, interview with author, April 8, 2002, in Namur. There would be two notable departures from this policy of nonviolence in Butare, namely, the *kubohoza* against the Nyabisindu burgomaster and the murder of the national CDR president in February 1994.

49. Sous-préfecture de Nyabisindu, *Note d'information du Sous-Préfet au Préfet de Butare*, May 17, 1992.

50. Ibid.

51. Sous-préfecture de Nyabisindu, *Formule de message n° 360/04.09.04/4*.

52. Préfecture de Butare, *Lettre circulaire du Préfet aux Bourgmestres du 17/03/92*.

53. Préfecture de Butare, Compte rendu de la réunion du comité préfectoral de sécurité tenue le 07/05/92.

54. Préfecture de Butare, *Lettre circulaire du Préfet aux Bourgmestres du 26/05/92*.

55. Commune de Mbazi, *Lettre du Bourgmestre au Préfet du 27/07/92*.

56. Des Forges, *Leave None to Tell the Story*, p. 354.

57. MDR, PSD, PL sections de Butare, *Lettre au Préfet du 25 août 1992 portant sur l'inquiétudeface au projet de meeting de la CDR dans la préfecture de Butare*.

58. Préfecture de Butare, *Lettre du Préfet au président de la section du MRND dans Butare du 21/08/92*.

59. Préfecture de Butare, *Compte rendu de la réunion du comité préfectoral de sécurité tenue le 19/08/92*.

60. Préfecture de Butare, *Lettre d'invitation aux représentants des partis politiques à la conférence-débat devant se tenir le 10 octobre 1992 du 21/09/92*.

61. Préfecture de Butare, *Compte rendu de la réunion du comité préfectoral de sécurité tenue le 18/09/92*.

62. Préfecture de Butare, *Compte rendu de la réunion du comité préfectoral de sécurité tenue le 26/09/92*.

63. Commune de Muganza, *Lettre du Bourgmestre au Préfet à propos de la tension causée par les départs de jeunes gens partis rejoindre les rangs des Inkotanyi du 18/09/92.*

64. Préfecture de Butare, *Compte rendu de la réunion du comité préfectoral de sécurité tenue le 02/01/93.*

65. Commune de Ngoma, *Lettre du Bourgmestre au Préfet à propos du communiqué publié par les partisans du PSD.*

66. Préfecture de Butare, *Compte rendu de la réunion du comité préfectoral de sécurité tenue le 02/01/93.* The security committee, comprising the heads of the local contingents of the army and police, showed political cohesion in contrast to the president's inner circle and the national army chiefs. This solidarity between civilian and military leaders would form the foundation of Butare's effort to resist the genocide.

67. Préfecture de Butare, *Compte rendu de la réunion du comité préfectoral de sécurité tenue le 19/01/93.*

68. République rwandaise, Ministère de l'Intérieur, *Note sur les manifestations des partis MRND et CDR les 19, 20 et 21 janvier 1993*, no date.

69. Commune de Ngoma, *Lettre du Bourgmestre au Préfet portant sur la sécurité dans la ville de Butare du 13/02/93.*

70. Préfecture de Butare, *Compte rendu de la réunion du comité préfectoral de sécurité tenue le 11/02/93.*

71. Préfecture de Butare, *Compte rendu de la réunion du comité préfectoral de sécurité tenue le 15/02/93.*

72. Ibid.

73. Préfecture de Butare, *Compte rendu de la réunion du comité préfectoral de sécurité tenue le 25/02/93.*

74. Ministère de l'Intérieur, Service d'Information et d'Enquête, *Formule de message du 15 mars 1993 à 10 h 20.*

75. Préfecture de Butare, *Lettre du Préfet au Ministre de l'Intérieur communiquant les résultats des élections des bourgmestres organisées le 23/03/93.*

76. Préfecture de Butare, *Procès-verbal de la réunion du conseil préfectoral de sécurité tenue le 20/04/93.*

77. Préfecture de Butare, *Procès-verbal de la réunion du conseil préfectoral de sécurité tenue le 24/05/93.*

78. Préfecture de Butare, *Compte rendu de la réunion de sécurité qui s'est tenue au stade Huye le 27/05/93.*

79. Ibid.

80. Préfecture de Butare, *Procès-verbal de la réunion du conseil préfectoral de sécurité tenue le 24/05/93.*

81. Parti libéral, Comité communal de Mbazi, *Lettre de la Présidente au Bourgmestre dénonçant des nominations occultes au sein du parti du 28/12/93.*

82. Sous-préfecture de Nyabisindu, *Compte rendu de la réunion du comité de sécurité sous-préfectoral du 03/12/93.*

83. Commune de Mbazi, *Lettre du Bourgmestre au Préfet du 22/02/94 lui annonçant les graves événements qui ont eu lieu le 22 février dans sa commune.*

84. Des Forges, *Leave None to Tell the Story*, p. 437.

85. PSD section de Butare, *Lettre du comité régional au Préfet du 22/02/94 lui communiquant le programme des manifestations suite au meurtre de Félicien Gatabazi.*

86. Joseph Ndahimana, Représentant du PSD section de Belgique, *Mise au point sur l'assassinat de Félicien Gatabazi, le 24/02/94.*

87. PSD section de Butare, *Communiqué de mobilisation adressé aux citoyens de Butare le 26/02/94.*

88. Des Forges, *Leave None to Tell the Story*, pp. 500–501.

89. Karemano interview. At the time he was the PSD Executive Secretary. The other privileged witness wished to remain anonymous; interview with author, April 2, 2002, in Brussels. Determining the most popular political party in the commune is based on the analysis of political events in the commune as well as on witnesses' impressions because no election by universal suffrage took place during this period. Recall that the seven elected burgomasters had been chosen by the "preselection" council, which brought together elites from the commune, heads of communal services, and members of the technical commission. Therefore the political affiliation of the burgomaster chosen by the elites could have been different from the most popular party in the commune. Because all communes had been MRND by default, a former burgomaster could retain his position either by changing political parties or playing down his MRND membership without officially changing his party membership. In rare cases the MRND might have maintained a significant influence in the commune.

90. "With Ntaganzwa's forceful tactics, the MDR stood a chance of taking Nyakizu, thus establishing a foothold in a region where the MDR had never been strong." Des Forges, *Leave None to Tell the Story*, p. 357.

91. Ruanda-Urundi, *Supplément au Rudipresse*, 1960, no. 184; d'Hertefelt, "Les élections communales," 1960, pp. 426, 433.

92. Ibid. See also next chapter on Kigembe.

93. Ibid.

94. Karemano interview

95. République rwandaise, Ministère du Plan, Service national de Recensement, *Recensement Général de la Population et de l'Habitat au 15 août 1991.* Official reports were known to underrepresent the number of Tutsis. For Gikongoro Prefecture, see Verpoorten, "Death Toll of the Rwandan Genocide," 2005.

96. Interviews, conversations, and public testimonies reveal that the large majority of those who survived the genocide in southern Butare chose to flee toward Burundi despite immense difficulties.

97. Des Forges, *Leave None to Tell the Story*, p. 499.

98. "In the period just before the genocide, there was little indication of the problems to be posed by the militia after April 6. The MRND, the CDR, and the MDR had too few adherents to have built up significant groups of trained men in the town or in most of the communes of Butare." Ibid., p. 436. The many MDR adherents in the south of the prefecture did not organize themselves into a formal militia and, even after the Hutu-power coalition was set up in October 1993, they had not shown unbridled hatred toward the Tutsis.

99. In general, because a faction of the army was doing the opposite around the same time, and from April 17 on went around the communes to incite people in the areas where they were favorable to genocide. This small group of less than a dozen soldiers drove around in a red pickup truck. On April 18, the pickup truck returned to Maraba to participate in the launch of the massacres and to distribute grenades. Ibid., p. 447.

100. By April 14, massacres of Tutsis orchestrated by the MDR had begun in Nyakizu Commune. Ibid., p. 376. On the afternoon of April 17, thousands of Tutsis had sought refuge in the church and the surrounding buildings in Simbi of Maraba Commune. Ibid., p. 447. That evening, in Kivuru Sector, dozens of people were massacred by mobs of political party supporters under the direction of the MDR. See Chapter 6 on the genocide in Kigembe.

101. Ibid., p. 448.

102. During this power vacuum in the prefecture, on April 18 at 9:00 a.m., the massacre of 3,000 to 5,000 Tutsis began in Simbi of Maraba Commune. Ibid., p. 452.

During that afternoon 10,000 Tutsis were killed in the Kansi Church in Nyaruhengeri Commune. Ibid., p. 453. On the same day, the siege of 2,000 to 3,000 Tutsis began in Kigembe. See Chapter 6 on the genocide in Kigembe.

103. Ibid., p. 460.
104. Ibid., p. 462.
105. Ibid., p. 467.
106. Ibid., p. 467.
107. Ibid., p. 446.
108. Ibid., p. 454.
109. Ibid., p. 496.
110. Ibid., p. 443.
111. Ibid., p. 499.
112. For election results of the June 1960 communal elections and July 1961 legislative elections, see Chapter 4.

6

Kigembe: A Social and Political History

In this chapter I focus on Kigembe Commune, in the southwest of Butare Prefecture, where the genocide began while the rest of the prefecture remained calm. This chapter and the next deal with the sociopolitical dynamics at the grassroots level that led to the radicalization of the population of Kigembe Commune, which embraced early on the order of the genocide. In this chapter I analyze the social and political evolution of the commune between 1959 and 1989, following three themes: the evolution of the relationship between citizens and the state, the interethnic relations, and the socioeconomic conditions. I pay particular attention to the National Revolutionary Movement for Development (MRND) system of government at the grassroots from 1976 onward and the dialectics of state action and the people's response. In Chapter 7, I will deal with the end of the one-party-state era, the democratic transition, and the war and genocide in Kigembe Commune.

The First Republic

The Geographical and Historical Context

Kigembe Commune is located in the extreme south of Rwanda, on the border with Burundi. It was established in 1963 at the crossroads of Mvejuru and Nyakare Regions, both previously chiefdoms of the precolonial era. The commune is situated on the margins of the major Tutsi settlement in the southwest of Butare Prefecture, at the center of which was the historical great Nyaruguru Region, which extended northward and westward. This area covered the northern half of Nyakizu Commune, the western half of Gishamvu Commune, and almost the entire Runyinya Commune as well as the south of Maraba Commune. The other half of Nyaruguru was located in Gikongoro Prefecture. Together with the historical Bashumba-Nyakare Region part of today's Kigembe Commune, the great Nyaruguru Region formed social/army settlements near the Kingdom of Burundi and was home to several Tutsi warrior lin-

Table 6.1   Ethnic Distribution of the Population in the Southwestern Communes of Butare, 1987

Commune	Tutsi	Hutu	Twa
Runinya	42.3	56.7	1.0
Gishamvu	27.6	71.8	0.6
Nyakizu	18.4	80.7	0.9
Nyaruhengeri	25.6	59.4	5.0
Kigembe	7.7	92.0	0.3
Butare Prefecture	**18.7**	**80.3**	**1.0**
Rwanda	**10.94**	**88.53**	**0.53**

Source: République rwandaise, Ministère de l'Intérieur et du Développement communal, *Recensement administratif de la population rwandaise durant la période de 1960–1987*, 1987, p. 42.

eages. The second historical region of Kigembe Commune is Mvejuru, on its southern side that reaches the Akanyaru River. In 1994, few Tutsi lived on that part of the commune. Before the 1994 genocide, the great Nyaruguru region held the largest concentration of Tutsis in Rwanda (see Table 6.1), if one includes the part in Kikongara prefecture which had even higher proportions of Tutsis.

The Bashumba-Nyakare historical region in the north of Kigembe Commune marks the southern end of this major Tutsi settlement. The section of the Bashumba-Nyakare Region within Kigembe consists of five sectors—Ngera, Murama, Kigembe, Kivuru, and Ngoma—and had the largest concentration of Tutsis in the commune (see Map 6.1). Tutsis made up 8 percent of the commune population, but 33.7 percent of Ngera sector, 21.8 percent of Murama, 16.2 percent of Ngoma, and 14 percent of Kivuru population. These four sectors out of the five situated in the Nyakare Region held 76 percent of the Kigembe Tutsi population.[1] In the south, in Kigembe, the historical Mvejuru Region is made up of seven sectors: Fugi, Karama, Kigali, Nyanza, Nyaruteja, Rubona, and Ruhororo. Mvejuru Region, which lies on the border with Burundi, was annexed from Burundi and shares close social and cultural ties with that country. The Kinyarwanda spoken in Mvejuru and to some extent in Nyakare is more similar to Kirundi than to Kinyarwanda in general. Also, in Mvejuru, it is not always easy to distinguish a Rwandan from a Burundian.[2] The border with Burundi is marked by the Akanyaru River; the Migina River also runs through the commune. The main tarmac national highway linking Rwanda and Burundi also passes through the commune, with the major border customs point located in Kigembe. A smaller dirt road headed toward Burundi also passes through the commune. The border post on this other road is only five kilometers from the Nyaruteja trading center, the commune's biggest as well as the administrative center.

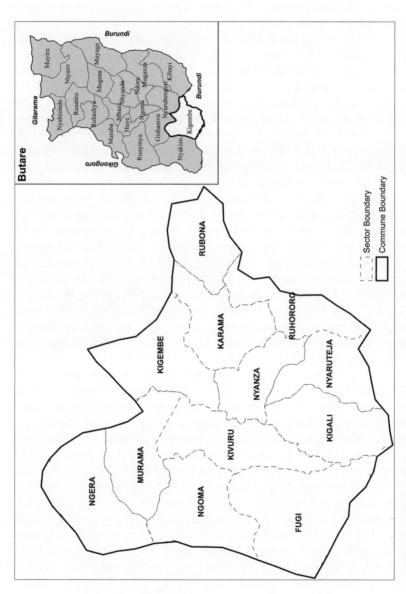

Map 6.1 Kigembe Commune

Political History of the Commune from 1959 to 1973

Kigembe Commune was created in 1963 out of the former Murama, Gatete, and part of Bimba Communes. The former communes were the scene of events of the 1959 revolution. The first instances of violence took place in April 1960 in the section of the present-day commune located in the former Mvejuru Chiefdom. In the June 1960 commune elections, the three communes voted overwhelmingly for APROSOMA, giving the party thirty-four out of a total of forty commune council seats, in comparison with four for the PARMEHUTU.[3]

The violence that took place in Murama Commune a few weeks before the September 25, 1961, parliamentary elections contributed to radicalizing the region and making it shift to the PARMEHUTU camp. On July 29, 1961, in present-day Ngera Sector, interim Burgomaster Alphonse Ngoga, a PARMEHUTU firebrand, accompanied by a contingent of the national guard, led a fight against a group of Tutsis apparently armed with traditional weapons.[4] On August 14, 1961, once again in Ngera Sector, Ngoga led what he called a "fierce war" against the "king's army."[5] In reality, the attacks were part of the larger PARMEHUTU campaign of intimidation and terror against Tutsi civilians.[6] These violent events also intimidated APROSOMA supporters and were carried out with the complicity of the Belgian military resident.[7] Soon after these military exploits, Ngoga was put in charge of spreading the PARMEHUTU propaganda in all the communes of Astrida Province. In Nyakare, many houses were burned, and cattle belonging to Tutsis were slaughtered. The majority of Tutsis sought refuge in the Nyumba Church of today's Gishamvu Commune, and in Kansi Church in Nyaruhengeri Commune. Also, a few people were killed.[8]

A few weeks after Tutsis had sought refuge, in each commune, the PARMEHUTU officials gathered the Hutu people around the churches to pick out the Tutsi refugees they wanted to return to the community and those they wanted expelled. This was done all over the region as a standardized procedure after violent clashes that caused displacement of Tutsis. The public nature of the process profoundly changed the relationships between Hutus and Tutsis and instituted a sentiment of collective power of the Hutus over the Tutsis.[9] Two factors determined the choice of who was banished: one was belonging to the political and social elite of the time, especially owning a significant amount of land.[10] The other was one's sociability; generally antisocial or condescending behavior toward Hutus could also lead to banishment. Families found themselves split; a son or husband could be expelled while the rest of the family remained.[11] Those sent away from the community were either deported to camps for the displaced within the country, for example in Nyamata, or sent to Burundi. Most often, those allowed to return to the community had to share their land with Hutus.[12] Others who had some property were slapped with fines so hefty that they had to pay them in installments over many months.[13] The land belonging to those expelled was seized by interim commune authorities who proceeded to redistribute the land. The first to benefit from the property transfers were the individual members of the new political institutions and those who had played a major part in the violent expulsion of Tutsis. Burgomaster Ngoga of Murama Commune, Burgomaster François Sezirahiga of Gatete Commune, Anastase Nyongira of Bimba Commune, councilors such as Sebabirigi, and other activists allocated to themselves several pieces of land.[14] These attacks against the Tutsis of Murama Commune traumatized the Tutsi population of the region and turned the commune into a PARMEHUTU stronghold.

In 1963, Kigembe Commune was created by merging Murama, Gatete, and Bimba (part) Communes. In the subsequent commune elections of August 1963, Epimaque Nkwaya, former interim burgomaster of Gatete Commune, was elected burgomaster of Kigembe Commune. In the meantime, the PARMEHUTU had become a de facto one-party state there; all other political parties had disappeared. In the commune elections of August 1967, Straton Semayenzi was elected burgomaster. He kept this post until 1992, demonstrating his exceptional political longevity. From 1959 to 1963, PARMEHUTU political organs at the grassroots comprised one party official and two propagandists responsible for "expanding and spreading the opinions and ideals of the party."[15] In 1967, the party was restructured, and from then on the local PARMEHUTU committees included all the councilors of the commune, all local members of the PARMEHUTU, and an equal number of propagandists voted in by the population. As with the rest of the PARMEHUTU machine, the primary mission of this structure at the commune level was to implement the ideology and programs of the party,[16] demonstrating the importance the party attached to spreading its messages at even the local level.

This brief historical overview of the politics in Kigembe Commune between the 1959 revolution and the end of the PARMEHUTU regime shows that the commune participated wholeheartedly in the political upheavals in the country. The changes implemented through violence, with the participation of the Hutus, which affected the Tutsis regardless of their status during the monarchy, instilled an enduring feeling that the Hutus held the power to decide the fate of their fellow Tutsi citizens. This situation contributed to creating two political identities ethnically defined by a traumatic experience.

The history of Kigembe Commune under the First Republic reveals a dynamic democratic life reserved for Hutus, with regular local elections and a change in leadership in 1967. After that, the political longevity of Burgomaster Semanyenzi seems to have been legitimized by his leadership qualities and by the satisfaction of his constituents.[17]

Economic Development of the Commune
Under the First Republic

Kigembe Commune always had poor public infrastructure. Without a significant church presence, it was not able to benefit from the educational and health care infrastructure that came with the establishment of Catholic and Protestant networks of churches. In 1962 a dispensary was finally constructed in the commune. Until 1987, Kigembe Commune had only twenty-five classrooms and no secondary school to its name.[18] During the First Republic, public services and government projects were centralized at the government ministries. The communes had lean administrations headed by the burgomaster and the commune councilors. The number of councilors met the quota of one councilor per 1,000 inhabitants. The councilors still pursued their private careers. Their main task was to assist the commune council, over which the burgomaster presided, and for that, they received an allowance. State technical officials such as agricultural officers, teachers, and health workers mainly led development activities. The burgomaster's role in these activities was to supervise the peasants in the implementation of the technical guidelines, to issue orders for popular mobilization, and to impose fines to punish any shortcomings. The principal development activities aimed at improving human and environmental sanitation, fighting against soil erosion, and performing the difficult task of persuading people to volunteer their labor in physically strenuous projects after forced labor was abolished. The other activities of the commune were compulsory cultivation of coffee, failure of which was subject to a fine, and marking the local roads.

During the First Republic, the peasants of Kigembe felt the tight grip of the colonial system weaken. Whereas compulsory community service and forced labor had been abolished, sufficient financial resources for development had not been allocated, leading to socioeconomic stagnation. In the people's memory, this period coincides with poverty and numerous food shortages, for example in 1962, 1967, and 1973.[19] The main mandate of the local administration structure was ideological indoctrination; commune councilors were matched by an almost equal number of propagandists elected by popular suffrage.[20] Moreover, given that interactions between the state and the people had long been characterized by the use of force, after being the de facto party-state in 1965, the PARMEHUTU claim to democracy meant that it used significantly less force and put considerable effort into persuasion. These moves, intended to encourage support for the regime, extended to only one part of society, the Hutus; the Tutsis continued to live in fear.

Kigembe Commune was spared the violence of the April 1973 crisis, which marked the end of the First Republic, partly because it had no secondary schools and, by extension, no teachers or students, the primary protagonists of the crisis.

The Second Republic

The MRND in Kigembe Commune

The Kigembe population felt the regime change when the new MRND structures were put into place. The commune structures were created in 1976; they comprised, from the lowest to the highest levels, the cell, the cell committee, the sector council, the commune committee, and the commune assembly. In 1981, these structures were modified and made more complex, with both a committee and an assembly established at every level—cell, sector, and commune.[21] At each level, the committee was the executive arm of the assembly or congress, and the assembly or congress was the policymaking arm. In 1975, the commune councilors elected the previous year retained their duties in the new structures, and elections were organized to appoint members of the cell committees.[22] Under the First Republic, the burgomaster was elected by direct suffrage in 1963 and 1967 and by indirect suffrage in 1971, when new laws required the commune councilors to elect a burgomaster from among themselves. Starting in 1973, the burgomaster was appointed by President Juvénal Habyarimana. Just as with the other administrative levels above the commune, the state structures at the grassroots were duplicated within the MRND. Thus, to the commune committee and the commune council was added an MRND assembly. At the lower ranks, the sector and the cell, the MRND and the administration merged.[23]

In addition to these administrative and political institutions, of which the staff generally had limited formal education, there was a technical commission responsible for planning development in the commune.[24] This commission consisted of five to ten members chosen according to their qualifications in the economic, social, cultural, and technical fields. They were appointed by the minister of the interior upon recommendation by the burgomaster and the advice of the prefect. The Kigembe Commune technical commission was launched in 1974. At the time, it was made up of nine members whose level of formal training varied from four years of postprimary education to two years of postsecondary education. During its thirteen years of existence, the technical commission "greatly helped the commune in the conceptualization and development of several projects in all areas."[25] It was also involved in seeking funding. The commission, the majority of whose members came from the commune but were not residents there, also opened a window for the commune to the outside world, especially by creating a link with people originally from the commune who had advanced levels of education and were most often working for the central government in Kigali. From 1982 on, Kigembe had also maintained international cooperation with the Belgian Commune of Edegem as its sister city. Contact between the authorities of both communes was rather sporadic, with the bulk of the cooperation being in the form of the Belgian partners financing different Kigembe Commune projects.

The commune had two important levels of political and administrative representation: that of the burgomaster and that of the commune councilor running the sector. In the official reports, the communal councilor was also called sector councilor. The commune councilor was the burgomaster's administrative and political representative in the sector; he facilitated the economic, social, and cultural development activities under the supervision of the burgomaster and regularly presided over sector meetings for sensitizing the people and for gathering and channeling the people's aspirations. He led the people in development activities, and he collaborated with the technical commission working in the commune.[26] Councilors were regularly chosen during elections preceded by actual campaigning. At the sector level the elected official knew each family within his jurisdiction and, as the representative of the population, he was regularly in direct contact with the state organs—the burgomaster and his administration and other state agencies working in the commune.[27] In short, the sociocultural profile of the councilors was similar although slightly higher than that of their constituents; they were generally more well off peasants with a slightly higher level of formal education than most of their constituents, which rarely went beyond primary school education.

The sector, or commune, councilors were the real point of contact between the state and the community. They were part of the state apparatus and represented state authority in the sector, but they were also close culturally and socially to their constituents. They received salaries and often had a small administrative building from which to work.[28] The heads of the cells, members of the sector committee, for example, had neither the same power nor the same aura because they were elected by indirect suffrage by fellow members of the cell committee and obtained neither a salary nor a real office in which to work. The sector councilors used the members of the cell committees to enforce court decisions upon orders from the burgomaster or to "round up" peasants for events such as *umuganda* or *animation* (entertainment). Kigembe Commune had twelve sectors, each headed by a commune councilor. Each sector had three to five cells, with a cell committee of five members. The burgomaster presided over the commune council comprising the councilors from the twelve sectors. Power relations within the commune council were strongly asymmetrical, with the figure of the burgomaster holding powers that far outweighed the capacities of the commune council.

Under the Second Republic, the state granted the burgomaster prerogatives that gave him far-reaching powers. As an administrator, the burgomaster was the president of the commune and development councils and a member of the technical commission.[29] Politically, the burgomaster presided over the congress and the MRND commune committee. He could easily mobilize the population using a chain of command passing through the commune councilors, the sector councilors, and the members of the cell committees who directly dealt with the population. The burgomaster was also the head of the police, and in 1987, he had one sergeant and seven officers under his command.[30] The burgomaster was responsible for the services provided by the commune administration, such as tax collection, health care, agriculture, veterinary services, water provision, and youth affairs.

The education sector did not fall directly under the burgomaster's control, but he had oversight powers over the entire staff. In 1988, the Kigembe Commune administrative personnel numbered thirty-five people, none of whom had finished secondary school. It also had other professionals, most of whom came from the ministries of the central government and some of whom were representatives of religious organizations and a few associations. Even these sectors felt the authority of the commune administration.

The most important institution in the commune in terms of the number of employees was the school. In 1988, the commune had nine primary schools and two integrated rural vocational and training schools (CERAI).[31] There was no secondary school in the commune. The education system employed 107 teachers whose level of education was quite low because none possessed a high school certificate. According to the compromise agreement still in force between the Catholic Church and the state, all the schools of the commune fell under the authority of the church except Murama primary school, the responsibility of the Union of Baptist Churches in Rwanda (UEBR). Different faiths were also represented in the commune. The Catholic Church had only one parish and a congregation, the Sisters of the Assumption. The church personnel included two priests, eight nuns, a parish secretary, and 276 parish advisers.[32] The UEBR had two institutions run by two pastors. The Free Methodist Church and the Pentecostal Church each had only one school with one pastor. The religious establishments in the commune were modest, especially those of the Catholic Church, probably because two long-standing churches, Nyumba and Kansi, were located in neighboring Gishamvu and Nyaruhengeri Communes, respectively.

Communes also had a number of cooperatives as well as farmers' societies. In Kigembe Commune there were only two such cooperatives, La Banque populaire, a branch of the national institution with 2,457 depositors in Kigembe in 1988, and CODAPAKI, a bank for seeds and agricultural produce. It collected foodstuffs for storage and redistributed them during food shortages. CODAPAKI had 2,293 members; it was run by the local citizens and experienced serious problems of fund embezzlement by its various managers.[33] Note that the commune authorities were part of the cooperatives' administrative council.[34] The fourteen "precooperatives" in operation in 1988 were small farmers' or fishermen's groups, each with an average of fourteen members.[35] There were also eight socioeconomic groups for youth committed to agriculture. Two of them were local branches of international organizations, such as the Scouts and Young Christian Workers. Together, these groups each had an average of twenty-nine members. Through the youth and cooperatives extension officer, the commune office played a supervisory role in the various cooperatives and youth groups. The youth officer was responsible for organizing the youths in their daily activities. He helped them find solutions to the local challenges they encountered; he organized meetings and checked in on these youths. The office was also responsible for providing a framework for youth groups such as the Scouts, the Young Christian Workers, and Xaveri (a Catholic youth group formed by missionaries in Central Africa). The youth officer supervised the political performance (*animation*) troupes and wrote reports on the youths.

The last nonpeasant socioeconomic group in the commune was that of small traders, called "smugglers," who engaged in smuggling in Burundi. In 1988, a census taken to facilitate collection of MRND membership dues put the number of these business people at thirty-two. The number of state technical agents attached to the ministerial departments, including teachers, was 158, whereas that of the commune agents was thirty-five.[36] If one adds to this number the thirty traders and about twenty religious workers, one can conclude that in 1988, the commune had a few more than 200 paid, educated workers out of a total population of 51,091 inhabitants, most of whom were peasants. Finally, still in 1988, the commune had seven police officers and three secret service agents attached to the office of the president of the republic.[37]

The burgomaster was the main political leader, the head of the commune administration, an officer of the judicial police representing the prosecutor, and the chief of the small commune police force. He was also the administrative chief of the employees of the commune county court.[38]

The burgomaster's power over all the state employees working in his commune meant that teachers working in churches and managing schools, the largest group of wage earners in the commune, fell under his jurisdiction. His authority over all state agents, who formed the great majority of the salaried workers in the commune, bestowed him mechanisms of influence practically unchallenged. The only limit of the law to the burgomaster's powers was the state power higher up in the hierarchy, namely, the prefect, to whom the burgomaster had to report even the smallest action. In this bureaucratized system, every decision, every meeting was an item to report to the prefect and the deputy prefect in order for the decisions to receive approval and validation. The burgomaster's nearly unlimited authority was nevertheless weakened by his little real coercive power with a small group of police officers with no means of transportation in a large commune of 114 square kilometers, and deployed only in an ad hoc fashion. The burgomaster's daily coercive powers rested on unpaid members of the cell committee with little to distinguish them from the general population.[39]

The Socioeconomic Evolution of the Commune

The population of Kigembe consisted almost entirely of peasants whose only income came from subsistence farming and coffee growing.

Kigembe was one of the most populated communes of Butare Prefecture. It was one of the top three communes that crossed the commune population threshold, set at 50,000 inhabitants in 1988. The Kigembe population grew between 1975 and 1989 at a rate of 2.8 percent. In comparison with the 1978 national density of 183 inhabitants per square kilometer, the population density of Kigembe was 333 inhabitants per square kilometer. There were considerable disparities between the population densities of the different sectors. Some sectors, Kivuru in particular, were among the most populated in the whole country. Kigembe Commune had areas of average, high, and very high density, increasing fast at 30 percent in eleven years (see Table 6.2).[40]

In 1989, 48.8 percent of the population above the age of fifteen knew how to read. The population was largely young, with 43.5 percent of the population between the ages of fifteen and forty-five.[41]

In Table 6.3 we can see the huge decrease in food production in the 1980s. In 1984, Rwanda experienced a severe food shortage resulting from drought. Hunger was reported in the commune, and residents began to steal tuber crops from their neighbors and even to make holes in the houses in order to steal food.[42] In 1987, the problem was the opposite; heavy rains destroyed the maize, potatoes, and beans.[43] In 1988, it was a bean disease.[44] From 1980 on it was a downward trend in food production in absolute figures accentuated by

Table 6.2 Population Density of the Sectors of Kigembe Commune, 1978 and 1989

Sector	Area (km²)	Density in 1978 (inhabitants/km²)	Density in 1989 (inhabitants/km²)	Change (%)
Fugi	12.1	392	496	26.5
Karama	8.8	368	491	33.4
Kigali	11.1	311	417	34.0
Kigembe	6.8	334	455	36.2
Kivuru	7	557	702	26.0
Murama	10.9	224	298	33.0
Ngera	9.6	245	298	21.6
Ngoma	8.4	367	497	35.4
Nyanza	7.5	426	546	28.1
Nyaruteja	10	373	531	42.3
Rubona	9	276	341	23.5
Ruhororo	13.3	243	314	29.2
Total	**114.5**	**333**	**438**	**30.7**

Source: République rwandaise, Ministère de l'Intérieur et du Développement communal, *Recensement administratif de la population rwandaise durant la période de 1960–1987*, 1987, p. 42.

Table 6.3 Growth in Food Production per Inhabitant in Kigembe

Year	Food Production (tons)	Population	Food Production per Person (kilos)
1980	221, 605	40,535	5,467
1981	45,843	41,863	1,095
1982	82,903	43,417	1,890
1983	36,340	44,851	810
1984	27,614	46,352	595
1985	30,802	47,775	644
1986	33,701	49,152	685
1987	33,234	50,289	660
1988	31,580	51,091	618

Sources: Commune Kigembe, *Lettre du Bourgmestre au Préfet du 26/01/87. Renseignements sur 25 ans de l'Indépendance nationale*; Commune Kigembe, *Rapports annuels*, 1987, 1988.

the ongoing increase in the number of mouths to feed. An analysis of the three types of food cultivated gives a more somber picture of the food situation.

In Table 6.4 we can see the decrease in cultivation of certain crops. Bean, soya, and banana production collapsed, and sorghum production dropped. These decreases indicate the continual exhaustion of the soil. When it came to food quality, production of the crops with the highest nutritional value, such as that of cereals and vegetables, dramatically fell, whereas production of tu-

Table 6.4 Food Crop Production in Kigembe, 1982, 1985, 1988 (tons)

Crop	1982	1985	1988
Beans	2,677	2,325	646
Peas	—	3	3
Soya	31,181	140	478
Sorghum	3,811	3,533	2,700
Maize	155	106	194
Rice	10	17	—
Peanuts	—	—	3
Potatoes	—	231	506
Bananas	21,811	14,874	14,420
Sweet potatoes	7,894	5,147	7,533
Cassava	13,879	3,981	4,305
Cocoyam	668	407	372
Yams	2	4	19
Total	**82,093**	**30,802**	**31,580**

Sources: Commune Kigembe, *Lettre du Bourgmestre au Préfet du 26/01/87, Renseignements sur 25 ans de l'Indépendance nationale,* pp. 3, 5; Commune Kigembe, *Rapports annuels,* 1982, 1985, 1987, 1988.

bers fell by 1985 and then stabilized. This imbalance led to acute deficiency in proteins, fats, and vitamins.[45]

The drop in bean production was particularly tragic because beans were one of the main sources of protein in the Rwandan diet. As Straton Nyarwaya put it, "When a family has no beans, it is in danger; the children can get kwashiorkor."[46] Kigembe Commune residents, who grew beans, now found that they too had to buy beans at the market. The repeated references to food shortages in the official reports of the 1980s indicate that the commune never produced any significant surplus, implying that the people persevered through the drop in food production by restricting daily consumption.

Kigembe Commune found a solution to its declining food production, at least a partial one, when it moved toward fruit production, as one can note from Table 6.5. In 1988, fruit production, which was 50 percent commercialized, brought in revenue of more than RF517 million. Revenue from commercial agricultural production (excluding coffee), mainly from fruits and bananas, rose to more than RF692 million. All other produce, raised largely for individual consumption, earned only RF72 million. The bulk of income from fruit production went to buying foodstuffs from outside the commune.

Coffee production was uneven between 1981 and 1988; a relatively good coffee harvest occurred in 1988 (see Table 6.6), but the fall in international and producer prices meant that the main industrial activity of the commune earned only RF47.9 million, or ten times less than the income of fruit production.

Total agricultural production similarly obtained an income of just more than RF740 million per year, or RF14,500 per head, making this production

Table 6.5 Fruit Production in Kigembe, 1981–1988 (metric tons)

1981	1982	1983	1984	1985	1986	1987	1988
3,316	5,343	5,489	21,383	21,588	27,644	33,894	29,558

Sources: Commune Kigembe, Lettre du Bourgmestre au Préfet du 26/01/87, Renseignements sur 25 ans de l'Indépendance nationale, pp. 3, 5; Commune Kigembe, Rapports annuels, 1982, 1985, 1987, 1988.

Table 6.6 Coffee Production in Kigembe, 1981–1988 (metric tons)

1981	1982	1983	1984	1985	1986	1987	1988
561,876	282,395	290,692	628,551	679,968	286,490	—	382,858

Sources: Commune Kigembe, Lettre du Bourgmestre au Préfet du 26/01/87, Renseignements sur 25 ans de l'Indépendance nationale, pp. 3, 5; Commune Kigembe, Rapports annuels, 1982, 1985, 1987, 1988.

above average compared with other communes in Rwanda. The average situation is notably reflected in the dynamic trading center of Nyarutega, the biggest town in Kigembe Commune, which had a large market and was relatively significant for Rwandan and Burundian traders. Nevertheless, the socioeconomic situation at the end of the 1980s demonstrates the national trends of extensive poverty and a precarious food situation.[47]

Integration Between Hutu and Tutsi Communities

All of the respondents in the interviews for this study talked of the high level of integration of Hutus and Tutsis from the early Habyarimana years up until 1991, when political parties arrived. One way to gauge this reality would be to analyze statistics on the frequency of "mixed" marriages between Hutus and Tutsis. The choice of marriage as an indicator comes from interviewees themselves, who systematically cite these marriages as proof that harmony existed between the two groups. In statistical reports, the commune did not mention

Table 6.7   Number of Registered Births in Kigembe by Parents' Ethnicity and Nationality, 1987

Parentage	Dec. 1986 to Jan. 1987	January	February	March	April	May	Total
Hutu father/ Hutu mother	85	61	52	69	71	70	408
Hutu father/ Tutsi mother	3	5	2	3	2	3	18
Tutsi father/ Hutu mother	4	0	0	3	2	4	13
Tutsi father/ Tutsi mother	9	5	8	5	6	7	40
Father unknown	151	107	91	120	78	89	636
Father a foreign national	0	0	0	0	0	0	0
Mother a foreign national	0	0	0	0	0	0	0
Twa father/ Twa mother	—	16	—	—	—	—	16
Twa father/ unknown mother	3	3	—	—	—	—	6
Total	255	197	153	200	159	173	1,134

Sources: Commune Kigembe, *Statistiques des mois de décembre, janvier, février, mars, avril, mai 1987.*

Table 6.8 Number of Registered Births in Kigembe by Parents' Ethnicity and Nationality, 1989

Parentage	March	April	May	June	July	August	September	Total
Hutu father/ Hutu mother	44	64	64	81	53	49	52	407
Hutu father/ Tutsi mother	2	4	3	2	0	3	3	17
Tutsi father/ Hutu mother	1	0	1	5	0	1	2	10
Tutsi father/ Tutsi mother	1	1	1	2	0	2	1	8
Father unknown	30	49	47	63	35	40	32	296
Father a foreign national	0	0	0	0	1	0	0	1
Mother a foreign national	1	0	0	2	3	0	1	7
Total	79	118	116	155	92	95	91	746

Sources: Commune Kigembe, *Statistiques des mois de mars, avril, mai, juin, juillet, août, septembre 1989.*

the ethnic identity of the people whose marriages they were officiating. However, from 1985 on, and from 1987 in an unsystematic but consistent manner, the commune indicated the ethnicity of the parents in its statistics on registered births. The authorities tried to discourage unregistered marriages as much as possible, but the practice persisted. With the deteriorating economic situation, more and more couples arranged to live together without involving their families or the commune, but even in these cases, births resulting from these "illegal" unions had to be registered. Officially, ethnic identity under the Habyarimana regime was passed down through the father. Tables 6.7–6.11 provide a sense of how close Hutus and Tutsis of Kigembe Commune were in the last years of the Habyarimana regime.

From Tables 6.7–6.11, the cumulative figures of children with at least one Tutsi parent are as follows:[48]

- Number of births to Hutu fathers and Tutsi mothers: 62
- Number of births to Tutsi fathers and Hutu mothers: 47
- Number of births to Tutsi fathers and Tutsi mothers: 90

There are therefore 199 births to at least one Tutsi parent: 45 percent are children born to two Tutsi parents, and 55 percent are children born to a Hutu

198 *Rwanda's Popular Genocide*

Table 6.9   Number of Registered Births in Kigembe by Parents' Ethnicity
and Nationality, June and August 1990

Parentage	June	August	Total
Hutu father/ Hutu mother	74	125	199
Hutu father/ Tutsi mother	4	3	7
Tutsi father/ Hutu mother	2	4	6
Tutsi father/ Tutsi mother	4	5	9
Father unknown	41	70	111
Father a foreign national	0	0	0
Mother a foreign national	1	1	2
Total	126	208	334

Source: Commune Kigembe, *Statistiques des mois de juin et août 1990.*

Table 6.10   Number of Registered Births in Kigembe by Parents' Ethnicity
and Nationality, 1991

Parentage	April	July	August	September	October	November	December	Total
Hutu father/ Hutu mother	49	73	78	65	39	26	36	366
Hutu father/ Tutsi mother	2	2	0	4	2	2	1	13
Tutsi father/ Hutu mother	3	1	4	3	0	1	1	13
Tutsi father/ Tutsi mother	2	7	8	4	0	1	0	22
Father unknown	28	42	52	36	25	17	12	212
Father a foreign national	0	1	0	0	0	0	0	1
Mother a foreign national	1	0	0	0	0	1	1	3
Total	85	126	142	112	66	48	51	630

Sources: Commune Kigembe, *Statistiques des mois de mars, avril, mai, juin, juillet, août, septembre 1989.*

Table 6.11 **Number of Registered Births in Kigembe by Parents' Ethnicity and Nationality, January–March 1992**

Parentage	January	February	March	Total
Hutu father/ Hutu mother	12	65	70	147
Hutu father/ Tutsi mother	1	1	5	7
Tutsi father/ Hutu mother	1	1	3	5
Tutsi father/ Tutsi mother	2	5	4	11
Father unknown	18	37	32	87
Father a foreign national	0	0	1	1
Mother a foreign national	0	0	1	1
Total	34	109	115	258

Sources: Commune Kigembe, *Statistiques des mois de janvier, février, et mars 1992.*

parent and a Tutsi parent. Of the children with at least one Tutsi parent, more are born into mixed unions than to two Tutsi parents. In other words, most mating among the Tutsi community in Kigembe Commune tended to be exogamous.

Although the frequency of marriage between Tutsi women and Hutu men was very visible before the 1990 war, a widespread notion has it that few Tutsi men married Hutu women.[49] However, the data show that in Kigembe Commune, the trend of Tutsis mating across ethnicity was only slightly higher among women. In the group of children with one Tutsi parent, 23 percent had a Tutsi father and a Hutu mother, while 31 percent had a Hutu father and a Tutsi mother. This high occurrence of both male and female Tutsis mating with Hutus tends to set Kigembe Commune apart from the main trend across the country as highlighted in the 1987 administrative census by the Ministry of Interior saying that the increased occurrence of mixed marriages was almost "always between Hutu men and Tutsi girls."[50]

This high participation in mixed mating definitely indicates a strong integration between the two communities. One could also point to a trend toward assimilation. Even though the transmission of ethnic identity in Rwanda was above all a social and political issue, and it was done through the father, such a high occurrence of mixed marriages must have increasingly diminished the *identity* significance of the difference between Hutus and Tutsis. The data presented here cover only the final years of the 1980s, but the multiplication of mixed marriages between Tutsis and Hutus in the commune seems to have started after the 1959 revolution. The Tutsis' consciousness of their vulnerability after the events of August 1961, as well as the nature of the new regime, were the primary reasons for the strong tendency toward interethnic marriage in the small Tutsi community of Kigembe Commune.[51]

Between 1976 and 1990, there was little Hutu-Tutsi ethnic tension in Kigembe. It never features in the local administration reports consulted, and only one Tutsi survivor of the genocide referred to it. He explained that the tension was confined to a quite specific segment of the population, mostly between families of former PARMEHUTU activists and formerly relatively prominent Tutsi families who remained in the commune and had become successful, for example families in which the father was employed and/or had children attending secondary school.[52]

MRND Political Control

The actions of the authorities between 1976 and 1990 may be characterized as intrusive and coercive to the citizens. The state officials intervened in both public and private life and made no distinction between politics and administration. They carried out intensive campaigns to both persuade and force the people to participate in different activities. However, imposing this new form of governance was not easy: a process of internal conquest of the people was required. Its success was short-lived because the people soon challenged the system. After setting up its party-state structure, the MRND spent the years immediately following on domesticating these new bodies and their operations. Elections held in 1976 appointed the local MRND administration. During this process, the MRND commune committee dismissed a number of elected members or heads of cell committees for unsatisfactory performance. In general, the new institutions were established in strict observance of regulations, and in the process a number of practices and activities became institutionalized in the communes.

The most important MRND activity institutionalized at the local level was *umuganda*, the compulsory community work. *Umuganda* was established in 1974, but its implementation intensified two years later when structures for mass mobilization were set up. The activity focused primarily on the fight against soil erosion, reforestation, construction and upkeep of roads, and maintenance of water resources. *Umuganda* also helped complete most of the commune projects that did not require specialized technical skills, such as building classrooms. The commune accounting system officially counted *umuganda* as work-investment and calculated it in terms of the number of the participants along with contributions from donors such as the sister commune of Kigembe in Belgium, Edegem, or funds coming from government. *Umuganda* took place once a week on workdays, in contrast to what was happening in the urban areas. The commune council was responsible for planning these days. The cell committees ensured that everybody attended and guided the people to designated work sites. *Umuganda* was one of the topics dominating discussions in deliberating organs of the commune, such as committees and congress assemblies. It was also a major focus of commune council work. Because participation in *umuganda* was compulsory, it was used as a tool to assess the performance of the local leaders, councilors, and cell committee members, along with people's obedience to the authorities.[53]

Another major practice institutionalized was *animation*, which consisted of sessions of song and dance in praise of President Habyarimana and the MRND. Every cell had to set up a singing and dancing troupe, and the performances were to take place once a week.[54] During these sessions, the cell committee was expected to sensitize the population on MRND ideology and on cultivating peace, unity, and development. Its members were also expected to explain that MRND actions were guided by "responsible democracy."[55]

Competitions for the dancing and singing groups were organized at the commune and prefecture levels. The groups performed during official celebrations welcoming important guests. Their goal was also to ensure that the "ideals of the MRND remain permanently ingrained in the whole population and be expressed through 'animation.'"[56] After initially setting up animation groups, the commune council expanded them to the schools as well: "In the schools, the songs have to integrate the chosen theme for animation, and the teachers should study ways in which to set up their *animation* groups."[57] The songs and dances during the competitions in 1988, for example, were about the president's theme for the year, such as "defense of the farmers' income," the presidential and parliamentary elections of December 1988, and the Fifth MRND Ordinary National Congress.

The commune authorities made significant efforts to sensitize the population on several themes, some of which were almost permanent whereas others changed according to the circumstances and slogans for a particular year. The sensitization had four main channels: animation, assembly meetings at the cell and the sector levels, ad hoc information meetings, and official state functions. In 1985, the commune inhabitants participated in at least four cell meetings, 6 sector meetings, fifty-two days of *umuganda*, and fifty-two animation sessions. A total of 118 meetings between the people and their authorities were held during which people were sensitized, exhorted, and instructed. This figure does not take into account ad hoc meetings. Last, the official celebrations repeated the same themes.[58] In 1985, the people of Kigembe Commune celebrated the eleventh anniversary of *umuganda*, the twenty-third anniversary of independence, the twelfth anniversary of the Second Republic, the tenth anniversary of the MRND, and the third anniversary of the harvest celebration, *umunganura*.[59] The meeting themes were of two kinds: political propaganda and instructions to people on social behavioral change.

All these social occasions, whether political and administrative meetings, *umuganda*, animation, or official celebrations, compelled participation with cell officials fetching people from their homes if necessary or fining them. The driving force of this coercion was the sector councilor, supported by the five cell committee members, whose responsibility it was to "drum up support."[60] Night patrols were another activity that required the forced participation of the people. They were carried out by men of the village and consisted of surveillance patrols, ideally supposed to last the whole night. The patrols were expected to be a permanent feature, but they were often abandoned until a particular event made it necessary to reactivate them.[61] The night patrols were carried out at the cell level, and the cell committees organized them and designated the people who were to participate.

The other important item that determined the relations between the people and the commune authorities was the collection of compulsory MRND membership dues. The annual fee increased during the 1980s to an average of RF100 for the peasants, RF630 for the workers of the commune, and RF2,650 for business people.[62] This subscription was a priority for the commune authorities, who wrote several reports every year assessing the rate of collection and including exhortations to attain 100 percent compliance.

Table 6.12 shows a high rate of collection from 1986 to 1988. However, one must read these figures with caution, keeping in mind the burgomaster's frequently stated target of 100 percent. Over the three years, the collection rates varied, except for commune employees who could not avoid the contributions because the party membership dues were deducted from their salaries. The collection of peasants' contributions decreased by 6 percent over three years, possibly because the peasants' socioeconomic situation did not allow them to meet their obligations as they once did. In contrast, the rise in collection rates from the traders reveals the pressure the commune must have ap-

Table 6.12   Rate of Collection of MRND Dues in Kigembe Commune (percentage)

Category	1986	1987	1988
Peasants	94	92	88
Commune employees	100	100	100
Businesspeople	81	88	100

Sources: Commune Kigembe, *Lettre du Bourgmestre au Préfet, Rapport sur le recouvrement de la cotisation au MRND pour l'année 1986;* Commune Kigembe, *Rapports annuels 1987 et 1988.*

plied on them. Given that collecting party membership fees was politically sensitive as an indicator of the burgomaster's performance, one may infer that this pressure may have increased on the peasants, but it was not as effective.

The MRND organs and operations in Kigembe Commune allowed the state to deeply intrude into the lives of the citizens through the use of coercion, leading several analysts to assert that the party-state had total control over rural society. The next section focuses on how the people responded to the MRND ambitions for power.

Conduct of the Masses

Internal political conquest (1976–1985). With the new local MRND structures in place, commune authorities regained control of the population, thereby breaking away from the prevailing situation during both the First Republic and the initial years of the new regime. The people needed to adjust to the new MRND structures before accepting them, and this took time and met some resistance. Toward the end of 1977, the MRND commune committee reported that "some sectors still experience instability because of persistent conflicts between the leaders and their constituents. This is the case of Nyaruteja, Rubona, Ruhororo, Kigali, Kivuru, and Murama Sectors. The commune committee desired that several meetings be organized in the cells with the purpose of bringing these misunderstandings to an end."[63]

A few years later, in 1984, the burgomaster wrote a report evaluating the performance of different sector councilors for the purpose of recommending them as candidates in the upcoming elections. In the report he described, sector by sector, how the social and political situation had evolved between 1976 and 1984. Within this period, the sectors had held two elections, one in 1976 and the other in 1980. A maximum of five candidates was to be chosen for each sector and "preselected" by secret ballot at the MRND commune congress twelve days prior to the election. The people in the sector would then elect their councilor from among these candidates.[64] The fifty-one candidates chosen to compete in the January 1985 elections for the position of commune councilor were all Hutu.[65] I present a few extracts from the burgomaster's report on the sociopolitical evolution in five of the commune's twelve sectors on the eve of the election.[66]

About Kigembe Sector, the burgomaster wrote,

> Kigembe sector has been headed by Antoine Kabutura since 1976. There has generally been no security problem in the sector. Throughout his tenure, this councilor has developed the sector. He fought against discord that had taken root in this sector. The people carry out development activities; there is no violence, no robberies, murders, or hatred. All that is over. Now a spirit of understanding prevails. The collaboration between the councilor and the cell

members is excellent. The MRND meetings at that level are held on time, and the resolutions are implemented. The councilor also follows the recommendations given in MRND Articles 51 to 63. The people follow what is stated in these articles, and the councilor gives reports to the commune MRND president.[67]

The burgomaster described Kivuru Sector as follows,

Councilor: Vital Munanira since 1976. The people in this sector spend so much of their time in disputes: never-ending court cases, violence, robbery, malicious gossip, etc. Consequently, one must have a councilor strong enough to deal with these bad people. Since his election, the councilor has tried to steer the population toward peace and unity in order to lead them to development. The people were difficult to convince. He taught them to work for their development, he fought the thieves who sowed insecurity, he closed the bars that were a source of violence, and he reduced the number of recalcitrant citizens who were not paying taxes. He revived umuganda to the point that it now takes place without him needing to supervise the cell members. The sector was ranked first in its development activities. All this was the fruit of the good relations between the councilor and the cell members. He was very strict, which earned him the nickname Cyamakare ["tough one"]. Those who feel wronged are taking their revenge against him: they have cut his coffee trees, uprooted the trees in his forest—all that in order to discourage him. Fortunately, he remains strict and courageous. Because he supervises people's participation in umuganda and does not allow people to be lazy, he receives few votes during the elections.[68]

On Nyaruteja Sector, the burgomaster wrote,

Councilor: Bicundamabano since 1976. Before taking charge of the sector, the people behaved like savages. Some lived in Burundi, others in the Akanyaru Valley. If one visited their homes, one found only women. The men lived in the banana plantations and in the bush. The majority of these wayward citizens and thugs did not pay taxes. When he was elected, the councilor, a teacher, approached the people and taught them not to hire out their fields and banana plantations. This contributed to an increase in income. The men began to work instead of spending their time in the bars. The MRND meetings were regular and the "animation" sessions started, which inspired the population. The conflicts because of ignorance disappeared, and the population collaborates with cell members for the sake of their development.[69]

Ngoma Sector:

The councilor has been in office since 1976 because in a democracy, the candidate who receives the highest number of votes becomes the leader. He is a councilor who stays silent, and the people do what they want. When a problem arises, he sends it to the cell members to resolve it, or he passes it on to the courts. He does not reprimand criminals, those who do not pay taxes or who do not participate in umuganda, and he does not send any report to the commune. The population is made up of lazy people who spend all their time sitting by the roadside. This means that during elections, he is overwhelmingly elected. You know that the people like someone who does not compel them to work. If his candidacy is not rejected, he will be elected, and things will always go wrong. Right now, the councilor's inaction after violent incidents is leading to revenge attacks that fuel insecurity. As for umuganda, it is not regularly held, and it has been neglected. The cell members are despised because the councilor does not act on their reports. This discourages the cell members. Even umuganda is not taken seriously given that there will be no repercussions. In the sector, only Gacumbi Cell remains active, thanks to two cell members influential in the community. But even the population of this cell is moving to work in other cells.[70]

Fugi Sector:

Councilor: Bagenzi since 1980. Upon his election, the population was unruly in different ways: conflicts, violence, theft, and fraud. The population was made up of crooks. Some were living in Burundi, the men were no longer paying taxes; in short, they behaved like beasts. After his election, the councilor insisted on animation. Six months later, people started being seen; before they used to cross the border at the mere sight of a person in authority. Because he was active, we collaborated in organizing meetings. The people were sensitized until the problem ended. Now they participate in umuganda, and the sector is the top in animation. Each cell has its own performance group, and the group from the sector represents the commune during the competitions at the prefecture level. Umuganda has reached a respectable level.[71]

The extracts above are about only five of the twelve sectors. The information from the seven other sectors, as with Kigembe Sector, seen above, gives a picture of prevailing harmony as well as the councilor's good control of the population. In general, the burgomaster's report captures the marked shift in the people's behavior after MRND structures were established in 1976, showing how effective these structures have been for managing people. However, this report also explains that on its own, the existence of these structures was not enough to inspire people to obey; the people had to be won over by coercion and persuasion. In the elections for councilors, the people were not passive. They had preferences the burgomaster feared in some cases, so he proposed that the state intervene, for example through rejecting an individual's candidature. Finally, all of the burgomaster's electoral choices prevailed.[72]

Despite the unequal relationship between the local organs of the state and a population without its own organization, there was a certain level of power struggle in the mid-1980s by a population using means at its disposal—both legal and illegal—to defend its interests and choices, although without much success. The MRND control over the Kigembe population in the mid-1980s was strong. This success was certainly also a result of its high popularity following the socioeconomic improvement in the first few years. A few years later, the people's behavior changed; acts of disobedience increased, and this time the people had the upper hand.

The rise in disobedience (1986–1989). If one wishes to demonstrate the political significance of the people's behavior in the context of the all-powerful local institutions of the state, it is not enough to cite the actions of Kigembe inhabitants during specific institutional milestones, such as commune council elections, or somewhat dramatic events officially termed *political*, such as payment of MRND dues. One must also study the reports written by the different commune institutions between 1977 and 1989 on the daily life and behavior of ordinary people. In these reports, acts of unruliness and criminal behavior are often mentioned. Here one must question the criminal label used by local authorities for some acts and behaviors to make a distinction between the delinquent behaviors of residents of the community and those of professional, asocial criminals.[73] In the dynamics of power relations between the people of Kigembe and the institutions of the party-state, two different periods emerge, one from 1977 to 1986 and the other one from 1987 onward.

During the first few years of the MRND regime, some social disorder continued to prevail in Kigembe Commune. For example, the commune council on July 15, 1977, mentioned "violence in the sector, robbers, people smoking cannabis, players of *urusimbi* [a betting game] as a source of crime, and criminals who stab people."[74] To redress the situation, the council decided to reestablish night patrols along Akanyaru River and to intensify the collaboration between sector councilors from adjacent communes in order to better control people's movement. During its meeting in late 1977, the council presented a mixed picture of the social and political situation in the commune. On the one hand, the council was satisfied with the successful completion of the projects such as the fight against soil erosion, road maintenance, water management, construction of bridges, and literacy campaigns carried out through people's participation in *umuganda*. On the other hand, the council condemned the consumption of cannabis, sexual licentiousness, and "some conflicts between leaders and their constituents that still persist." In 1978, the minutes of the commune council of June 16 note a clear improvement in the security situation, stating, "The situation in all the sectors is generally good apart from a few cases of petty crime."[75]

The minutes of the July 16, 1979, meeting on security recommended that all councils flush out all criminals, urusimbi players, and cannabis smokers. Similar vigilance was demanded of councilors in order to stamp out smuggling. One could argue that these were normal delinquent acts of some people who did not follow the standards of public morality laid down by the commune. These infringements of the law and of local regulations were relatively benign acts of individual indiscipline.

In late 1979 a significant resurgence of crime and robbery originated outside the commune and continued throughout 1980, traceable to the power struggles at the top levels of the state. Colonel Théoneste Lizinde, chief of security, allegedly encouraged prisoners to escape in order to create political instability in the country. During this time, crime levels suddenly shot up in many regions. In the minutes of its meeting on December 1979, the Kigembe Commune council speculated about the external and political origin of this resurgence: "This security becomes more and more precarious because of a sharp increase in criminals, smokers, and smugglers." The council resolved to organize night patrols in all the sectors as a countermeasure.[76] On October 14, 1980, the commune council "noted that there is a kind of thuggery which targets public administration buildings and individuals, such as the cases of Taba, Mabanza, and Nshili (communes outside Butare Prefecture). The meeting also noted a big problem at the Nyaruteja trading center that makes security control difficult."[77] One of the resolutions made was to control people's movements. The members of the cell committees were to find out which guests were visiting the trading center and the length of their stay. Visitors staying for more than three days were required to have a residence permit. Bars were to respect the opening hours and close at 7 p.m. The council also declared a curfew between 8 p.m. and 5 a.m.[78]

In 1984, the commune experienced a food shortage. Harvests had been poor because of drought. In his report to the prefect on the sectors of his commune in November 1984, the burgomaster stated that the drought had caused an increase in theft. "People are stealing sweet potatoes, cassava, and coco yams. They are even digging holes through houses to steal." In spite of these cases of desperate acts of theft caused by hunger, people in all the sectors were generally taking part in *umuganda* and animation.[79]

Between May and June 1985, reported acts of theft were more violent, and first attacks against local authorities appeared:[80]

- A gang of thieves stole coffee at the market in Ruhororo Sector and fled to Burundi.
- In Fugi Sector, youths engaged in foreign-exchange, black-market selloff and fraud. Cannabis was smoked.
- In Mutakwa and Ruli Cells, food was stolen from the fields. The same was reported in Nyaruteja, Murama, and Kigali Sectors.
- In Kivuru Sector, a member of the cell committee was attacked by an unidentified person; also a certain Nyamulindwa was walking around with a machete threatening to kill the local authorities.[81]

- In Nyanza Sector, thieves entered the home of an unidentified elderly woman and stole her coffee harvest as well as her clothes.
- In Kivuru Sector, the home of a certain Nzabamwita was burned. Investigations were ongoing.
- In Karama Sector, Barambanza Léonidas attacked Bahizi, a member of the cell committee.

In 1986, the commune reports gave an uneven picture of the local authorities' handling of the population. The minutes of the commune council meeting of May 7 recorded the security situation as generally good, except for some cases of insecurity in some sectors, consisting mainly of banana theft because of the food shortage.[82] In May 1986, the burgomaster wrote to the prefect informing him of the "case of a certain Josée Mukamana, who hails from Ruhororo Sector. The young woman claims that she receives apparitions of the Virgin Mary." The burgomaster cites ten people who joined Mukamana to head together to Kibeho, in a neighboring commune, and he adds that she gathered quite a number of new followers.[83] This event in Kigembe Commune is part of the larger wave of apparition claims that originated from Gikongoro Prefecture in 1981.[84] One month later, the burgomaster played down the event when he wrote that the security meeting of May 21, 1986, analyzed the prevailing security situation in the commune and noted that it was generally good, except for a few cases of people in Ruhororo Sector claiming to have received visitations.[85] The commune committee meeting at the end of 1986, regarding the March of Remembrance, recommended "sensitizing the people in order to get maximum participation, even though most people are beginning to understand."[86]

During the MRND commune congress of December 1986, members of the cell committees were criticized for their lack of interest and for leaving all the work to the heads of the cells. The congress also lamented that parents had abandoned their responsibilities and were no longer concerned about raising their children. It was also mentioned that parents could no longer afford to pay school fees regularly or buy school materials for their children. Parents therefore avoided running into the school staff so that they were not asked for money. The last issue raised was that of parents' dissatisfaction with the educational system, with parents maintaining that the children who finished their eighth year simply returned home, and those who finished their vocational training could not find employment.[87]

From 1987 forward, the tone of the reports and commune minute proceedings changed rather abruptly, revealing that the local authority of the state structures was eroding. At the same time relationships between ordinary people and authorities started to change, different types of social problems arose. One of the main problems facing Kigembe Commune had to do with court cases concerning the sharing of land after death of the family head or a divorce. In addition to an increase in land litigation, a new phenomenon was the rise in the number of land disputes taken to court but never resolved.[88] The burgomaster was increasingly unable to enforce court decisions. One such case was the land dispute between Rubandako and Kamuzinzi, about which the burgomaster wrote, "Enforcement of the court ruling was impossible; on the one hand, the losers did not want to surrender the property they had seized, and on the other, a second court action was instituted on the same piece of land."[89] In other instances, rather than respect the court's decision in her divorce case, Mukadanga and her sons attacked and injured her ex-husband with a machete.[90] In the dispute between Semutwa and Nderabanzi over the land left to them by their grandfather, one did not want to parcel the land, and the other did not want to go to court to settle the matter. The burgomaster betrayed weariness with this issue and explained that the court decision was yet to be enforced.[91] In another case, the court ordered Shumbusha and his son Karekezi to return land they had illegally seized. The councilor of Kigembe Sector had authorized the winners of the court case to retrieve their land, but Karekezi seized the same land again. The burgomaster requested the prosecutor to sanction Karekezi, but the latter did not want to obey instructions.[92] Another case was that of a certain Ribakare of Kivuru Sector, who hired groups of criminals to seize other people's land by force in broad daylight.[93]

In addition to their refusal to respect court decisions and tendency toward social violence, Kigembe residents increasingly carried out physical attacks against local authorities. In a security meeting of April 15, 1987, Councilor Munanira of Kivuru Sector complained of traders threatening him for having asked the trade inspector to shut down shops that did not have the necessary licenses. He said these people had slapped his wife and burned his coffee trees. In Ngoma Sector, Mabinga was arrested for beating up cell committee members who had caught him for failing to participate in *umuganda*.[94]

In a security committee meeting on September 16, 1987, the commune council noted that alcohol abuse was causing a number of problems in the commune, and it had therefore decided all bars were to be closed at 6 p.m. It also discussed the violence targeted at local authorities. The council called for heavy penalties for those who had attacked cell committee members.[95] The meeting report drew a vivid picture of the social disorder in the commune. It noted cases of rape, theft by prostitutes, players of *urusimbi*, and idlers who spent their time by the roadside at Nyaruteja trading center. It also mentioned cannabis sellers, instances of violence, night attacks, women who chased away their cowives, bars that did not respect opening and closing hours, and rich people who exploited the ignorance and despair of others to rent the latter's lands when they had no other livelihood. It also referred to drunkards who attacked the night patrols, banana thieves who used knives, injuries caused by machete blows, and the attempted murder of a sector councilor.[96] All this disorder and sometimes violent insubordination had an impact on the implementation of *umuganda*.

The commune council on May 19, 1987, noted some level of negligence and recommended that after each incident, the members of cell committees write reports that would help in punishing the criminals.[97] Three months later, the council expressed concern that *umuganda* was not well implemented in most of the sectors because the "population was abandoning itself to alcohol and spending most of its time in the bars."[98] At the same meeting, the councilors noted that most of the marriages were not legally officiated.[99]

In 1989, the commune experienced a serious food shortage. The commune council response exposed not only the cause of the crisis but also the limitations of commune administration action as vague and repetitive of past resolutions. To fight against the famine that ravaged the population, the council requested the agricultural officers to exert more effort and urged the people to abandon idleness and ignorance. All who attended were encouraged to implement the prefect's orders to all the administrators to fight against laziness and vagrancy within the population and to encourage youths to form associations and to look for work. The council also decided that uncultivated land not reserved for pastures would be given to the landless to cultivate cassava. The commune administration had to fight against idlers who passed time at the Nyaruteja trading center, and the restaurants and bars had to respect the hours of operation.[100]

In Kigembe Commune, the late 1980s were clearly marked by party-state institutions overwhelmed by social problems: land shortage, recurring food shortages, unemployment, a rise in violence, and an increase in acts of insubordination sometimes turning into violent rebellion against the authorities. Finally, the local MRND institutions had fulfilled their ambition of obtaining almost total control over the population of Kigembe Commune, but for a relatively short time because from 1987 onward, there were increasing signs that the authority of these institutions was crumbling.

Notes

1. Kigembe Commune, *Résultats du recensement mené en août 1989.*
2. Innocent Rwamigabo, interview with author, May 4, 2001, Karubanda Prison, Butare.
3. Ruanda-Urundi, *Supplément au Rudipresse.*
4. Alphonse Ngoga, *Lettre au Préfet de Butare du 10/02/90 demandant une médaille de mérite pour les prouesses et le courage dont il a fait preuve depuis le début du pouvoir républicain au Rwanda jusqu'à aujourd'hui.*
5. Ibid.
6. Joseph Habyarimana, interview with author, April 26 and 27, 2001, Butare; Isaïe Buyenzi, interview with author, May 26, 2001, Kigembe.

7. Reyntjens, *Pouvoir et droit au Rwanda,* p. 299. According to a journalist from the *Sunday Times,* it was only in Astrida Province (the future Butare Prefecture) where in August and September 1961, 150 people were killed, 3,000 homes burned, and 22,000 refugees fled. Lemarchand, *Rwanda and Burundi,* p. 195.

8. Buyenzi's brother was killed at this time. Buyenzi interview; Antoine Kabutura, interview with author, May 18, 2001, Kigembe; Habyarimana interview; Sephorien Karekezi, interview with author, May 3, 2001, Rwandex Prison, Butare.

9. Interviews. Those who participated in it remember this process vividly, as do their descendants from many places in Rwanda.

10. Kabutura interview.

11. Habyarimana's aunt was the only member of the family to be banished. Ibid. Buyenzi's brother's wife, but not Buyenzi's brother, was also banished, although both eventually returned to their home. Ibid.

12. Kabutura interview.

13. Habyarimana interview.

14. Anastase Niyongira personally seized the land belonging to the former sub-chief. Ibid.; Kayumba, interview with author.

15. Commune Kigembe, *Note du Bourgmestre au Préfet du 26/01/87, Renseignements sur 25 ans de l'Indépendance nationale.*

16. République rwandaise, Ministère de l'Intérieur et du Développement communal, *Bilan des 25 ans d'Indépendance du Rwanda: 1962–1987,* 1987.

17. Straton Nyarwaya, interview with author, May 26, 2001, Kigembe; Kabutura interview.

18. République rwandaise, Ministère de l'Intérieur et du Développement communal, *Bilan des 25 ans d'Indépendance du Rwanda: 1962–1987.*

19. Nyarwaya interview.

20. These individuals were officially called *propagandists*, and they functioned as political managers.

21. République rwandaise, Ministère de l'Intérieur et du Développement communal, *Bilan des 25 ans d'Indépendance du Rwanda: 1962–1987,* p. 146.

22. Commune Kigembe, *Lettre du Bourgmestre au Préfet du 26/01/87, Renseignements sur 25 ans de l'Indépendance nationale.*

23. The intertwining of the party and the state is evident in the statement, found in the burgomaster's handbook, that the burgomaster facilitates the implementation of court decisions with the help of the sector councilors and the members of the MRND cell committees. Commune Kigembe, *Lettre du Bourgmestre au Préfet du 13/01/87, Renseignements sur le Guide du Bourgmestre.*

24. République rwandaise, Ministère de l'Intérieur et du Développement communal, *Bilan des 25 ans d'Indépendance du Rwanda: 1962–1987,* p. 116.

25. Commune Kigembe, *Lettre du Bourgmestre au Préfet du 26/01/87, Renseignements sur 25 ans de l'Indépendance nationale.*

26. Commune Kigembe, *Rapport annuel 1985.*

27. In 1989, for instance, the commune had about 50,161 inhabitants, roughly an average of 4,180 inhabitants for each of the twelve sectors and 836 households per sector, based on the estimates of the commune's administration of 5 people per household. Commune Kigembe, *Résultat du recensement mené en août 1989,* p. A-2.

28. The head and the members of the cell communities received only a modest annual allowance.

29. The development council is a decisionmaking body that oversees development. It is comprised of the sector councilors of the commune, of those in charge of the

services of the commune administration and other state services working in the commune.

30. Commune Kigembe, *Lettre du Bourgmestre au Préfet du 13/01/87, Renseignements sur le Guide du Bourgmestre.*

31. These two-year professional training centers were added to primary schools to provide a version of multidisciplinary vocational training.

32. These advisers were generally members of the community attached to the parish.

33. One of the first managers of CODAPAKI cooperative, created in 1980, embezzled a significant amount of the cooperative funds, to the extent that the minister of the Interior and Cooperative Development, under whose jurisdiction cooperatives fell, was obliged to bail out CODAPAKI. The leader of the cooperative in 1999, Kayisire, also embezzled money, and the burgomaster issued a warrant for his arrest. Calixte Kayisire, interview with author, May 3, 2001, Karubanda Prison, Butare; Commune Kigembe, *Lettre du Bourgmestre au Procureur de la République du 07/06/89, Instruction d'une affaire de détournement de fonds de la coopérative CODAPAKI.*

34. Kayisire interview.

35. Commune Kigembe, *Rapport annuel 1988*, p. 22.

36. Ibid., p. 60.

37. Ibid.

38. In 1988, the county court of Kigembe Commune had a presiding judge, two other judges, and two court clerks. Ibid., p. 54.

39. In 1988, the commune had seven police officers for a population of 51,000 inhabitants spread over a territory of 114 square kilometers, with, for the whole commune administration, only a single truck, which often experienced problems of inadequate fuel supply.

40. Nzisabira, "Accumulation du peuplement," p. 39.

41. Commune Kigembe, *Résultats du recensement mené en août 1989*, p. A-8.

42. Commune Kigembe, *Lettre du Bourgmestre au Préfet du 08/11/1984, Situation dans les secteurs administratifs de la commune Kigembe.*

43. Willame, *Aux sources de l'hecatombe*, p. 133.

44. Commune Kigembe, *Rapport annuel 1988*, p. 4.

45. Bézy, *Rwanda*, p. 17.

46. Nyarwaya interview.

47. Bézy, *Rwanda*, p. 32.

48. Most often, the reports for one specific month compiled the number of births spread over several months. For example, the commune registered 1,691 births in 1985 and 1,504 in 1988. These two figures suggest a drop in the country's birth rate during the last half the 1980s. By taking the 1988 figure of 1,504 births and extrapolating it to 1987, 1989, 1990, 1991, and 1992, one can argue that the data presented in Tables 6.7– 6.11 cumulatively represent 41 percent of the total births for the years under consideration.

49. République rwandaise, Ministère de l'Intérieur, Division Recensement et Statistiques, *Recensement administratif de la population rwandaise durant la période de 1960–1987*. Document for internal reference, October 1987, p. 10.

50. République rwandaise, Ministère de l'Intérieur, Division Recensement et Statistiques, *Recensement administratif de la population rwandaise durant la période de 1960–1987*, p. 10.

51. Joseph Habyarimana, who survived the genocide in Kigembe, drew our attention to the fact that in Kigembe before the genocide, many Tutsi men were marrying Hutu women. He explained that the rise in these marriages, which started in the 1960s, was a search for social and political protection. Habyarimana interview.

52. Ibid.

53. Commune Kigembe, *Lettre du bourgmestre au Préfet, Situation dans les secteurs administratifs du 08/11/1984.*

54. Commune Kigembe, *Procès-verbal de la réunion du comité communal du MRND du 14/05/77.*

55. The component of responsibility in this democracy was a coded concept used to justify single-party rule. Commune Kigembe, *Procès-verbal de la réunion du conseil communal du 15/07/77.*

56. Commune Kigembe, *Rapport annuel 1988*, p. 60.

57. Commune Kigembe, *Procès-verbal du Conseil Communal du 27/04/80.*

58. Commune Kigembe, *Rapport sur la fête de l'Indépendance du 1 er juillet 1987.*

59. Commune Kigembe, *Rapport annuel 1985*, p. 34

60. None of the minutes of these sensitization meetings mentions the people's reactions or even questions. If there was any, the burgomaster did not consider it worth mentioning in his reports.

61. Commune Kigembe, *Procès-verbal de la réunion du conseil communal du 15/07/77.*

62. Commune Kigembe, *Rapports annuel 1982*; Commune Kigembe, *Rapports annuel 1985* ; Commune Kigembe, *Rapports annuel 1988.*

63. Commune Kigembe, *Procès-verbal du Comité communal du MRND du 27/12/1977.*

64. République rwandaise, Ministère de l'Intérieur et du Développement communal, *Loi du 27 novembre 1984 portant organisation des élections des conseillers communaux.*

65. Commune Kigembe, *Lettre du Bourgmestre au Préfet du 14/10/84, Liste des candidats retenus pour les élections des conseillers communaux du 20 janvier 1985.* The MRND commune congress was made up of all the cell committees. The members of the committees were elected directly by the people without any ethnic restrictions, which implied that the commune congress had both Hutus and Tutsis. The systematic ethnic exclusion of Tutsis from political posts began at the position of head of cell committee.

66. Commune Kigembe, *Lettre du Bourgmestre au Préfet du 08/11/84, Situation dans les secteurs administratifs de la commune Kigembe.*

67. Ibid.

68. Ibid.

69. Ibid.

70. Ibid.

71. Ibid.

72. Commune Kigembe, *Rapport annuel 1985*, p. 1.

73. Commune documents make this distinction by labeling professional criminals as thugs. Commune Kigembe, *Procès-verbal de la reunion du conseil communal du 2 avril 1979, Liste des bandits qui vivent dans la commune Kigembe.*

74. Commune Kigembe, *Procès-verbal de la réunion du conseil communal du 15/07/1977.*

75. Commune Kigembe, *Procès-verbal de la réunion du conseil communal du 27/07/1977.*

76. Commune Kigembe, *Procès-verbal de la réunion du conseil communal du 10/12/1979.*

77. Commune Kigembe, *Procès-verbal de la réunion du conseil communal du 14/10/1980.*

78. Ibid.

79. Commune Kigembe, *Lettre du Bourgmestre au Préfet du 08/11/84, Situation dans les secteurs administratifs de la commune Kigembe.*

80. Préfecture de Butare, *Tableau récapitulatif de l'état de la situation de sécurité dans la préfecture de Butare entre le 17/05 et le 27/06/85.*

81. Commune Kigembe, *Procès-verbal de la réunion du conseil communal du 25/05/85.*

82. Commune Kigembe, *Procès-verbal de la réunion du conseil communal du 07/05/1986.*

83. Ibid.

84. These visitations generally correspond with a time of social turmoil; in similar contexts in Africa they are considered symptoms of the people's disengagement from the state. See Mbembe, *Afriques indociles.*

85. Commune Kigembe, *Lettre du Bourgmestre au Préfet transmettant le procès-verbal de la réunion de sécurité du 21/05/1986.*

86. Commune Kigembe, *Procès-verbal de la réunion du comité communal du MRND du 26/12/1986.*

87. Commune Kigembe, *Procès-verbal du congrès communal du MRND du 15/12/1986.*

88. The comparison between the report on rulings in 1982, 1983, and 1984 with that of rulings for 1985 reveals a significant increase in land court cases. Commune Kigembe, *Rapport portant sur les exécutions des jugements pour les années 82, 83, 84*; Commune Kigembe, *Rapport sur les exécutions des jugements pour le 1er, 2eme, 3eme, 4eme trimestre 1985.*

89. Commune Kigembe, *Lettre du Bourgmestre au Sous-Préfet du 19/02/1987.*

90. Commune Kigembe, *Lettre du Bourgmestre au Sous-Préfet du 08/10/1987.*

91. Commune Kigembe, *Lettre du Bourgmestre au Sous-Préfet du 24/07/1987.*

92. Commune Kigembe, *Dossier judiciaire adressé au Procureur le 13/11/1987.*

93. Commune Kigembe, *Lettre du Bourgmestre au Sous-Préfet du 02/09/1987.*

94. Commune Kigembe, *Procès-verbal de la réunion du conseil communal consacrée à la sécurité de la commune du 15/04/1987.*

95. Commune Kigembe, *Procès-verbal de la réunion du conseil communal consacrée à la sécurité du 16/09/1987.*

96. Commune Kigembe, *Procès-verbal de la réunion du conseil communal consacrée à la sécurité du 16/11/1987.*

97. Commune Kigembe, *Procès-verbal de la réunion du conseil communal du 19/05/1987.*

98. Commune Kigembe, *Procès-verbal de la réunion du conseil communal du 05/08/1987.*

99. Marriages not officiated in the commune in the late 1980s that were therefore illegal generally did not take place in traditional ceremonies either. Faustin Matabaro, interview with author, May 3, 2001, Karubanda Prison, Butare; Joseph Nzabonimpa, interview with author, May 2, 2001, Karubanda Prison, Butare.

100. Commune Kigembe, *Procès-verbal de la réunion du conseil communal du 06/04/1989.*

7

Political Radicalism
and Genocide in Kigembe

Kigembe is one of the communes in the southwest of Butare Prefecture where the genocide began while the rest of the prefecture remained calm and peaceful. In this chapter I examine the reasons why the population of Kigembe participated massively and early on in genocide while until at least 1989 a strong process of integration between Hutu and Tutsi communities had been taking place. Before considering the period of the genocide itself, I look at the behavior of the population of the commune in two preceding events: the war of October 1, 1990, launched by the Rwandan Patriotic Front (RPF) and the establishment of multiple parties in June 1991. My analysis in this chapter answers three underlying questions. The first is to determine what role the state, as opposed to social actors, played in the Kigembe mass participation in the genocide. The second is the role both socioeconomic and ideological factors played in the process of mobilizing the people. The last question is related to the agency of the local population in perpetration of the genocide.

The Impact of the 1990 War on Kigembe

Social Cohesion Rediscovered

The war set off by the RPF on October 1, 1990, was confined in the initial years to the fringes of the extreme northeast of Rwanda, opposite the geographical location of Kigembe Commune. In 1990 and 1991, the commune experienced the conflict from a distance. Given its proximity to the border with Burundi, out of solidarity with the regime the commune authorities adopted a number of measures. One of their first actions was to hold meetings to sensitize the people on security and national unity in order to "seal the cracks through which the enemy could penetrate."[1] During these meetings night patrols were established and roadblocks erected to check identity cards. Again, to reinforce security, the commune expanded its police force from four to eight officers by recruiting Rwandan Army reservists. To avoid upsetting the tight

215

budget of the commune, four technical service agents were suspended. Recruitment of soldiers for the national army was relaunched, and the commune council selected forty-seven candidates for enlistment.[2]

The National Revolutionary Movement for Development (MRND) congress on October 20, 1990, established a "voluntary" monetary contribution by all citizens according to their means, "including members of the public who were not on salary," that is, peasants and traders.[3] Collection of these "voluntary" contributions was bound to cause problems. At the end of January 1991, in his report to the prefect on a meeting for supporting the army, the recently chaired burgomaster thanked the teachers for their contributions and called for the continuation of the exercise. He instructed teachers in each school to give this contribution to the inspector "on pay day, since after that it would become impossible."[4] During the meeting, the burgomaster said he did not understand why some people displayed a lack of diligence and asked that "leaders use all means necessary to convince everyone to participate voluntarily."[5] Despite the fact that the MRND of Kigembe had decreed that everyone should contribute voluntarily, there is no trace in official documents of such a request being made to the peasants. The idea probably had to be abandoned. A month after the initial attack, the regime pushed back the RPF and officially declared victory. On November 7, 1990, Kigembe Commune held a march in support of the armed forces similar to the marches taking place in the rest of the country. During this victory march, banana stumps were buried to symbolize the death of Fred Rwigema, the RPF military chief who had been killed in combat several weeks before.[6] According to the burgomaster, 15,000 people attended the demonstration.[7]

The burgomaster also took it upon himself to inform his foreign partners of the ongoing situation in the country in order to counter the "enemies of Rwanda, who have also used the international media, such as the radio and newspapers, to tarnish the country's true image abroad." During the last four months of 1990, he held two meetings with his Burundian counterparts in charge of bordering Mwumba and Busiga Communes. The three parties agreed to establish special permits for inhabitants of their communes who regularly crossed the border.[8]

Four days after the RPF attack, there was a wave of arrests across the country of alleged RPF accomplices, almost all Tutsis. In Kigembe, Tutsis were arrested but then released. After their release, the commune authorities asked them to return to their homes, and at subsequent meetings, the participants were asked to leave in harmony and not to be carried away by ethnic hostility.[9] Even as the authorities adopted a conciliatory tone, they simultaneously put a number of Tutsis under surveillance and imposed some restrictions on them. These Tutsis could not, for example, sell cattle or withdraw more than RF500 from their bank accounts.[10] Tutsis who crossed the border in either direction were also under surveillance. In this case, the authorities were trying to discourage young Tutsis from Rwanda who were tempted to pass through Burundi to join the RPF, and to prevent the infiltration of RPF agents from Burundi. Young Tutsis found fording the Akanyaru River, between the countries, were systematically arrested, and criminal charges were filed against them.[11] Sometimes political developments in Burundi affected the burgomaster's collaboration with the authorities of the Burundian border communes to increase security. Thus he wanted to organize a meeting between the councilor of Nyaruteja Sector in Rwanda and his Burundian counterpart from Rwanyege Sector in Busiga Commune. However, Burundian military officials, most likely Tutsis, did not want to allow the Burundian councilor to pass through the border post, so the councilor had to go back and cross the river, close to his home. During their meeting the two councilors, hinting at their shared Hutu ethnicity when they noted the fact that inhabitants had relatives on either side of the border, facilitated surveillance in their sectors. They also discussed the issue of "a Tutsi" originally from Murama Sector of Kigembe Commune. The Burundian councilor stated that the Tutsi had been arrested and tortured in his sector by the population, but the councilor had decided to organize the Tutsi's escape when he saw the severity of the latter's wounds. The burgomaster ended his report to the prefect by mentioning that this Rwandan Tutsi had been the victim of the interethnic crisis in Burundi.

The burgomaster, the councilors, and the members of the cell committees committed the most effort, out of all the actions they took upon the outbreak of the war, to the day and night patrols. The patrols consisted of small groups of men doing rounds in the cell and stopping people to check their identity cards. Participation in the night rounds was a good indicator of the degree of obedience to authorities because it was compulsory. In the beginning, the rounds were successfully implemented with good participation by the people, and the burgomaster considered the security situation generally good.[12] At the end of January 1991, things started to become more lax, first in Rubona Sector. In response, the burgomaster decided to organize a sensitization meeting there. In his security report of January 21, 1991, the burgomaster mentions that he had been in Fugi Sector to help sensitize the people because the patrols had been neglected in some areas.[13] In Kigembe Sector, a certain Museruka incited people not to participate in the patrols. In Kivuru Sector, the number of thefts at farms and houses multiplied.[14] This decrease in participation in the patrols leaves the impression that when mobilization failed, the usual security problems resumed in the commune.

The rounds were satisfactorily implemented only in the interior of the commune. The sectors situated along the border with Burundi experienced a number of problems, especially for the patrols of the Akanyaru River crossings.[15] The rounds in these routes were a hindrance to smugglers in particular. On January 6, 1991, five people were arrested in Ruhororo Sector after quarrelling with members of the patrol; residents of the area then came to their rescue and threw stones at the patrol, which helped the smugglers cross with their cargo of potatoes. The next day, the burgomaster went to meet with the smugglers and their accomplices and explain to them that during this period of war, it was not a good idea to cross the Akanyaru River illegally. On January 11, 1991, smugglers in Nyaruteja Sector fought with the men on patrol and were arrested.[16] On January 16, 1991, another group of smugglers from Nyaruteja and Ruhororo Sectors was arrested and transferred to Karubanda Prison in Butare Prefecture. As a result of these problems, the burgomaster decided to have six people patrol these fording sites during the day and ten people at night.[17] Frequent confrontations led to reinforcement of the peasant patrols of the river routes toward mid-January 1991 with military officers from the small troop of soldiers stationed at the two border posts.[18]

Fear of the RPF

Another national event after the October 1, 1990, attack that had important repercussions for Kigembe Commune was the surprise RPF incursion of Ruhengeri Town in the northwest on January 23, 1991, which caused rumors of potential Inkotanyi attacks in other regions of the country.[19] Also in Kigembe, after the RPF attack on Ruhengeri was announced on the radio, the rumor of a possible RPF attack on the commune office caused panic, leading many peasants to flee toward Burundi while others took up arms and headed toward the headquarters to defend it.

The incident reveals the fear the RPF inspired among the Kigembe peasants, largely a result of official propaganda diffused on the radio.[20] The people spontaneously reacted by closing ranks with the commune authority and considering the RPF the enemy. The burgomaster's account shows how porous the ethnopolitical situation between Rwanda and Burundi was in Kigembe Commune, given that some of the causes of the panic came from across the border. This incident caused a spontaneous increase in participation in the patrols.[21] This reaction was not uniform throughout the commune, however, and a few days later, the incidents challenging the patrols resumed.[22]

The population of Kigembe Commune didn't react much to the launching of the war by RPF in October; most of the events in response to the distant attack were organized by the commune. RPF's attack in Ruhengeri caused more reactions in the border areas of the commune because of an incident from across the border in Burundi. Overall, the beginning of the war led to greater unity of the population under the commune authorities and to a general reduction in crime. After the incident, the usual rhythm of social life in Kigembe resumed with its accompanying social problems. It is important to note that during this period of reinforced unity in support of the authorities and against the RPF enemy, which the official propaganda portrayed as a Tutsi revenge mission, the commune authorities took measures to carry out surveillance on particular Tutsis. However, neither commune documents nor interviews with witnesses reveal rising ethnic tension among the residents during this period, even around the time when fear gripped the commune. Despite its fear, members of the local Hutu population seem to have seen their Tutsi neighbors as distinct from the RPF.

The Resumption of Violence

Between late February 1991, when mobilization for the war effort declined, and August of that same year, when political pluralism was established, residents of Kigembe Commune experienced a resurgence of insecurity and crime. The sharp rise in social instability can be traced to the surge of hunger experienced in the commune once again. Most of the crimes, which consisted of crop theft in the fields and violent attacks on homes to steal food, demonstrated the intensity of the food crisis facing the people. As a response to the food shortage in the commune, food aid was promptly delivered to vulnerable groups. On January 8, 1991, the burgomaster sent to the prefect a list of 780 people suffering from hunger in the commune.[23] On February 5, the French region of Loiret donated 850 kilos of beans to Butare Prefecture, and it was distributed to the eighty-five families most affected by hunger in Kigembe Commune, with each family receiving ten kilograms.[24] At the beginning of March, 1.3 tons of sorghum, 1.3 tons of beans, and 557 kilograms of maize were distributed to 123 families "in situations more critical than others and according to the number of members of those families."[25] On June 7, 156 families repatriated from Tanzania received emergency food aid; at the end of February 1992, 237 families were assisted; and 217 families received aid at the end of the following month.[26]

Others, however, did not wait for food aid and preferred to survive through theft and extortion. On January 23, 1991, the burgomaster indicated in his security report that thieves had attacked three families at their homes in Ngoma Sector and a family in Fugi Sector. In the four cases, the motive was to steal food.[27] A March 20, 1991, security report stated, "The population continues to carry out surveillance patrols of routes which the enemy could pass through to attack us, while at the same time watching out for those stealing food from the fields and the homes."[28] However, in his security report of March 21, 1991, the burgomaster wrote that in Nyaruteja and Fugi Sectors, on the border, rounds were neglected. In Kigembe Sector, a certain Museruka continued to incite people not to participate in the rounds, and in Kivuru Sector the burgomaster observed another rise in theft in the fields and homes.[29] On April 5, 1991, the burgomaster wrote that some incidents had disturbed the peace of the commune, that the majority of infractions were theft of produce in the fields, and that there were too many people accused for him to write down their names.[30] On April 12, five people were arrested and repatriated after they attempted to steal food from Burundi.[31] In the security report of May 17, 1991, the burgomaster identified hunger and theft as the problems in the commune.[32] On May 16, 1991, food crops were stolen from fields and coffee from houses.[33] On May 27, 1991, there were reports of more cases of food theft, and peasants were organizing patrols of their fields.[34] On December 16, 1991, the burgomaster once again reported the theft of beans and potatoes in Kigembe Sector. The people were asked to set up surveillance to patrol their fields.[35] Theft from the fields and attacks on the homes were particularly destabilizing. The attacks were often physical assaults, and when they occurred in the context of such a precarious food situation, the effects on the victim family were disastrous.

Against this backdrop of rising social tension, acts of disobedience increased in the commune. At the end of February 1991, the burgomaster wrote to the judicial police inspector to request that a certain Sebugabo be prosecuted for refusing to obey the court decision that obliged him to return a particular piece of land.[36] Two days later, the burgomaster asked that Mukakizimana be prosecuted, also for refusing to respect a court decision in a land dispute.[37] On March 12, the burgomaster wrote to the prefect explaining the conflict between Museruka and the councilor of Kigembe Sector, arguing that the councilor was not implicated in the conflict. Museruka had been convicted of stealing bananas and of inciting his neighbors against any participation in the rounds.[38] A security committee meeting of May 15 noted that a group of women wanted to prevent a certain Bidi from cultivating his field in Migina Valley despite warnings from the councilor.[39]

The Multiparty Era

The Republican Democratic Movement (MDR) Hegemony

Even before political parties were legalized at the national level, the people of Kigembe Commune were so keen on the development of the national multiparty movement that at the end of April 1991, the burgomaster felt the need to call on the population not to "be distracted by the political intrigues of the day."[40] Shortly after the law on political parties went into effect in July, in August 1991 the MRND and the MDR began their political activities in Kigembe Commune.[41] The Social Democratic Party (PSD) established itself in the commune a little later, but the Liberal Party (PL) presence in the commune was short-lived, almost fleeting.

The history of political parties in Kigembe Commune is primarily that of the MDR, which managed to dominate the commune. Political parties sent their prefecture and national leaders, accompanied by a strong delegation from Kigali or Butare Prefectures, to meetings and rallies they used as a platform to popularize the party and recruit members.[42] After the rallies, the visitors would hold discussions with the residents at public places such as the marketplace, after church mass, and mostly in bars, where the visitors would generously offer drinks.[43] The MDR organized a first, small public meeting at the end of June 1991 on the initiative of Bonaventure Nkundabakura, a wealthy trader from Kigembe. It brought together Kigembe Commune residents as well as people from Kigali. The burgomaster, a member of the MRND, described the residents who responded first to the MDR call as "bandits, thieves who are always being arrested, people who have lost their court cases, those struck off the candidate list for local elections, and those who had lost their jobs."[44] This profile of the earliest members of the MDR was confirmed by other witnesses, who added that for many, the possibility of free drinks was one of the most important motivations for joining the party. Generally, the fact that no "intellectual" was among the first members of the MDR was highlighted.[45] In mid-August 1991, the burgomaster wrote that the Kigembe Commune MDR branch had ninety-seven members and that in the previous month three members of a cell committee had joined it.[46] However, the party rapidly grew over the next eight months, and 5,990 people, 10 percent of the entire commune population, took part in the elections for the MDR commune committee and MDR sector committees April 26, 1992.[47] After these elections, the burgomaster also noted that the profile of MDR supporters and leaders had changed; according to him, "some MDR supporters left the party because the local people had not voted for them; they were thugs and robbers who had presented their candidacy but had not been elected, even though they had been the ones who had forced their relatives to join the party."[48]

At the end of these eight months of activity, the MDR was strongly established in the commune, and its support base had expanded. However, during this whole period, the leaders and supporters were mostly peasants and "smugglers." The president of the MDR branch, Nkundabakura, was a smuggler and was known to be particularly violent. He was nicknamed "Kabyankwese" ("if you push me, I will beat you up") because as a child, he had attempted to strike his father with a spear.[49] His father was Alphonse Ngoga, a forefront PARMEHUTU activist during the 1959 revolution and one of the main leaders of the August 1961 violence. Ngoga's activism resulted in his election as burgomaster of the newly created Kigembe Commune.[50] Whereas the national MDR was divided by a heated debate between those who wanted to continue with the MDR-PARMEHUTU legacy and those who wanted a new MDR, in Kigembe Commune the MDR under Nkundabakura declared itself staunchly PARMEHUTU.[51] Later, when the national MDR split into the majority "power" and the "new" party, in Kigembe Commune, the MDR also split, and the majority under Nkundabakura naturally became MDR-power.[52] At the beginning of 1992, most "intellectuals" in the commune were still loyal to the MRND, especially when they were still civil servants or teachers on the government payroll. Following elections for the various MRND institutions on

January 26, 1992, the ten-member MRND commune committee comprised the burgomaster, a member of parliament, three heads of schools, the education inspector, the veterinary officer, the accountant/collector, a retired teacher, and a businessman. This situation would change after the MDR takeover of June 1992, which definitively expelled the MRND from the commune.[53]

At the commune level, the main goal of the parties was to recruit the highest possible number of members in view of the upcoming elections. The main method used to accomplish this goal was political rallies—the primary partisan political activity in the commune.

Table 7.1 shows that an average of two rallies per week took place in the commune for the eight months listed and that each sector had held an average of five meetings. This record demonstrates intense political activity in the commune. The sectors that received the most visits from the political parties were the two administrative centers, that is, the commune offices in Nyaruteja Sector and Ngoma Sector; the administrative center of the Mvejuru Region, Ruhororo Sector; and Kivuru Sector, which had long been most defiant toward local authorities. Finally, the level of activity of the three main parties represented in the commune differed slightly during this period: the MDR held twenty-five rallies, the MRND held twenty-one, and the PSD held twenty. The PL, a late arrival in the commune, held only one rally, at the end of the period.[54]

The arrival of political parties contributed to sowing suspicion in daily relationships in the commune. There was strong social pressure for everyone to be affiliated with a party because it touched on personal security. Anyone who still did not belong to a party became a target for forced party membership, especially by MDR supporters.[55] Faustin Matabaro, a young villager who could not read or write, tells of the fear the MDR instilled in some of the villagers:

> All I knew was simply that I was a member of the MDR because whoever refused to join the party was condemned. Joining the party was a way of redeeming oneself. You think that we joined the party voluntarily? . . . It was by force. For example, if you did not join the party of your neighbors, or the families nearby, they would beat you; they would destroy your house. You became a member despite yourself, not knowing what to do. That is the way in which most people joined that party. It was done by force. . . . The party held rallies. We spent the whole day dancing. Those who could dance, danced; those who could not stayed in the house but with their cards, so that if they were surprised by anyone, they would display those cards to show the others that they were also party members. That was how we survived.[56]

The commune rallies discussed the same topics rallies did elsewhere in the country, with the notable exception of the MDR, which was more openly violent and not shy about issuing threats in public. According to the burgomaster's summary of the topics discussed by the political parties throughout 1991, Nkundabakura and his assistants almost always made the same speech, "criticizing the MRND government from the president of the republic down to the

Table 7.1   **Political Rallies in Kigembe Commune Between August 1991 and April 1992**

Political Party	Date	Venue
MRND	August 19, 1991	Commune office in Nyaruteja Sector
	September 20, 1991	Ngoma Sector
	September 28, 1991	Ngera Sector
	September 29, 1991	Commune office
	October 6, 1991	Ngoma Sector
	November 3, 1991	Commune office
	December 29, 1991	Karama Sector
	January 5, 1992	Commune office (Mvejuru region)
	January 12, 1992	Nyakera region
	February 16, 1992	Ngera and Murama Sectors
	February 23, 1992	Rubona Sector
	March 1, 1992	Kivuru and Ruhororo Sectors
	March 8, 1992	Nyaruteja, Kigali, and Ngoma Sectors
	March 15, 1992	Fugi and Kigembe Sectors
	March 22, 1992	Karama and Nyanza Sectors
MDR	August 25, 1991	Commune office
	September 22, 1991	Nyakare region
	September 29, 1991	Fugi Sector
	October 6, 1991	Ruhororo Sector
	November 10, 1991	Nyanza and Kigembe Sectors
	November 17, 1991	Kivuru and Ngoma Sectors
	December 22, 1991	Kigali Sector
	December 29, 1991	Ngoma Sector
	January 12, 1992	Karama and Ruhororo Sectors
	January 19, 1992	Kivuru, Kigembe, Kigali, and Nyanza Sectors
	February 8, 1992	Ngera Sector
	February 9, 1992	Fugi and Rubona Sectors
	February 15, 1992	Ruhororo Sector
	February 23, 1992	Murama and Kigali Sectors
	March 29, 1992	Mvejuru region
	April 5, 1992	Kigembe Sector
	April 12, 1992	Kivuru Sector
PSD	November 6, 1991	Commune office
	November 11, 1991	Ruhororo, Nyaruteja, and Kigali Sectors
	November 17, 1991	Ngera and Murama Sectors
	December 22, 1991	Kivuru, Fugi, Kigembe, and Karama Sectors
	January 5, 1992	Nyanza Sector
	February 1, 1992	Kivuru Sector
	February 22, 1992	Ngera Sector
	March 7, 1992	Rubona Sector
	March 8, 1992	Karama Sector
	March 14, 1992	Ngoma Sector
	March 15, 1992	Nyanza Sector
	March 21, 1992	Murama Sector
	March 22, 1992	Nyaruteja Sector
	March 29, 1992	Ruhororo Sector
PL	April 12, 1992	Commune office

Sources: Commune Kigembe, *Rapport de l'inspection communale du 22/01/92*; *Commune Kigembe, Autorisations à tenir un meeting politique délivréesentre le 1er janvier 1992 et le 15 avril 1992.*

cell members and trying to incite the people against the authorities."[57] They demanded that MRND leaders return to their home in Bushiru Region in the northwest and performed songs and dances to that effect. Extracts from the opposition newspapers criticizing the regime were read out loud. The articles held the government responsible for the war with the RPF. They accused authorities of the commune, from the burgomaster to the members of the cell, of embezzling food aid for the needy. Finally, they incited the population to engage in civil disobedience.[58] Between its establishment in the commune and mid-April 1992, the MDR held two large rallies graced by high-profile guests. Donat Murego and Agathe Uwilingiyimana (president of the Butare MDR branch), both members of the national party leadership, participated in the rally of January 19, 1992.[59] Nkundabakura issued threats against the authorities. He explained that the MDR in Kigembe Commune was going to organize demonstrations to "seize the sector councilors, tie them up, and do what they wanted to them"[60] and disarm the commune police officers because the police weapons were instruments of intimidation. Finally, they were going to attack the burgomaster and abuse him until the Habyarimana government fell. In support of Nkundabakura's threats, Murego appealed to the Kigembe burgomaster, to defect from the MRND, to choose the path of democracy and stated that the residents would thank him for liberating himself from the yoke of the Bashirus (people of President Habyarimana's region of origin). The other speakers also made the usual arguments against the MRND, accusing it of being alien to Kigembe Commune, with no real attachment to the people.[61] During the rally held on March 29, 1992, again in Uwilingiyimana's presence, Nkundabakura asked the supporters "to seize the councilors of Ruhororo, Kigembe, Rubona, Kigali, and Murama Sectors and bring them to him."[62] Between 3,000 and 4,000 people attended the rally. Both Nkundabakura's personality and the fact that he repeatedly issued threats in front of the national party officials show that the violent behavior of the party representatives in the commune were condoned at the national level.

The political rallies also provided the opportunity to demonstrate popular strength. Before the rallies began, there was a whole protocol of singing and dancing troupes chanting political slogans, known as *animation*, intended to liven up the atmosphere as people waited for the audience to reach its peak numbers. Groups of young men and women and even children dressed in the party colors and marched in line. Supporters were called by the beating of drums. The drums were also used to accompany chanting of slogans during the rally.[63] In more improvised meetings other than rallies, groups were sometimes formed to dance to and sing songs insulting authorities or members of other political parties. These improvised animations often provoked fights between supporters of the different parties.[64] Late on the evening before a January 19, 1992, rally a group of about fifty children between the ages of five and nine spent about an hour in procession chanting songs demanding a national conference and hurling insults outside the door of the Nyaruteja councilor.[65] Party paraphernalia, including flags, was displayed to the hilt. Caps, clothes, and distinctive signs carried by the supporters also frequently caused arguments.[66] Neutrality, especially for the most vulnerable members of the community, had become risky. To protect oneself from being forced to join parties or be beaten, one had to affiliate with a party. Often for the most vulnerable, this choice was not made freely but after strong pressure from family members and neighbors to join their parties.[67] This competition between the parties to gain members led the members to resort to violence. This was especially the case for the MDR. The political violence encouraged by the MDR spilled over into both gratuitous and calculated violence. MDR supporters exploited the opportunity under the banner of the party to form gangs to carry out their own projects.

The New Rise in Violence

These violence-tainted partisan actions were part of a larger context in which similar acts, not politically motivated, were also committed. In mid-December 1991, in Karama Sector, a group of cannabis smokers armed themselves with machetes so that no one could come near them.[68] In the same sector, a peasant cut down trees in the commune forest.[69] In late December, a certain Claver Nyilimana—armed with a bow, arrows, and a sword—protected his assistant Ruganiki as the latter stole produce from the farm that belonged to Nzabamwita.[70] In late January 1992, a scuffle between seven people over a land issue was reported in Kigali Sector.[71] In late March, in Kigembe Sector, a young member of a violent gang of thugs threatened to kill his mother and sister with a machete and a knife, but people intervened just in time.[72] During the same period, a certain Habimana of Nyaruteja Sector was reported to have attacked local authorities who had come to arrest him.[73] On January 31, 1992, there was an attempted murder in a bar that belonged to a councilor. On February 2, 1992, in Nyaruteja Sector, a peasant attempted to kill a councilor for allegedly having struck the peasant's child.[74] During the same period, bandits attacked a family with knives, injuring the husband, his wife, and their daughter.[75] The security report of February 19, 1992, mentions attacks in Ngoma and Kigembe Sectors on police officers who had just collected taxes for cattle ownership.[76] On March 2, 1992, a man attempted to forcibly snatch a gourd of sorghum beer from another person at the Ngoma market; when he was unsuccessful, he spilled the contents on the ground. The gourd owner injured the attacker with a machete, and the attacker sought refuge at the burgomaster's home while he was in a meeting, saying that someone wanted to kill him. The burgomaster asked him to wait until the following day for investigation of the case because it was late in the day. The man in question tried to physically attack the burgomaster, who was saved when people intervened.[77] The attacks on homes continued. In late March, in Kigembe Sector, thieves attacked a peasant at his home and stole his pig and all his clothes.[78] In Nyanza Sector, two youths attacked a family, broke through the door, and carried away fifty kilograms of soya and thirty kilos of beans.[79] To fight back the proliferation of thieves, the burgomaster advised the patrols to narrow the area they covered in their rounds from the cells to groups of ten homes, otherwise known as *nyumbakumi*.[80] During the commune council meeting on April 22, 1992, the councilors expressed their uneasiness, saying that the members of the cell committees no longer wanted to collaborate with them and that others took sides with the troublemakers. They felt despised by the population.[81] During the meeting of all members of the cell committees on May 5, 1992, the burgomaster told his colleagues that nothing should interfere anymore with the successful implementation of *umuganda* (compulsory community labor).[82] On May 12, 1992, it was reported that in Kivuru Sector, thugs had attacked two homes and made away with coffee, beans, and clothes.[83] The following week, in Ngera Sector, the residents hunted down a man accused of fatally poisoning a resident. He fled to the home of a certain Balirwanda, who injured him with a spear. The people then beat him to death.[84] Finally, on May 29, 1992, the burgomaster sent a list of 871 homes containing 3,260 people who needed emergency food aid. These people were mostly handicapped, elderly, widowed, orphaned, or from large families.[85]

One can also note that the social climate did not change during the months before and after the establishment of political pluralism; it remained characterized by social violence instigated by poverty that sometimes targeted the local authorities as well.

Following the introduction of political pluralism, similar acts were committed, but this time they took on a semblance of partisan significance. In early 1992, for example, one of the first members of the MDR hurled a stone at a police officer who had come to collect the cattle tax from him; the officer picked up the stone and hurled it back, injuring the latter's head. The MDR supporter then took up a spear to defend himself but was overpowered just in time. In early February 1992, it was reported that the right to draw water from a public well had been restricted to MDR members only.[86] A report of March 2, 1992, made mention of people injured following a bar fight between supporters of different political parties.[87] At the Nyaruteja trading center, MDR members accused the sector councilor of killing the infant just born to his daughter.[88] On March 26, 1992, the burgomaster wrote to the prefect requesting a contingent of gendarmes to help him maintain law and order because the MDR had planned a big rally on March 29 that would coincide with an MRND rally. According to the burgomaster's sources, on that occasion the MDR intended to carry out a *kubohoza* operation on the councilors of Karama and Ruhororo Sectors in order to force them to change their party allegiance.[89] A few days before the MDR rally, some MDR and MRND supporters nearly came to blows but were successfully separated. One MDR supporter began screaming, claiming that the Ruhororo councilor had sent people to kill him.[90] The rally itself was relatively peaceful, but afterward in the evening MDR supporters spent the night singing and dancing in different sectors. In Ruhororo Sector, these demonstrations took place in front of the councilor's home.[91]

After the Kigembe MDR internal elections took place on April 26, 1992, the burgomaster wrote to the public prosecutor requesting that charges be brought against eight MDR members who on elections day had attacked members of a cell committee, including an MRND official. They beat up two cell committee members and took them by force to the polling stations, but one of the captives managed to escape. The gang also struck the president of the cell committee. The burgomaster asked that those found guilty be punished because the criminals were also part of a twenty-six-member gang that had invaded the commune land and destroyed crops.[92] On May 10, 1992, a certain Lazare known to be an MDR partisan was caught in Kigali Sector at an Akanyaru River crossing. He was accompanying Nestor Cyiza, president of the Palipehutu party branch in Ngozi Province in Burundi. The Burundian was also arrested for being in the company of a person armed with a grenade. As they approached the commune office, Lazare incited a group of MDR supporters to attack the guards who arrested them as well as the members of the cell committee. The Burundian fled, and Lazare returned home. Charges were filed against him.[93]

Predatory Behavior by MDR Supporters

After political pluralism was established in Kigembe Commune, a new pattern of behavior emerged: its public land and, increasingly, individual farms were invaded. These acts were unique partly because they went beyond the simple theft of food; the raiders destroyed, rather than harvested, the crops they found in the fields with the aim of making their hold on the land permanent. This predatory behavior appeared two months after political pluralism took root in the commune.

On October 10, 1991, the burgomaster reported that twenty-six people in Kigembe Sector, some of whom were MDR members, seized land that belonged to the commune on which sweet potatoes and beans were cultivated that had helped 276 families.[94] The invaders uprooted the sweet potato seedlings and planted sorghum instead. The sector councilor, accompanied by seven other people, went to arrest the troublemakers. The latter chased them away, insulting them and telling them that they no longer had any power.[95] In early November 1991, twenty-nine people in Ngoma Sector invaded pastures protected by the commune. The invaders continued to cultivate the land despite a ban by the councilor.[96] A month later, a peasant in Kigembe Sector invaded and farmed an area reserved for the cultivation of sweet potato cuttings.[97] On February 24, 1992, the burgomaster reported that in Kivuru Sector, a group of thirty-four peasants invaded farms in Migina Valley that belonged to the Tulikumwe Association. They began by digging the field and destroying the crops already there. The burgomaster asked the farm owners to stay calm and told them that their issue would be resolved by the deputy prefect. Three days later, in a report on the same problem, the burgomaster wrote that he had returned again to the site and asked the cultivators why they had not obeyed the orders of the deputy prefect.[98] The cultivators responded that everyone could see that the decisions were not being enforced, so both invaders and entitled members of the registered association continued to cultivate haphazardly. Finally, the burgomaster decided that clear boundaries would be marked on every person's land and a management committee would be appointed to settle disputes.[99]

On February 27, 1992, the burgomaster wrote that peasants in Kivuru Sector continued to defy the Tulikumwe Association and forcefully seize its fields. In Kigembe Sector, bananas were stolen, and in the process the commune forests were damaged.[100] On April 16, 1992, the burgomaster wrote to the deputy prefect that the commune residents, generally MDR members, continued to seize others' farms.[101] On April 18, 1992, it was reported that people in Murama Sector had seized land by force.[102] In late April 1992, twenty-seven people seized grazing land protected by the commune. The invaders immediately began to cultivate, and when arrested, they claimed they were MDR supporters.[103] The security report of May 19, 1992, stated that MDR supporters invaded grazing land in Kigembe Sector, and other MDR supporters in Nyaruteja Sector invaded fields that belonged to residents of the Akanyaru Valley.[104] On May 22, 1992, the burgomaster informed the deputy prefect that MDR supporters had invaded the peasants' farms located in both the marshy areas and pastures. These acts were reported mostly in Kigembe Sector.[105] The security report of May 27, 1992, noted that farms continued to be invaded in Kivuru Sector, and in Kigembe Sector sixty-one people claiming to be MDR members invaded the pastures of two breeder associations as well as the commune veterinary dispensary, where they broke windows.[106] A security report of June 12, 1993, reported that pastures all over the commune along with the public papyrus fields in Kivuru Sector had been invaded, and in Kigembe Sector people assaulted the owner of a private farm, invaded it, and cultivated it.[107]

Faced with the invaders' determination, the number of lawbreakers, and often the residents' support for the invaders, the authorities felt powerless to defend the established order. When the invasions succeeded—and most of them did—the authorities' lack of reaction led even the victims to eventually align themselves with the attackers and their political party, the MDR, considering that almost all these acts were carried out under its banner. Even though only a minority engaged in these acts, the predation was a sign of the thirst for land that affected a sizable proportion of the population. Interviewees attest to the destabilizing effect on ordinary people of this rise in acts of rebellion against the authorities and violent land-grabbing, producing a sense of chaos. For many it prefigured dynamics that would appear during the genocide. These acts signified that the status quo was not desirable and perhaps not even sustainable for a section of the population, considering the level and recurrence of hunger. The top MDR officers found receptive listeners for their repeated incitement of the local population to politically motivated violence. Some residents of the commune exploited MDR promotion of violent behavior to cope with their own survival challenges.

The MDR Takeover

The rising authority of commune MDR president Nkundabakura eventually led to a bitter conflict with Burgomaster Straton Semayenzi. Nkundabakura acted as if his party supporters were under his sole authority. In turn, certain MDR militants became victims of attacks by local authorities, such as sector councilors and members of cell committees, most of whom were still loyal to the MRND. In an exchange of letters with the burgomaster, Nkundabakura warned that his militants would take revenge. The burgomaster in turn advised Nkundabakura to tell his militants to go to court.[108] In a letter to the prefect, the burgomaster defended himself from Nkundabakura's accusations, explaining that residents of the commune had many court cases against each other and that the procedure for similar cases was to either appear in court or, in less serious cases, to appear before the community reconciliation forum of *gacaca*. In his letter, the burgomaster lamented that the MDR president was encouraging his supporters to resolve their cases through the structures of his party.[109] On May 12, 1992, the police inspector followed the burgomaster's orders and filed charges against Nkundabakura for beating a cell committee member trying to resolve a dispute between residents; Nkundabakura had torn the cell member's hat and made him sit down in the mud.[110]

Nkundabakura brought the commune under his control. The people no longer attended the meetings organized by the burgomaster, and the only cell committee members who could arbitrate people's disputes were those endorsed by the MDR.[111] In order to earn the people's trust and affection, Nkundabakura bought people drinks, told them that the MRND had oppressed the population, that the party was incapable of providing jobs, and that it was behind the times.[112] The rivalry between the burgomaster and the local MDR president would lead to an ever greater outpouring of violence.

Between May 30 and June 3, 1992, the following events took place. First, a large MDR rally was held in Busoro Subprefecture administrative center in the neighboring Gishamvu Commune "during which the speakers threatened to hurt MRND members, calling them *Interahamwe*, and deliberately aroused and incited Hutus against Tutsis."[113] Next, MDR supporters in Kigembe seriously beat a councilor from Kigali Sector because they considered him loyal to the MRND. According to public opinion, the burgomaster sought revenge by asking a commune police officer to let an MDR member escape from the commune prison and then shoot him to death. The local MDR reacted by carrying out a *kubohoza* operation over almost the entire commune, attacking the most prominent MRND members. MDR supporters blocked the roads with tree trunks; attacked the councilors from Ruhororo, Nyaruteja, Kigali, Rubona, and Nyanza Sectors; and looted, burned, and completely destroyed the councilors' homes. Sixty-seven homes were burned in the five sectors.[114] The political rationale of carrying out *kubohoza* against administration officials was the desire to align the local authorities with the political party that enjoyed the most popular support; in other words, *kubohoza* was implemented in party supporter strongholds. These five sectors were all located in Mvejuru Region, where the Tutsi population was minimal.

For three days, the MDR supporters held councilors, cell committee members, traders, and villagers known to be MRND supporters in the newly built dispensary in Ngoma Sector. They slaughtered the councilors' cows and ate them.[115] A number of residents, including the councilors and their families, took refuge in the Higiro Church. The MDR supporters attacked and unsuccessfully attempted to destroy the commune office, after which they headed for the burgomaster's home. They chased and pursued the burgomaster with spears, but he managed to escape and fled toward Butare Town by car. In the meantime, many residents had fled toward the commune office and others to Burundi. The MDR supporters exploited the opportunity to cultivate the fields that belonged to the commune.[116] This was a humiliating end to his career for Burgomaster Semayenzi, who for a long time enjoyed the respect of the residents of Kigembe who appreciated his administrative and leadership abilities as well as his having greatly developed the commune since he took office in 1967. He had regularly received an "elite" grade from his superiors and had been honored with the order of national merit.[117]

A unit of gendarmes was sent to the commune to restore order. The prefect and a delegation from the ministry of the interior visited the area. First, the gendarmes assured the prisoners detained by the MDR supporters of their safety but did not dare use force to free them. Nkundabakura was obliged to order the prisoners' release following "pleas" from the prefect and the military commander of Butare.[118] The display of strength had been commandeered and led by the local MDR president, with "physically robust thugs" as his close allies.[119] All of the commune officials had been removed from office because people did not want them anymore according to the MDR, but the councilors were reinstated upon the prefecture's intervention. Burgomaster Semayenzi did not resume his duties, and above all, the MRND was effectively banished from the commune. The violence by the MDR planted fear in the commune.

The main perpetrators of these actions, as well as Nkundabakura, were arrested and transferred to Butare Prison. A few weeks later, they were released because the procedures for retaining them in temporary custody had not been properly followed.[120] Some instigators of violent actions, such as those in Ruhororo Sector, were not even charged because the judicial police inspector lacked the courage to arrest them.[121] The majority of witnesses attribute the releases to the intervention of Uwilingiyimana of the MDR, who had become minister of education.[122] The impunity enjoyed by the troublemakers was not reassuring. After this MDR takeover, MRND members defected to the MDR and the PSD, with the majority opting for the MDR. The majority of councilors of the sector, including the former burgomaster, joined the PSD not out of conviction but because they did not want to join the party that had humiliated them.[123]

The commune carried on without a burgomaster and was under the jurisdiction of the deputy prefect until March 1993. The excessive MDR violence in Kigembe Commune weakened its president's standing among the intellectuals as well as the authorities of the ministry of the interior and Butare Prefecture.[124] This lack of respectability of MDR power allowed the PSD to assert itself even though the party did not enjoy the support of the majority of the population. The MDR and PSD quickly entered into open conflict, and this bad blood between them would be the main agenda of the security committee meeting of the commune council on August 7, 1992, chaired by the deputy prefect in Kigembe Commune. During the meeting, Nkundabakura complained that while he was in prison, the PSD had committed violence against MDR members, that PSD members had recently held a rally during which they hurled insults at the MDR, and that PSD members were arrogant because they said their party was made up of educated people.[125] Nkundabakura explained that the increasing violence was caused by the people's anger at the injustice against him, and the anger was still strong.[126] Regarding the appointment of the next burgomaster, Nkundabakura threatened that the people would rise up again if a PSD burgomaster was imposed on them against the will of the majority. He called for the arrest of the gendarmes who had abused and beaten the people with the complicity of some councilors. He ended his speech by promising to ask the people to stay calm. In their response, the local PSD leaders pointed out that the burgomaster was appointed by the president of the republic and that they were inclined to welcome whoever would be appointed. The leaders also admitted that some former MRND members who had "taken refuge" in the PSD had provoked the violence against the MDR.[127]

Nkundabakura was far from remorseful; instead, he talked with confidence of his public support. On March 23, 1993, elections to replace rejected burgomasters were organized throughout Butare Prefecture and the rest of Rwanda.[128] A week before these elections, a new incident occurred in Kigembe Commune when local agents attempted to collect taxes. MDR supporters had rebelled, saying that they would not pay as long as they did not have a burgomaster. The prosecutor then proceeded to arrest the culprits. On their way back, the MDR supporters seized five sector councilors and locked them in the Ngoma Sector office for two days. The captors said that they would not release the councilors as long as their recently arrested party comrades remained in jail, but upon the request of Nkundabakura the councilors were freed.[129]

The replacement of the "defective" burgomasters gave way to a limited electoral process that consisted of "preselection" by an electoral college composed of sector heads, members of the commune development council, project directors working in the commune, and representatives of political parties and churches in the commune.[130] Sephorien Karekezi, a member of the PSD, was elected but MDR supporters refused to recognize his victory. In July 1993, the Butare Prefecture security council reported that MDR supporters in Kigembe Commune had thrown grenades at PSD supporters, only the latest episode in the war between the two parties since June 1992.[131]

The new burgomaster reported obstacles set up by Nkundabakura, such as preventing people from attending the official meetings he called. In his interview, Burgomaster Karekezi acknowledged MDR hegemony in the commune during his tenure.[132] Already, before it forcefully took control in June 1992, the MDR was the first political force in the commune that had managed to greatly diminish the influence of the former MRND party-state. After its violent abuses, the MDR became the political movement with the greatest influence in the commune, and this despite its being ostracized by the prefecture administration and despite the disfavor of the electoral college in March 1993.[133]

The MDR, Vehicle of Ethnic Hatred

The majority of people interviewed for this study explained that the resurgence of ethnic animosity in Kigembe Commune corresponded with the advent of political parties. Joseph Nzabonima compares the effects of the political parties on the commune with those of other important events: "Even when there was a regime change [to the Second Republic], there was no problem. And that was not only in Kivumu Sector; it was the same elsewhere. Things began to change only when political parties came, when the leaders of the parties began their campaigns; the parties, especially the MDR, had evil intentions."[134]

The elderly Antoine Kabutura was of the same opinion, having stated, "The ethnic conflicts themselves emerged in 1992. This was the moment when things changed. Everything happened because of political parties."[135] Martin Ntamishimiro situates the emergence of ethnic hatred in Kigembe Commune sometime later, during the rising competition in 1993 between the MDR and the PSD, the two biggest parties in the commune at the time. "Ethnic hatred had not yet reappeared because hatred, strictly speaking, was reported around

1993, approximately in March. That is where hatred began to appear, but it was not serious because nobody could run away. There was some mistrust between parties, and one felt that something was going to happen."[136]

According to witnesses of the events, ethnic hostility first appeared with the rising competition between the MDR and the PSD during the "election" of the new burgomaster. The anti-Tutsi ethnic hostility ushered in by the MDR was used as an argument not against the PL, practically nonexistent in Kigembe Commune, but more against the PSD, which counted several socially prominent Hutu men married to Tutsi women among its ranks.[137]

The Kigembe branch of the MDR proclaimed its affiliation with the MDR-PARMEHUTU from the beginning. The leaflets posted on the doors of houses in sectors where the MDR held its meetings called the MDR the party of former president Kayibanda, whose objective was to defend the interests of the Hutus. At rallies, former 1960s activists boasted about the violence of the revolutionary period.[138] According to Straton Nyarwaya, the local MDR insisted on its ethnic character because of the large number of Hutus in the commune.[139] In Kigembe Commune, no Tutsis affiliated with the MDR.[140]

In March 1992, official commune documents reported ethnic tensions within the population for the first time since 1977, when administrative reports became regular.[141] On March 19, 1992, it was reported that rumors of ethnic violence to come in Ngoma Sector led a Tutsi, Augustin Nyirikindi, and his family to spend three nights outdoors fearing for their safety.[142] A few days later, in Kivuru sector, frightened Tutsis spent the night at the home of someone called Karekezi.[143] Following the political developments in the capital Kigali in mid-1993 where the MDR split, the Kigembe Commune's branch of the party followed suit in late 1993, and the Nkundabakura faction joined the MDR side.[144] After the split, Prime Minister Uwilingiyimana, one of the leading figures of the minority "moderate" faction of the MDR, visited Kigembe Commune again to lead a rally during which she criticized the Kigembe MDR-power faction and its president.[145] Later, she could no longer go to the commune because of the strength of MDR-power opposition to her.[146] The MDR-power intimidation, in the form of threats and false rumors, was increasingly defined in ethnic terms. In late 1993, Nkundabakura spread the rumor that any Tutsi home with flowerpots had hidden weapons, and the latrines of Tutsi homes would be used to bury Hutus.[147] Gaston Mazina, whose Tutsi identity was combined with his social vulnerability as a frail villager who could neither read nor write, was repeatedly beaten during MDR-power rallies in Ngera Sector, which had the largest proportion of Tutsis in the commune at 33 percent of the population. During the routine animations that preceded its meetings, MDR-power supporters used blows to force some Tutsis of Ngera Sector to dance while chanting the praises of the party. The Tutsis would be sent away after the animation because they were not allowed to attend the rally. Some people affiliated with the PSD were also beaten.[148]

The fact that the MDR had many followers in Kigembe Commune substantially affected local Hutu-Tutsi relations. Calixte Kayisire explains how social relations in the commune evolved after the emergence of political parties:

> Personally, I think that the relations between Hutus and Tutsis began to change in 1992, 1993, but even that was not to the point of killing each other, but there was an atmosphere of mistrust following the creation of political parties. . . . Yes, you could be my friend with whom I share everything. But with the creation of parties, you could join a certain party of which I am not a member. So there, you believe in a party that is different from mine . . . that's already a misunderstanding; we no longer speak the same language. In that case, this group organizes its rallies, another its rallies, and so on. . . . Things did not change to the point where people would hurt each other, but we could no longer confide in each other because we said, "after all, I don't know what they say at their meetings." There you have it: mistrust.[149]

The Social Democratic Party (PSD)

The second most important political party in Kigembe Commune between 1991 and 1994 was the PSD. As it did elsewhere in the country, the PSD recruited its members mainly from among the elite of the commune, educated and employed people. Some of the civil servants in the MRND before the party was forcibly expelled from the commune by the MDR joined the PSD. A large majority of teachers also belonged to the PSD. One of the PSD political strong points in Kigembe was its opposition to ethnic animosity.[150] The MDR carried out its takeover by *kubohoza* in June 1992 only in Mvejuru Region sectors of Kigembe Commune, which had a small Tutsi population. In Nyakare Region, the other part of Kigembe, with a much larger Tutsi population, the PSD was the most popular party. Yet Tutsis joined the PSD with little enthusiasm, so that when the PL appeared, they left the PSD to join the PL.[151] In Kigembe Commune, the PSD did not enjoy the support of the majority of Tutsis, but did attract young Hutu progressive schoolteachers and Hutus who had family ties with Tutsis.[152] The PSD political strategies in the commune centered mostly on denouncing the MRND regime failure in the socioeconomic sphere resulting from its corruption and incompetence; the PSD promised to reform conditions primarily in terms of people's welfare. The PSD also played the regionalist card and criticized the Bashiru domination of the country.[153] Generally, witnesses of the democratization period in the commune emphasize that the PSD was peaceful. However, with the arrival of the Hutu-power movement in mid-1993, the PSD president in Kigembe Commune (of Burundian origin nicknamed "Compagnie" Nderabanzi) led a portion of his party members into declaring itself "power," thus participating in the anti-Tutsi campaign.[154]

The third party represented in the commune was the Liberal Party (PL), which attracted only Tutsis. The party held its first rally on April 12, 1992, about eight months after the MDR, PSD, and MRND had arrived in the commune. This rally, which took place near the official commune building, did not attract a big crowd. When the MDR-power party began to turn increasingly violent at the end of 1993, PL activities became increasingly clandestine.[155]

Finally, the arrival of Hutu political refugees regularly crossing the border from Burundi exacerbated the ethnically and politically charged atmosphere in Kigembe Commune. Previously, security reports from early 1992 had mentioned the occasional arrival of refugees when Burundi was putting in place the "politics of unity."[156] After Burundian president Ndadaye was assassinated by Tutsi army officers on October 21, 1993, and after the subsequent massacres, Kigembe Commune received almost 50,000 Burundian Hutu refugees in just a few months, thereby doubling its population.[157] The arrival of these refugees fleeing interethnic civil war had strong political and social consequences in the commune by reinforcing the atmosphere of ethnic tension. The majority of refugees allied with the Hutu-power faction.[158] Nevertheless, maybe because of a history of persecution, despite the increasing threats and the rising interethnic tension by the end of 1993, the Tutsis never thought that their lives could be at risk before April 1994. The genocide caught them completely by surprise.[159]

Genocide in Kigembe

I present the events leading to the extermination of the Tutsi population of Kigembe Commune—and of the Tutsis from the neighboring communes caught on their way to seek refuge in Burundi—in three phases. First, I discuss the political events as they led to leaders of political parties taking over control of the commune. Second, I discuss the main massacre in the commune, which took place at the commune office and at the neighboring integrated rural vocational and training school (CERAI) from April 19 to 21, 1994. Finally, I will analyze how events unfolded in the different sectors of Kigembe Commune.

In March 1992, the Tutsis of Kigembe numbered 3,712.[160] Not all of the Tutsis from Kigembe who died were murdered in their own commune; many had taken refuge in the large churches near the Nyakare Region, such as Nyumba and Kansi Churches in Gishamvu and Nyaruhengeri Communes, respectively, the sites of massive massacres. However, between 2,000 and 3,000 people were killed in the commune, most of them during the massacres of April 19–21; many were local Kigembe Tutsis, others were Tutsis from outside the commune passing through while fleeing Burundi.[161] Both Kigembe and Nyakizu Communes were points of contact with the border of Burundi.

This was an area of high Tutsi concentration that covered the northern part of Kigembe Commune and the neighboring Nyakizu Commune and then stretched to the north. With no official institution set up to control the Kigembe Commune's territory and its border with Burundi—that is, no organized militias and very few security officers—the local people along with the Burundian refugees exercised control of movement of people and effectively prevented Tutsis from crossing into Burundi.

Political Parties Seize Control of the Commune

On Monday, April 11, 1994, four days after the massacres began nationally, Prefect Jean-Baptiste Habyarimana of Butare called a meeting of the prefecture council security committee on maintaining local peace and security.[162] The military commandant of Butare, Lt. Col. Tharcisse Muvunyi, who was present, assured burgomasters of army support if necessary.[163]

During the same meeting, it was announced that neighboring Gikongoro Prefecture had turned into a bloody battlefield, and burgomasters were requested to do all they could to maintain peace in their respective communes. The following day, Tuesday, April 12, 1994, after massacres had begun in Mubuga Commune of Gikongoro, neighboring Nyakizu Commune, and a little farther north of Kigembe Commune, Burgomaster Karekezi went to sensitize the people on maintaining peace in Fugi, Ngoma, Murama, and Ngera Sectors, adjacent to Nyakizu Commune. On the evening of April 12, the first refugees from Nyakizu fleeing the massacres in Gikongoro Prefecture arrived in the Kigembe Commune and were sent to Higiro Parish. On Friday, April 15, the burgomaster, accompanied by commune police officers and people of Ngera and Murama Sectors, stationed himself at the border between Ngera Sector and Nyakizu Commune to repulse the attackers in pursuit of the refugees. From then on, the flood of refugees swelled, comprising not only those fleeing the Gikongoro massacres but also the Nyakizu massacres, which had just begun. With the descent of Nyakizu into the violence, the atmosphere in Kigembe became tense. On Saturday, April 16, the priest of Higiro Parish asked the burgomaster to get rid of the refugees, numbering about a hundred, who according to the good father were disturbing the "smooth functioning of parish activities" and for whom he no longer had enough food.[164]

The burgomaster brought the refugees into the CERAI building near the Nyaruteja training center, five kilometers from the border with Burundi. Nyaruteja Sector had many Burundian Hutu refugees, and the proximity of the two groups caused concern for the burgomaster, who decided to convene the heads of the political parties in the commune to decide on the security measures for the refugees. Present at the meeting were the presidents of the MDR-power and of the MDR moderate factions, of the PL and of the PSD. The meeting participants decided to ask the prefect to move the refugees to a more secure location. Until Saturday, April 16, the burgomaster had the situation in the commune under control, and his authority was still respected.[165] However, the villagers took advantage of the disorder in the surrounding regions and the charged atmosphere and, spontaneously and without orders from above, set about threatening their Tutsi neighbors with the goal of seizing their properties.

On Sunday, April 17, the relative calm was overturned. In Ngera Sector, at around 4:00 p.m., the first attacks against the Tutsis began, and afterward, in Kigembe Sector, a house was burned down in the early evening. At around 9:30 p.m., in Kivuru Sector, a massacre began. On Monday, April 18, in Kivuru Sector, the killings resumed, and in Ngera, Murama, Kigembe, and Kigali Sectors, the Hutu population encircled, gathered, and led the Tutsis in a procession to the commune office. On Monday, April 18, unaware of the development and final objective of these actions, the burgomaster headed to Kivuru Sector to the home of one of his deputies, where about fifty Tutsis from the sector had sought refuge. He addressed the attackers encircling the house, asking them to allow the Tutsis to return to their homes. The Tutsis cried out, asking what they were returning to because their houses had just been reduced to ashes.[166] The burgomaster led the refugees to the parish near his home. This group included the family of his Tutsi wife.[167]

On the same day, Nkundabakura, president of the local MDR-power faction, came to take the refugees at the Higiro Church and the primary school and brought them to the CERAI and the commune office building. On the morning of April 19, the presidents of the various Hutu parties in the commune—the MDR-power faction, the "moderate" MDR, the PSD, and the CDR—came to "attack" the burgomaster at his home. They came for the members of his wife's family in his home, telling him that if he resisted, they would burn down his house, kill him, and seize the Tutsis he was protecting.[168] After consulting with his in-laws, he saw that he did not have many options, and he finally gave them up. The burgomaster then went to the home of the PSD president, a former comrade in the party, to plead that the children and the women held at the CERAI and the commune office be allowed to return to their homes. At the home of the PSD president Compagnie, he found four party leaders in a meeting. The four made fun of him. The party presidents resolved to hire five of their own "police officers" and give them weapons found at the commune office.[169] The party leaders assigned themselves this armed force because they could not rely upon the regular commune police officers, who remained loyal to the burgomaster to the last.

Also on Tuesday, April 19, the burgomaster went to Butare Town to request help from the army in restoring order to Kigembe Commune. Arriving on the outskirts of the town, he came across a group of about twelve soldiers in a red van that happened to be heading for Kigembe. The soldiers dissuaded him from going to see the military commandant of Butare, Muvunyi, saying they were in fact on their way to restore order in the commune. On the way there, the soldiers realized they did not share the same objectives with the burgomaster, so they dropped him off at his home, advising him not to move, and they went to the commune office.[170]

The killings that had begun in Kivuru Sector on the evening of April 17, along with rounding up Tutsis from various sectors and taking them to the commune office building and the CERAI, constituted the first stages of the plan to exterminate the Tutsis of Kigembe Commune. The group that covertly organized the activities revealed itself the next day during the attack on the burgomaster at his home to take his wife and her family members.

After the burgomaster and his small group of police officers had been neutralized, the genocide in Kigembe went forward. The representatives of the parties of the former opposition turned out to be the key promoters of the extermination.

The Massacres at the Commune Office Building and CERAI

As a result of the political party presidents' meeting at Compagnie's home, Nkundabakura toured the commune in his truck, equipped with a loudspeaker. He called on the population to take arms and go to the commune office building, "which had been attacked from Burundi by the Inkotanyi."[171] There was also beating of drums to rouse the population. Hundreds of men from the surrounding areas arrived carrying traditional weapons and covered with banana leaves.[172] Among them were MDR supporters who had participated in the takeover of power from the MRND in June 1992, along with many Burundian refugees.[173] All of the neighboring areas, the roads and paths that passed by the CERAI and the commune office building, were filled with armed men, with women and children.[174] During the day of April 19, Nkundabakura delivered three truckloads of men from the farthest sectors armed with traditional weapons at the commune office building.[175] In the early afternoon, Nkundabakura ordered the Tutsis of Kigembe who had assembled at the commune office building to move and join the other Tutsis from Gikongoro Prefecture and Nyakizu Commune who had assembled at the CERAI, 200 meters away from the commune office building. The Tutsis refused to move. Four of them acquiesced and left the main commune compound with their cows. They had hardly reached the road before they were killed with machetes.[176] A young man hurled a spear at Nkundabakura, who withdrew with his group.[177] A few minutes later, at around 2:00 p.m., the twelve soldiers with whom the burgomaster had ridden back arrived and began to shoot and throw grenades at the CERAI as well as the commune office building. The massacre lasted two hours, until around 4:00 p.m., and then the soldiers withdrew. Immediately, the inhabitants, who included a significant number of Burundian refugees, encircled the two buildings, prevented the Tutsis from escaping, and entered the buildings to finish off the survivors.[178] The killings by machete began the evening of April 19 and were finished on April 22, 1994. Under cover of night, while the moon was rising, some men managed to cross the river five kilometers away and reach Burundi.[179] When the massacre was over, the commune PSD president, the businessman Compagnie Nderabanzi, was given the responsibility of burying the victims. Also on April 19, the soldiers went to the Nkomero marketplace in Ngoma Sector, where Tutsi refugees had gathered, and massacred the refugees.[180] Afterward, groups of killers made up of people from the neighborhood continued to comb through the neighborhoods in search of Tutsis who had managed to survive by hiding.[181]

The Genocide in the Sectors

The first spontaneous acts of hostility and attacks by Hutu villagers against Tutsis independent of orders from above were consistently motivated by the desire to feast on Tutsi cows and, more generally, loot their property.[182] From April 9 to 12, 1994, Joseph Habyarimana, a young Tutsi intellectual from Murama Sector, participated in the patrol rounds. One day the villagers doing the rounds caught a refugee coming from Gikongoro Prefecture with his cow and its calf. They told the refugee that they would seize his cow and that if he wanted it back, he had to pay RF10,000. The refugee had to give up his calf in place of his cow, and the men cut it up and shared the pieces on the spot.[183] Habyarimana said that "in this locality of Runyinya (Murama Sector), people began to kill the cows that belonged to the refugees from Gikongoro. The burgomaster jailed four people, but after one day he released them, and they returned home. After that, one could understand what was going to follow."[184]

In Kivuru Sector, on Sunday, April 10, Katabirora, a Tutsi and friend of Ignace Nsengimana "was worried by threats from his neighbors, who swore that they would eat the cow Katabirora had received as dowry for his daughter, Rose Mukagatare. He asked me to keep the cow at my place."[185] This extract from Nsengimana's written testimony shows some local dynamics underlying the massacre orchestrated from above:

> On Saturday, April 16, 1994, I was forced to do the rounds by the authorities of my cell, Akabuye, who were in turn under pressure from the residents who said that even intellectuals had to collaborate, whether they liked it or not. When I arrived at the Kivuru bars where others were gathering, I realized that a certain Karengera, son of Munyankiko, was in the process of inciting people, telling them that just nearby, at Nemba, were families of "accomplices" who were sheltering Inkotanyi and who should be searched. When I heard these lies, I was the first to speak out and explain to this man and his gang the following: (1) that according to the Arusha accords between the Rwandan

government and the RPF-Inkotanyi, all Rwandans were the same; they were all equal before the law, without any discrimination. And that therefore nobody should give himself the right to accuse others of this or the other; (2) there was no RPF soldier in Nemba because I was there for the burial of the grandson of the late Charles Karera; and (3) that the patrol had been launched to guarantee the peace of the people, and they therefore had no right to spend nights ransacking the homes of families. In no way would I support anyone intending to attack the Nemba population, and whoever did that would be clearly responsible for the consequences. On hearing these remarks, Karengera was filled with rage and approached with the intention of striking me with his spear. I stepped back five meters, and I was saved by the late Katabirora and Kambanda (Mugobe Cell), Niyibaho alias Seromba (Mugobe Cell), and Anastase Gizimana, who was in charge of Akabuye Cell. Karengera calmed down but insisted on carrying out his plans. He told me: "You can go and order university people around, but as for the people of Kivuru, they will do what they decide to do." He spat in my face and challenged the people present, asking "Is that not true?" and the others relented, "Yes! Yes!" He then added, "Comrades in arms, forward!" The majority of them did not dare; only six people followed him. I was not able to know their names because it was dark (it was around 9:00 p.m.). When they arrived in Nemba, they met the people of this hill, including Faustin Nshiyimana, who was the deputy burgomaster. Karengera addressed them, saying, "The other people who are on patrol at the school sent me to come fetch you." The others said, "Let's go!" They returned together. When Karengera arrived where we were, he said, to save face, "These are the men I had gone looking for; I found them carrying out the patrol." Meanwhile, the rest of us immediately booed, saying, "Tell them clearly the criminal intentions that sent you there, rather than lie to us!" At that moment, a certain Mpakaniya (a resident of Kinyambo in Akabuye Cell) said, "This patrol is a patrol of cowards" and immediately left."[186]

Because his intervention made the attackers abort their mission, Nsengimana was chased and threatened by the residents of his village. "On April 19, 1994, almost all the men and youths of Akabuye and Mugobe Cells led an attack on my home at 4:40 p.m., intending to kill us should they find the Katabirora family (Mugobe Cell) or any other Tutsi."[187]

This extract depicted the armed villagers gathering again for a surveillance patrol without orders from anyone, personally planning to attack and loot although order still prevailed in the commune. For that, they adopted the politicians' rhetoric, which accused the Tutsis of collaborating with the enemy. When Karengera and Nsengimana were engaged in an altercation, Gizimana, the head of the cell, intervened with the others to calm Karengera down. Karengera was also forced to make a retreat when he met the deputy burgomaster accompanied by several men protecting the neighborhood. The change in the routine was also demonstrated by the villagers asserting themselves by insisting that "intellectuals" participate in the patrols. During such moments of trouble, the violent villagers took a leading role.

In addition, on Saturday, April 16, in Ngera Sector, attacks on Tutsis were aimed at taking their cattle. According to Gaston Mazina, a Tutsi survivor, Hutus from Nyakizu incited the people of Ngera Sector to attack their Tutsi neighbors. "Everything began at Nyakizu. The Hutus from there said that the Hutus here were useless, that they were just lazy, while they on the other side had already found something to eat."[188]

> On Saturday, April 16, they came at us with machetes. Here on Ngera hill. They began to cut down our cows with machetes. We were still there . . . they formed groups of close to fifty people. They attacked one homestead, came across a child, cut him down, came across cattle, cut them down. They distributed the tasks, saying, "Such and such a team should go there, the other there." They called that working. They said they were going to work. . . . They created such a terrible racket. . . . As for us, we went to hide in the anti-erosion ditches. While they were busy eating our cows, we ran away. You could not leave with a child like this one here. The child would go one way, and you would go the other. Nobody could leave with his child or wife. They ate our cows and looted our property on Saturday. As for me, I fled toward Nyumba [Church], and on Sunday and Monday, they started killing.[189]

Mazina lost his wife and nine of his ten children to the massacres. Joseph Nzabonima recounts how on the afternoon of April 17 in Kivuru Sector, the villagers formed groups according to their party affiliations and attacked Tutsis of their neighborhoods.

> I think it was Sunday. I was chatting with others. There were some young people, but there were also married men, people of all ages, but all male. In our area, there were political party activities, and sometimes some confrontations between the residents because of these parties. The MDR and the MRND fought the most. That is how things happened. A Tutsi from the neighborhood, Straton Habimana, had entrusted his cow to a Hutu herder, who had brought it back for fear that people would eat it. The cow refused to stay at its owner's home and followed the herder. While the cow was following him, this group of MDR members, led by a man called Samura Laurien (he is in fact in prison here at Rwandex) seized the cow, slaughtered it, and ate it. Afterward, those who could not return home with the meat brought it to be grilled on my garden fire. In fact, we argued violently because I considered that abuse. I did not know what was going to follow. Later in the evening, when we had just begun doing the patrol, the men, neighbors with whom I was to go on patrol, told me to go with them to Evariste Ntirushwa's home to take his pig for us to eat. I told them, "You, you have just eaten Pascal's cow, with no one telling you a thing—you are now also going to eat this man's pig—how do you think this will end?" Because the MDR was strong in our area, the locals rushed to join the parties, but I was a PSD member. So at that moment, people continued to crowd around. Those who were killed in our area included a certain Kabirwa Apollinaire, who was my neighbor, a Tutsi; Pascal Habineza, whose cow had been eaten, Straton Bizumuremyi, and Ladislas Ngezi, who was with us on the patrol. Canisius Munyentwari, the farmer who had formed this gang—I think he was not arrested, unfortu-

nately—went in front and led our attack on the home of Ntirushwa. We did not find him at home, so we looted some items. Personally I took a small National Panasonic radio. We then returned, and honestly, I did not think that massacres were going to take place.[190]

This group of villagers, whose first aggressive action was looting, carried out murderous attacks the following day. Also on April 17, in Kivuru Sector but in a neighboring cell, as Nsengimana testified, "The residents seized the cow of their Tutsi neighbor called Cyprien (he lived in Nyagasozi in Akabuye Cell) and ate it in public 1:00 in the afternoon. While they were slaughtering it, Cyprien went in search of the authorities of Kivuru Sector and the members of the cell committees, and the latter answered: 'What do you want us to do?' The man left in tears."[191]

The first house burned down in Kigembe Sector was also the work of villagers seeking to loot, as Burgomaster Karekezi recounts:

On the evening of April 17, I was coming from one of the cells of the sectors neighboring Nyakizu Commune; it must have been Ngoma. I arrived at home toward 8:00 in the evening. It was at this time that I was alerted and informed that someone's house had just been burned. This was the first incident in my commune, at 8:00 in the evening, at the house of Elie Kubwimana, someone warned me, saying, "They are destroying his house—as someone in authority, do something." It was in Kigembe Sector. I got a police officer and left with him for the scene. I went to stop people in the process of destroying the house. It had a tile roof. The people climbed on the roof. They had chased away the family. His wife and children had taken refuge at my house, and as for Elie, I don't know where he went. I went to scare off the attackers. This was the season when the sorghum stalks were high. As soon as I had scared them off, they took refuge in the sorghum field, waiting for me to leave so that they could return and finish the job. We chased them away one more time. They did not go far. This man owned cows, small livestock, pigs, and goats, and then he was not there, so I was compelled to spend the night to ensure the safety of his property with some residents of this area in Kigembe Sector. It was the evening of Sunday April 17.[192]

The events in the Kigembe Commune gained momentum from the evening of Sunday, April 17, with the first murders occurring in Kivuru Sector. This was the only sector in which a real massacre occurred without the participation of soldiers. The following day, people in the other sectors proceeded to enforce physical control over the Tutsis by preventing them from fleeing. The nights of April 17 and 18 marked a turning point. In his letter, Nsengimana recounts how the killings began in Kivuru Sector.

That night of April 17, around 9:20 p.m., I was in the house and heard the movement of people from Nyagacaca (Mugobe Cell) heading toward Gihishabwenge, and they were screaming: "Here come these Inkotanyi, watch out!" A few minutes later, I saw houses in Gihishabwenge burning, from the place called Kivumu to Mwumba. They killed every person they found in the homes. . . . That attack, which consisted of a whole night of killing, appears to have been carried out by authorities of cells such as Mugobe—by Firmin Bahizi and Demokarasi in particular. Another attack started from Kabuye (in Rugogwe), and all those who did not yet know what was happening and who had not yet fled were massacred. Afterward, people such as Maniraho, Sebahire's son; Noël Rwakunswe; Ruremesha; Minani, Martin's son; and their accomplices publicly sang about their murderous exploits.[193]

On Monday, April 18, in Kivuru Sector, as people on the other hills screamed, "The Bahutu revolution has begun,"[194] other attacks with the motive to kill occurred, such as the one that began at around 10 a.m. led by the councilor of Kivuru Sector, the chief magistrate of the local court, and his son, Firmin Mazimpaka, the accountant.[195] "It was they who led Monday's attack on the home of Marius Kabonera; they fought—I was watching from somewhere—they fought, and at one time even I was part of it. Finally, Kabandana; his son Mugemana; his son Narcisse; his neighbor Joseph Mutarambirwa; Mutarambirwa's wife, Anésie Mukaruhingo; and a child were killed."[196]

Nzabonima, a repentant killer, continued his account by explaining the mass mobilization in this murderous attack:

> In general, those were the people who stood out, but if you carry out a meticulous investigation, you will find that nobody in our village remained behind. There's only one person I can say didn't do anything, a young man called Célestin Nkundimana, who had an ailing stomach. He is the only person who I can say was not implicated. Everyone else, all the male residents of all categories and without exception, participated in the attacks. Even if it was not there, in the field [here he uses the French term "sur le terrain," literally "on the ground"] they were close and they were helping.[197]

On the same day, Nzabonima participated in another *igitero* (group attack), a killing spree on which he did not want to elaborate. "In the meantime, it was there that Canisius and his friends, the Karekezis, Kabahizi, the Bahizis, led an attack, *igitero*, and I was one of them—I was so visible that if you asked, 'I want to know those who were in that *igitero*,' my name would distinctly come up."[198]

The Bahizi in question was a member of the Mugobe Cell committee. In contrast to the previous attacks, primarily motivated by looting, these killing sprees were systematically managed by the local authorities, members and heads of the cell committees, sector councilors, and the intellectuals of the commune. In these killings, the looting villagers were at the forefront, as we have already seen with Munyetwari, who on one occasion led a looting expedition and on another took a leading role in an attack aimed at killing. When it came to possession of the personal property looted from the victims or stolen from the victims' homes, there was no organized distribution of the loot; everyone helped themselves on a first-come, first-served basis. Yet, as things went along, the first arrivals were also the most directly threatening or even the first to strike the blows. Kayisire explained the importance of looting as a motivation for the killers: "The people involved in these killings were primarily driven by their personal interests, so the most implicated were the ones who looted. The simple villagers were pursuing their interests. In some cases those who had just killed would order everybody not to touch the property of the person whose throat he had just slit. Thus, he seized the property."[199]

On Monday, April 18, Tutsis were gathered in various sectors and then taken to the commune office building. In Murama Sector, Tutsis were surrounded in their homes and then rounded up, but before carrying out the transfer, the Hutu population, as soon as there was a chance, took time to eat the cows that belonged to the victims. Isaïe Buyenzi, a Tutsi survivor, explained:

> One would come to the house and lead the whole family out. . . . They surrounded us in the same area. I lived at a little higher elevation. They distributed our cows among themselves right before our eyes. We were still there. Toward 10:00 in the morning, they said to us: "Hey—go, your safety is guaranteed in the commune!" . . . They herded us away as one herds goats to market. They stripped us. We were left with nothing. Everyone took what he could. But when it came to the cows, they distributed them as we got out of our houses. They feasted on the cows in front of us. We had many cows. The rest of the cows were sold. As they looted, someone would grab a coat, for example, a hat, and so on. . . . The people from Murama transferred us to the people of Kigembe Sector, and so on and so forth. Those from Kigembe Sector gave us up to the killers of Nyanza Sector. And we had already arrived at the commune building [in Nyaruteja Sector]. You think we left voluntarily? Not at all! If it had been so, some of us would have been able to escape. They were behind, we were walking in front, and whoever strayed was cut down.[200]

This testimony shows the importance of mass participation in the essential stage of the extermination process, which consisted of controlling and transferring the large Tutsi population of Murama Sector.[2021] This was done in the absence of a prepared system of mass transportation and incarceration for the victims. When it came to the number of people who participated in the raids, Buyenzi strongly asserted,

> For example, at Nyarugano Cell, if we counted the families that belonged to this village, there were approximately two hundred and fifty. Let's say there were roughly two hundred killers or maybe two hundred and twenty. . . . Everyone participated: girls, women, children, and the elderly. Nobody re-

mained at home; everyone was very involved. . . . I even think that they did not have time to prepare meals; maybe they were doing that at night. Even the one who did not kill shouted. . . . They beat pans and pots; they aroused fear like hunters pursuing their prey.[202]

According to Buyenzi, people were called to participate in the operations by blowing whistles; in any case, that was not necessary because they were always there, close by. They had to stay vigilant to gather people to kill."[203]

When asked whether pressure was put on people in the neighborhood to act in this way, Buyenzi replied: "No, on the contrary, people went voluntarily. There was no pressure. If it was because of pressure, nobody would have died because they would have helped people to escape. The people needed to kill, they were thirsty. . . . What is striking is that they were like angry dogs. They were like mad dogs. The people behaved as if they had been possessed."[204]

Buyenzi also insists on the organized nature of the operations:

> They were like warriors, they had chiefs. . . . It was sometimes the intellectuals, sometimes the traders; for example, Karayenga was the school director. People like Murara, Kadafi, and Nzabonima were traders. They came to the commune to see the number of people still alive. They even led an attack at Nyumba [Church]. They took cars to go kill those who had taken refuge at Nyumba.[205]

To go back to the issue of material rewards as a motive for participation, one must also raise the issue of land. In his testimony, Nzabonima gives, not without nuances, insight into the intensity of the fight over distribution of land.

> Personally, I cannot say that we did that, nobody can say that they did that to acquire land. Even the fierce battles for land that followed—that is where I got this scar on my forehead, when we were fighting for the Tutsi farms—the goal was not to say, "I'm going to own this piece of land"; it was more that, "I'm going to give this amount of money so that so-and-so does not get ahead of me"; if he gives RF1,000, I will give RF1,500 so that it will be given to me." The goal was to gain access to a large and fertile piece of land but not to make it our own. Our ideas were not the same at that time. That is why the weight of our crimes is not the same. But according to me, nobody was looking for land.[206]

What Nzabonima said here is that concerning land, the killers' objective was not to own it but rather to be able to pay a good price to have access and farm it. One of the questions Nsengimana asked at the end of his testimony also points to the violence that dominated the distribution of the loot. He stated that it was important to identify "those who incited others to kill, those who killed each other during the looting, those who took the property of the people who were killed or had fled."[207]

When it comes to knowing whether the people who engaged in the massacres thought they would benefit from the land that belonged to the victims, Kabutura, respected for his integrity in the sector, explained: "The people knew, given what had happened in 1959. Those who had been chased away in 1959, 1960, and 1961 had not returned. And their land was distributed in 1962. They feared nothing because they wanted to grab these pieces of land whose owners would not return."[208]

Kabutura explained in this way the procedure for gaining access to the land that belonged to victims of the massacres:

> When it came to the farms and the food, these were entrusted to the councilors of the sector. Whoever wanted to occupy these properties had to pay some money. At first, people sold the loot and kept the money. Later, all the properties fell into the hands of the commune. For two months, that is, May and June, the authorities accumulated money from property owned by the people killed. One went to the location, and the money was paid to the councilor. You went to the councilor and told him, "I want to buy this banana farm." The councilor then asked you to go visit the place first, and if it was a large farm, two or three people had to rent it. Then he distributed the land among all of you, you all gave him money, he wrote a receipt, and he deposited the money with the commune. I don't know the purpose for the money—that was the procedure—but in the meantime, during the three months, money from the village was paid to the commune.[209]

On the question of whether those who had not participated in killing could gain access to the land, Kabutura responded,

> Oh no! On the contrary, that person had accounts to settle. He would be publicly brought to a place where everybody was, and he would be asked to explain his inaction. These individuals had problems; they were not to receive a thing. Even if you wanted to rent land with your own money, you were declined. They said, "You were of no help to us. There are brave men." The "brave men" were rewarded first and the others taken aside and made to explain where they were during the events.[210]

Therefore a strong competition existed, even between killers, for access to the victims' land. This land was leased and not ceded in a definitive manner. Even in these exceptional circumstances, the authorities quickly wanted to restore some semblance of order and display some sort of legalism. The violent competition for access to land, coupled with this legalism, perversely further incited the murder of Tutsis by their Hutu relatives. In fact, Hutu members of mixed families could inherit the property of their dead Tutsi relatives. That's how Joseph Habyarimana explained the murder of his young nieces and nephew by their own Hutu father-in-law.[211]

The Political Supervision of Villagers Who Killed

The first attacks against Tutsis aimed at looting were initiated by the villagers. These attacks took shape during the patrols, and those taking part were often men from the same political party, but in this case party membership was only a passive basis for common action. The attacks aimed at killing or rounding up Tutsis directly involved political party structures. Kabutura explained:

> Within each party in the rural areas, there were high and low ranks. Among the members of each party were propagandists responsible for spreading the ideology. In fact, it was members of the committees of the parties who said that people had to stand strong in order to fight the Tutsis' objective, discourage the return of the Tutsis, and thus fight the Inkotanyi. In fact, they took people and enlisted them in the war to kill—to kill without cause.[212]

In his interview, Faustin Matabaro brings in the question of the power relations within the groups that led the killings at the sector level. "It is of course members of political parties; they went to the meetings, they had turned themselves into great authorities, into councilors; they had assumed power in the sectors."[213]

Almost all of the witnesses questioned said that the roundups of Tutsis and killings in the sectors were led by sector councilors, heads of cells, and intellectuals, and all of the members of political parties were working in a collegial fashion. Similarly, the various political factions, except the PL of course, carried out the genocide at both the commune and sector levels in the same collegial manner. The formal administrative authorities were not necessarily the most involved. In April 1994, all the incumbent councilors had been elected in September 1991 under the banner of the MRND. All had since changed parties following the takeover by the MDR, and out of the twelve councilors, ten joined the PSD and the remaining two the MDR. The unity of the moment did not erase the difference in political strength, so the MDR-power faction assumed leadership when raw violence prevailed. The important role political party affiliations, especially the MDR, played in the direction of and participation in the massacres can also be read in the words of the commune police officer, Martin Ntamishimiro, who witnessed firsthand the staging and implementation of the massacre at the commune office building on April 19, 1994. "In my view, there is a relationship between the killings that took place in our area and the destruction of houses in 1992: because the culprits saw that they would not be prosecuted, they began doing it again. . . . Those I was able to identify may not be many, but they were the same ones who spent their time in the streets beating drums; they were mostly MDR members."[214] The 1992 event to which Ntamishimiro refers was the violent MDR takeover of the commune.

Political party leaders and other ordinary individuals seem to have had two major motivations for taking a leading role in the massacres at the commune and sector levels. Some of the politicians had been turned by their personal and family experience into depositories of the hostile anti-Tutsi ideology inherited from the days of the revolution and the First Republic. MDR-power president Nkundabakura was a thick lout whose temperament naturally inclined him toward the use of violence in his quest for power. However, his choice of the MDR faction loyal to PARMEHUTU was definitely influenced by the fact that his father, Ngoga, had been an MDR-PARMEHUTU activist and one of the main promoters of violence against Tutsis in Kigembe during the revolution, and as a result, the first burgomaster of the newly created commune.[215] During the genocide, a "roadblock" where Tutsis were stopped or often killed on the spot was located in front of the Chez Ngoga Bar, which Nkundabakura's father had owned in his working-class neighborhood of Cyarwa in Butare Town. The barricade was guarded by Micomyiza, Ngoga's son and Nkundabakura's brother, a university student who had organized a gang of Burundian thugs to guard the roadblock and kill many people.[216]

The other prominent PARMEHUTU loyalist, Thaddée Karayenga, director of the CERAI of Ngoma Sector, was accused of having led the roundups and killings of Tutsis from Marama and Ngera Sectors as well as the massacres at Nyumba Church in Gishamvu Commune. Karayenga was the son of Sebabirigi, one of the PARMEHUTU propagandists who also played a key role in the anti-Tutsi violence of August 1961.[217] When Karayenga was a primary school teacher in Murama Sector in the 1980s, he was openly hostile toward Tutsis and tried to transmit that hostility to the children in his charge. In March 1992, he was elected to the MRND commune committee, then elected president of the MRND committee of Murama Sector. He joined the MDR after its takeover of the commune. Karayenga belonged to the same group of rural intellectuals who preserved the historical memory of the MDR-PARMEHUTU.

Nkundabakura and Karayenga's loyalty to the original MDR-PARMEHUTU ideology was part of a larger lineage. Both belonged to the Abasozo clan. This clan was heavily implicated in MDR-PARMEHUTU activism and in the party's anti-Tutsi violence in Kigembe in 1961. It had allowed clan members to accumulate land, acquire political posts, send their children to school, and exercise influence in the community. These influential dynasties, which owed their social ascension to the 1959 revolution, definitely helped ensure the political revival of the PARMEHUTU and of its violently sectarian politics in Kigembe Commune. It is a strong bet that such families must have existed in other communes in the southwest of the prefecture, where an important segment of the Hutu population had subscribed to the PARMEHUTU in the 1960s and where the genocide in Butare Prefecture began.

The participation of several intellectuals, especially from the PSD and from the "moderate" MDR, in the genocide in Kigembe Commune was strongly linked to the military and political circumstances in late 1993 and in the month of April 1994 at the national level. The case of Innocent Rwamigabo, a member of the PSD political bureau of the Butare branch, was revealing of the sudden change of heart of some of the intellectuals in the commune. Rwamigabo fit the profile of a Hutu intellectual supporter of the PSD: he was a former midlevel civil servant in the central government, had a university education, came from a family of well-to-do Hutus during the monarchy and the colonial era, and his mother and wife were Tutsis.[218] His sudden change of perspective, like that of many other PSD supporters, was the apparent culmination of the debate between those who saw the war against the RPF as an existential struggle between Hutus and Tutsis and those who interpreted it essentially as a political fight for change. The assassination of Burundian president Ndadaye, the shooting down of President Habyarimana's plan in April 1994 (depicted as the work of the RPF), and the resumption of an all-out war worked to the advantage of those who had always presented the conflict as one between Hutus and Tutsis and changed the minds of many in the killers' camp who had resisted the propaganda of hatred until those events.

Rallying PSD members to the genocidal agenda was catastrophic because it created a united political front for the massacres in the commune. This unity added cohesion to the control of Kigembe Commune and the Tutsis. Given that this was a remote region bordering Burundi and a potential border crossing for tens of thousands of Tutsis who lived in the wider southwest region of Butare Prefecture, any breaches in the control of the area might have allowed more Tutsis to find refuge in Burundi.

Manipulation

In order to encourage mass participation, the strategy of the leaders of the genocide in Kigembe Commune was to create fear and count on a violent reaction. This strategy emerged from the official propaganda on the radio asking Hutus to defend themselves by killing their Tutsi neighbors because their own lives were threatened by the RPF.[219] On April 19, 1994, Nkundabakura toured the commune in a truck equipped with a loud speaker, announcing that the RPF had attacked the commune from Burundi and asking the population to take up arms and defend themselves from the enemy. Dramatizing the threat the RPF was supposed to represent by making it immediate and close bore fruit. People heard this appeal as well as drumbeats summoning them to the commune office building. As Ntamishimiro explains, "People came without anyone going to look for them—of their own free will. They came from everywhere. They were many, including Burundian refugees and many other people coming from the surrounding sectors."[220] Burgomaster Karekezi "saw some individuals passing near [his] home, quite disgruntled, who were heading for the killings."[221]

Seven years later, Matabaro explained how ordinary people easily accepted the official propaganda and started attacking their neighbors for their alleged complicity with the RPF:

> As for me, I was in my cell, and not many people were killed there in any case. Someone came from the commune, for example, let's say a soldier, and was telling people to liberate themselves since they were at risk of being captured. So people asked: "We'll be captured by whom?" He replied: "You will be captured by the RPF." So we started seeing people burn houses, the police started to shoot, and the residents attacked their neighbors; they began to kill them and to eat their cows. That is how I saw things.[222]

Ambiguities in Local Participation

Propaganda and manipulation indeed played an important role, but certain ambiguities in the behavior of the killers tend to mitigate the idea of ideology blinding the participants. Among these ambiguities was that many killers sought to camouflage themselves. After Nkundabakura's call to arms against the Inkotanyi and the drumbeats to rally the population, Ntamishimiro, who was at the commune office building, explained that people responded in the neighborhood as well as in the neighboring sectors en masse. Their attire greatly surprised him.

> Almost everyone was covered in banana leaves. . . . I did not know what the leaves meant because that was my first time seeing such a thing. It seems that it was a sort of camouflage to avoid being identified because with the banana leaves, everyone looked the same. . . . In fact, they were in camouflage because they knew the things they were doing were not permitted. They knew very well that nobody had given them that order.[223]

Regarding Ngera Sector, Mazina pointed out that the people who had come to attack "were making a terrible racket, dressed in banana leaves. They covered themselves in banana leaves. They were screaming as they approached."[2264]

One can also highlight the roles some killers assumed, as if to justify their own actions to themselves. In his testimony, Nsengimana tells of being at his home in Kivuru Sector at around 9:20 p.m. on the night of April 17. He heard the movement of people from Nyagacaca (Mugobe Cell) heading toward Gihishabwenge as they yelled, "Here are the Inkotanyi, stay alert!"[225] "They were killing every person they found in the houses. As they arrived at each house, they tried to pretend by calling each other by military titles such as soldier, corporal, sergeant, captain, major, etc."[226]

Tutsi neighbors were transformed from the initial accomplices of the Inkotanyi, to being the Inkotanyi themselves when they were being killed, and in the thick of the action, the killers tried to convince themselves that they were soldiers, as if it was difficult for them to face the stark reality of their actions.

Finally, there were the *ibitero*, attack mobs, composed of a significant proportion of the male population of the area, who participated in the first weeks of the genocide. Not everyone in these groups—which could number from as few as ten to a few hundred—had the same intentions, and the extreme violence of the genocide did not neutralize the already existing relationships between the villagers.

> There was also some mistrust among the Hutus, who thought that at any moment they could be killed by other Hutus with whom they did not get along. In fact, each person was doing the best he could to save his own life. . . . They were closely following the situation so that, if necessary, they could find an escape or help their loved ones escape. . . . It was possible for you to take part in an attack with no intention to kill, but maybe with the intention to save your friend, for example, or when, for example, you were the brother-in-law of a Tutsi or even the husband of a Tutsi. After all, this individual could not wish his wife's brothers ill. That is why one had to follow the others, to know who was being targeted, to be able to help them to escape should the opportunity arise. Not all of the people who joined in the attack mobs intended to kill; there were some who wanted to know the murderers' evil intentions.[227]

By participating in the attacks, those who did not support the attacks but who joined in, often out of fear for their own security and sometimes to protect the people they were hiding, had the perverse opposite effect of giving the massacres the legitimacy of consensus.[228]

Instances of Resistance to the Genocide

The most significant attempt to resist the genocide was undoubtedly that of Burgomaster Karekezi, who did everything within his power to maintain peace in his commune and to save lives. However, his attempt at resistance yielded only limited results. The burgomaster succeeded in saving only three people but not his in-laws. He abandoned resistance when he resumed his duties as burgomaster in late April, as people in hiding continued to be killed and killers followed the interim government directive to cast the net wider to include Tutsi wives and young women, who until then had not been systematically targeted.[229] Finally, as burgomaster, he contributed to organizing the civil defense program during the month of May, which in reality was the state taking charge of the killing operations.

Hutu families who hid Tutsis provided other instances of resistance carried out in secret and therefore more effectively. Joseph Habyarimana's story provided a good illustration. He survived thanks to his Hutu cousin, who hid him for some time before other Hutu family friends took over.[230] Unfortunately, the fact that Kigembe Commune had few survivors means that such cases were rare. Finally, given that the roundup operations and killings were decentralized at the grassroots within the sectors and the cells, resistance to the genocide could have been a matter of local power relationships. Openly refusing to collaborate seemed not to have been impossible, and on occasion to be strong and determined enough to dissuade the mobs of actively engaged killers. This was how Habyarimana, a genocide survivor, saw it:

> Those who fought against the genocide and those who did not support it are only those who hid people. There was, for example, this man at whose home about ten Tutsis were found at the end of the genocide. His name was Isaïe Twagirayezu. He hid my two nephews as well as a girl called Immaculée Mukashyaka and other nephews and nieces of hers. Only these acts show that the people who saved others did not support the killings, but nobody took a microphone or organized a meeting to say that what was being done was wrong. Twagirayezu had several sons with violent tempers, which means that nobody touched him. He was also an influential person in the village, and he did not belong to the Abasozo clan. His sons were active looters, but they did not kill. Their aggressiveness scared the others. Ironically, one of those who saved people was the teacher, Karayenga, who helped a young man flee to Burundi. I know everyone in our sector of Murama. Only those hidden at Twagirayezu's home survived the genocide. Nobody else.[231]

When one has not lived through such terrifying moments, one should be very cautious when analyzing the behavior of the massacre victims. However, that should not impede a critical analysis of the victims' behavior as long as one is not making a moral judgment. The Tutsis of Kigembe tried to resist the genocide, but that resistance was more of a survival reflex when almost all was lost. Thus some Tutsis in Kivuru Sector died fighting with weapons in their hands. Before the soldiers arrived at the commune office building from Butare Town, the refugees had armed themselves with stones and kept the killers at a distance. Until the soldiers joined them, the killers feared not being able to kill the surrounded Tutsis. The fact that the refugees let themselves be rounded up and led to the commune office building and the CERAI and that they stayed there without breaking out and heading for the Burundi border about five kilometers away demonstrates a certain amount of passiveness, but above all, that the refugees had not grasped the gravity of what was going to happen.[232] With the roundup and transfer operations almost complete by the evening of April 18, thousands of Tutsis who were to be massacred the following day spent the night at the commune office building and the CERAI, missing the chance to forcefully escape to the Burundian border nearby.

Some of the Tutsis from the former Nyaruguru Region further north had a different attitude. After escaping from the Kibeho and Cyahinda Parishes (in

Gikongoro Prefecture and Nyakizu Commune, respectively), where thousands of people had already perished on April 15 and 16, thousands of Tutsi from different places in the region gathered at Bitare Hill in Gishamvu Commune near the border with Nyakizu Commune.[233] Some Tutsis from Kigembe, Murama, and Ngera Sectors joined them and later managed to reach Burundi after passing again through their sectors. After the deadly attacks of Monday, April 18, in Ngera Sector, Mazina and other Tutsis went to the deputy prefect's office in Nyumba Parish (Gishamvu Commune) to ask for protection. They did not find anyone, but at Nyumba Church, where hundreds of Tutsis were gathered, Hutu residents were eating the cows and goats that belonged to the Tutsis. Mazina decided to proceed to Bitare hill. The day after his departure from Nyumba, soldiers with guns and grenades massacred thousands of Tutsis who had sought refuge there. Bitare hill, located at the border with Nyakizu Commune, was famous for the Tutsi population that had successfully fought back Hutu attackers during the 1959 revolution. According to Mazina, the Tutsis of Gikongoro Prefecture said to others in Butare Prefecture, "We, we have been fighting with the Hutus for two weeks, and it is useless, so we have to leave for Burundi."[234] "They took spears, they put their wives, children, and livestock in the middle, and a group of men went in front and another behind, and they took arrows, machetes, and clubs. No Hutu could penetrate without a gun. They were determined to arrive at the border post even if only three of them remained."[235]

The Tutsis left at dawn on Wednesday, April 20. According to Mazina, they formed three groups.

> Each team had about 1,500 people. The third team was made up of about 400 people. Nobody was able to go in front of these three groups. . . . They left in the daylight, they took the path that led them to the macadamized road [in Kigembe Commune] up to the customs office, and nobody was able to stop them. . . . When the first team arrived at customs, a soldier fired on the crowd, which trampled him to death. The Burundian custom officials welcomed them saying: "Come, come, come." . . . The first team arrived in Burundi at noon. I left with the second group, and we reached the road at 1:00 p.m. and arrived at 4:00 p.m. Our group must have numbered about 2,000 people because we formed a procession of a kilometer long. The third group left on Thursday.[236]

According to Mazina, the trucks full of soldiers quickly arrived on Thursday at the border, but it was too late because the majority of refugees in the last group had already crossed.

Last Word: The Causes of Mass Participation in the Genocide

The opinion of the participants themselves should have a bearing on the discussion about the reasons the Kigembe Commune population mobilized in such massive numbers in the extermination of Tutsi neighbors.

Buyenzi, a genocide survivor, explains his inability to understand the reasons for the behavior of people from his village. "We too, we did not understand. Nobody could understand why people were killed by those with whom they shared everything. I cannot tell you why. If it was because of propaganda, if the time had come, if I gave a reason, I would be lying to you."[237]

The burgomaster of the commune suggested that the mass participation was a result of manipulation of the villagers' poverty:

> I already told you that those who participated in the genocide were those who had nothing; they killed the Tutsis in order to grab their land. Before, hatred as such was not widespread, but if someone said, "Kill a Tutsi, you will have his land, you will get his banana farm . . .," you can see that he is stimulating savage instincts; he is provoking greed, savagery, and guilt put together, and then killing becomes very easy. . . . When it comes to the role played by the people, one could quote the Kinyarwanda proverb: Umuntu ananira umuhana nta we unanira umushuka ("You can resist whoever advises you but not whoever lies to you").[238]

For a long time, the elderly Kabutura was the councilor of Kigembe Sector and a member of the commune MRND committee. During the genocide, the killers did not look for him or try to enlist him, and he did not participate in the killings. "The way I see it, it was mostly because of ignorance. The first thing that struck me in all this was the ignorance. In my opinion, everything was because of ignorance. The second thing was greed, this desire for self-interest. That was all I noticed, but the main issue was ignorance."[239]

Two villagers who admitted participating in the killings pointed an accusing finger at the political parties. Joseph, a literate member of the PSD who admitted having taken part in several attacks and personally killed people, gave his final word: "If you asked me, this would be my only answer. I would say that the political parties dragged us into the evil we committed."[240]

Matabaro, an illiterate villager and MDR member who confessed to having killed people, accused the MDR: "The MDR dragged us into the killings. We, the villagers, accuse the party because the party was violent and strong and was sensitizing people. I am not lying to you."[241]

These perpetrators, of different sociocultural profiles, who played different roles in the tragedy offered complementary and coherent answers to the question on the cause of the mass participation. The educated protagonists who did not participate gave an abstract answer in terms of the powerful influence of more educated people, manipulation, and poverty. The villagers who killed saw themselves as victims of the influence of political parties and especially of the MDR, the most powerful party. The responses were also striking because they referred neither to the role of the state nor to coercion—nor even to ethnic hatred.

The issue of influence and manipulation was more complex than one may think. First, the one who manipulated was not always the one people thought would do so, as in the following extract from Nsengimana's testimony on an altercation between himself, a university student, and a group of villagers who wanted to force him to participate in the killings.

> "Kill me if you want because that is your intention, but I cannot join in your attacks of murder and looting. Continue to collaborate with these intellectuals you like so much. The cows you are now eating, you will one day be compelled to return them with their horns and tails. You will pay for it." After hearing these words, Ruremesha shot back disdainfully, "For all that we are doing, it is you intellectuals who will pay."[242]

One can see the level of autonomy exercised by the villagers who lucidly followed the intellectuals in actions from which they benefited and for which they could evade responsibility, should a problem arise.

As for Buyenzi, it was not surprising that after losing his wife, eight of his nine children, and all his brothers and sisters, he still could not understand why his neighbors took part in the genocide.

Notes

1. Commune Kigembe, *Rapport administratif du quatrième trimestre 1990*, pp. 1–2.

2. Ibid.

3. Commune Kigembe, *Lettre du bourgmestre au préfet, Rapport sur la réunion portant sur la contribution de soutien à l'armée.*

4. Ibid.

5. Ibid.

6. Ibid. Kayumba, interview with author, May 17, 2001, Kigembe. Fred Rwigema was the military head of the RPF, killed in the first days of the war.

7. Commune Kigembe, *Rapport administratif du quatrième trimestre 1990*, p. 3.

8. Ibid.

9. Kayumba interview.

10. Ibid.

11. Between January 31, 1991, and March 25, 1991, sixty young Tutsis suspected of heading for Burundi were arrested and their files sent to the prosecutor. Commune Kigembe, *Rapport de sécurité du 31/01/91, du 09/03/91 et du 18/03/91*; Commune Kigembe, *Lettre du Bourgmestre au Procureur introduisant les dossiers judiciaires de six personnes du 25/03/91.*

12. Commune Kigembe, *Rapports de sécurité des 11, 16 et 19/01/91.*

13. Commune Kigembe, *Rapport de sécurité du 25/01/91.*

14. Ibid.

15. There were twenty-seven crossing points on the Akanyaru River in Kigembe Commune; they were well known to the authorities. These river crossings were necessary during the flood season. When the river level was low, one could cross at any point without needing a boat. Commune Kigembe, *Lettre du Bourgmestre au Préfet du 11/06/91, Liste des passages à gué sur la rivière Akanyaru.*

16. Commune Kigembe, *Rapport de sécurité du 11/01/91.*

17. Commune Kigembe, *Lettre du Bourgmestre au Préfet du 15/01/91 portant sur le problème des gens qui traversent pour vendre des pommes de terre.*

18. These are the border posts of the Lower and Upper Akanyaru, both located in Kigembe. Commune Kigembe, *Rapport de sécurité du 19/01/91*.

19. This was the RPF attack and occupation for a few hours of Ruhengeri Town in the northwest on January 23, 1991. The attack took place after the regime had announced and celebrated its victory over the RPF. During this raid, RPF fighters released important political prisoners incarcerated in the town prison. Ruhengeri was located in the regime's regional stronghold.

20. In late 1990, there were 1,161 radio sets in the commune, and when one considers that the people listened to the radio in groups or as families, one can say that official government information penetrated the population at a significant rate in the commune. The most unexpected figure is that of 1,700 subscriptions to magazines and newspapers in a commune in which relatively few people were educated and/or employed. It shows how closely the local elites were following national events.

21. On February 7 and 12, 1991, the burgomaster wrote that the population had become more vigilant and increased their participation in the rounds. Commune Kigembe, *Rapport de sécurité du 07/02/91* and Commune Kigembe, *Rapport de sécurité du 12/02/91*.

22. On February 16, 1991, smugglers disrupted the group on patrol, and on February 19 a group of seven people attacked the patrol. Commune Kigembe, *Rapport de sécurité du 20/02/91*; Commune Kigembe, *Rapport de sécurité du 20/02/91*.

23. Commune Kigembe, *Lettre du Bourgmestre au Préfet du 08/01/91, Liste des victimes de la faim*.

24. Commune Kigembe, *Lettre du Bourgmestre au Préfet du 06/02/91, Rapport de distribution de l'aide aux personnes souffrant de la faim*.

25. Commune Kigembe, *Lettre du Bourgmestre au Préfet du 07/03/91, Rapport de distribution de l'aide aux personnes souffrant de la faim*.

26. Some months after the October 1, 1991, outbreak of the war, Tanzania forcibly repatriated thousands of Rwandan economic migrants. Commune Kigembe, *Lettre du Bourgmestre au Préfet du 05/08/91, Rapport de distribution de l'aide alimentaire aux rapatriés de Tanzanie*; Commune Kigembe, *Lettre du Bourgmestre au Préfet du 21/02/92, Rapport de distribution de l'aide alimentaire aux rapatriés de Tanzanie*; Commune Kigembe, *Lettre du Bourgmestre au Préfet du 23/03/92, Rapport de distribution de l'aide alimentaire aux rapatriés de Tanzanie*.

27. Commune Kigembe, *Lettre du Bourgmestre au Préfet du 23/03/92, Rapport de distribution de l'aide alimentaire aux rapatriés de Tanzanie*.

28. Commune Kigembe, *Rapport de sécurité du 23/01/91*.

29. Commune Kigembe, *Rapport de sécurité du 21/03/91*.

30. Commune Kigembe, *Rapport de sécurité du 05/04/91*.

31. Commune Kigembe, *Rapport de sécurité du 12/04/91*.

32. Commune Kigembe, *Rapport de sécurité du 17/05/91*.

33. Commune Kigembe, *Rapport de sécurité du 16/05/91*.

34. Commune Kigembe, *Rapport de sécurité du 27/05/91*.

35. Commune Kigembe, *Rapport de sécurité du 16/12/91*.

36. Commune Kigembe, *Lettre du Bourgmestre à l'IPJ du 20/02/91*.

37. Commune Kigembe, *Lettre du Bourgmestre à l'IPJ du 22/02/91*.

38. Commune Kigembe, *Lettre du Bourgmestre au Préfet du 12/03/91* (explanation of the Museruka case).

39. Commune Kigembe, *Procès-verbal de la réunion du conseil communal de sécurité du 15/05/91*.

40. Commune Kigembe, *Rapport de sécurité du 24/04/91*.

41. The first meeting of an opposition party, the MDR, was held on August 25, 1991, at the Nyaruteja trading center, the administrative center of the commune. Commune Kigembe, *Rapport d'inspection communal du 22/01/92.*

42. Innocent Rwamigabo, interview with author, May 4, 2001, Kabutare Prison, Butare.

43. Straton Nyarwaya, interview with author, May 20, 2001, Kigembe.

44. Commune Kigembe, *Rapport de sécurité du 29/07/91.*

45. Name given in Rwanda to people who have attended secondary school and hold white-collar jobs. For instance, Rwamigabo says that despite Bonaventure Nkundabakura's limited education, he was the most educated member of his group. See Rwamigabo interview; Nyarwaya interview; Symphorien Karekezi, interview with author, May 3, 2001, Rwandex Prison, Butare.

46. Commune Kigembe, *Rapport sur l'activité des partis politiques du 13/08/91.*

47. Commune Kigembe, *Rapport sur les élections du parti MDR à Kigembe du 30/04/1992.* This proportion is even more important than the age pyramid of the commune, which shows that the majority of residents were less than fifteen years old. Commune Kigembe, *Résultats du recensement tenu en août 1991.*

48. Commune Kigembe, *Rapport sur les élections du parti MDR à Kigembe du 30/04/1992.*

49. Rwamigabo interview.

50. Joseph Habyarimana, interview with author, April 26 and 27, 2001, Butare.

51. Nyarwaya interview.

52. Ibid.

53. Karekezi interview.

54. The PL was considered the Tutsi party in Kigembe Commune. Its quasi-clandestine status reflects the political marginalization of Tutsis in the commune during the multiparty era.

55. Faustin Matabaro, interview with author, May 3, 2001, Karubanda Prison, Butare.

56. Ibid.

57. Commune Kigembe, *Rapport portant sur les meetings des partis MRND, MDR et PSD durant les mois de décembre 1991 et janvier 1992.*

58. Ibid.

59. Agathe Uwilingiyimana, who came from neighboring Nyaruhengeri Commune, was the minister of education and then the prime minister beginning in April 1992. She was considered one of the leading moderate figures within the MDR. Historian Donat Murego, seen as MDR-PARMEHUTU, became one of the leaders of the MDR-power faction when the party split in 1992.

60. Commune Kigembe, *Rapport portant sur le meeting du MDR du 19/01/92.*

61. Ibid.

62. Commune Kigembe, *Rapport portant sur le meeting du MDR du 20/03/92.*

63. Nyarwaya interview.

64. Commune Kigembe, *Procès-verbal de la réunion rassemblant les autorités communales et les responsables des partis politiques oeuvrant dans la commune du 21/02/92.*

65. Commune Kigembe, *Rapport portant sur le meeting du MDR du 19/01/92.*

66. Ibid.

67. Matabaro interview. This vulnerability was often the result of a combination of factors, such as widespread poverty, lack of social contacts, and illiteracy. Such was the case of Matabaro, a Hutu accused of genocide, and of Gaston Mazina, a genocide

survivor, both of whom underwent such pressure. Mazina was beaten. Mazina, interview with author, May 27, 2001, Kigembe.

68. Commune Kigembe, *Rapport de sécurité du 13/12/91*.
69. Commune Kigembe, *Rapport de sécurité du 16/12/91*.
70. Commune Kigembe, *Rapport de sécurité du 24/12/91*.
71. Commune Kigembe, *Rapport de sécurité du 24/01/92*.
72. Commune Kigembe, *Rapport de sécurité du 30/01/92*.
73. Commune Kigembe, *Rapport de sécurité du 31/01/92*.
74. Commune Kigembe, *Rapport de sécurité du 03/02/92*.
75. Commune Kigembe, *Rapport de sécurité du 15/02/92*.
76. Commune Kigembe, *Rapport de sécurité du 19/02/92*.
77. Commune Kigembe, *Rapport de sécurité du 09/03/92*.
78. Commune Kigembe, *Rapport de sécurité du 25/03/92*.
79. Commune Kigembe, *Rapport de sécurité du 04/04/92*.
80. *Nyumbakumi* was the new structure of surveillance put into place the day after the outbreak of the war; all ten homes voted one person to be in charge of watching entrances and exits. Commune Kigembe, *Procès-verbal de la réunion du conseil communal de sécurité du 12/03/92*.
81. Commune Kigembe, *Procès-verbal de la réunion du conseil communal du 22/03/92*.
82. Commune Kigembe, *Procès-verbal de la réunion du conseil communal élargi aux membres des comités de cellules du 05/05/92*.
83. Commune Kigembe, *Rapport de sécurité du 13/05/92*.
84. Commune Kigembe, *Rapport de sécurité du 21/05/92*.
85. Commune Kigembe, *Liste des personnes souffrant de la faim du 29/05/92*.
86. Commune Kigembe, *Rapport de sécurité du 27/02/92*.
87. Commune Kigembe, *Rapport de sécurité du 02/03/92*.
88. Commune Kigembe, *Rapport de sécurité du 12/03/92*.
89. Commune Kigembe, *Lettre Bourgmestre au Préfet du 26/03/92, Demande de renfort de gendarmes*.
90. Commune Kigembe, *Rapport de sécurité du 26/03/92*.
91. Commune Kigembe, *Rapport de sécurité du 30/03/92*.
92. Commune Kigembe, *Lettre du Bourgmestre au Procureur de la République du 27/04/92*; Commune Kigembe, *Rapport de sécurité du 27/04/92*.
93. Commune Kigembe, *Lettre du Bourgmestre au Sous-Préfet du 22/05/92*.
94. We know that at least some of these people belonged to the MDR and that they had attacked MRND supporters on the day of the MDR elections.
95. Commune Kigembe, *Rapport de sécurité du 10/10/91*; Commune Kigembe, *Lettre du Bourgmestre au Président de Tribunal de Canton du 19/12/91*.
96. Commune Kigembe, *Rapport de sécurité du 05/11/91*.
97. Commune Kigembe, *Rapport de sécurité du 09/12/91*.
98. Commune Kigembe, *Rapport de sécurité du 24/02/92*.
99. Commune Kigembe, *Lettre du Bourgmestre au Sous-Préfet du 27/02/92, Rapport sur le problème des champs de la vallée de la Migina*.
100. Commune Kigembe, *Rapport de sécurité du 27/02/92*.
101. Commune Kigembe, *Rapport de sécurité du 16/04/92*.
102. Commune Kigembe, *Rapport de sécurité du 18/04/92*.
103. Commune Kigembe, *Rapport de sécurité du 27/04/92*.
104. Commune Kigembe, *Rapport de sécurité du 19/05/92*.
105. Commune Kigembe, *Rapport de sécurité du 22/05/92*.
106. Commune Kigembe, *Rapport de sécurité du 27/05/92*.

107. Commune Kigembe, *Rapport de sécurité du 12/06/92.*

108. Commune Kigembe, *Lettre du Bourgmestre au Président du parti MDR dans Kigembe du 10/04/92.*

109. Commune Kigembe, *Lettre du Bourgmestre au Préfet du 27/04/92.*

110. Commune Kigembe, *Rapport de sécurité du 12/05/92.*

111. Martin Ntamishimiro, interview with author, May 4, 2001, Karubanda Prison, Butare.

112. Ibid.

113. République rwandaise, Ministère de l'Intérieur et du Développement communal, *Rapport portant sur la situation de sécurité dans le pays du mois de juin 1992.*

114. Karekezi interview.

115. Joseph Nzabonima, interview with author, May 3, 2001, Karubanda Prison, Butare.

116. République rwandaise, Ministère de l'Intérieur et du Développement communal, *Rapport portant sur la situation de sécurité dans le pays durant le mois de juin 1992.*

117. Commune Kigembe, *Rapport de l'inspection communale du 22/01/92.*

118. Ntamishimiro interview.

119. Ibid.

120. Préfecture de Butare, *Procès-verbal de la réunion du comité préfectoral de sécurité du 24/07/92.*

121. Ibid.

122. Karekezi interview; Nyarwaya interview.

123. Kigembe residents say that the former MRND members had hidden in the PSD without necessarily having changed their views. Ibid.

124. At that time, the Ministry of the Interior and Commune Development portfolio was held by an MRND member within the coalition government; the prefect of Butare was a PL member, and the prefecture authorities as well as the Butare population were generally more inclined toward the PSD.

125. This rally was chaired by PSD leader Félicien Gatabazi, then minister of energy and public works.

126. He implied that the people were angry because they had not gotten the leaders they wanted, in other words leaders from the MDR.

127. Commune Kigembe, *Procès-verbal de la réunion du conseil communal consacré à la sécurité du 07/08/92.*

128. This election to replace only the "defective" burgomasters took place throughout the country. The majority of burgomasters to be replaced had been overthrown by the political parties or were incapable of carrying out their duties because of the widespread opposition of their communes.

129. Préfecture de Butare, *Procès-verbal de la réunion du comité préfectoral de sécurité du 05/04/93.*

130. Ministerial Directive No. 46/04.09.01 of March 11, 1993, on the preselection of candidates for burgomaster.

131. Préfecture de Butare, *Procès-verbal de la réunion du conseil préfectoral de sécurité du 16/07/93.*

132. Karekezi interview.

133. Straton Nyarwaya, the longtime commune accountant and a member of the commune MRND committee, estimated that three-quarters of the commune population belonged to the MDR in 1993. Nyarwaya interview. Prefect Jean-Baptiste Habyarimana, a Tutsi, was a member of the Liberal Party (PL), which was closer to the PSD than to the MDR. The PSD was the most influential party in Butare Prefecture.

134. Nzabonima interview.
135. Ibid. Several similar testimonies blame the massacres on the rising animosity for which political parties were responsible.
136. Ntamishimiro interview.
137. Habyarimana interview; Kayumba interview; Nzabonima interview; Ntamishimiro interview.
138. Habyarimana interview; Kayumba interview.
139. Karekezi interview; Nyarwaya interview.
140. Habyarimana interview.
141. One can follow the evolution of Kigembe Commune from 1977 on because that was when the reports became regular.
142. Commune Kigembe, *Rapport de sécurité du 19/03/92*.
143. Commune Kigembe, *Rapport de sécurité du 23/03/92*.
144. The Hutu-power movement crystallized the day after the assassination of Burundian president Ndadaye. The change in the political situation in Burundi could not be without effect in Kigembe Commune.
145. Nyarwaya interview.
146. Habyarimana interview.
147. Ibid.
148. Mazina interview.
149. Calixte Kayisire, interview with author, May 4, 2001, Karubanda Prison, Butare.
150. Karekezi interview.
151. This is probably a sign of the ethnic polarity of a portion of the Tutsi population of Kigembe Commune at the time. Explaining this as the result of official propaganda, some Tutsis of the commune associated the PL with the RPF. Habyarimana interview; Mazina interview.
152. Habyarimana interview.
153. Karekezi interview. Commune Kigembe, *Rapport portant sur les meetings des partis MRND, MDR et PSD durant les mois de décembre 1991 et janvier 1992*. The Bashiru are the inhabitants of Bushiru, a historical region and the place of origin of President Habyarimana and his inner circle.
154. Habyarimana interview.
155. Mazina interview.
156. Thus, the security report of March 7, 1992, discussed a meeting between the burgomaster and his Burundian counterpart, along with the administrator of the border post of the Lower Akanyaru River, who informed him about the constitutional referendum and Burundian authorities' fear that refugee members of Palipehutu would attempt to sabotage the process from Rwanda. Commune Kigembe, *Rapport de sécurité du 07/03/92: Arrivée de trois étudiants réfugiés*; Commune Kigembe, *Rapport de sécurité du 02/01/92: Arrivée de quatre réfugiés*; Commune Kigembe, *Rapport de sécurité du 07/01/92*.
157. Karekezi interview.
158. Ibid.; Habyarimana interview.
159. Habyarimana interview; Mazina interview; Isaïe Buyenzi, interview with author, May 26, 2001, Kigembe.
160. Commune Kigembe, *Rapport démographique du mois de mars 1992*.
161. These estimates were from discussions with the former burgomaster, Karekezi, as well as two survivors of the massacre, Kayumba and Buyenzi. Des Forges proposed the same estimates. Karekezi interview; Kayumba interview; Buyenzi interview; Des Forges, *Leave None to Tell the Story*, p. 341.

162. Karekezi interview.
163. Ibid.
164. Karekezi interview.
165. Ibid.
166. Ibid.
167. Karekezi interview.
168. Ibid.
169. Ibid.
170. Ibid.
171. Habyarimana interview; Ntamishimiro interview.
172. Ntamishimiro interview.
173. Ibid.
174. Buyenzi interview.
175. Ntamishimiro interview.
176. Kayumba interview.
177. Ibid.
178. Ibid.; Ntamishimiro interview.
179. Kayumba interview; Buyenzi interview.
180. Nsengimana testimony.
181. Habyarimana interview; Nsengimana testimony.
182. In spite of the loss of social prestige that comes with owning a cow in contemporary Rwanda, the act of feasting on a cow that belongs to someone else was still a serious outrage to the owner.
183. Habyarimana interview.
184. Ibid.
185. Nsengimana testimony.
186. Ibid.
187. Ibid.
188. Mazina interview.
189. Ibid.
190. Nzabonima interview.
191. Nsengimana testimony.
192. Karekezi interview.
193. Nsengimana testimony.
194. Ibid.
195. Nzabonima interview.
196. Ibid.
197. Ibid.
198. Ibid.
199. Kayisire interview.
200. Buyenzi interview.
201. According to the August 1989 census, 21.8 percent of the population of Murama Sector was Tutsi. Commune Kigembe, *Résultats du recensement mené en août 1989*.
202. Buyenzi interview.
203. Ibid.
204. Ibid. The extreme hysteria of the crowds during the killing is often invoked by the escapees of the genocide. During the commemoration of the genocide in April 2001 at the University of Butare, a student testifying about his experience stated that he forgave those who had pursued him and left him for dead because he knew some of his killers and sincerely thought that in the heat of the moment they had been overcome with folly.

205. Many Tutsis from the region, some of whom were from Murama and Ngera Sectors, had sought refuge at Nyumba Church in neighboring Gishamvu Commune. The church was the scene of a massive massacre. Mazina interview.

206. Nzabonima interview.

207. Nsengimana testimony.

208. Kabutura interview.

209. Ibid.

210. Ibid.

211. Habyarimana interview.

212. Kabutura interview.

213. Nzabonima interview.

214. Ntamishimiro interview.

215. Kabutura interview.

216. Des Forges, *Leave None to Tell the Story,* pp. 471–472.

217. The intergenerational transmission of fidelity to the PARMEHUTU within families was found at all levels of the party. See Bertrand, *Rwanda,* p. 87.

218. Habyarimana personally witnessed and heard Innocent Rwamigabo arriving at the building of the fish farming project where Habyarimana was hiding in a truck with a group of killers armed with machetes. Rwamigabo asked Habyarimana's cousin to show him the Tutsis he had hidden, and Rwamigabo and his companions searched the building. Habyarimana interview.

219. Chrétien, *Les Médias du génocide.*

220. Ntamishimiro interview.

221. Karekezi interview.

222. In Kigembe, a small detachment of soldiers was stationed at the border. Matabaro interview.

223. Ntamishimiro interview.

224. Mazina interview.

225. Nsengimana testimony.

226. Ibid.

227. Kayisire interview.

228. The same phenomenon is highlighted by the Human Rights Watch report. Des Forges, *Leave None to Tell the Story,* p. 350.

229. See Nsengimana testimony; Habyarimana interview. On the widening of the circle of people targeted on orders of the interim government, see Des Forges, *Leave None to Tell the Story,* p. 191.

230. Habyarimana interview.

231. Ibid.

232. On April 18, 1994, when all of Rwanda was a literal bloodbath, a part of Butare Prefecture also ignited, for example, in Nyakizu Commune, adjacent to Kigembe Commune. Some Tutsis in the commune had shortwave radios, so they knew what was going on in the rest of the country. According to Joseph Habyarimana, the Tutsis of Kigembe Commune did not try to leave en masse for Burundi because they believed they could count on the resistance of the prefect of Butare and the head of the gendarmes. Things were not simple across the border either, because the Burundian Hutus had armed and positioned themselves at the crossing points of the Akanyaru River. Habyarimana interview. The Burundian authorities were experiencing a deep crisis following the assassination of President Ndadaye and seem not to have provided much support in terms of free access of Tutsi refugees beyond the official border posts guarded by the army.

233. Des Forges, *Leave None to Tell the Story,* pp. 166, 295.

234. Mazina interview.
235. Ibid.
236. Ibid. Des Forges estimates the number of people able to cross in these groups at several hundred. Des Forges, *Leave None to Tell the Story*, p. 382.
237. Buyenzi interview.
238. Karekezi interview.
239. Kabutura interview.
240. Nzabonima interview.
241. Matabaro interview.
242. Nsengimana testimony.

8

Kibuye:
A Story of Power Relations

Like Butare Prefecture, Kibuye Prefecture was far from the battlefield of the war between the Rwandan Patriotic Front (RPF) and the Forces armées rwandaises (FAR), the government army. Kibuye was also the prefecture with the highest Tutsi population. In comparison with Butare, it was slightly less hostile to the National Revolutionary Movement for Development (MRND) regime, and unlike Butare, it plunged into the genocide the day after the death of President Juvénal Habyarimana with mass participation. In order to shed light on the historical, political, and social context of the genocide in Kibuye, in this chapter I first analyze the development of the prefecture during the 1980s and early 1990s before discussing the genocide itself in Chapter 9. The common thread running through this analysis is the power relations between the political actors and the people: the acts of the MRND party-state, those of the different political parties in the multiparty era, and the people's response. I pay particular attention to the social, economic, cultural, and ideological context in which these political interactions took place.

Historical and Social Context

Geography and History

Kibuye Prefecture is located in the west of the country with Lake Kivu, which separates Rwanda from Zaire, forming its backdrop.[1] A chain of mountains that make up the Congo-Nile Ridge splits Kibuye into two. All of the communes are located on either the western or eastern slope, apart from Gisovu Commune, which straddles the crest. Kivumu, Mwendo, and Bwakira Communes, to the east, along with Gisovu Commune, are all located in a remote hinterland isolated from the urban centers. On the western slope of the ridge, Rutsiro, Mabanza, Gitesi, Gishyita, and Rwamatamu Communes surround Lake Kivu, with only Rutsiro not reaching the shore (see Map 8.1). North of the western part of the prefecture is Gisenyi Prefecture, which opens into

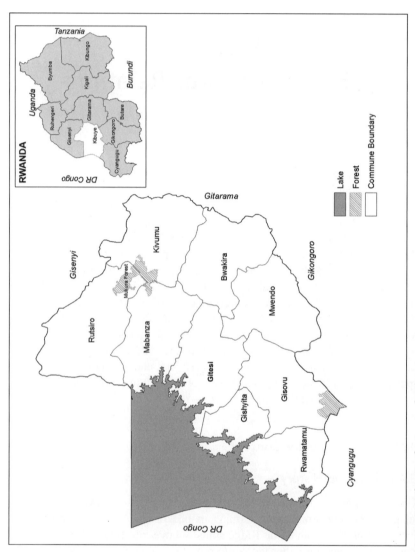

Map 8.1 The Prefecture of Kibuye

Zaire. Gisenyi Town, the administrative center, is a place of dynamic exchange with Goma Town on the Zairean side. To the south of Kibuye Prefecture is Cyangugu Prefecture, with Cyangugu Town, another important exchange point with Bukavu Town on the Zairean side. Kibuye Prefecture had only one road that linked it to the rest of the country, unsurfaced and often in a poor state. This isolation of Kibuye Prefecture from the rest of Rwanda meant that its people interacted more with the regions in the west bordering the lake and facing Zaire.

The major part of the genocide took place in the western side of the prefecture where the majority of Tutsis lived, as shown in Tables 8.1 and 8.2.

The earliest human settlement in this region was on the western slope, which provided historical passages for pioneers who cleared the land and settled in large numbers to the west, especially along the shores of Lake Kivu, to avoid the most rugged terrain, cold weather, and weak soil.[2] The Bwishaza and Rusenyi Regions thus had large and long-settled Tutsi populations. Immigration from the Bugoyi Region in the north (in Gisenyi Prefecture) and from Kiyaga Region in the south (in Cyangugu Prefecture) also boosted these pop-

Table 8.1   Ethnic Distribution in the Communes of Kibuye Prefecture on the Eastern Slope of the Congo-Nile Ridge, 1987 (percentages)

Commune	Tutsi	Hutu	Twa
Gisovu	13.5	86.0	0.5
Mwendo	12.8	87.0	0.2
Bwakira	11.3	88.0	0.7
Kivumu	9.0	90.7	0.3

Source: République rwandaise, Ministère de l'Intérieur et du Développement communal, *Recensement administratif de la population rwandaise durant la période de 1960–1987, 1987.*

Table 8.2   Ethnic Distribution in the Communes of Kibuye Prefecture on the Western Slope of the Congo-Nile Ridge, 1987 (percentages)

Commune	Tutsi	Hutu	Twa
Rwamatamu	32.6	67.0	0.4
Gishyita	37.5	62.0	0.5
Gitesi	34.7	65.0	0.3
Mabanza	21.0	78.5	0.5
Rutsiro	1.8	80.3	0.4
Kibuye Prefecture	**19.3**	**80.3**	**0.4**
Rwanda	**10.94**	**88.53**	**0.53**

Source: République rwandaise, Ministère de l'Intérieur et du Développement communal, *Recensement administratif de la population rwandaise durant la période de 1960–1987, 1987.*

ulations. The significant settlement in the regions between the ridges and along the lakeshore was also a result of the terraced topography between the ridgetops and the lowlands, which favors diverse farms and livestock.[3] According to Vansina, Kibuye Prefecture was slowly conquered by the Rwandan monarchy around Kinyaga in the south and Bugoyi in the north in the late eighteenth century.[4] The expansion westward was more the integration of a previous colonization rather than a conquest by the Rwandan minority. For a long time, there existed in the north (Gisenyi Prefecture), in the south (Cyangugu Prefecture), and in the center (Kibuye Prefecture) autonomous communities that did not recognize the king's authority, such as Nyantango Commune in present-day Kibuye Prefecture.[5]

In the more recent past, the Rubengera Region in Mabanza Commune was quite famous. While returning from a military expedition in present-day North Kivu, Mwami Kigeli Rwabugiri had stayed over in Rubengera near Lake Kivu, where he established a new type of royal residence around 1880.[6] The former royal residences scattered around the country were small chiefdoms often led by one of the king's wives and including only a few hills. The new royal residences established by Rwabugiri, especially in the north and west of the country, were huge chiefdoms of which the administrative influence reached several surrounding regions; these were entrusted to Rwabugiri's new but powerful officials who often did not belong to the old aristocracy. Rwabugiri established these new residences as part of his move toward centralizing his power. The Rubengera residence was entrusted to the powerful Bisangwa, Rwabugiri's adopted son of Hutu origin, chief of the Ingagurarugo, the royal guard.[7] Thus despite its apparent geopolitical remoteness, the Rubengera residence brought together members of aristocratic lineages.

Finally, the tip of Gishyita Commune, which enters Lake Kivu, was for a long time an important royal port, from which Rwabugiri launched his war expedition toward the western shore of the lake. In addition, Gishyita was the capital of the Rusenyi Chiefdom during the colonial period. This important political profile in relatively recent history explains the dense population, especially of Tutsis, in this region.[8] Whereas Bwishaza and Rusenyi Regions were intimately integrated into the monarchy, Kanage, Budaha, and Nyantango Regions were considered part of Rukiga, a high-country, socioculturally different area that corresponded to present-day Gisenyi, Ruhengeri, and Byumba Prefectures farther northeast. The Bakiga Mountain inhabitants were notorious for their defiance of the monarchy and their unique identity. This sociopolitical contrast between the Rukiga Region and the rest of the country was also felt in Kibuye Prefecture under the Second Republic. Local elites from the historical Kanage, Budaha, and Nyantango Regions (Rutsiro, Kivumu, Bwakira, and Mwendo Communes) were politically closer to President Habyarimana and the MRND, whereas elites from the historical Bwishaza and Rusenyi Regions (Mabanza, Gitesi, Gishyita, and Rwamatamu Communes), who were more distant to the regime.

During the 1959 revolution, Kibuye Prefecture experienced violence in the form of arson against Tutsi huts. The only community to experience serious violence was Bwishaza Region on November 7, 1959, when arsonists and looters from Kayove and Rutsiro Communes in Kanage Region attacked Bwishaza Tutsis, particularly in Mabanza and Gitesi Communes in the Rubengera Region.[9] The Tutsis fought back, and the attackers suffered dozens of casualties.[10] The following year, hundreds of huts belonging to Tutsis were burned throughout the prefecture. Under the First Republic, the prefecture was long ostracized because the regime blamed it for being lukewarm toward the revolution. By virtue of its significant Tutsi population, the region on the edge of Lake Kivu betrayed its inclination toward the promonarchy party, the Rwanda National Union (UNAR).[11] At the end of the 1960s, President Grégoire Kayibanda, faced with the increasing isolation of his regime and on bad terms with the elites from the north and south of the country, sought to close ranks with some of the political figures originally from Kibuye Prefecture and appointed two of them into his government. Kibuye Prefecture would soon pay the price for this late reconciliation. In 1973, the regime of the Second Republic in turn neglected the region. However, President Habyarimana faced an increasingly complicated environment at the end of the 1980s and similarly initiated a belated reconciliation with the political icons of the prefecture. Even though these twists and turns took place among political personalities, they also had direct repercussions on the residents of the region. Because of this lengthy political marginalization, Kibuye Prefecture received less than a fair share in terms of the construction of infrastructure and facilities in comparison with other areas. Along with Gikongoro Prefecture, Kibuye was reputed to be the poorest region of the country.[12] One issue in particular drew the resentment of the residents: the failure to pave the national highway connecting the prefecture to the rest of the country despite repeated promises to do so.

The Socioeconomic Context of the 1980s

In this section I examine the severe socioeconomic crisis in Kibuye Prefecture over a long period. I begin with a synthesis of the socioeconomic development of the western slope of the Congo-Nile Ridge, then present a social chronology of the period from 1984 to 1990, with the goal of providing a picture of the lived reality of the inhabitants.

At the heart of the social crisis in this region was the sharp rise in population density. In 1978, Rwamatamu, Gishyita, Gitesi, Mabanza, and Rutsiro

Table 8.3   **Population Density on the Western Slope of the Congo-Nile Ridge of Kibuye Prefecture, 1991**

Commune	Population	Area (km²)	Density (inhabitants/km²)
Rwamatamu	55,740	103	541
Gishyita	42,070	86	498
Gitesi	61,030	132	462
Mabanza	63,980	158	404
Rutsiro	58,250	190	306
Region	**321,250**	**819**	**392**
Rwanda	**7,149,215**	**25,338**	**271**

Source: Z. Mulindwa, *Les contraintes du surpeuplement,* pp. 79, 88, 89; République rwandaise, *Recensement général de la population et de l'habitat au 15/08/91,* p. 9.

Communes, on the western slope, together had a population of 199,304 inhabitants, a gross density of 283 inhabitants per square kilometer and a real population density of 315 habitants per square kilometer on available arable land.[13] In 1991, the situation had greatly changed, as is evident in Table 8.3. Between 1978 and 1991, the population of the region had increased by 62 percent. In 1991, its density on arable land was 508 inhabitants per square kilometer.

In 1978, there were huge disparities in the internal distribution of the population that varied according to three different levels of altitude in the region.[14] The higher population density was on the edge of Lake Kivu as well as on the headlands, the less uneven hillsides, and the flatter zones. The average densities were in the middle level, and finally the sectors with low population density were at the top level of the Congo-Nile Ridge and its secondary crests. The increase in population density meant a gradual occupation of all of the cultivable land. The various strategies of expansion of this arable area had negative repercussions; they dragged the crop yields downward leading to a "demographic entrapment."[15]

The occupation of all cultivable land combined with the increase in population led to a constant decrease in the size of farms. Gradually, especially between 1950 and 1960, land ownership went through transformation from collective family ownership, which gave each household of the clan a plot of land, to individual ownership by the head of the home, otherwise known as *isambu*, or the management by one family. The system of inheritance resulted in the constant partitioning of land among all the married male heirs. Picking up the development of single-family cultivation along successive generations, Zebron Mulindwa notes that:

The decrease in land inherited by each individual was determined by the number of heirs. The more heirs, the smaller the size of the land they inherited; as a result, family cultivation decreased by at least half with each generation. . . . The reduction of a family's cultivable land, and the subsequent exhaustion of the land, only increased the vulnerability to poverty and the exhaustion of the soil, a precious capital for this rural population with no other source of revenue. It is within this context that "oversaturation" of the land, coupled with slow progress in agricultural techniques, threatening the different elements of the physical environment, especially in the form of extreme soil degradation, came with a practically permanent food shortage.[16]

Demographic pressure, the decrease in cultivable land, and soils exhausted from excessive use led to several socioeconomic problems that hardened social relations.

Among the most serious problems was that of property disputes and resulting conflicts. The source of these conflicts is partly historical, being related to land appropriation under the monarchy and the changes brought about during the 1959 revolution:

Within the native administration, a wealthy authority (chief, deputy chief, etc.) could seize the best lands suitable for cultivation and grazing in their constituencies, depriving some of his constituents. Or he usurps from someone (kunyaga) in order to give larger pieces of land to one of his loyal and most submissive subjects (kugaba). From the 1959 revolution until 1963, victims of such land-grabbing got back their land either by chasing away the "political" occupant or by taking the matter to court. The pieces of land under dispute included properties that belonged to a single tenant of one of the various farming areas as well as vast stretches as large as a hill. Underlying these court cases was the desire to obtain the greatest amount of cultivable land because ownership was proof of one's wealth during this period when the socioeconomic values based on cattle were being challenged. This transformation into capital of land that the grabbers did not immediately need always complicated the resolution of disputes. Thus many court cases would go through all the levels of the judiciary system before the loser of the case would decide to abandon it. That is why, although disputes of this kind were officially settled through the legal process, they fueled bitterness and resentment between the two opposing sides, not to mention often tragic endings such as poisonings and murder.[17]

However, the vast majority of land disputes during the 1980s and the early 1990s involved micro-properties.

Indeed, numerous families facing acute shortage of farmland squabbled over a few square meters, whole parcels of land of varying sizes, or property that belonged to less productive and thus socially weaker neighbors. On some occasions, families who had inherited land from the same person but not enough to divide among their children would fight over the ownership of a specific parcel of land. Because land inheritance was not written down, and considering that there was no land registry in the rural area, the slyest person usually won the case. These lawsuits were fueled above all by a vague and unreliable system of boundary demarcation combined with the corruption of the officials carrying out the demarcation.[18]

The scarce land was no longer enough to occupy manual laborers all day long, and the seasonal nature of farmwork brought the villagers together for only part of the year. "Various studies show that traditional cultivation uses only 30 percent of the available manual labor and lasts for only 40 percent of the working hours. This is evidence of the 'unemployment in disguise' prevalent on all the Rwandan hills."[19]

Growing dependence on the market, which contradicted the self-reliance of their traditional vocations, compelled peasants to look for sources of income besides their family farms. The region had few opportunities for work. The main ones were daily wage labor at the homes of people such as businessmen, teachers, and civil servants as well as road maintenance and construction. Churches, communes, and health care centers also offered some limited employment opportunities. Some peasants engaged in hawking wares. One of the main strategies of seeking employment was migrating to the large towns, and despite its small size, Kibuye Town was the only real urban center in the region. The jobseekers also migrated farther, toward Gisenyi Town or Kigali Town or even to foreign countries Zaire, Burundi, and Tanzania. In the countryside, they worked as agricultural laborers, and in the towns they worked as night security guards or in construction of buildings and roads. The different modes of migration were determined by age and marital status. Men with families most often left on a temporary basis; that is, for a few months. The situation of the uneducated youths such as those who did not get admission into high school, was more precarious. The youths, who were the majority, were the most acutely affected by the shrinking size of family farmland. A large number of them helped with the farmwork, but most of them abandoned it for lack of pay. Many left the countryside and spent the day idling about the nearest trading centers, still very rural. They worked in the informal sector as house servants, cobblers, and porters. After they had earned enough money for a bus ticket, these youths left home for Gisenyi Town or Kigali Town, which held the greatest attraction for the youths of Kibuye. In the towns, some of these young men and women worked as house servants, nannies, and bar servers, and others committed petty crime and prostitution.[20]

This situation on the western slope of the Congo -Nile Ridge existed during the early 1980s. With almost all the cultivable land used and with no new ways out of this agricultural impasse, the situation only worsened over the years, as I show in the chronology that follows.

The Final Years of the MRND Party-State

The Social and Security Situations (1984–1990)

This period began with a food shortage in Kibuye Prefecture in early 1984. In March, violent rainfalls damaged the crops. The rains stopped abruptly and were followed by sunlight that dried up the crops. This harsh weather left peasants with almost nothing to harvest. The worst-affected were Gishyita, Mabanza, Mwendo, Rutsiro, and Rwamatamu Communes.[21] In order to survive, people stole crops from other farms, and families fled for Zaire. In Giko Sector of Gisovu Commune, a "certain Nyilindekwe who lived alone, without a wife or child, and who worked as a casual agricultural laborer, fell sick and died in his bed because he was unable to earn money to buy food."[22] In Gikaranka Sector, "men left saying they were going to look for food for their families but did not return. Young men stole from the farms during the night and raped the women who had been abandoned. There were also cases of men bringing food home and sharing it only with their wives and the youngest children, and telling the older children that they were left up to their own devices."[23] In Gitabura Sector, three men fled with a family's pot of food. In Twumba Sector, a "man called Livugabaramye died of hunger. One of his sons abandoned his wife and children, who were in terrible condition. The theft of crops from the fields has attained worrying proportions; some Batwas acted as if they were suicidal by stealing from farms in broad daylight."[24]

The Kibuye Prefecture security council meeting in November 1984 noted the increase in theft and concluded that these thefts were not organized crime but were mostly a result of the food shortage the region was experiencing, so its members decided to organize roundups in the four urban centers of the prefecture.[25] The following year, a census by the Kibuye Prefecture security council in September stated that the number of vagrants living in the different centers but originally from a different commune was 748. However, it criticized Mabanza and Rwamatamu Communes for giving figures far lower than the actual numbers.[26] In general, the burgomasters accused the vagrants of making a living from theft, of committing violence, and often of being prison escapees from their home communes. At the same meeting, the prefecture council security committee examined a list of Rwandan illegals incarcerated in Burundi and noted that at least ten of them were residents of local communes.[27]

Kibuye Prefecture also experienced a wave of murders in the same period. At the prefecture council security committee meeting of November 1985, the prefect said in his opening address that murders had been reported in almost all of the communes in the months of July, August, and September.[28] The council noted that the main culprits of the resurgence in violent robbery and murders were the vagrants living in the surrounding area and on the islands of

Lake Kivu. These criminals could be found in Rwamatamu, Gishyita, Gitesi, Mabanza, and Kayove Communes along the lakeshore in Gisenyi Prefecture. "These people help themselves to land on the islands for cultivation, without a care about plundering the communes."[29] The council lamented that when the list of the dead was circulated in the communes, nobody responded by reporting the disappearance of a relative. The committee provided a list of murder victims identified between July and September 19:

- In Rwamatamu Commune, a certain Mpatsagatwa was killed on August 7, 1985, over a land dispute.
- In Rwamatamu Commune, Mubumbyi was killed by some drunkards on August 31, 1985.
- In Gishyita Commune, a certain Mukomeza was caught stealing and killed on July 21, 1985.
- In Gishyita Commune, on August 4, 1985, a certain Batibaza was killed while stealing.
- In Rutsiro Commune, a decomposing corpse of a woman was found on August 14, 1985.
- In Rutsiro Commune, a certain Balihenda, accused of rape, was beaten and burned on September 18, 1985.
- In Kivumu Commune, a certain Munyandamutsa was killed for stealing a cow.
- In Bwakira Commune, a certain Nyirankundabanyanga was killed along with her two-year-old child on July 11, 1985, because the local authorities did not monitor the land dispute within the family.
- In Gitesi Commune, the body of a certain Nyirabugingo, who was killed because of a court dispute over land, was found on September 14, 1985.
- In Mabanza Commune, the strangled body of a ten-year-old child called Nahayo was found on July 29, 1985.
- In Mabanza Commune, the body of a trader called Nzamwita, killed for money that he had just borrowed from the Banque populaire in Kigali Town, was found on September 2, 1985.
- In Mabanza Commune, a certain Mwiseneza was castrated, and his arms were cut off, on September 26, 1985. He had provoked people by eating in small taverns and refusing to pay.
- In Mabanza Commune, the corpse of a woman never identified was found on September 27, 1985.[30]

To this list of thirteen murder victims within the communes, one must also add the corpses found floating in Lake Kivu. It is therefore not possible to get an accurate number of murders committed in the prefecture during the three months in question. Nevertheless, one can appreciate the significance of the problem through the reaction of the prefecture council members, who seem to have concluded that the frequency of these murders was very important. However, the motives for the murders are also significant, and in this case, land disputes were the motives of a significant number of the murders. Another fraction of these murders was committed by robbery victims who took the law into their own hands and killed the thieves. Neither kind of case involved career criminals but ordinary people, members of families or people living in the same neighborhood.

During a prefecture council security committee meeting in May 1987, the Kibuye Prefecture prosecutor communicated the findings in the attorney general's report for the year 1986 on the murders in the prefecture. The Kibuye prosecutor added that the figures cited did not reflect reality because some communes had no judicial police inspector, so files had not been handed over to the attorney general. He also mentioned that the number of murders had declined from the previous year. But overall, the Kibuye prosecutor indicated that the judicial police inspectors were overwhelmed by the increasing number of criminal cases to prosecute. The attorney general thus proposed that the commune police chiefs and the brigadiers be allowed to resume the role of the judicial police. The figures provided in the prosecutor's report indicated that of the 119 cases in court of murder, 91 of the accused were men, 19 were women, and 9 were children. After a discussion of the report conclusions commune by commune, "meeting participants noted that most of the crimes, including murders, were connected to land problems."[31]

Three years later, the prefecture council security committee in January 1990 took stock of the security during the year 1989.[32] Its members took note of not only the many thefts of crops from the farms in the previous year but also the huge drop in the number of murders. Only forty-one homicides were reported for 1989. The security committee did not give an explanation for this decrease in violent crime. For the months of January and February, the security situation was considered generally good.[33]

In early February 1990, thousands of people in Mabanza, Mwendo, and Bwakira Communes lost their crops to hailstorms.[34] At the end of that month, heavy rains in the region caused considerable damage to the farms and destroyed bridges. The government came to the rescue of the affected communes and gave money for food to those in need as well as metal sheets to rebuild their houses.[35] In his letter dated April 17, 1990, the prefect reported a resurgence in violence.[36] The security report for March 1990 also indicates a rise in crime at the end of February.[37] This change seems to closely follow the sudden deterioration of the food situation. The same document reported that most of the violence was committed by repeat offenders who had previously served at least one prison term. The prefecture council security committee expressed the hope that the criminals would be severely punished because they had been receiving light sentences, after which they returned home to taunt people and commit more violence given that they were not afraid of prison. They were therefore arousing anger within the population. Finally, the report also criticized the limited reliability of the prison system given that many prisoners escaped.[38] During its meeting of August 24, 1990, the committee drew attention to different violent occurrences in July and August and noted that the "murders rooted in land disputes are a persistent problem, and the solution lies in raising the level of education among the population."[39]

This short chronology of the late 1980s simply confirms the conclusions of Mulindwa's study, limited to the western part of the prefecture in the first half of the same decade. There was a significant level of violence caused by land problems and the precarious equilibrium of the food situation in the prefecture. Any upset in this balance seemed to be immediately followed by abrupt surges in violence. I would like now to explore the extent to which the violence in this social climate had acquired an ethnic dimension.

Interethnic Relations in Kibuye Prefecture

Until the 1990s, some Hutu circles in Kibuye Prefecture defended the idea that the revolution had not been fulfilled there given that Tutsis, in their view, continued to enjoy undue influence.[40] This was probably behind the fact that in 1973, Kibuye was one of the rare prefectures where the violence spilled from the urban and educational centers into the hills. The local authorities instigated an arson campaign against Tutsi homes in Gitesi Commune and others, also under pressure from looters from Rutsiro Commune.[41] Just as in 1959, in 1973 gangs of looters attacked Tutsis in Mabanza and Gitesi Communes. Hutu and Tutsi residents, in solidarity, repulsed the looters.[42] Official documents at the time, and before 1973, betrayed frustration with what was considered the strong Tutsi presence, especially in state services such as education. Citing the prefect of Kibuye, the minister of the interior and judicial affairs, under President Kayibanda, in January 1973 stated,

> Primary school education in Kibuye Prefecture is flooded with Tutsi teachers who are unhappy with our regime, thus the predicament of our children who need to be taught by these people who are indifferent to our regime, especially in terms of patriotism. . . . In the secondary schools, teaching is in the hands of Europeans and some Tutsi teachers; it is high time we thought about encouraging Hutu children to pursue higher education in humanities and pedagogical institutes, with a view to train teachers who can teach our children.[43]

Thus in the 1973 crisis Tutsi students were expelled from schools and, in some regions, Tutsi homes were burned and their cows eaten. These events did not last and had limited repercussions on the coexistence between Hutus and Tutsis.[44] They definitely provided the opportunity for new adjustments, however, such as reduction of land that belonged to Tutsis. The Tutsis of Gitesi and

Gishyita Communes took refuge in the mountains and returned to their homes a few days later.[45] Often, the Hutus who had burned down their houses helped them rebuild. A certain number of Tutsis, especially the "intellectuals," that is, secondary school students, teachers, and state officials chose exile, some in Burundi and others in Zaire.[46] Many Tutsis also fled to Idjwi Island, next to Rwamatamu Commune.

After President Habyarimana took power on July 5, 1973, the new government also sought to contain the Tutsis while simultaneously affirming its desire to fight ethnic discrimination. In his first meeting with newly appointed prefects on July 31, 1973, Lt. Col. Kanyarengwe asked the prefect of Kibuye to monitor in particular the return of refugees and directed, "He should watch the Tutsi ethnic group, which, by virtue of forming the majority in some communes, wields control over the rest of the population by imposing its feudal role."[47] Although President Habyarimana publicly preached peace and reconciliation, in Kibuye Prefecture, just like everywhere else, his new regime was not keen on refugees returning home. A strict selection process for candidates seeking to return was implemented to discourage more returns. In March 1974, the Kibuye prefect sent the following memo to burgomasters of the communes:

> As a result, we are experiencing a massive return of refugees in our prefecture, especially those coming from Idjwi Island without valid documents and under several pretenses. Given that most of these people with irregular status are women, who often have no money on them to pay fines, and that imprisoning them under Article 1 of the ordinance-law of December 29, 1962, regarding national passports would discredit the country, I have the honor to ask you to observe the following: (1) Refugees returning to the commune to be reintegrated (and these are rarely unaccompanied women) will be sent to the prefecture as usual for a review of their cases in accordance with Presidential Decree 25/01 of February 26, 1966; (2) Every refugee, man or woman, who claims to be visiting relatives or friends should definitely be issued a pass from the appropriate authorities of the country of departure and stamped with a visa by our department of immigration services. If the individual has not been furnished with the required documents, the individual has a maximum of twelve hours to definitively leave the commune; and (3) Every refugee without the required documents who comes to see if peace has really been restored or on any other pretext but with a similar goal, that refugee has no trust, and it is on trust that you will build up your commune. Twelve hours is the maximum time allowed for definitively leaving the commune. Should this period expire in the second and third instances, Article 7 of the same ordinance-law must immediately come into effect.[48]

The presidential degree of February 26, 1966, required, among other things, that the refugee present himself or herself at the prefecture, and it vested in the prefect alone the power to determine whether the refugee was to resettle. Subsequently, the decree stipulated that all of the property left behind by the refugee and already occupied or granted to a third party by the state could not be reclaimed under any circumstances. In a prefecture such as Kibuye with a huge, largely peasant Tutsi population living in relative harmony with peasant Hutu neighbors, the stakes in respecting these procedures were high. However, between the Hutu and Tutsi elites, tensions existed. In 1973, some Tutsis had believed the reconciliatory speeches of the new government and were accused of displaying an air of triumph. During Habyarimana's grand tour of all of the country's prefectures between April and August 1976, the prefecture's "intellectuals" who came to listen to the president reacted to the idea of reconciliation proposed by the newly created MRND. The public views of the Kibuye population were recorded by the president's office in a summary of the discussions as follows:

> On the problem of Hutu-Tutsi relations: It was said that harmony must prevail, but in reality, hypocrisy prevails. The Tutsis now say that the 1973 coup restored to them the social status taken from them by the 1959 revolution. Because the reason for their conflict is power, reconciliation would necessarily mean that such-and-such people should regain the power they had. (For a long time, the room is filled with loud expressions of doubt about achieving this reconciliation).[49]

After the crisis of 1973 was over, and the new refugees were contained outside the borders, the few mentions of the ethnic question in the prefecture official documents over the subsequent years refer to minor conflicts with an ethnic angle in the schools.[50] Pacifying speeches and efficient control by MRND institutions established in 1976 influenced this near disappearance of open ethnic tensions in the prefecture.

The only mention of some ethnic tension I was able to find in the official documents appears in the prefecture security council May 1987 report, which mentions that "murders, and problems related to ethnic and religious affiliation are beginning to decrease."[51] Given the official policy, the regional and local administrators engaged in self-censorship and did not report such incidents, but that would not have been possible had not such conflicts been rare. The good relations between Hutus and Tutsis in the prefecture were confirmed by different people who had lived in Gitesi, Gishyita, and Mwendo Communes.[52]

Mass Disobedience

As already mentioned, before 1990 the popular expressions of disobedience toward the state at the grassroots comprised crime, vagrancy, and rural exodus. These types of behavior were largely what Jean-François Bayart and colleagues refer to as "infrapolitical."[53] However, one type of movement of dissent against authority was expressed rather clearly: religious dissidence, particularly in Kibuye Prefecture. The arrests mentioned in the following Kibuye prefect report took place in Mabanza, Gisovu, Rwamatamu, Bwakira, and Gishyita Communes:

> I am honored to let you know that since February 21, 1986, thirty-three self-proclaimed abarokore, who clearly displayed rather subversive and perverted behavior, have been arrested. From our analysis of their actions, we have reason to fear that they have formed groups of subversives among the population who express contempt for the Supreme Authority of the country. . . . These groups of abarokore roam specific areas (Cyangugu, Kibuye, Gikongoro, Nyanza) preaching against animation, wearing lapel pins with President Habyarimana's portrait, singing the national anthem, applauding authorities, and so on. Above all, these people are known for their vagrancy, for making too much noise all night long, for the arrogant and subversive attitude inherent in their attempts to convince the people not to respect human authority because Jesus alone deserves respect![54]

These movements, labeled sects by the authorities, seemed to be in response to the heavy weight of MRND social control over people at the grassroots, and their subversive intent was quite obvious.[55] In the forwarding letter of his report, the minister in the president's office informed the minister of the interior and the secretary-general of the National Central Intelligence unit that the head of state was asking that "all energies be put into identifying this propaganda network in order to bring it to a halt permanently."[56]

Three months later, the minister wrote to the public prosecutor of Kibuye instructing that the thirty-three people arrested in Kibuye be charged with "threatening the security of the state."[57] But the arrest was not enough to deter this initial group of *abarokore*, as the prefecture council security committee report of May 1986 indicates:

> Ever since the arrest of groups of abarokore leaders in the communes of Kibuye Prefecture, other abarokore appear even more determined. The prefect told the council that he had implemented the decision of the prefecture authorities to completely eradicate this movement that threatens public safety by ordering burgomasters to arrest all those who formed abarokore groups and charge them in court. For this problem to be eradicated once and for all, any person implicated, whether a woman, a sickly person, or anyone else, should be arrested. . . . The burgomasters carried out these orders, and several abarokore were arrested and taken to court. What remains now is to send them to Kigali. Some have asked the military base in Kibuye for help with trucks to transport the suspects to Kigali.[58]

As one can see, the movement proved determined. It was systematically and resolutely suppressed; even the highest organs of the state took charge of the issue. Four months later, in September 1986, a report of the security committee mentioned that arrests of the *abarokore* were ongoing but that the movement had lost its momentum.[59] Such a display of open rebellion against the authorities was rare at the time. Five years later, when political parties were established, mass insubordination toward authorities had become almost the norm.

Mass Mobilization, War, and the Transition to Democracy

To better understand how the population in Kibuye Prefecture would respond to the calls by the national and regional political elites, it is important to once again describe the economic and social context of that period of the early 1990s.

Socioeconomic Context

In early 1991, the commission responsible for soil protection and conservation raised concern about the food situation in Kibuye Prefecture. The commission had just carried out a one-week tour of all the communes between March 25 and 31, 1991. It noted that almost all of the communes in the prefecture were suffering from food shortage. The commission classified the food situation in the following three categories:

1. The communes experiencing permanent food shortage, led by Rwamatamu, followed by Gishyita;
2. The communes whose food situation varied with the seasons: Mwendo, Gisovu, Gitesi, and Bwakira; and
3. The communes attempting to overcome the food crisis: Rutsiro, Mabanza, and Kivumu.[60]

The communes in the first group were the most densely populated, but they also had the largest Tutsi population.[61] When combined with the sensitive political situation at the beginning of the 1990s, these three factors proved to be explosive.

The prefecture security report for April 1991 explains that despite the outbreak of the war with the RPF and the ensuing tensions, the cases of violent behavior among the Kibuye population had more to do with the usual social problems. "A resurgence of banditry has been noted in the communes, and crime is not decreasing. Nevertheless, in most cases, this crime is caused by family conflict, drunkenness, and hatred between individuals not linked to the tension beginning to emerge in some groups following the Inkotanyi attack on the country."[62] The report of the following month explained the causes of the food shortage:

Although the climate remains relatively good compared with previous years, and this despite the few periods of sunshine in Lake Kivu, famine is far from disappearing from the prefecture, since the underlying causes are severe land shortage, infertile soils, plant diseases, bad weather, and poverty of the peasants as well as the gullies left behind by previous floods. . . . The most recent report from the communes indicates that 56,539 people need emergency assistance.[63]

This means that at that time, the Kibuye inhabitants in a critical situation comprised 12 percent of the total prefecture population.[64] Once again, the shortage and deterioration of land as an important cause of hunger within the population is emphasized. In the extract below, another effect of land shortage is highlighted:

May witnessed an unprecedented resurgence in crime caused by interpersonal hatred as much as by the "struggle for life" caused by family tussles over limited land. It was for this reason that a young man was killed in Kivumu Commune by his older sister, his own mother, and his nephews. A similar case was reported in the same commune on the night of May 14–15 when a family of five, parents and children, was killed by the son of the second wife of the father of the murdered family because of problems of inheritance typical of polygamy. The criminal also slaughtered three sheep, which he placed on the bodies of the dead. In Bwakira Commune, a widow and her four children were killed on the night of May 18–19. The criminals were arrested but the investigations have not yet revealed the real causes behind the crime. In the same commune, a young man was killed by three people, including his younger brother (who had escaped the commune jail) in revenge for his having participated in the investigations leading to his arrest. . . . The cases of serious crime reported this month occurred especially in the communes of Birambo Subprefecture, specifically in Kivumu and Bakwira Communes. As the security council of June 1 noted, the main causes are linked to problems associated with polygamy, family disputes over land, the attitudes in this region, and most of all the "bargain market" of court sentences the people consider too lenient and annoying; they are therefore quick to dispense justice on their own, most times in the form of death.[65]

Although the serious violence, including murder, was concentrated in Birambo Subprefecture in the highlands of the eastern slope of the Congo-Nile Ridge during this period, such incidents were not unique to this part of the prefecture.

The May–June 1991 report refers to the manner in which murder had become commonplace for the youths and people who had not attended school.

Crime is still on the rise, especially in Birambo Subprefecture. The main causes are described in previous reports. According to the analysis of the Kibuye Court, most of the criminals are illiterate people who act without considering the consequences. In fact, they commit murder just to get a drink or just for a pittance. The other category of criminals is young people who have left prison having learned from hard-core criminals whom they met in prison.[66]

Although acknowledging that the food situation had slightly improved, the prefect explained that there was still a growing need for assistance, with the latest estimates indicating that 117,313 people were in need of food assistance but not necessarily in a critical situation.[67]

The July 1991 security report does not mention any violence; it also explains that the food situation was temporarily good, with the sorghum and potato harvest in full swing.[68] Between August 15 and September 6, 1991, seven murder cases were filed in court, most of the crimes committed in Rwamatamu Commune.[69] Prefecture security reports after August 1991, when political parties were established in the prefecture, no longer mention the socioeconomic conditions of the prefecture residents; the intensity of the multiparty political battles among the population took up all the attention.

In my review of the socioeconomic evolution of Kibuye Prefecture and its consequences for public safety between the end of 1990 and August 1991, we see the continuity with previous periods almost perfectly matching situations of socioeconomic distress with rising violence.

The Outbreak of the War in Kibuye Prefecture

The launch of the war by the RPF on October 1, 1990, had an impact on interethnic relations within some circles and in defined local areas. In his report of November 1990, the prefect reported some interethnic tension around Lake Kivuin Mabanza, Gitesi, Gishyita, and Rwamatamu Communes, home to a significant number of Tutsis, and some of them rejoiced at the news of the RPF attack.[70] Further on, the prefect specifies that the tension in Gishyita Commune was found primarily in intellectual circles.[71] Serious incidents that occurred in Kivumu Commune were instigated by outsiders to the commune and the prefecture, that is, from Kibilira Commune in Gisenyi Prefecture.[72] "In Kivumu Commune, Tutsi families were victims of vandalism by people, especially from Kibilira Commune. Despite fierce resistance from the Kivumu residents, a sign of their unity and solidarity, the attackers managed to burn twelve houses, destroy the roofs of eight houses, and steal eleven cows, four sheep, two pigs, and several household items."[73] In Mabanza Commune, pro-RPF leaflets were distributed a few days after the attack. On October 13, 1990, the prefect chaired an extraordinary meeting of the commune MRND congress for the purpose of further sensitizing political leaders to the dangers of a possible confrontation between the populations in the naive belief that they are part of resolving the ethnic problem facing the country, a situation that might work to the advantage of the enemy, whose goal is to destroy and destabilize. During the conference, the prefect also denounced the disgraceful attitude of some Tutsis who were fanning ethnic hatred and agitating Hutus in order to provoke disorder and panic within the population. He explained that everyone, Hutu as well as Tutsi, would respond to these acts, which might benefit or be aimed at benefiting the enemy's cause.[74]

During the same period, the prefect chaired an extraordinary MRND commune meeting in Gishyita Commune. Gishyita and Mabanza Communes had been "identified as extremely high-risk areas."[75]

On October 14, 1990, the burgomaster of Mabanza toured the commune, where he met with cell committee members to sensitize them to remaining united and to fighting against the unhealthy atmosphere spreading within the population. The next day, the councilor of Kigeyo Sector led the population in resisting an attack by residents of Kibilira Commune (Gisenyi Prefecture) and from Rutsiro and Kivumu (in Kibuye Prefecture) who sought to burn Tutsi houses, rob them, and feast on their livestock.[76]

In the following section of his report, the Kibuye prefect expressed fear that the prefecture would become a base of operations for RPF soldiers.

> In fact, just as I had indicated in my report sent to you through a letter dated October 11, 1990, the peaceful environment in Kibuye is unstable; the slightest spark could set the structure alight. The coast of Lake Kivu is susceptible to being used by the Inkotanyi: the Tutsi population, which does not hide its satisfaction with any hint of the slightest defeat suffered on our side, is almost a majority, and the porous border favors infiltration from the lake into Nyungwe Forest. In addition to these two social and geographical factors, the military officers assigned to Kibuye are insignificant, and the enemy cannot be ignorant of this.[77]

The day after the outbreak of war, the situation in Kibuye Prefecture had two dimensions: on the one hand, tensions emerged in the four communes along Lake Kivu, particularly in Mabanza and Gishyita Communes and in Kibuye Town (Gitesi Commune) to some extent because of the strong Tutsi presence, some of whom rejoiced over the RPF attack. In Rwamatamu and Gishyita Communes and Kibuye Town, there were tensions particularly among the intellectuals. The extracts presented above do not identify with precision the Tutsis provoking the tensions in Mabanza.

The second dimension concerns the north of the prefecture, on the border with Gisenyi Prefecture. This time, the issue was less about ethnopolitical tensions, and more about attacks by gangs of looters looking to steal Tutsi property. The most affected by this violence were Kivumu and Mabanza Communes. Mabanza Commune therefore fell into both categories along sociogeographical lines. Of the three communes along the lake, it was the commune with the smallest Tutsi population, mostly concentrated in the south around the historical Rubengera Region. On the other hand, the northern part of the commune was also part of the social dynamics of northern Kibuye, sociologically and politically close to Gisenyi Prefecture.[78]

A third important element was the significant efforts by prefecture and commune authorities to maintain peace and security following the announcement of the RPF attack, in an attempt to control the tension driven by ethnic politics and by the desire to loot. Also worth noting is that only the looters from the northern side of the prefecture committed actual acts of violence. In the period that followed, beginning in mid-1991, the relative calm still prevailing in Kibuye Prefecture would be seriously threatened.

Multiple Parties in Kibuye Prefecture

I present this section in two parts. In the first, I look at the events on the prefecture level, and in the second, I trace how the events unfolded in the different communes.

The Prefecture Perspective

Between January and August 1991, Kibuye Prefecture experienced unrest in the form of protest against the political monopoly of the MRND, calling for the establishment of multiparty rule. This agitation was a reflection of the same struggle taking place in other regions of the country, especially in Kigali Prefecture. In his security report for March 1991, the prefect affirmed that his prefecture was calm but that

> this peace was almost shattered in some sectors of Mabanza and Rutsiro Communes bordering Kayove Commune [Gisenyi Prefecture], where interethnic conflict had broken out. . . . Vigorous measures were taken to stem the tide coming from Kayove and threatening to engulf our area. We praised the collaboration of the military officers stationed in Kibuye who accepted our request to organize patrols as deterrents in the sectors under threat.[79]

In the same report, the prefect adds, "Mabanza Commune is a very sensitive area with underlying tensions." Permission was granted for special efforts to maintain order and to monitor this commune where the explosion of tensions had the potential to engulf the "entire region, if not the whole country."[80] When it came to politics, the prefect explained that according to the local leaders, the residents remained silent on their political preferences. He nevertheless raised two issues facing the prefecture when the issue of political reform was raised; first were the "promises the head of state and president of the MRND made to the people, which have not been fulfilled." One of the promises the people considered the most important was the construction of the Gitarama-Kibuye road and the Kibuye Town market. The people did not accept the reasons for the postponement of these projects. "Some no longer hesitated to declare that the MRND had done nothing for Kibuye and that it was therefore reasonable to try one's luck in another party." The second point was raised by the sector councilors, who said that their salary was too low and had not been increased despite numerous promises. These councilors emphasized the important role they would play for the MRND during the establishment of the multiparty system.[81]

In his report of April 1991, referring to the release of people jailed beginning in October 1990 after the launching of the war by the RPF, the prefect explained that tensions had reasonably subsided despite the people's uneasiness about the release of suspected Inkotanyi accomplices. Some people did not welcome the massive release of people whose innocence was still in doubt, and they feared that the latter would dig out hidden weapons. From April 7 to May 4, 1991, the prefect toured all the communes of the prefecture. He met with about sixty MRND propagandists and potential leaders to defend the party colors in the prefecture and explained the new manifesto and statutes of the new MRND.[82]

On May 23, 1991, the minister of public works held a public meeting to refute MRND opponents and reassure the Kibuye population that construction of the Gitarama-Kibuye road was starting soon. To appear more credible, he brought representatives from the European Development Fund, the World Bank, and the Swiss Agency for Development and Cooperation. On May 31, 1991, the prefect called for a meeting with the heads of the prefecture administrative departments, school inspectors, and representatives of different faith communities. The aim was to exchange ideas on what approach to adopt during the transition period to multiparty rule. "Everyone was asked to avoid fanaticism, to be objective, and to safeguard the social peace."[83]

Two months before the legalization of political parties, the Republican Democratic Movement (MDR) appeared to be already putting pressure on Kibuye Prefecture.

> In order to prepare the people for multiparty democracy, the number of sensitization meetings in the sectors increased recently; an evaluation tour of all the communes carried out by the prefecture commission discovered that the MRND was still the overall leading party in the villages, even though the villages were still seeking more information about other political parties. Meanwhile, the state officers were split between the MRND and the MDR, and up to that time, the other parties were not known well enough. In any case, MDR propagandists were unrelenting in using educated people, especially teachers, to attract sympathy from villagers vulnerable to the ideology of this political institution, still part of their memories. It is also useful to point out that the preparations for the census have been entrusted to students, and that generally, the students' secondary motivation is to spread pro-MDR propaganda.[84]

In his security report for July 1991, the prefect related the visit of the head of state to Kibuye Prefecture, where he opened a school in Kivumu Commune. The prefect explained to President Habyarimana the prefecture and commune authorities' efforts to spread MRND propaganda. Kibuye Prefecture seemed to have entered the MRND good books with the appointment of a Kibuye native, Edouard Karemera, as secretary-general of the party. The prefect suggested that this appointment had rallied the MRND troops in the prefecture and influenced many residents to acquire party membership.[85]

In August 1991, the prefect ordered the burgomasters to implement a series of security measures in response to the so-called incursions by the Inkotanyi, who according to prefect were "no longer imaginary but real given that some institutions have reported infiltrators being officially issued visitor or tourist passes" and to rectify the negligence in the issuance of passes. Intelligence-gathering from the population was reinforced, roadblocks were erected on the paths and roads into the communes, the registration of cars and their passengers passing through was recorded, and directives from the ministry of the interior on issuing permits to move from one commune to another were strictly implemented.[86] The RPF first arrived in Kibuye prefecture during the genocide in 1994.

On August 18, 1991, the first MDR political rally at the Gatwaro Regional Stadium marked the beginning of public activities of opposition parties. A sizable crowd attended this meeting in Kibuye Town, and the immediate outcome was a movement of disobedience against local authorities. At the end of the month, criminals were reported to have started major forest fires in Mwendo and Gitesi Communes.[87]

The participants of the prefecture security council meeting of August 28, 1991, suggested three possible explanations for the fires, including

> propaganda directed by supporters intoxicated with the excessive fanaticism of some political parties. Some said this would be a kind of prelude to the violent fire, which would follow the imminent MDR victory in the upcoming elections, just as in 1959. A third possible explanation is that those who committed these crimes hoped to destroy the forests, where the Inkotanyi could hide. In fact, some believe that the administration authorities are not neutral and accuse them of being MRND pawns. Consequently, the council concludes that the arsonists want to destabilize the current government.[88]

The August 1991 report of the prefect explained that the MRND and the MDR were the most popular political parties in Kibuye Prefecture. He criticized the insulting, disruptive, and disparaging claims of MDR propagandists who attacked even the person of the head of state.[89] "In fact, they incite the people to civil disobedience, to stop carrying out civic duties such as paying taxes and taking part in *umuganda*, even in its current democratic form, supposedly because umuganda is an MRND project. They also encourage people to set the bushes and forests on fire."[90] Further on in his report, the prefect described the political offensive of opposition parties, but mainly by the MDR, in all the communes of the prefecture. In the same report, the prefect regretted the lack of dynamism and initiative of the MRND in the prefecture, with the party being forced to trail after MDR supporters to refute the latter's claims.[91] "The way it conducts its campaigns seems closely modeled on the old MRND and its weak propaganda and gives the impression that the leaders have not grasped the extent of the influence of opposition parties. One has the impression that the MRND is relying on government authorities, who have to respect the principle of neutrality even though in reality they support the MRND."[92]

In an October 23 meeting of the prefect and all the burgomasters of the prefecture, the latter reaffirmed their support for the MRND and the president of the republic. The country was experiencing a significant political crisis after the parties refused to recognize the president's appointment of Sylvestre Nsanzimana as prime minister. The Kibuye burgomasters expressed their regret that the RPF was achieving its goal of "dividing the Hutu parties— MRND, MDR, [Social Democratic Party (PSD)], and [Christian Democratic Party (PDC)], then of gaining power" and "establishing parties that are traitors and accomplices of the RPF—[Liberal Party (PL), Rwanda Socialist Party (PSR)] and that are together preparing for the return of the refugees." In their final statement, the burgomasters asked the MRND not to give in to radicalization but instead to look for ways to initiate negotiation with the other Hutu parties (MDR, PSD, PDC) to safeguard the power of the majority.[93]

In his October 1991 report, the prefect explained that the burgomasters of the prefecture reaffirmed their loyalty to the MRND and condemned democratization, which they called a "threat to Hutu unity." In the communes, violence, especially against councilors of the sectors, increased. Several opposition party representatives in the sectors behaved as if they were the ones providing state administration services to their party members and therefore overlooked the legal authority. The prefect also noted that the MDR had increased its rallies in the prefecture.[94]

Fearing an Inkotanyi attack launched from Zaire and Idjwi Island, the prefect asked the burgomasters at a November 1991 prefecture security council meeting to watch over strategic public facilities and buildings as well as roads and bridges. It was decided that roadblocks would be sporadically installed in order to mobilize the population without causing fear. The prefect also noted in his report that the march in support of the MRND in the communes took place peacefully but that the "attendance was not as high as one would have liked" given that the "communes reported that the demonstrators numbered between 500 and 800."[95]

In March 1992, the prefect described the consternation of the prefecture security council following the increase in violence, including criminal attacks using grenades and people attacking burgomasters and seeking to forcibly fire them from their duties. The report criticized the abuse of MDR and PL members against local authorities as well as the fact that on the eve of the political rallies, party supporters spent the night beating pails and saucepans. The report drew attention to the theft of produce from the fields because of hunger, the fact that court decisions were no longer implemented because losers refused to comply, the theft of livestock, the gambling, and the rapes.[96] In February 1993, after the violent demonstrations and counterdemonstrations of January 1993, the government suspended political rallies in some prefectures, including Kibuye.[97]

This overview of political developments in the prefecture just before and during the first years of the multiparty period reveals that the former party-state, quickly overwhelmed, was on the defensive, and its representatives had difficulty controlling the population. Violence also spread.

Political Parties in the Communes

In this section I summarize commune reports on the most important political and security events.

Mwendo Commune. In August 1991, forest fires set off by arsonists that caused serious destruction were reported.[98]

In September 1991, a forest was set on fire, apparently by people returning from an MDR rally on September 22.[99]

This commune was not able to pay its staff until December 31, 1991. According to the burgomaster, revenue for the commune was no longer regularly collected because of the influence of opposition parties.[100]

In March 1992, a crowd of 200 people occupied by force grazing land assigned to a group of producers. The invaders drove away the two herds they found, sending them to the commune.[101] A hectare of commune forest was burned by people who could not be identified.[102] The villagers who had seized the grazing land continued to cultivate the land daily.[103]

On March 24, 1992, two men destroyed the house of Ayirwanda after taking off the tiles. The attackers injured his wife in the foot and chased away the councilor of the sector, who wanted to intervene; the councilor broke his leg as he fled.[104]

On April 21, 1992, a trader was attacked in a small trading center by bandits; passers-by who came to his aid caught one of the thugs and beat him to death.[105]

In January 1993, MRND failed at its attempt to organize a demonstration in Mwendo Commune as part of its reaction to the signing of the January 9 Arusha protocol agreement on power-sharing. Tension between MRND and MDR supporters was reported to be high.[106]

In March 1993, there were eight warnings of grenade attacks, and gendarmes were dispatched to carry out night patrols in the commune.[107]

In 1993, Barnabe Rumarana, a teacher, was killed by unidentified people on July 12.

Bakwira Commune. In August 1991, MDR propagandists tried to sensitize the people to disrupt the progress made under the MRND and *umuganda* in particular. Local administrative authorities were confused and attempted to control the situation.[108] A large majority of the people supported the MRND, whereas the remainder, who supported the MDR, mostly consisted of petty criminals whose propaganda partly consisted of openly insulting the incumbent political authorities. The criminals also incited the people against participating in *umuganda*.[109]

On March 15, 1992, six woodland areas were set ablaze, two of which belonged to the commune and together covered forty hectares; the remaining four belonged to individuals.[110]

In Ngoma Sector, villagers seized a field that belonged to the commune. They fled when the councilor intervened. The troublemakers later explained that the MDR cell committee authorized them to cultivate the field. Some villagers vacated the field, but others continued to cultivate.

In Nyabinombe Sector, Nzaratsi Cell, a bar declared loyalty to the MDR, and no Tutsis were allowed to enter. This was instigated by a certain Gatabazi, found with a list of Tutsis of the Nzaratsi Cell to be attacked.

The MDR commune representative and his supporters walked out of a meeting of political party representatives called by the burgomaster on March 19, 1992, declaring that as long as the party was not in power, the commune MDR branch would not contribute to such a meeting and that such a meeting was useless. The party would implement its own ideas when it took over power in the commune.[111]

On April 19, 1992, Hitimana hacked his older brother Munyantwali to death with a machete because his brother had chased away their parents from the family homestead and injured their father.[112]

A group of villagers forcibly seized a forest belonging to the commune to convert it into a brickyard.[113]

In November 1992, one person went to Nyabarongo to carry out a *kubohoza* operation on the Batwas.

In January 1993, as part of its national strategy to oppose the signing of the Arusha protocol agreement, the local branch of the MRND organized a demonstration in Bwakira Commune. The MDR held a counterdemonstration. The Young Republican Democrats (MDR youth wing) attacked and drove back the Interahamwe (MRND youth wing), which had blocked access to the Kilinda Hospital.

On January 23, MDR supporters revolted because of a rumor about the death of the MDR cell committee secretary, called Munyadamutsa. Carrying cudgels, machetes, and clubs, the supporters from different sectors of Bwakira attacked the commune office building and sequestered the burgomaster, Tharsisse Kabasha. Kabasha was freed upon the intervention of the gendarmes. At the same time, the commune MDR secretary came back to Bwakira from Kibuye Town, where he was released from prison after he had been detained on accusation of murdering a certain Kiragi. The gendarmes carried out patrols in the region.[114]

On August 10, 1993, a gendarme on duty killed Ezéchiel Nkundizanye after the gendarme found Nkundizanye and others brazenly defying the legal prohibition against the felling of trees.[115]

On October 24, 1993, Nkurikiyinka, son of Nzamurambaho, was killed by his four brothers on suspicion of poisoning their father.[116]

The villagers caught and beat to death Ruhorahoza, member of a group of thugs who had attacked the civil servant neighborhood of Birambo.[117]

On November 13, 1993, Nkundiye was killed by his son Phéneas; the two were engaged in a legal dispute over land.[118]

A group of thugs attacked the court at Birambo to thwart the hearing of a case because the organizer of the attack feared being sentenced.[119]

On November 27, 1993, Bihoyiki, daughter of Muberandinda, was killed by her father's younger brother.[120]

Kivumu Commune. In August 1991, MDR propagandists fiercely fought the MRND. They sought to show their party supremacy by convincing people that the only member of the MRND in the commune was its president.[121]

Only two parties were known in this commune: the MRND and the MDR. People's attention was drawn to political ideologies and promises made by the parties. Some individuals were "already corrupted by MDR supporters" who incited them not to fulfill their civic duties, such as payment of taxes, participation in *umuganda*, and the fight against soil erosion. The councilors of Sanza and Kigali Sectors were with MDR supporters.[122]

In September 1991, a forest was set on fire.[123]

On February 14, 1992, five bandits carried out a grenade attack in Rukoko Sector with the goal of looting and caused fear in the population.[124]

In March 1992, three thugs from the neighboring Kibilira Commune (Gisenyi Prefecture) attacked Gasave Sector of Kivumu Commune, where they reunited with two of their accomplices.[125] The thugs had come for the purpose of *gukora* ("work") against the Tutsis in Kivumu.[126] They caused panic in Gasave Sector. Realizing that they were under attack, the Tutsis of the sector fled. The prefect dispatched some military officers there who restored order. In a meeting with the population, the prefect asked the people to maintain their unity and not to allow themselves to be influenced by attempts to divide them. He restricted the bar opening hours to between 4 p.m. and 8 p.m. He asked the people to resume their community patrols and to remain in their homes should they hear sounds of attack because the attackers sought to deliberately distance the residents from their houses in order to make looting easier. The prefect finally assured the people of the support of law enforcement, but he also asked the people to take responsibility and not let themselves be intimidated.[127]

Following the Gasave attack, 300 Tutsis from Nyange, Kigali, Ngobagoba, Kivumu, Mwendo, Kibanda, and Ndaro Sectors sought refuge in Nyage Parish; they returned home the following morning.[128]

Still in Kivumu Commune, thirty acres of forest belonging to a Tutsi, two acres belonging to a Hutu, and two acres belonging to a commune police officer were burned on the night of March 10–11, 1992.[129]

In his letter to the minister of the interior and commune development dated March 11, 1992, the prefect explained that he went to Kivumu Commune once again to visit the forests burned in Ngobagoba, Nyange, Kigali, and Sanza Sectors.[130] As a result of the visit, the prefect held a meeting with the cell committees of Ngobagoba, Nyange, and Sanza. He asked the cell committee members not to let themselves be intimidated by a few troublemakers in their communities and not to play the same game as the RPF by spreading fear and internal conflict. He informed them that they had to ensure their own security because not enough military officers to maintain security could be found.

Cell members attending the meeting admitted that they had failed in their duties and that they no longer were telling the truth. They stated that during these turbulent periods, they no longer had any clue which way to go, yet they had been abandoned by their superiors in administration and been destabilized by opposition parties. The members of the cell committees explained that the state institutions had left them at the mercy of thugs, and after the thugs were arrested, they would be released instead of being punished, free to taunt the cell members who had arrested them. The committee members explained that this was why, in the face of the disturbances, they preferred to keep quiet for fear of also becoming victims. The prefect's report on the situation in Kivumu continues to explain that ethnicity was not the major cause of the violence despite the fact that thugs were using ethnicity as an excuse.

However, the prefect acknowledged that the atmosphere did cause friction between ethnic groups because the Tutsis were telling their Hutu neighbors that they would defend themselves, and the Hutus would respond that they had endured the Tutsis for too long. Cell committee members explained that the ethnic issue arose when the Hutus were alone in quelling the fires. The prefect told the cell members this was normal because in the prevailing climate the Tutsis were afraid of being attacked, even more so because the attacks took place at night. On the role of the political parties, the prefect wrote,

> One would not be mistaken to say that the parties are partly responsible for what is happening because when the fires occur, shouts calling for "national

conference" (rukokoma) can be heard.[131] During the rallies, the villagers would be told that they should retake the land the state had claimed for reforestation. It is sad to note that the villagers do not properly understand rukokoma; they see it as a time when they shall have food to eat or when they shall seize the property of others by force, when they shall have land because many people will die and leave land available.[132]

In November 1992, people from Bulinga Commune (Gitarama Prefecture) came to Kigali Sector to incite the residents to stop paying taxes to the commune.[133]

On August 31, 1993, two families were seriously beaten, leading to the death of three people.[134]

On September 11, 1993, Fidèle Mugarura was killed by his son Bagambiki, who had booby-trapped him with a grenade. When it exploded, the family turned a deaf ear, and his body was found only the next day by passersby.[135]

On October 14, 1993, Godefroi Mbarubukeye was killed by his father, Kabayiza.[136]

On December 3, 1993, Ayabagabo, son of Bajyumugambi, was killed by his older brother.[137]

Rutsiro Commune. In August 1991, prominent PL propagandists including Secretary-General Agnès Ntamabyaliro, Monique Mukamana, and Elikan Uzabakiliho went to Rutsiro, where they vehemently attacked MRND policies and the party president.[138]

MRND leaders held an important meeting aimed at sensitizing the population against the corruption in the other political parties. They called the meeting a "resounding success."[139]

In September 1991, another forest fire was set.[140]

On November 24, 1992, between 70 and 120 people held a demonstration and blocked the commune road with tree trunks. The aim of the demonstration was to reject the dismissal of Rutsiro school inspector Elie Basenyeruwenda, who was also vice president of the Rutsiro MRND committee.[141]

On January 21, 1993, the MRND organized a demonstration in Rutsiro as part of the nationwide MRND protest against the signing of the 1993 Arusha protocol on January 9. Roadblocks were erected near the Congo-Nile Ridge market.[142]

From January 21 to 25, the MRND reacted to the opposition's counterdemonstrations by instigating ethnic unrest in its stronghold communes in Ngororero Subprefecture, south of Gisenyi Prefecture. The official toll of Tutsis killed was 133. On the first day of this movement, about 1,400 people invaded Gitebe and Bwiza Sectors next to Kayove Commune (Gisenyi Prefecture). They attacked the Bagogwes, a Tutsi subgroup, many of whom lived there. According to official figures, three Bagogwes died in Rutsiro.[143]

Mabanza Commune. In August 1991, the administration noted that many rural cell committee members of the MRND, especially in three sectors, defected to the MDR. A certain Jean Rwabukwisi, an influential businessman with businesses in Kigali, gave up his shop in the Kibirizi commercial center to be used as an MDR office, and the party flag was raised there.[144]

Multiparty rule divided the cell committee members. There were frequent fights resulting from the discussions between members of the different political parties.[145]

On September 22, 1991, a forest was set on fire after MDR meeting participants declared it was located in an area suitable for human settlement.[146]

In March 1992, villagers coming from Rutsiro to sell their potatoes at the Kibingo Sector market were beaten and robbed on their way back. Several injuries and one death were reported.[147]

On the night of March 15–16, 1992, criminals set ablaze four houses in Buhinga Sector and attacked a young girl with machetes. The girl had to be hospitalized. The thugs stole two goats and a hen. The commune authorities intervened and were able to arrest fourteen people. The thugs had just participated in the MDR elections, attacked with the intention of looting, and claimed to be members of that party. As houses burned, other members of the group set the commune forest in the same sector on fire.[148]

On the night of March 16, 1992, in Kibingo Sector, a certain Munyambonera from Rutsiro stole two traditional gourds belonging to a certain Gasasira. The latter captured and fought with the thief until Gasasira called his family for help. The thief Munyambonera also called for help, saying that the Tutsis would kill him. The Hutus from the neighborhood, who included his brothers-in-law, intervened. Moreover, since the previous day, a rumor had been circulating in the sector that Tutsis were to be killed and their property destroyed because they had refused to participate in the MDR elections. MDR supporters, led by a certain Séverin Gakunde, just elected head of MDR in the sector, along with friends of the thief Munyambonera, attacked Tutsis who chose to flee after they saw the scale of the attack. The assailants destroyed houses and burned a coffee plantation. Several people were injured, but only Munyambonera and one of his brothers-in-law needed hospitalization.

On the night of March 19–20, 1992, once again in Kibingo, a Tutsi called Munyabarame was attacked by a group of Hutus who could not be identified. Military officials intervened, but Munyabarame died from his injuries, and his wife was seriously hurt. Those who attacked him were seeking to avenge Munyambonera, who was rumored to have died but was still alive, although with crippling leg injuries.[149]

On January 28, 1993, three MRND regional officials originally from Mabanza Commune but residents in Kigali arrived to help the MRND prefecture committee. A rumor spread that Interahamwe were going to attack MDR supporters. Members of the Youth for a Democratic Republic (JDR, the MDR youth wing), gathered at the Gitikinini area, where they attacked Ndarayabo, an MRND supporter, who fought back with a bow and arrows. The commune police intervened to prevent any injuries. As a result the MDR supporters, led by the teacher Munyandoha, attempted to attack the home of the Mabanza burgomaster, who was forced to call on the military officers stationed in Kibuye Town to protect him.[150]

Gishyita Commune. In August 1991, the MDR carried out sensitization campaigns with the goal of destabilizing all levels of the administration in order to disrupt the state services. Some MDR supporters tore up MRND membership cards.[151]

Forgetting their obligation to remain neutral, cell members "persecuted" members of opposition political parties.[152]

In October 1991, the councilor of Murangara Sector was beaten and handicapped for life. The burgomaster was also physically attacked in public.

In March 1992, following the massacre of Tutsis in the Bugesera Region of the Kigali-rural Prefecture, many people, the majority of them Tutsis, returned their MRND membership cards, saying that the MRND wanted to exterminate them and that the MDR could protect them.[153]

On March 27, in Musenyi Sector, someone named Gafurere had gone to drink in a bar in Gashyaka. Toward 9:00 p.m., the bar manager and his friends beat Gafurere to death for refusing to pay what he owed.

On the night of April 1, 1992, a certain Harora attacked Nshogoza and his wife with a machete; neighbors were brought to the scene by the screams for help, and the couple's sons beat the attacker to death.[154]

On the night of April 7, 1992, in Gishyita Commune, a certain Ngirabatware attacked his neighbor Nyamutezi with a machete, and Nyamutezi had to be hospitalized. The attacker sought refuge in the commune office because Nyamutezi's parents were looking for him to kill him.[155]

From August 20 to 22, 1992, killings of Tutsis occurred.

From November 19, 1992, onward, Tutsis in the commune no longer stayed in their houses out of fear of the people imprisoned for the August killings, whom the prosecutor had begun to release. Some people hid their livestock and their property.[156]

In April 1993, the preselection for burgomaster of Gishyita yielded the following results:[157]

1. Charles Sikubwabo, a reservist of the Rwandan Armed Forces, Hutu (MDR): twenty-three out of thirty-seven votes
2. Casimir Gatarayiha, teacher, Tutsi (PL): twelve out of thirty-seven votes
3. Canisius Niyonzima, assistant burgomaster, Hutu (PSD): four out of thirty-seven votes

The PL and MDR parties had vigorously campaigned. PL president Justin Mugenzi and Secretary-General Ntamabyaliro personally campaigned. The report by the minister of the interior indicates that the poll was tainted with major irregularities carried out by Prefect Clément Kayishema. The PL contested the results and denounced the irregularities in the election and the climate of intimidation created by MDR threats of anti-Tutsi violence in the commune if a Tutsi was elected. A second poll was organized that yielded the same result.[158]

In October 1993, the competition between political parties gave rise to ethnic tension between the local Hutu-power coalition of the MRND, MDR, and CDR against the Tutsi PL.[159]

Rwamatamu Commune. In August 1991, MDR propagandists accused the MRND of favoring the Tutsis and of having provoked the ongoing war. They criticized onerous school tuition fees and promised to spread disorder.[160]

There were four parties in the commune: the MRND, with the largest influence, followed by the MDR and the PSD, trailed by the PL. Insubordination against the local authorities (sector councilors and heads of cell committees) was reported.[161]

On the night of October 18, 1991, a sordid crime almost degenerated into an ethnic confrontation. A group of known thugs, all of them Hutu, that included a certain Mudacumura, killed a Tutsi shop owner who was also a teacher. The thieves stole various items. Mudacumura's hat was found next to the victim's body. Some of the stolen property was found at the home of Mudacumura's father, who was taken and beaten by a crowd of neighbors, the majority of whom were Tutsis. As he fought back, he injured one of his attackers with a machete and hid in the house. The Tutsi family of the murdered store owner burned down the house, and as the father tried to escape, beat him to death with sticks and hoes and seriously injured his wife. The Tutsis from the neighborhood grouped together in gangs for fear of revenge attacks by Hutus, and rumors of a general confrontation started going around. Normalcy returned after law enforcement intervened.[162]

In addition to general insubordination, it was noted that some sector councilors had actually slackened and some even gave in to the political party representatives, who in turn behaved like state administration officers.[163]

In March 1992, a Hutu peasant who had sold his land to a Tutsi a long time previously gathered members of his family to attack the Tutsi buyer, intimidate him, and reappropriate the land. When the plan was discovered, the Tutsis from the area withdrew to a hill where they waited to fight back. The next day, the burgomaster managed to restore the peace.[164]

On March 14, 1992, a woman was raped in Cyiya Sector by three men and died from her injuries. The sector councilor arrested the criminals, but the woman's relatives came to demand them from the councilor, who refused to release them. The relatives of the victim seized the accused men by force and killed them.[165]

On March 20, 1992, in Mahembe Sector, a man was killed with a hoe by a known criminal who had come to rob him.

On April 1992, still in Mahembe, a young Tutsi man called Masabo, a known vagrant, left to join the RPF. He was not the only one. Investigations revealed that several young Tutsis from Kibuye and Cyangugu Prefectures had also gone to join the RPF. They passed through Kirambo and Gatare Communes in Cyangugu, then crossed the lake to arrive on Idjwi Island. From there, they were welcomed by a refugee called Mutsinzi, originally from Mabanza Commune, who led them to Habiyambere, another refugee, who in turn helped them cross Lake Kivu to Bukavu Town, Zaire. From there, they took a flight to either Uganda or Burundi. An investigation cited in a report of the prefecture council security committee meeting of April 16 revealed that a rumor was going around Idjwi Island of an attack planned by the RPF for June, to be launched from different points on the boundaries of Rwanda, particularly from Zaire.[166] During the attack, the Inkotanyi were to unite in Rwanda with the young Tutsis who had left to join them and had returned home with weapons. This attack was expected to be the last. The security committee report also stated that the atmosphere was tense in the home sectors of the young Tutsis leaving to join the RPF, with the Hutus saying that the youths were going to return to attack them. However, the frequency of these departures was decreasing because the authorities tightened their control of the movement of young Tutsis, and on Idjwi Island, one of the main crossing points, Tutsis without valid documents were arrested and sent back to Rwanda by Zairian authorities.[167]

On the night of April 1, 1992, in Cyayi Sector, two brothers were killed with machetes by members of another family. On April 20, a certain Mazimpaka was attacked with machetes and seriously injured by unidentified people and was later hospitalized.[168]

In the early evening of May 2, 1992, a certain Munyansoza, who had spent the day buying coffee from the villages, was killed 200 meters from the bar where he had just been. In Kilimbi Sector, Tutsis carried out patrols without informing the authorities beforehand, which raised the suspicions of Hutus in the sector. With the rising anger of the Hutus, the burgomaster organized a reconciliation meeting.[169]

From August 20 to 22, 1992, killings of Tutsis occurred.

From November 22, 1992, on, Tutsis in Nyagahinga Sector were no longer sleeping in their homes and had begun to hide their cattle and property following rumors that the next fracas would kill not only Tutsis but also Hutu members of the MRND.[170]

In October 1993, tension arose between members of the MDR-power faction and Tutsis in Nyagahinga Sector following an MDR-power meeting called by the local party president. Tutsis began to move toward the mountains.[171]

Gisovu Commune. In August 1991, it was reported that some Tutsis were trying to sensitize others to join the PL. MDR members attacked the administration and even accused the head of state of poorly governing the country.[172]

According to a poll taken by the local authorities, the MRND would be able to garner 60 percent of the vote in the commune and would be followed by the MDR. It was reported that Tutsis secretly supported the PL and that multiparty politics had spread lack of discipline among the peasants.[173]

In September 1991, the commune secretary and commune MDR representative beat up the chief judge of the court in a bar because he had talked about the MRND.[174]

In March 1992, acts of violence took place especially in the development projects. In one of these projects, a certain Simon Muhunde was attacked with machetes by criminals who also robbed him and took away his daughter. The gang attacked a project manager in his house and carried out several items. Its members then attacked a project vehicle ferrying large sums of money three times. On the tea plantation, female farmworkers were repeatedly raped. The thugs also attacked and robbed the plantation agricultural officer. In Gisovu Commune, there was a serious land conflict; fields were assigned to peasants who refused to settle on them and farm them, but when the previous owners wanted to repossess the land, the new people entitled to the land came running, and the situation degenerated into fighting.[175]

Rumors spread that the burgomaster would be forcibly relieved of his duties on March 22 during a *kubohoza* operation.[176]

On May 6, 1992, in Muramba Sector, four thugs armed with grenades attacked and killed a certain Nyandera. The son of the deceased had recently visited his father, and the thugs thought he had left behind some money. The following day, as people were still trying to locate their stolen property, they noticed a group of strangers in the neighborhood and chased them. One of the thugs tried to throw a grenade, which did not harm anyone, and he finally dove into Lake Kivu and drowned. Following these incidents, the prefect visited Gisovu Commune. Discussions with the local authorities exposed the following security problems: murders of fathers by their sons over land issues, thugs armed with military weapons, violent conflicts between people who had refused land on the steep hills allocated to them by the commune and the former owners, and cases of poisoning.[177]

In November 1992, the prefect wrote to the interior minister to request urgent intervention by law enforcement officers in Gisovu Commune. Over the previous two years, some residents of Gisovu had been rebelling against Burgomaster Joseph Bugingo. During a meeting November 22 at Ngoma (Gishyita Commune), the people were invited to join the people of Gisovu to put an end to Bugingo's power. By July 27, the people had already told the visiting prefect, "Kayondo [the previous prefect] deceived us just like Bugingo, but you will not fool us a second time." Prefect Kayishema urgently asked the minister to intervene; otherwise, he wrote, "I know that the people here are fierce and will riot, causing serious damage to life and property."[178]

In January 1993, the MRND, in accordance with its national reaction against the signing of the January 9 Arusha protocol, organized a demonstration in Gisovu Commune and blocked a commercial road to Rushishi.[179]

In April 1993, the results of the preselection of the Gisovu burgomaster on April 25 were as follows:[180]

1. Aloys Ndibubati (MRND): twenty-three out of forty-three votes
2. Martin Ntamukunzi, garage manager (MDR): twenty out of forty-three votes
3. Michel Nduwamungu, teacher (PL): zero out of forty-three votes

Violence Against Tutsis in Rwamatamu and Gishyita Communes. From August 20 to 22, 1992, massacres were committed against Tutsis in Gishyita and Rwamatamu Communes.

The violence affected almost all the sectors in Gishyita, especially Mara and Murangara. Houses, woodlands, and coffee plantations were burned, banana plantations cut down, and cows slaughtered and eaten. On August 22, 202 houses that belonged to Tutsis were burned in two sectors, some in broad daylight. Tutsis from these sectors sought refuge in the Mubuga Parish, in the neighboring sector. On August 24, Prime Minister Dismas Nsengiyaremye (MDR), accompanied by the ministers of defense and of the interior and commune development, had held a meeting with the Mara residents. Nsengiyaremye asked the people to stop giving in to the violence and to carry out surveillance patrols. The army and the gendarmes were dispatched to the area, and the prosecutor launched an investigation.

In Rwamatamu Commune, the violence was even greater. It spread over three sectors in particular, Gihombo, Nyagahinga, and Butimbo, where 306 houses were burned. Violence was perpetrated by MDR youths and targeted Tutsis in general, some of whom were members of the MDR as well as the MRND. The Rwandan Association for Individual Rights and Civil Liberties (ADL), put the toll at 85 dead, 200 injured, 500 houses burned, and more than 5,000 people displaced.[181]

According to a report from the Ministry of the Interior, the Rwamatamu burgomaster wanted to intervene, but the arsonists caused him to flee. Prime Minister Nsengiyaremye, in the company of the defense minister, army chiefs of staff, top officers of the gendarmes, and officials from the president's office met at the Rwamatamu commune office building with the people in order to stop the violence. At the meeting, the prime minister made efforts to reassure the people and specifically promised to increase the number of soldiers and gendarmes patrolling the commune. He committed himself to ensuring that those responsible for the violence were arrested and charged regardless of their ethnicity or political party.[182]

As Prefect Kayishema was writing his report on these events, ninety-six people had been arrested, and the prefect indicated that on August 26, peace had begun to be restored in Gishyita, although Rwamatamu remained tense. In his report, the prefect explained that the officials from the public prosecutor's office who had gone to Gishyita to carry out the investigation were releasing the criminals caught in the act, and the soldiers and gendarmes were raping women and young girls. In Rwamatamu, the public prosecutors complained that soldiers they sent to arrest the criminals were interfering with investigations and releasing the suspects. There were vehement arguments between gendarmes who wanted to release the accused and gendarmes who wanted them prosecuted. According to the prefect, this showed that the residents knew the troublemakers, people they had lived with backed up by the instigators.

Most observers explained the violence as a reaction from hard-liners in the MRND to the signing of the first protocol of the Arusha accords on August 18, 1992, which they saw as a humiliation. The signing of the second protocol of the Arusha accords on January 9, 1993, was also followed by orchestrated ethnic massacres. The novelty of the massacres in Kibuye Prefecture was the subcontracting of the killings to local supporters of the MDR who at the time were supposed to be at odds with the MRND. Almost a year later, the Association of Peace Volunteers (AVP) wrote to the Rwamatamu burgomaster asking him to investigate the roles played in the August 1992 violence by André Ntahomvukiye of MDR; André Kayishema, a teacher in Nyagahinga Sector (MDR), Jean-Damascène Minani, a trader at Kibatsi; and Jean-Paul Mujyambere of Gihombo Sector, also of the MDR. According to the letter, witnesses could identify these individuals as the main organizers of the violence.[183] In an interview, Burgomaster Augustin Karara of Gitesi explains how his Gishyita counterpart, Burgomaster Charles Sikubwabo, at the time told him the violence had been planned and carried out by MDR supporters without the knowledge of their party at the instigation of the military officers based in his commune. Yet during this period, the violence was a great blow to the MDR, the driving force behind the Arusha peace talks in the government of the coalition. Finally, military officers' interference in the investigation cited in the prefect report and their arbitrary release of criminals also indicate they were protecting the people implicated.

From the early 1980s, the peasants of Kibuye Prefecture were stuck in demographic entrapment characterized by landlessness, endemic food shortage, and the rise in intense social violence. There was a significant level of violence caused by land problems and the precarious equilibrium of the food situation in the prefecture. Any upset in this balance seemed to be immediately followed by abrupt surges in violence, as in 1984 and 1989. The occurrence of killings in many communes, mainly in land disputes, was strikingly high for the population size of the prefecture. Even before the legalization of opposition political parties, the hardening of the social conditions led also to the erosion of state authority.

With the advent of opposition parties, specifically of the MDR, social violence took on political coloration, with criminals often using their adherence to the MDR as an excuse to commit violence and loot property. The MDR propaganda also raised ethnic animosity against the Tutsis, specifically in communes where there were many. Here, the motives of material gain and more ideological inclinations appeared inseparable. One can illustrate this with the manner in which some MDR supporters in early 1992, at the height of the political confrontation when newly approved political parties were fighting the MRND for the formation of a broad-based transitional government, understood the significance of the national conference (*rukokoma*) for which they appealed.

Danielle de Lame, who carried out an ethnographic study of Bwakira Commune, clearly associated this wish for a time of widespread violence to the desire for a "second" 1959 revolution and its predatory anti-Tutsi violence: "The precarious food situation of 1989 had aroused a sense of urgency. From mid-1990 on, propaganda was active in the hills, and the ethnic divisions had been revived. Anyone could clearly see the method for reducing the huge population and proceeding a second time to distribute land that had become too crowded."[184] As we shall see in Chapter 9, when in April 1994 the opportunity presented itself again, these grassroots political entrepreneurs would not miss out on it.

Notes

1. I will use the name "Zaire" in reference to the years 1971–1997 as that was the official name of the country during that period.
2. Zebron Mulindwa, "Les conséquences géographiques de la pression démographique" (1985), p .54.
3. Ibid., p. 59.
4. Vansina, *Antecedents to Modern Rwanda*(2004), pp. 200–201.
5. Ibid., p. 205.
6. Ibid., p. 217.
7. Ibid., p. 239.
8. Mulindwa, "Les conséquences géographiques de la pression démographique," p. 85.
9. Royaume de Belgique, Ministère des Colonies, *Rapport soumis par le Gouvernement belge à l'Assemblée générale des Nations unies au sujet de l'administration du Ruanda-Urundi pendant l'année 1959*, 1960, p. 26.
10. Lemarchand, *Rwanda and Burundi*, p. 163. According to Lemarchand, these *jacqueries* (violences) in late 1959 were the deadliest of the entire revolution.

11. Augustin Karara, interview with author, June 1, 2001, Kibuye Prison; Damascène Gakwerere, interview with author, June 13, 1998, Kigali.

12. Karara interview; Donatien Rugema, interview with author, June 12, 1998, Kigali.

13. Mulindwa, "Les consequences géographiques de la pression démographique," p. 79.

14. Ibid.

15. Bonneaux, "Rwanda" (1994), pp.1689–1690; King, "Rwanda" (1994), pp. 11–19.

16. Mulindwa, "Les conséquences géographiques de la pression démographique," p. 79.

17. Ibid., p. 159.

18. Ibid., p. 160.

19. Mouchiroud et al., quoted in Mulindwa, "Les consequences géographiques de la pression démographique," p. 163.

20. Ibid., p. 165.

21. Préfecture de Kibuye, *Procès-verbal de la réunion du conseil préfectoral de sécurité du 10/10/84.*

22. Préfecture de Kibuye, *Rapport portant sur la situation alimentaire du mois de septembre 1984.*

23. Ibid.

24. Ibid.

25. Préfecture de Kibuye, *Procès-verbal de la réunion du conseil préfectoral de sécurité du 05/11/84.*

26. Préfecture de Kibuye, *Procès-verbal de la réunion du conseil préfectoral de sécurité du 03/09/85.*

27. Following the serious famine of 1984, thousands of Rwandans illegally migrated to Burundi in search of work, and in 1985 and subsequent years, Burundian authorities arrested them.

28. Préfecture de Kibuye, *Procès-verbal de la réunion du conseil préfectoral de sécurité du 11/11/85.*

29. Ibid.

30. Ibid.

31. Préfecture de Kibuye, *Procès-verbal de la réunion du conseil préfectoral de sécurité du 21/04/87.*

32. Préfecture de Kibuye, *Procès-verbal de la réunion du conseil préfectoral de sécurité du 26/01/89.*

33. Préfecture de Kibuye, *Procès-verbal de la réunion du conseil préfectoral de sécurité du 26/01/90*; Préfecture de Kibuye, *Procès-verbal de la réunion du conseil préfectoral de sécurité du 02/03/90.*

34. Préfecture de Kibuye, *Procès-verbal de la réunion du conseil préfectoral de sécurité du 02/03/90.*

35. Ibid.

36. Préfecture de Kibuye, *Lettre du Préfet au Ministre de l'Intérieur et du Développement communal présentant le rapport de sécurité du 01/03/90.*

37. Préfecture de Kibuye, *Procès-verbal de la réunion du conseil préfectoral de sécurité du 27/04/90.*

38. Ibid.

39. Préfecture de Kibuye, *Procès-verbal de la réunion du conseil préfectoral de sécurité du 24/08/90.*

40. Rugema interview.

41. Edouard Serugendo, interview with author, June 1, 2001,Kibuye Prison; Anne-Marie Nyampuza, interview with author, June 8, 2001, Kibuye.

42. Ibid.

43. Ministère de l'Intérieur et des Affaires judiciaires, *Transmission au Ministre de l'Éducation nationale d'un extrait du rapport trimestriel pour les mois de novembre et décembre 1972 et janvier 1973 envoyé par le préfet de Kibuye en date du 30 janvier 1973*, 1973.

44. Gakwerere interview. See also Chapter 9, on Gitesi Commune.

45. Ibid.

46. Karara interview.

47. République rwandaise, Ministère de l'Intérieur et des Affaires judiciaires, *Procès verbal de la réunion des Préfets tenue à Kigali le 31 juillet 1973 sous la présidence du lieutenant-colonel Alexis Kanyarengwe*.

48. Préfecture de Kibuye, *Directives relatives aux réfugiés du 15/03/1974*.

49. République rwandaise, Présidence de la République, *Synthèse des échanges tenus lors de la tournée présidentielle dans les préfectures en avril-mai 1976*.

50. Ministère de l'Intérieur et de la Fonction publique, *Synthèse des rapports de sécurité pour le mois de février 1975*; Ministère de la Défense nationale, *Lettre du ministre de la Défense au ministre de l'Intérieur et de la Fonction publique du 11/04/75*; Préfecture de Kibuye, *Rapport de sécurité du mois de mars 1977*.

51. Kibuye Prefecture, specifically on the western slope of the Zaire-Nile Ridge, is one of the strongholds of Protestantism in Rwanda.

52. Assiel Kabera, interview with author, May 28, 1998, Kigali; Gakwerere interview; Rugema interview; Esther Kami, interview with author, June 9, 2001, Kibuye Town; François Ndahimana, interview with author, June 9, 2001, Kibuye Town. See also Chapter 9, on Gitesi Commune.

53. Bayart, Mbembe, and Toulabor, *Le politique par le basen Afrique noire,* 1992, p. 44. Numerous examples of this kind of behavior are found in Chapter 9, on Gitesi Commune.

54. Préfecture de Kibuye, *Rapport circonstancié sur l'arrestation des prétendus "abarokore" des communes Mabanza, Gisovu, Rwamatamu, Bwakira et Gishyita du 04/03/86*.

55. See Chapter 7, on Kigembe, for a detailed look at this system and its operation.

56. Ministère à la Présidence, *Lettre au Ministre de l'Intérieur et du Développement communal et au Secrétaire général du Service central de renseignement concernant l'affaire des Abarokore du 26/03/86*.

57. Ministère de la Justice, *Lettre au Procureur de la République, Parquet de Kibuye concernant l'arrestation des Abarokore du 09/03/86*.

58. Préfecture de Kibuye, *Rapport du conseil préfectoral de sécurité du 16/05/86*.

59. Préfecture de Kibuye, *Rapport du conseil préfectoral de sécurité du 04/09/86*.

60. Préfecture de Kibuye, *Rapport de sécurité du mois de mars 1991*.

61. See Table 8.1.

62. Préfecture de Kibuye, *Rapport de sécurité du mois d'avril 1991*.

63. Préfecture de Kibuye, *Rapport de sécurité du mois de mai 1991*.

64. République rwandaise, *Recensement général de la population et de l'habitat au 15/08/91*, p. 9.

65. Ibid.

66. Préfecture de Kibuye, *Rapport de sécurité du mois de juin 1991*.

67. Ibid.

68. Préfecture de Kibuye, *Rapport de sécurité du mois de juillet 1991*.

69. Préfecture de Kibuye, *Rapport de sécurité du mois d'août 1991.*

70. Préfecture de Kibuye, *Rapport de sécurité du mois de novembre 1990.*

71. Ibid.

72. On October 11, 1990, at least 348 Tutsis were killed in Kibilira Commune (Gisenyi Prefecture) and 550 houses were destroyed. The Tutsis' livestock, food reserves, and household appliances were destroyed or looted. According to the International Commission of Inquiry into the violation of human rights in Rwanda in 1993, this massacre, carried out by the population, was initiated by local authorities, sector councilors, cell heads, and cell committee members under orders of the burgomaster or deputy prefect. International Federation of Human Rights et al., *Report of the International Commission of Inquiry on the Violations of Human Rights in Rwanda Since October 1, 1990*, 1993, pp. 18–21.

73. Préfecture de Kibuye, *Rapport de sécurité du mois de novembre 1990.*

74. Ibid.

75. Ibid.

76. Commune de Mabanza, *Rapport portant sur les actions entreprises mettant en application les directives du chef de l'État depuis que le pays a été attaqué du 18/03/91.*

77. Préfecture de Kibuye, *Rapport de sécurité du mois de novembre 1990.*

78. The attacks by looters on Tutsis in Kivumu and northern Mabanza Communes occurred on October 12, 1990, the day after the massacre of Tutsis in Kibilira Commune, bordering Kivumu.

79. Préfecture de Kibuye, *Rapport de sécurité du mois de mars 1991.*

80. Ibid.

81. Ibid.

82. Préfecture de Kibuye, *Rapport de sécurité du mois d'avril 1991.*

83. Préfecture de Kibuye, *Rapport de sécurité du mois de mai 1991.*

84. Ibid.

85. Préfecture de Kibuye, *Rapport de sécurité du mois de juillet 1991.*

86. Préfecture de Kibuye, *Note d'instructions aux bourgmestres concernant les mesures de sécurité à prendre du 14/08/1991.*

87. Préfecture de Kibuye, *Résolutions dégagées de la réunion du conseil de sécurité du 28 août 1991.*

88. Ibid.

89. Préfecture de Kibuye, *Rapport portant sur l'évolution politique dans la préfecture de Kibuye du 28/08/91.*

90. Ibid.

91. Ibid.

92. Ibid.

93. Préfecture de Kibuye, *Rapport de la réunion des Bourgmestres du 23/10/91.*

94. Préfecture de Kibuye, *Rapport de sécurité des mois de septembre et octobre 1991.*

95. Préfecture de Kibuye, *Recommandations du conseil de sécurité et événements récents dans Kibuye du 26/11/91.*

96. Préfecture de Kibuye, *Rapport de sécurité du mois de mars 1992.*

97. République rwandaise, Ministère de l'Intérieur et du Développement communal, *Synthèse des rapports préfectoraux de sécurité du mois de février 1993.*

98. Préfecture de Kibuye, *Rapport portant sur l'évolution politique dans la préfecture de Kibuye du 28/08/91.*

99. Préfecture de Kibuye, *Rapport de sécurité des mois de septembre et octobre 1991.*

100. Préfecture de Kibuye, *Rapport de sécurité du mois d'août 1991.*

101. Préfecture de Kibuye, *Lettre du Préfet au Ministre de l'Intérieur et du Développement communal du 04/03/92.*

102. Préfecture de Kibuye, *Lettre du Préfet au Ministre de l'Intérieur et du Développement communal du 20/03/92.*

103. Ibid.

104. Préfecture de Kibuye, *Rapport du conseil préfectoral de sécurité réuni le 16/04/1992.*

105. Préfecture de Kibuye, *Rapport du conseil préfectoral de sécurité du 9 mai 1992.*

106. République rwandaise, Ministère de l'Intérieur et du Développement communal, *Synthèse des rapports préfectoraux de sécurité du mois de janvier 1993.*

107. République rwandaise, Ministère de l'Intérieur et du Développement communal, *Synthèse des rapports préfectoraux de sécurité du mois de mars 1993.*

108. Préfecture de Kibuye, *Rapport portant sur l'évolution politique dans la préfecture de Kibuye du 28/08/91.*

109. Préfecture de Kibuye, *Rapport de sécurité du mois d'août 1991.*

110. Préfecture de Kibuye, *Lettre du Préfet au Ministre de l'Intérieur et du Développement communal du 20/03/92.*

111. Préfecture de Kibuye, *Rapport du conseil préfectoral de sécurité réuni le 16/04/1992.*

112. Préfecture de Kibuye, *Rapport du conseil préfectoral de sécurité du 9 mai 1992.*

113. Ibid.

114. République rwandaise, Ministère de l'Intérieur et du Développement communal, *Note sur les manifestations des partis MRND et CDR les 19, 20 et 21 janvier 1993*; République rwandaise, Ministère de l'Intérieur et du Développement communal, *Rapport sur la sécurité dans les préfectures*, no date.

115. République rwandaise, Ministère de l'Intérieur et du Développement communal, *Synthèse des rapports préfectoraux de sécurité du mois d'août 1993.*

116. République rwandaise, Ministère de l'Intérieur et du Développement communal, *Synthèse des rapports préfectoraux de sécurité du mois d'octobre 1993.*

117. Ibid.

118. République rwandaise, Ministère de l'Intérieur et du Développement communal, *Synthèse des rapports préfectoraux de sécurité du mois de novembre 1993.*

119. Ibid.

120. Ibid.

121. Préfecture de Kibuye, *Rapport portant sur l'évolution politique dans la préfecture de Kibuye du 28/08/91.*

122. Préfecture de Kibuye, *Rapport de sécurité du mois d'août 1991.*

123. Préfecture de Kibuye, *Flash d'information du 27/09/91.*

124. Préfecture de Kibuye, *Rapport de sécurité du mois de mars 1992.*

125. Préfecture de Kibuye, *Lettre du Préfet au Ministre de l'Intérieur et du Développement communal concernant la sécurité dans Kibuye du 11/03/9.*

126. The term *gukora*, which means "to work," specifically in the context of *umuganda*, or working as a collective under the orders of the state, became a code word for attacking and killing Tutsis during turbulent periods.

127. Préfecture de Kibuye, *Lettre du Préfet au Ministre de l'Intérieur et du Développement communal concernant la sécurité dans Kibuye du 11/03/92.*

128. Ibid.

129. Ibid.

130. Préfecture de Kibuye, *Lettre du Préfet au Ministre de l'Intérieur et du Développement communal du 13/03/92.*

131. Before March 13, when the parties signed with the president the agreement protocol on the modalities of a government broadened to include the internal opposition, the national convention, called Rukokoma in Kinyarwanda, was one of the major demands of the opposition parties, especially the MDR.

132. Préfecture de Kibuye, *Lettre du Préfet au Ministre de l'Intérieur et du Développement communal du 13/03/92.*

133. Préfecture de Kibuye, *Note du Préfet au Ministre concernant la sécurité dans la préfecture du 26/11/92.*

134. République rwandaise, Ministère de l'Intérieur et du Développement communal, *Synthèse des rapports préfectoraux de sécurité du mois d'août 1993.*

135. République rwandaise, Ministère de l'Intérieur et du Développement communal, *Synthèse des rapports préfectoraux de sécurité du mois de septembre 1993.*

136. République rwandaise, Ministère de l'Intérieur et du Développement communal, *Synthèse des rapports préfectoraux de sécurité du mois d'octobre 1993.*

137. République rwandaise, Ministère de l'Intérieur et du Développement communal, *Synthèse des rapports préfectoraux de sécurité du mois de décembre 1993.*

138. Préfecture de Kibuye, *Rapport portant sur l'évolution politique dans la préfecture de Kibuye du 28/08/91.*

139. Préfecture de Kibuye, *Rapport de sécurité du mois d'août 1991.*

140. Préfecture de Kibuye, *Flash d'information du 27/09/91.*

141. Préfecture de Kibuye, *Note du Préfet au Ministre concernant la sécurité dans la préfecture du 26/11/92.*

142. République rwandaise, Ministère de l'Intérieur et du Développement communal, *Note sur les manifestations des partis MRND et CDR les 19, 20 et 21 janvier 1993*; République rwandaise, Ministère de l'Intérieur et du Développement communal, *Rapport sur la sécurité dans les préfectures*, no date.
2

144. Préfecture de Kibuye, *Rapport portant sur l'évolution politique dans la préfecture de Kibuye du 28/08/91.*

145. Préfecture de Kibuye, *Rapport de sécurité du mois d'août 1991.*

146. Préfecture de Kibuye, *Rapport de sécurité des mois de septembre et octobre 1991.*

147. Préfecture de Kibuye, *Rapport de sécurité du mois de mars 1992.*

148. Préfecture de Kibuye, *Lettre du Préfet au Ministre de l'Intérieur et du Développement communal du 20/03/92.*

149. Ibid.

150. Préfecture de Kibuye, *Lettre du Préfet au Ministre de l'Intérieur et du Développement communal du 23/02/93.*

151. Préfecture de Kibuye, *Rapport portant sur l'évolution politique dans la préfecture de Kibuye du 28/08/91.*

152. Préfecture de Kibuye, *Rapport de sécurité du mois d'août 1991.*

153. Préfecture de Kibuye, *Lettre du Préfet au Ministre de l'Intérieur et du Développement communal concernant la sécurité dans Kibuye du 11/03/92.*

154. Préfecture de Kibuye, *Rapport du conseil préfectoral de sécurité réuni le 16/04/1992.*

155. Préfecture de Kibuye, *Rapport de sécurité du mois d'août 1991.*

156. Préfecture de Kibuye, *Note du Préfet au Ministre concernant la sécurité dans la préfecture du 26/11/92.*

157. The preselection rationale was explained in the discussion of Kigembe Com-

mune in Chapter 7. Simply recall that the idea was to replace burgomasters too often challenged or dismissed from their duties by a section of the members of the commune. Their replacements were elected by a small electoral college.

158. République rwandaise, Ministère de l'Intérieur et du Développement communal, *Synthèse des rapports préfectoraux de sécurité du mois d'avril 1993*; Parti Libéral, Lettre du président du PL au Ministère de l'Intérieur et du Développement communal, *Irrégularités dans la présélection du bourgmestre de Gishyita,02/05/93.*

159. République rwandaise, Ministère de l'Intérieur et du Développement communal, *Synthèse des rapports préfectoraux de sécurité du mois d'octobre 1993.*

160. Préfecture de Kibuye, *Rapport portant sur l'évolution politique dans la préfecture de Kibuye du 28/08/91.*

161. Préfecture de Kibuye, *Rapport de sécurité du mois d'août 1991.*

162. Préfecture de Kibuye, *Rapport sur un événement survenu dans la commune de Rwamatamu le 18 octobre 1991.*

163. Préfecture de Kibuye, *Rapport de sécurité des mois de septembre et octobre 1991.*

164. Préfecture de Kibuye, *Lettre du Préfet au Ministre de l'Intérieur et du Développement communal concernant la sécurité dans Kibuye du 11/03/92.*

165. Préfecture de Kibuye, *Lettre du Préfet au Ministre de l'Intérieur et du Développement communal du 20/03/92.*

166. Idjwi is a large island located between Rwanda and Zaire above Rwamatamu Commune and is part of Zairean territory.

167. Préfecture de Kibuye, *Rapport du conseil préfectoral de sécurité réuni le 16/04/92.*

168. Préfecture de Kibuye, *Rapport du conseil préfectoral de sécurité du 9 mai 1992.*

169. Ibid.

170. Préfecture de Kibuye, *Note du Préfet au Ministre de l'Intérieur concernant la sécurité dans la préfecture du 26/11/92.*

171. République rwandaise, Ministère de l'Intérieur et du Développement communal, *Synthèse des rapports préfectoraux de sécurité du mois d'octobre 1993.*

172. Préfecture de Kibuye, *Rapport portant sur l'évolution politique dans la préfecture de Kibuye du 28/08/91.*

173. Préfecture de Kibuye, *Rapport de sécurité du mois d'août 1991.*

174. Préfecture de Kibuye, *Flash d'information du 27/09/91.*

175. Préfecture de Kibuye, *Rapport de sécurité du mois de mars 1992.*

176. Préfecture de Kibuye, *Lettre du Préfet au Ministre de l'Intérieur et du Développement communal du 20/03/92.*

177. Préfecture de Kibuye, *Rapport du conseil préfectoral de sécurité du 9 mai 1992.*

178. Préfecture de Kibuye, *Lettre du Préfet au Ministre de l'Intérieur et du Développement communal portant sur la sécurité dans la commune Gisovu du 02/11/92.*

179. République rwandaise, Ministère de l'Intérieur et du Développement communal, *Note sur les manifestations des partis MRND et CDR les 19, 20 et 21 janvier 1993*; République rwandaise, Ministère de l'Intérieur et du Développement communal, *Rapport sur la sécurité dans les préfectures*, no date.

180. République rwandaise, Ministère de l'Intérieur et du Développement communal, *Synthèse des rapports préfectoraux de sécurité du mois d'avril 1993.*

181. Cited by Prunier, *Rwanda Crisis*, p. 162.

182. République rwandaise, Ministère de l'Intérieur et du Développement communal, *La situation de sécurité après le discours du Premier ministre du 28/07/92.*

183. Association des volontaires de la paix, *Lettre au Bourgmestre de Rwamatamu concernant les meneurs des événements d'août 1992 du 11/09/93.*
184. De Lame, *A Hill Among a Thousand,* p. 75.

9

Moderate Politics
and Genocide in Gitesi

In this chapter I focus on the participation of the people of Gitesi
Commune in various events in the commune between 1990 and 1994, from the
war launched in October 1990 to the establishment of multiple parties in July
1991 and finally to the genocide from April to July 1994. I begin my discussion with a chronology of the years immediately preceding (1984–1990) in an
attempt to provide the social and political context in which these events took
place. Again, my guiding principle is the desire to understand the modalities
of mass participation in the genocide by raising the questions posed in preceding chapters: In the mobilization of the people of Gitesi Commune, what was
the role of the state versus the role of other social and political actors? What
role was played by socioeconomic, as opposed to ideological factors?

In Gitesi, despite the political dominance of the Republican Democratic
Movement (MDR) in the commune after multiple parties were established, the
violence resulting from the severe economic and social crisis the commune
was experiencing did not transform into ethnic animosity. These moderate politics delayed its plunge into the genocide by a few days after the surrounding
communes had succumbed.

Gitesi is one of the nine communes of Kibuye Prefecture. It is home to
Kibuye Town, the administrative and economic center of the prefecture. The
commune is located on the western slope of the Congo-Nile Ridge, which di-
vides the prefecture into two, and it is one of the four communes bordering
Lake Kivu. Historically, Gitesi was located in the Bwishaza Region and was
for a long time part of the Nyiginya Dynasty. With Tutsis constituting 34.7 percent of the population, the region of Gitesi and Gishyita Communes was second only to the Tutsi settlement spread across Butare and Gikongoro Prefectures combined in the concentration of its population.[1]

Gitesi Commune is made up of twelve sectors. Kibuye Town stretches
across part of the Bwishyura, Gasura, and Gitarama Sectors. During colonial

309

times, the administrative center of Kibuye Province was located in the current administrative center of Kibuye Prefecture, making Kibuye a small, urbanized community. Until 1985, the town population had not yet reached 5,000. It was a small town that, in 1994, held some public infrastructure, such as a large hospital, a prison, a gendarme office, a few schools, the prefecture office, a small hotel, two banks, and a post office. The town residential area was of modest size. The core of the town population lived either in the working-class neighborhoods in the urban sections of the three sectors that made up the town or in the rural sections of these sectors, and the other sectors were clearly located in the countryside.[2] Until 1994, Gitesi Commune was linked to the rest of the country by an unpaved road from Kibuye to Gitarama Town. The road was hardly passable, which meant that just like the rest of the prefecture, the commune remained isolated from the rest of the country.

1984–1990: Social Crisis and the Rise of Subversive Behavior

The Food Shortage of 1984

Like most of Rwanda in 1984, Gitesi Commune experienced a serious food shortage caused by drought. Eleven out of its twelve sectors were seriously affected. In his report on the food situation in September 1984, the prefect pointed out that in Bubazi Sector, one of the most affected, people were eating only porridge. Some resorted to stealing, others to begging. Finally, those with property, livestock, or farms began to sell them to buy food. In Burunga Sector, people began to steal mature crops in the field and from banana plantations. The victims of these thefts were generally the very people who were themselves living on the bare minimum. In Buye Sector, also among the most affected by the shortage, children went to school on empty stomachs, people stole root crops from the farms, and an elderly lady was killed in her home by robbers who made away with her stocks of beans and sorghum. In Gasura Sector, one of the least affected, people did not have much to eat either, and those who were sick generally did not recover because of their weak condition. The residents of Kagabiro Sector were seriously hit by the famine; at least four families urgently needed emergency aid. Kayenzi Sector was better off, but if the drought continued, the people would soon no longer be able to buy food. In Mbogo Sector, the residents were selling their cattle to traders who profited from their desperation. In Rubazo Sector, seriously affected residents stole crops from the fields, and four people were suffering from advanced stages of starvation. Finally, in Bwishyura, Gitesi, and Ruragwe Sectors, few people could afford beans because they were almost completely unavailable, and the status of the other commodities was not much better. Many people were forced to steal crops from the farms.[3]

In late 1994, there was an outbreak of dysentery in the commune.[4] According to the prefecture security council meeting of August 27, 1984, Kibuye Town experienced a number of problems in addition to the widespread hunger and disease, such as the prostitution of young women arriving by bus from neighboring rural Rwamatamu, Gishyita, and Mabanza Communes at the end of the week, in the early evening so as not to be recognized. According to the council, the young women were spreading diseases and were causing fights in the bars. Another problem noted was that of young vagrants, apparently homeless, who spent their days in the towns and nights sleeping in the schools and damaging the facilities. The youths also robbed homes. The security committee noted the problems caused by the cabarets, which sold banana beer; customers stayed there for a long time and ended up drunk, after which they fought and were hospitalized with injuries.[5] In August 1985, there were still reports of theft of produce from farms.[6]

Rising Petty Crime and Unchanged Political Control

On September 1, 1985, elections for cell committee members were held in Kibuye Prefecture. According to the authorities, the elections ran smoothly in Gitesi Commune despite some contested cases. In the urban Kiniha Cell of Bwishyura Sector, residents protested that those elected were either state officials or people working for Europeans, who did not have time to devote to their new duties. In Kigezi and Gomba Cells of Gitarama Sector, residents challenged the election results, arguing that the results did not reflect how they had voted.[7]

The prefecture council security committee report for November 1985 discusses in detail the murders and violent robberies committed by gangs of criminals attacking people living around the lake or on the boats sailing the lake. These people, originally from the communes surrounding the lake including Gitesi Commune, were not registered as residents anywhere; some of them illegally claimed cultivated land for themselves on the islands. The security committee requested that local authorities revive community security patrols to address the insecurity prevailing on the lake and in the surrounding communes.[8]

In late December 1985, there were reports of a riot in Kibuye Prison by prisoners complaining of the abuse and mistreatment suffered under the prison director. In the security council meeting, the prefect took the time to categorically refute ongoing rumors that Colonel Théoneste Lizinde, incarcerated for political reasons since 1981 at Ruhengeri Prison, had escaped with the prison director. The Gitesi Commune burgomaster also reported on a person named Rubandora, the Gitesi Sector councilor under the First Republic, who was spreading rumors that "Tutsis were going to resume their massacres of Hutus, and no one would escape."[9]

In the prefecture council security committee meeting of March 13, 1987, the public prosecutor reviewed the problems experienced in Gitesi Commune throughout 1986 and gave examples of murders generally tied to land disputes, violence in entertainment spots, polygamy, prostitution, vagrancy, and stubborn hatred resulting in more court disputes over land.[10]

In the commune council meeting on November 6, 1987, the burgomaster and the councilors planned the burgomaster's tour of the sectors. Among the items for discussion were *umuganda*, issues of security, education, the fourth development plan, and payment of compulsory contributions to the MRND as well as taxes. Those at the meeting debated these themes, and only a few problems, such as polygamy, were addressed. The councilors explained that they had done all they could to get husbands to chase away their second wives, but the men secretly brought them back, thereby leading to conflict with the legal wives. The burgomaster asked his councilors to act against only those on whom they had tangible evidence and to take these cases to court rather than create conflicts based on the people's personal bad behavior. The meeting also made reference to the councilors of Burunga and Buye Sectors who were regularly accused of extortion by their constituents. The other councilors asked that the cases of their two colleagues not be discussed during the commune security council meeting, which included many people not working for the commune, but rather that they be cautioned at the commune council meeting; if their behavior persisted, the councilors would be denounced in public. In this meeting, which ran through the main MRND pillars of local governance, the councilors discussed *umuganda*, animation, and various contributions and raised only minor problems related to their constituents' obedience.[11]

In the security committee meeting on January 6, 1988, the tone slightly changed following a review of the political activities of 1987. Bwishyura and Buye Sectors were asked to put more effort into animation because they were trailing. The burgomaster declared, "A threat to security is not only a question of committing violence but also of refusing to properly fulfill one's duty to contribute to the MRND and to pay taxes." He affirmed that revenues for 1987 had decreased by 10 percent compared with the previous year. A report from a meeting held in June 1988 noted that the security was generally good. On November 8, 1988, President Juvénal Habyarimana visited Gitesi Commune as part of his campaign for the presidential elections late that year. The 1988 political year ended with preparations for the presidential elections on December 19 and legislative elections on December 26.[12]

In his opening address at a function for the cell committee members and heads of Kayenzi, Mbogo, Ruragwe, Bubazi, Rubazo, and Gitarama Sectors to receive their annual bonuses, the Gitesi burgomaster stated that their constituents knew how they were to vote in the coming presidential election, and there was therefore no need to give them only one colored card; they had to be given the two different colored cards as required by law.[13]

The burgomaster went on to say that on December 19 they would keep their promise to the president and give him 100 percent of the vote: "To vote for President Habyarimana is to support peace, strengthen unity, and promote progress and love for the nation." When it came to the legislative elections of December 26, 1988, the burgomaster regretted that some people were engaging in slander, asserting that one person or another had been useless to the commune. The burgomaster asked the cell committee members to ensure that people's votes were not influenced by gifts of free crates of beer or jerry cans of banana beer. He went on to deplore the fact that cell members were quarreling with the councilors as the elections for councilors approached. The burgomaster advised the councilors, who had just received an early bonus, to put it to good use. Finally, he stated that a proper politician wore a lapel pin with the president's portrait and that those who did not yet have one should buy one without delay because he did not want to see any more people not observing the dress code.[14]

In a meeting on November 19, 1988, with the officials of the polling stations preparing for the "election of President Habyarimana," the burgomaster stated, "The people usually vote for President Habyarimana but not under any pressure or duress; in other words, they vote in a completely democratic matter." He ambiguously reminded them that the goal of the election was to elect the president with 100 percent of the vote.[15]

In January 1989, the commune council revisited parliamentary elections and noted that in general, the elections went smoothly except in Gasura, Kagabiro, and Rubazo Sectors, where the people's intentions did not seem clear. It recommended organizing meetings with the residents of these sectors so that they shared the same goal. The assembly also decided that all those requesting any official document would from then on have to present proof of payment of taxes and the compulsory contribution to the MRND. It also observed that people no longer wanted to take part in *umuganda* because they had "voted well." The council decided that meetings would be organized to sensitize the population on the importance and value of *umuganda* and that if people still refused to take part, the council would arrest two people in every commune to intimidate the others.[16]

The commune quickly recovered from the serious food shortage of 1984. Even after the end of that difficult year, the social turmoil continued: vagrancy and prostitution among youths migrating from the hills and murders and court trials for crimes related to land. During this period, the MRND party-state continued its political and social control of the population without guilt, presenting itself as a gentle dictatorship. Nevertheless, the population sometimes exhibited disobedience here and there; for example, in the case of presidential and parliamentary elections, in which the people sought to trade submissive behavior for a refusal to participate in *umuganda*. In another case, three communes refused to follow the instructions on voting for the parliamentary candidates. Resistance to authority was also evidenced by the difficulties in collecting the compulsory MRND party contributions and the retaliatory measures taken by the commune council. In short, even if the MRND party-state control of the people was effective, it did not make them completely passive.

The situation changed rapidly with the commune's second serious food shortage (1989–1990) in five years. Not only did social problems take a more dramatic turn but the population asserted itself with acts of disobedience that sometimes expanded into violent rebellion.

1989–1990: Violence, Famine, and Political Protest

At a huge public meeting on June 29, 1989, at the Gatwaro Regional Stadium to discuss different problems facing Kibuye Town, the burgomaster observed that the youths living on the streets and squatting in houses still under construction were behind the resurgence of theft in the town. He talked of insecurity along the lakeside and criticized the town's residents for no longer responding to distress calls during attacks. He also spoke of the emergence of cannabis consumption in the town. Finally, as he announced the elections for commune councilors set for January 1990, he regretted that some individuals had already started their campaigns. The response from the residents of the town and the surrounding areas was to express their concern about unenforced court decisions and lax treatment of violent criminals who attacked with machetes and destroyed people's property, only to spend a single night in the commune cells before being released the next day. The criminals then returned to taunt their victims, the cell committee members, and the councilors who had contributed to their arrest.[17]

In a note to the prefect listing the items to address during his planned tour of different sectors of Gitesi Commune, the burgomaster suggested, among other things, that residents help each other resolve the numerous litigations and disputes, especially those regarding land inheritance, which pitted the people against each other. The burgomaster also talked about hatred; intrigues; violence; low participation in *umuganda*; and delayed payment of compulsory MRND contributions, levies, and taxes.[18]

In a letter dated September 26, 1989, the burgomaster informed the prefect of the problems experienced by the commune. Hunger continued to tor-
ment the residents and had been the main cause of resurgence in theft. He
pointed out that the residents of Ruragwe and Gitesi Sectors, armed with machetes, chased away the councilors coming to implement the court decisions
generally related to land disputes. The culprits went into fields and uprooted
the boundary markers set by the councilors.[19]

The commune elections for leaders of sectors on January 21, 1990,
sharply divided the people. During a commune council meeting on March 14,
the councilors painted a gloomy picture of their sectors, with attempted rebellion by some of their constituents. The councilor for Gitarama Sector reported
theft of bananas as well as other produce from the fields because of hunger.
Crops were stolen from the farms in Nyarusanga Cell (Rubazo Sector) and
sold in Gishyita Commune. There were also people who extorted others' property. In Burunga Sector, crops were stolen from the fields, generally by people
who had sold their farms but wanted them back. Bananas and crops were also
stolen in Twimbogo and Nyamarebe Cells. Several thefts because of hunger
and "deviancy" were reported in Kagabiro.

Cases of theft caused by hunger were reported in Bwishyura and Gitesi
Sectors. In Buye Sector, there was theft of bananas, cassava, and sweet potatoes as well as embezzlement of funds from farmer cooperatives and
never-ending court cases in addition to land-related conflicts. Gasura Sector
reported thefts driven by hunger and the refusal to pay fines imposed by the
courts. There were conflicts linked to the elections for councilors, such as in
Gafuruguto Cell, where the work ordered by the elected councilor was not
carried out but where others made residents work in private concessions. In
the same cell, people spread slanderous rumors about the councilor. Kayenzi
Sector reported theft of produce in the fields as well as bananas because of
hunger. In that sector, a man called Munyabarame refused to recognize the
councilor's authority to assign land to farmer cooperatives. The issue was a
past election rivalry.

In Mbogo Sector, groups of people slandered the councilor in a letter to
the prefect accusing the councilor of having killed a goat. People sold their
farms, saying they did not want to die of hunger while hanging on to property;
extortion within farmer groups was also reported. Bananas were being stolen
from Bubazi and sold in Mabanza Sector. Ruragwe Sector reported coalitions
formed during elections to incite others to uproot crops in the fields. When
summoned to court, culprits would not appear; they instead spread vicious rumors to discredit the councilor. In order to beef up security, the commune
council decided to sensitize the "population to carry out community security
patrols and to take any thief they caught to the commune to be sanctioned, so
that in cases where it was impossible to get the victims to release the thieves
they had caught, both parties would be taken to the communes instead of leav-

ing the thieves to be killed."[20] A decision was also made to ban residents from selling all their land just so that they could buy themselves food. When this ban was defied, both the seller and the buyer were to be punished.[21]

A comparison of the social and political impact of the two major food crises Gitesi Commune experienced in 1984 and 1989–1990 reveals major differences. Although the 1984 food shortage was more acute, it also led to an increase in theft but did not develop into violent conflicts. In 1989–1990 the crop theft victims tended to kill the thieves they managed to catch. The differences at the political level were also striking. In 1984 and subsequent years, the government maintained almost total social and political control of the population. Over the 1989–1990 period, the peasants of Gitesi Commune started to exhibit significant civil disobedience.[22] This defiance was targeted primarily at the state officials who were easily accessible; the commune councilors and cell committee members. The concurrent food crisis and the council elections definitely helped embolden the protests. Electoral coalitions were formed independently of the authorities, and they continued even after the elections; they made life difficult for the newly elected officials. The people supported these coalitions because the coalitions allowed them to launch predatory projects against the interests of needy farmer groups benefiting from land allocated by the commune.

Interethnic Relations

The 1994 genocide did not change the memory of interethnic relations in the commune. When asked to trace the history of interethnic relations in Gitesi, both the victims and those who committed genocide systematically begin with a reference to the 1973 crisis and then insist on good relations between Hutus and Tutsis from 1973 to 1994.

Former Gitesi burgomaster Augustin Karara, in 1973 a student at the junior seminary of Nyundo in Gisenyi Prefecture, explained that upon his return to the commune, he noticed the violence had gone beyond the school setting, and people were burning Tutsi houses in the Gasura Sector. However, calm was quickly restored, those who had burned the houses helped the Tutsis to rebuild them, and the peaceful coexistence between Hutus and Tutsis resumed. According to his testimony, no bitterness remained between the two communities in Gasura, few inhabitants of the sector left the country because of this violence, and those who did were mainly the intellectuals.[23] Anne-Marie Nyampuza, a genocide survivor, was in a secondary school in the commune in 1973. She saw how authorities manipulated the Hutu students to set upon their Tutsi friends. These students travelled around by car from school to school, armed with traditional weapons, to chase away the Tutsis. Upon returning home, she saw that trouble was starting in the countryside, particularly in her neighborhood, where all the houses that belonged to Tutsis were burned. According to her, people were injured during the violence, but no one was killed. She considered the local authorities the main instigators of the violence. She explains that after the unrest had ended, the Tutsi and Hutu communities reconciled.[24]

Several of the people I interviewed insist that the ties between Hutus and Tutsis were not severed during the 1973 violence. Edouard Serugendo explains that some Hutus protected the houses of their Tutsi friends from arsonists.[25] Before fleeing, some Tutsi neighbors left their young children, cows, and crops with the relatives of Benoît Usabyumuremyi.[26] According to Eliezer Mbonabande, the councilor of Gitesi Sector, called Mashyaka, instigated the violence that occurred there.[27] Mashyaka ordered Hutus to eat the cows that belonged to Tutsis. By complying, the peasants were targeting people they did not like, and more well-off Tutsis were the main victims of the aggressors.[28] All the people interviewed explained that when calm was restored, the Hutu and Tutsi communities reconciled, and even though the relations were weakened by the war that broke out in 1990, they held strong until 1994.

From 1973 to 1990 in Gitesi Commune, the contrast between good Hutu-Tutsi social relations and the state marginalization of Tutsis was confirmed. Nyampuza was not able to return to school after she was expelled. She too had to go into exile, joining her relatives who had fled to Zaire in 1959, in order to continue with school.[29] Upon returning from Zaire after finishing her studies, she spent two years following the administrative procedures to find work in the public sector but was unsuccessful. The Hutu husband of a Tutsi friend eventually found her a job.[30] Several of Usabyumuremyi's neighbors, males from a Tutsi family, also went into exile in Zaire in large numbers to pursue their secondary school education, and their sisters left to get married.[31] Usabyumuremyi refers to the state marginalization of Tutsis in political representation when he explains that under the Habyarimana government, Tutsis in the commune could not become councilors.[32] In periods of crisis like from 1983 to 1984 during the tension in the state summit between Hutu northern factions, Tutsis were made scapegoats, with each adversary accusing the other of being too conciliatory toward them.[33]

In Gitesi Commune, the state of the ethnic relations did not change with the shifting economic environment. Despite the rise in instability and violence during the severe food shortages in 1984 and 1990, official documents mention only one case of ethnic hostility, the one already cited of a former PARMEHUTU sector councilor who kept chanting the PARMEHUTU refrain about a Tutsi plot to exterminate Hutus during the political infighting at the top of government.[34]

The statements by protagonists in the genocide show the good relations between Hutu and Tutsi communities between 1973 and 1990. Catherine Kandamutsa, who confessed her role in the genocide in Bwishyura Sector, puts it this way:

> We shared everything; there was a perfect harmony [between Hutus and Tutsis]; we visited each other, and during ceremonies we were all there. Sometimes some Tutsis put me in charge of the drinks during their festivities. There was no bad blood between us. They gave us cows, and we gave them cows too, so there was perfect harmony. It is just this war that erupted that caused all this trouble; before the killings, there was no difference between us.[35]

Alphonse Nsengimana of Burunga Sector, a confessed genocide participant, explained, "Before the war (I was already an adult), I noticed that Hutu-Tutsi relations were good; there were many interethnic marriages; in fact, there was no problem. I, for instance, lived with Tutsis, and I had no problem with them."[36]

Mbonabande, a genocide survivor from Gitarama Sector, testified, "We lived in harmony; we were all Rwandans; we helped each other in the fields; we celebrated interethnic marriages. It was in 1973 that people started to form groups. Hutus started to say that they did not want Tutsis, but after things returned to normal, they continued to marry young Tutsi women until the war of 1994."[37] All the other people I interviewed, both survivors and confessed killers, gave a similar answer. They all mentioned the frequent interethnic marriages as proof that both groups lived in harmony. Mbonabande specified that mostly, Hutu men married Tutsi women.

I have tried to measure the frequency of interethnic marriages interviewees mentioned as an indicator of harmonious relations between the two communities. The administration statistics on registered births allow one to see the frequency of mixed matings. I also managed to find statistics for eight months over two different years, thus accounting for, in theory, a third of the births registered during this period.

The total number of children with at least one Tutsi parent are in Tables 9.1 and 9.2 as follows:

• Number of births to a Hutu father and Tutsi mother: fifteen
• Number of births to a Tutsi father and Hutu mother: eight
• Number of births to two Tutsi parents: fifty-seven

There were eighty babies born to at least one Tutsi parent, 71 percent of whom were born to two Tutsi parents, and the remaining 29 percent born to one Tutsi and one Hutu parent. Of those, 19 percent of the births were to a Hutu father and Tutsi mother, and 10 percent were to a Tutsi father and Hutu mother.

Of the children born to at least one Tutsi parent, more than two-thirds had two Tutsi parents, and the remainder had one Tutsi and one Hutu parent. These figures reveal that in the majority of Tutsi matings in Gitesi Commune, both partners were Tutsi, and there were a significant number of mixed matings

Table 9.1   **Number of Registered Births in Gitesi Commune by Parents' Ethnicity, 1987**

Parentage	January	February	March	April	May	Total
Hutu father/ Hutu mother	33	32	18	38	34	155
Hutu father/ Tutsi mother	0	0	6	2	1	9
Tutsi father/ Hutu mother	1	1	0	2	0	4
Tutsi father/ Tutsi mother	8	8	7	2	6	31
Father unknown	15	16	4	25	23	83
Mother unknown	24	9	22	5	19	79
Total	81	66	57	74	83	361

Source: Commune Gitesi, *Statistiques des mois de janvier, février, mars, avril, mai 1987.*

Table 9.2   **Number of Registered Births in Gitesi Commune by Parents' Ethnicity, 1989**

Parentage	March	April	May	Total
Hutu father/ Hutu mother	29	26	57	112
Hutu father/ Tutsi mother	2	1	3	6
Tutsi father/ Hutu mother	2	2	0	4
Tutsi father/ Tutsi mother	4	7	15	26
Father unknown	4	22	16	42
Mother unknown	0	0	2	2
Foreign father	2	0	1	3
Foreign mother	0	0	0	0
Total	43	58	94	195

Source: Commune Gitesi, *Statistiques des mois de mars, avril, mai 1989.*

with Hutus. In this latter group, the number of Tutsi women who married Hutu men was twice that of Tutsi men who married Hutu women. Although the Tutsi community was open to mixed marriages, most Tutsis preferred to marry within their group. One way to assess the importance of the frequency of in-

terethnic unions is to consider the perceptions of those people most directly involved. Despite the apparently limited frequency of Hutu-Tutsi marriages in
the mid-1980s, the people themselves were quite pleased with the number of
such marriages given that most of them cited it as the main proof of interethnic
harmony.

During the period between the political crises of 1973 and 1990, the
shortage of land sometimes caused conflicts, which, though private nevertheless put Hutu and Tutsi families on opposing sides. As the amount of
available land shrank over the years, some Hutu families tended to set upon
Tutsi families, notables during the monarchy. Some Tutsi families benefited
from land seized from certain Hutu and Tutsi lineages, which thereafter was
considered pastoral land controlled by state officials, or *ibikingi*. During the
revolution, such land was redistributed. If former notables did not have deep
roots in the region, their land might have been expropriated from local lineages. But families of lower-level Tutsi former notables, generally the only
ones who had remained on their land after the revolution, often in the 1980s
still owned their original family land. Dividing land given the different types
of land ownership was delicate, but the revolutionary activists who seized
Tutsi land generally went first for *ibikingi,* or politically acquired land.

In the 1980s, some Hutu families claimed parcels of land belonging to
Tutsi families on the grounds that the latter had extorted the land from them
during the period of the monarchy. These disputes presented for resolution in
court were often the basis for repressed ethnic animosity and thus a motive for
the massacre or flight of Tutsi families during the genocide.[38] The question remains whether the claims to the land in these kinds of cases were legitimate
and well founded or whether they were a means to take advantage of the vulnerability of the families of former lower-level Tutsi notables. The former burgomaster stated that Tutsis in his commune had the best land—even after the
redistribution of the 1960s—and suggested that was no longer the case in the
early 1990s, implying a continous process of redistribution of land that belonged to Tutsis.[39]

War and Multiparty Rule

Social Context of the Period

To better understand the mass participation in political party activities and
later on in the genocide, I start by sketching the social context underlying these
two events between 1990 and 1994. In a report on assistance to the poor dated
January 10, 1994, the burgomaster wrote,

Gitesi Commune has about 2,641 families experiencing chronic hunger. This shortage of food is tied to that of cultivable land, to weather conditions and low productivity of the little land available, as demonstrated by an investigation carried out by the Free Methodist Church in 1992 and a census launched by the minister of the interior in 1991. To this number are added 4,590 families seriously affected by famine during the 1992 fiscal year in need of food aid and 6,167 families who may join the above group if weather conditions do not return to normal.[40]

In 1991 Gitesi Commune had 61,030 inhabitants; if we conservatively consider that a family has four members on average, then 47 percent of the commune population was either experiencing chronic hunger or was seriously affected by the food shortage and 40 percent were food insecure.[41]

Desperate for land, some people contested transfers of land ownership made years or decades earlier. Thus, in May 1991 a peasant woman named Uzamuranga asked the commune for permission to cultivate a piece of land she used to exploit informally that the commune had granted to the Evangelical Church of Rwanda in 1988. At the time, Uzamuranga contested the grant in court, but her claim was dismissed. Three years later, she took up the fight again.[42] In January 1993, the Presbyterian Church of Rwanda, Kibuye Parish, presented an appeal against a Mr. Bigirimana farming a field in Bwishyura Sector that the state had legally granted to the church on June 14, 1963. In his defense, Bigirimana explained that his parents used to live there and that the land was ancestral property the state had seized. In 1969, he had received from the commune a plot to cultivate. The burgomaster requested urgent assistance from the head of the land registry of Kibuye Town because Bigirimana had fenced and cultivated the plot, yet the Evangelical Church was claiming that the crop belonged to the parish minister.[43] In March 1994, the burgomaster wrote to the councilor of Gitesi Sector asking him to intervene on behalf of a young man who asked the commune for help against his parents, who were selling their land without leaving any for him. The young man had started to build a home on the family land, but his parents had just sold the plot where he was hoping to live without assigning him somewhere else to build. The burgomaster asked the council to investigate the issue and see if the sale of the land complied with the law.[44]

At the height of the multiparty era, some used political parties' cover to grab land. The minutes of the commune council security committee meeting of September 7, 1993, observed,

> On the violence used in the grabbing of land, the burgomaster explained that some people, especially in Ruragwe, Kayenzi, and Burunga Sectors, had sold their land in 1974 and even earlier, but now they were repossessing it by force. This violent action, which the peasants called kubohoza, was also car-

ried out on commune land in Burunga Sector, the Nyamarebe marshland, the Nyagatovu technical school, and many other places.[45]

Six months after this report, a letter from the burgomaster still reported similar acts; in Bwishyura Sector, for example, in Kibuye Cell alone, six seizures of land took place at almost the same time. A Mr. Habimana was accused of forcibly taking a banana plantation a Mr. François Munyeperu had bought from Habimana's father in 1975. Habimana had taken the dispute to court and lost the case. He wanted to fight and was arrested, and upon his release from prison, he returned to take over the banana plantation. A Mr. Nkubito grabbed the land of Adrien Sengorore by force. Nkubito's father had sold the land to Sengorore's father. While the case was in court, Nkubito repossessed the land. A Mr. Ntilivamunda forcibly took away the land his father had sold to Halindintwali in 1969. Ntilivamunda had already harvested many crops from the farm under dispute. The report cited many other cases.[46]

Between 1990 and 1994, deadly violence increased in the communities. In 1991, the prefect noted in his report that a man from Gitesi who went to Mabanza Commune to steal cocoyams was killed at a farm.[47] In Gitesi Commune, a Mr. Uwimana was caught stealing at a cassava farm and killed.[48] The minutes of the security committee meeting of September 7, 1993, recorded, "The burgomaster explained that there was a strong resurgence in murders: many bodies were found in Lake Kivu, but closer examination revealed that the individuals had not died from drowning but had been killed. We are also witnessing a resurgence of murders committed in public as part of the cycle of revenge."[49]

Two months later, the burgomaster wrote in a letter to the prefect that there was a wave of unresolved murders in Bubazi and Kayenzi Sectors. Many of those killed were isolated individuals who were not particularly wealthy.[50] He said investigations were in progress, but he did not anticipate a decrease in the killings. He noted that on September 22, 1993, in Ruhande Cell of Kayenzi Sector, the body of Eliel Ndahayo, a resident and night guard at the national electricity company, was found on the banana plantation belonging to Ezechiel Munyambibi. It had been two days since Ndahayo had come home, and it was thought that he had been killed because of money he had borrowed from the bank plus the amount he had earned from selling an ox in order to pay for school materials for his son, who had just been admitted to secondary school. The neighbors immediately suspected Nzabihimana, a known murderer. Around that time, Ndahayo's wife had quarreled with Nzabihimana's mother and had struck the latter on the shoulder with a machete. Nzabihimana's mother had later died at the hospital from her injuries. The residents then grabbed Nzabihimana and beat him to death. Two days later, in the same banana plantation, residents called the authorities when they found the body of a corpulent man they did not recognize. Finally, the burgomaster stated that on the night of September 23, 1993, in Kavumu Cell of Bubazi Sector, a group of men attacked the home of a trader called Sostène Rusekabuhanga, seriously injuring him, his wife, and his sister. The night guards said there were several attackers, and they wore military uniforms and were armed with machetes and grenades. A few days later, members of the gang suspected to have killed someone with a grenade were arrested.[51] In a letter to the prefect dated February 4, 1994, the burgomaster wrote that in Nzoga-Nweya Cell of Kagabiro Sector on the night of January 24, 1994, a cow that belonged to Sekimonyo and another to Mudahunga were injured with machetes. The next day, the residents looked for Fidèle Nzamurinda and for Sekimonyo's son Safari. When the residents found the two, they beat them up. Safari died from the beating, and Nzamurinda was seriously injured. Sekimonyo went and surrendered to the prosecutor, explaining that he had killed his son because of harassment and violence he had suffered at the hands of Safari. The burgomaster explained that the two victims were in dispute with their fathers, and that Nzamurinda's father had even fled his home out of fear of his son.[52]

On January 31, 1994, in Nemba Cell of Gitesi Sector, a young man called Edison Ndahimana went to rob the house of a Mr. Habiyambare in broad daylight while the owner was away. When he left the house, the residents chased him and threw stones at him. He fell and was taken to the cell head. A few hours later, the young man died of his injuries. According to the burgomaster, Ndahimana was a well-known cattle thief who had walked out of Kibuye Prison just two days earlier.[53]

On March 19, 1994, in Nyamarebe Cell of Burunga Sector, a group of four men attacked the home of a certain Sentoki. They reduced the home to ashes and assaulted Sentoki, injuring him seriously. The group accused Sentoki of being a thief, yet according to the burgomaster, there was no reason to think so. The burgomaster requested gendarmes to accompany commune police officers to arrest the criminals because the men of this cell considered themselves untouchable.[54]

The few examples presented here reveal a rise in social violence that intensified in 1993 and early 1994. On the one hand, this violence was carried out by individuals and was increasingly extreme at the hands of hardened criminals who attacked in broad daylight; on the other hand, the violence was social because it came from the residents, who increasingly tended to take justice into their own hands and punished stealing with death. Finally, there was violence directly linked to the prevailing political environment. In the last example of Nyamarebe Cell, a group of people decided to assume the functions of the police, and the burgomaster was forced to request reinforcements in the form of gendarmes. Also in Nyamarebe a few months earlier, the people had forcibly (*kubohoza*) evicted groups of farmers to "free" the marshland that belonged to the commune. Nyamarebe Cell had been "liberated" and had come under the control of MDR supporters.[55] In general, despite the increasingly harsh social relations and the consuming rise in violence and despite the pervasive propaganda aimed at arousing ethnic antagonism throughout the war and multiparty period (1991–1994), there were few reports of ethnically motivated violence.[56]

Reactions to the Outbreak of the War in 1990

Before assessing the reactions, it is important to distinguish between the people at the grassroots in the commune, mainly peasants who lived in the countryside neighboring or distant from Kibuye Town, and the "intellectual" urban people working in the town. None of the peasants or semiurban residents I interviewed mentioned any ethnically motivated reaction to the outbreak of the war. Usabyumuremyi explained to us that in the Bwishyura Sector, the war felt far removed and of little concern to people in his area.[57] Nyampuza was a Tutsi civil servant working at the Kibuye Post Office and married to a Hutu small-scale businessman. They lived in the countryside close to the town. According to her, any reactions of ethnic hostility were directed at Tutsis who aroused jealousy because, for example, they had a son studying abroad or, in the case of her and her husband, they had social status.[58]

In the November 1990 report on the security situation in Kibuye Prefecture addressed to the president's office, the prefect summarized the situation since the October 1 attack. The prefect explained that after the Inkotanyi attack, the prefecture generally remained peaceful, and then he mentioned the following incidents:

> Ethnic tension was detected in Mabanza, Gitesi, Gishyita, and Rwamatamu Communes along Lake Kivu, with significant Tutsi populations. The tensions still brewing elsewhere, far from disappearing quickly, are the result of the inflammatory attitudes of Tutsis who have not hidden their satisfaction [with the attack] and their hatred for Hutus since the war broke out, whom they say they would not save from the massacres given that they are waiting to receive weapons directly after the takeover of the capital.[59]

In the early days of the political change, by the end of 1990, the government had promised to issue new identity cards that did not indicate ethnicity.[60] In his report, the prefect commented on this issue as follows:

> It should be noted, however, that a broad survey on this issue in Gishyita and Gitesi Communes revealed that Hutus were not happy with the move to remove the mention of ethnicity on the identity cards. They said it was a shrewd camouflage move by Tutsis in order to seize power and massacre Hutus. For their part, the Tutsis did not hide their pleasure and explained that they would no longer be called "Inkotanyi" and "accomplices," epithets directed at them by Hutus since the last inyenzi ["cockroach," or rebel] invasion.[61]

On the day after the RPF attack, in Gitesi Commune there was a wave of arrests of prominent Tutsis and progressive Hutus in which they were accused of colluding with the enemy. A month after the attack, the Kibuye prosecutor had completed drawing up twenty-four charges "for which the triage commission had already gathered sufficient evidence. Fifteen other accused will remain in detention and subject to thorough investigation."[62]

The other issue directly related to the war that had an impact on the social climate was the fact that some young Tutsis were leaving to enlist in the RPF. Usabyumuremyi insisted that this played a crucial role in the deteriorating trust between Hutu and Tutsi families in Bwishyura Sector after 1990.[63] Karara, burgomaster at the time, offers a different opinion:

> In 1990, with the war against the Inkotanyi, political problems affected Gitesi Commune, considered a Tutsi-dominated area. The Tutsis were considered the country's attackers and were not trusted. However, even before they reached here, the tensions had first begun in Gishyita and Rwamatamu Communes, especially Gishyita because many young people who joined the Inkotanyi ranks came from these communes. Here in Gitesi, that was not the case. I think that the Tutsis of the commune were not informed about these things, but that did not prevent them from becoming victims of what was going on elsewhere. Some tension came from Gishyita—it was an Inkotanyi commune; the Inkotanyi were popular there. The people here who had friends in Gishyita or who had sons studying abroad began to be suspected, but in general, there was no one you could consider actually committed here in Gitesi. There was no way this tension caused by Tutsis who had attacked Rwanda to overthrow the government could not have had an impact on the local Tutsis. They lived with this reality until political parties were established.[64]

No other interviewee mentioned young Tutsis rallying around the RPF; neither did the documents from Gitesi Commune and Kibuye Prefecture. One can thus share with the burgomaster his opinion that the news of the war with the RPF did not cause the spread of ethnic hostility in the commune, even though, as he explains, it created some mistrust.

Activities of Political Parties

During the multiparty period (1991–1994), the political environment in Gitesi Commune was strongly determined by various regional sensibilities in Kibuye Prefecture. The administrative capital of the prefecture, Kibuye Town, is located in the commune, and several employees originally from other regions worked and resided there. Among the intellectuals in the prefecture, those from areas politically close to the Habyarimana government were the majority, and many of them lived in Kibuye Town.[65] However, as the three other communes bordering Lake Kivu, Gitesi had a significant Tutsi population with its strong feeling of alienation from the central government. Most of the Hutus and Tutsis of the lower economic classes residing in Gitesi Commune whether in the town or the countryside, supported the opposition, whereas the political and administrative elite remained loyal to the MRND. Because of the strong influence of prefecture decisionmakers, the majority MRND, many junior civil servants did not dare show their true political sympathies out of fear for their jobs. Although publicly supporting the MRND, many had their hearts with the opposition. Among these people, the only ones who revealed their true political colors, essentially those of the MDR, were labeled the "dissatisfied," that is, those who had personal grudges against the regime or "the opportunists" who joined the strongest party in the hope of one day realizing personal ambitions they had not achieved under the MRND regime. This preponderance of MRND supporters in top positions restrained the town intellectuals from openly showing their political allegiance.[66]

Things were different for lower-income Hutus in both the urban and rural areas, most of whom were loyal to the MDR. Since the first MDR public appearance in the commune at a rally on August 18, 1991, at Gatwaro Regional Stadium, the party had "uplifted" the population, to use the expression of the prefecture security council.[67] Under the influence of the MDR, the people undertook a sabotage campaign of setting bushes on fire. The prefecture security council analyzed the situation as follows:

> In Gitesi Commune, people scoff at the sector and cell administrations. The only authority they listen to is the burgomaster; hence the neglect of the communal work for development (umuganda). A bogus democracy promising anarchy is slowly gaining ground. In the same manner, those who set off bush fires proudly claim to be acting under the banner of democracy. . . . In Gitesi Commune, the wave of forest and bush fires was set off beginning August 25, 1991, in Kayenzi Sector, after residents returning from the local parish of the Presbyterian Church of Rwanda spontaneously held a rally. The password for the supporters of these actions is the destruction of MRND achievements because, they say, the MDR will take over. They also base their actions on the fact that the state transferred the land they owned to ongoing rural development projects in the prefecture. That is how they revealed their intention to cause damage by destroying the forests planted by the former forestation pilot project. Some of the forests destroyed belonged to the commune and others to the state; even individually owned woodlands were not spared. The criminals celebrate upon seeing the forests burn and openly wish MRND supporters would burn in the same way. Some of the suspected troublemakers have already been arrested and will soon be interrogated. When they were arrested, they expressed their opinions and stated that the fire meant nothing other than the destruction of MRND work and that for the MDR, fire historically symbolized the light of democracy.[68]

After the presentation of the facts, the council members listed the causes of the situation in the prefecture as follows:

- The criminals are manipulated by supporters of some political parties.
- Some people who were starving wanted to slaughter others' livestock and reclaim land for cultivation, even if some of them claimed that Tutsi livestock owners wanted to spark the bush fires in order to clear land as pasture for their livestock.
- The MDR rally of Sunday, August 18, 1991, at Gatwaro Regional Stadium aroused the people; open resistance to the authorities by the population was observed after the rally.
- During the popular rally directed by MRND propagandists on August 27, 1991, in Gitesi Commune, the authorities were booed to the point of humiliation.
- Members of the security council noted that even if the sector and cell authorities are no longer listened to as before, they were duty bound to denounce the criminals.
- The parties' leaders needed to know the public they were addressing and adapt their language appropriately.[69]

To attract members, the MDR became vehemently critical of the government and played upon the alienation and frustration among the youth; it also had no qualms about making numerous promises. Silas Kanani explained his reasons for joining the MDR:

> As for me, I chose the MDR. When we attended the rally at the stadium, things were said about the MRND. They said that no leader's son went to study at the integrated rural and vocational school (CERAI); they said that the sons of leaders always had access to secondary school, but the sons of peasants were all condemned to go to the CERAI. When they finished their studies, they could not find employment; they would live in endless unemployment. So the MDR was saying: "At the very least, these sons of peasants—after they finish training in tailoring, masonry, and carpentry—could be helped to acquire equipment they could pay for over time, but at least they would have a livelihood." We supported this idea, and most of us chose to support this party.[70]

Serugendo gave the following reasons for his joining the MDR:

> Personally, I joined the MDR; I thought it was a party whose objectives and principles seemed very commendable. The MDR criticisms of the government matched exactly the problems I had with the authorities who oppressed us without us being able to protest, so I told myself that there is a party on my side. The authorities had taken our land and our cows in public, without our being able to protest. That had really hurt me.[71]

In addition to these reasons for joining the MDR based on its social and political critique and focus on the future, others introduced a combination of identity issues and the violent history of the MDR-PARMEHUTU. The burgo-master explained:

> When one spoke of the MDR, people understood it was the MDR-PARMEHUTU, and even at the rallies, one would speak of the MDR, but the people would add PARMEHUTU. In any case, that is what drew a good number of people to join the party. . . . [The MRND] was afraid that the MDR-PARMEHUTU would return under the name of the MDR and monopolize all those nostalgic for the MDR-PARMEHUTU. Some were proud of that because being Hutu gave them an identity.[72]

Ultimately, said Karara, "There would be those for whom this was the opportunity to return to the life of the distant past. In general, this is how people at the grassroots saw it."[73]

Here, the prefecture security council explained people's motivations to join the MDR by the desire for participating in its civil disobedience campaign to destabilize the local authorities that would allow them to satisfy their predatory desire for land-grabbing. The security council decided to ask political parties to be careful with the speeches they made to the people given the explosive potential of the conditions in which the people lived.

A few days after the first MDR rally, the prefect noted that the political change became stronger:

> In Kibuye Prefecture, the political climate began to evolve significantly since propagandists of some political parties, notably the MDR, visited and held rallies in the prefecture administrative center and in some communes, especially those of the PSD [Social Democratic Party], whose visit was meant to be secret and currently those of the MRND. . . . The people of Gitesi Commune do not dare openly declare their stand. The most popular bodies, namely the MRND and the MDR, are both fairly well represented separately in the sectors. Forest fires continue to ravage this commune.[74]

Despite the prefecture security council report of the MDR success, the prefect observed a few days later that the people supported the opposition parties in secret.

Despite the significant increase in social violence and hunger between 1991 and early 1994, Gitesi Commune experienced few ethnically motivated violent incidents. MDR supporters instigated all three main events in which ethnic tension might have deteriorated into open violence. Burgomaster Karara, who played an important part in stifling the conflict, was a direct witness:

> I can tell you of three instances. The first was here in Burunga Sector, Nyamarebe Cell. Many MDR followers lived in that area, and they attacked Ruyenzi Cell, where many Tutsis lived, and they seized a cow,

which they ate. This was some kind of looting, but the objective was to use this opportunity to make something explosive happen. Meanwhile, the people of Ruyenzi considered it nothing more than the theft of livestock (ubushimusi), so they chased after the cow. The thieves had slaughtered the cow in public view. The people of Ruyenzi wanted to seize the criminals, which is normal, but others wanted to give the incident a new dimension, and people said that the Tutsis had attacked Hutus of Nyamarebe. So the people of Nyamarebe rushed to defend their people. Luckily by that time, we had created committees to resolve problems that arose. These committees were made up of all kinds of individuals, including the presidents of the parties at the sector and cell levels. Among them, the MDR leader for Nyamarebe Cell disagreed with what was going on. I was therefore informed of the situation before violence broke out. If it had broken out, anything could have been possible. I summoned this MDR leader to the commune, and in the evening, I returned to the scene. I had taken police officers with me but I did not want them to accompany me to the place itself, so I left them at a short distance because I did not want the people to get the impression I was coming to start a fight. I left on my own, so all of a sudden, they saw me among them, at night, by surprise. They were in a small meeting. In the meantime, one of those who had stolen the cow had been caught and beaten by the Tutsis in pursuit. They took him to the prosecutor, and on the way there the thief died from the beating he had received. Upon their friend's death, the other bandits and their associates decided to take revenge. The problem became ethnic. I arrived there toward 7:00 p.m.: their meeting was taking place in the local bar, while the others were mourning for the one who had died. They were peasants; there were no intellectuals among them. Even the president of the cell MDR, my informant, was a simple peasant. After apprising me of the events, he sought refuge in Mabanza Commune; he fled from his friends, but he came back when he heard I had come to the place. I saw that there were many people, maybe about twenty, and they were angry because their man had been killed, and they were feeling that they should avenge him, no matter the cost. They wanted to proceed as the people from Kayove and Rutsiro Communes had done. The people from Nyamarebe Cell wanted to call on their friends from Kayove and Rutsiro for help; these were people who knew and visited each other. The conflict affected only two cells, Ruyenzi and Nyamarebe, out of the five cells of the sector, and they needed help. So when I surprised them, they did not know what to say and changed the subject. I asked them what they were doing. I asked them to go home because a curfew had been declared. I warned of dire consequences to anyone caught by surprise outside because the soldiers were on their way. Toward 9:00 p.m., police officers arrived, and people thought the soldiers were also coming, so everyone went to bed, and the coup aborted. We had to organize yet another meeting to clarify the issue so that the people of Ruyenzi Cell felt safe, the people of Nyamarebe Cell recognized their mistakes, and the guilty were punished.

The second incident took place in 1992 in the cell on the border with Gishyita Commune. At the time this commune was on fire, and the killings were threatening to spill over into Gitesi Commune. Here in Gitesi, people burned houses, but fortunately also there were reconciliation committees, which had informed me. While I was in this cell on the border with Gishyita, the conflict arose from the Tutsis' fear that the Hutus would attack them, and the Hutus also thought Tutsis would attack them. Everyone thought they would be attacked, tried to be vigilant, and then everything exploded. Again, these were simple peasants; there was no intellectual implicated, but the things they said were terrible. I held a meeting there, but peace was restored thanks to the prime minister's visit to the Rusenyi Region [Rwamatamu and Gishyita Communes]. He organized a meeting during which he calmed down the people from the MDR. Each time, in these events, the political parties were implicated. MDR supporters were trying to repeat the events of 1959 with the fires and replicate the revolution, but because the prime minister did not agree with what was going on, and neither did the members of the other parties such as the PL, they were able to suppress the conflict. During that time, the motivation was political, and some people paid the price. Even though ordinary people carried out the acts, behind them were the authorities secretly inciting them, such that one could not clearly identify the source of the event. The initiators of these acts could not have been simple peasants; messages had been given. The MDR used the same tactics of acting under cover, just like in 1959 when only the perpetrator was seen. The conflict was diffused this way.

The third case occurred in Gasura Sector, just near here. It was during the same period. The CDR [Coalition for the Defense of the Republic] had just been established in the sector. There were fishermen who spent the whole night fishing. Then, CDR supporters arrived from Gisenyi Prefecture and led an attack here on Gasura. A boat carrying a large number of people came to carry out the attack. The people of Gasura mobilized. Some people spread a rumor that the assailants had come by boat to attack Gasura just as had happened in Gishyita Commune. Gasura was a sector inhabited by many Tutsis, and I lived there. I often passed through there on my way back home; that is how I heard the rumor. I was told about the place where the attackers would disembark. I went to see, and there was a boat, and the local Tutsis were making security rounds. I asked them: "What is happening?" They explained to me their fear, so I told them: "You think that they can really surprise us here? That is why you are doing the patrols? That's good; continue with the patrols." It would not have been wise to prevent them from doing the patrols, because if they had been attacked, another problem would have been created. Even I was not sure that the attack was not for real. However, when the Hutus of Gasura saw Tutsis mobilizing and doing the rounds, they said to themselves that the Tutsis were going to attack the Hutus. The CDR and the MRND of Kayove Commune [Gisenyi Prefecture] launched the attack against the PL and the MDR of Gasura; the Tutsis of the sector felt most threatened and arose to defend themselves, and in this movement, another dimension was added, that of Hutus led by the MDR. Curiously, the MDR in the sector was represented by a Hutu and a Tutsi, the two having arisen to mobilize Hutus of the sector. From a war between political parties we arrived at ethnic confrontation; we were swimming in confusion. Then we held a meeting, and everybody came to the sector office. I invited all the civil servants as well as the former burgomaster, originally from the local area. I told them all to shut down their classes and accompany me to Gasura so that we could resolve the problem together.[75]

Thus, according to the burgomaster of Gitesi Commune at the time, these attempts to create ethnic unrest were the work of MDR supporters, ideologically inspired by the MDR-PARMEHUTU. Note that these initiatives were implemented before the creation of the Hutu-power coalition in late 1993. In Gitesi also, the peasants used their membership in the MDR as a tool for grabbing land by political force under the *kubohoza* label. Cases of *kubohoza* happened in different locations in the commune.[76] These operations occurred above all in areas where the MDR had significant influence. One of the factors that determined the strength of that influence was the proportion of Hutus in the population. The case of Nyamarebe Cell was revealing. This cell with many Hutus was controlled by the MDR, and here the first violent interethnic conflict in the commune started. Also in Nyamarebe, one of the most important *kubohoza* operations in the commune took place.[77] Even in the sectors and cells where MDR control was not as complete as in Nyamarebe, the party successfully overruled the local authorities installed during the MRND hegemony.

Nyampuza, who lived in Gitarama Sector, explained, "Because the MDR was the strongest in our village, its leader seemed to be stronger than the serving councilor, who was MRND. MDR supporters said they would be the strongest, and they would be in power. For example, when the council organized a meeting, they would try to prevent people from attending."[78]

Despite the fact that state power was in the hands of the MRND, the MDR succeeded in gaining significant political control over Hutus at the grassroots. Because of MRND's power and of the significant Tutsi population, the MDR supporters still could not exercise complete control over the people or engage in excessive violence or destruction.

The other opposition parties were also present in the commune. The PSD was, as usual, established among the intellectual circles, and Burgomaster Karara was one of its most active leaders. However, as a matter of caution, PSD recruitment activities remained largely clandestine.[79] That did not prevent party delegations from arriving to hold rallies. In the following extract from the prefect report of August 28, 1991, the uneasiness of the PSD and the PL during the initial activities of the political parties in Kibuye Prefecture is palpable: "Nevertheless, only the MRND and the MDR remained popular; the other parties remain relatively unknown by the residents. It is important to observe and to deplore the fact that PSD and PL leaders have to visit the area in secret, yet the administration is ready to receive them and facilitate any contact they would like to have with the population."[80]

On its part, the PL seemed to have a stronger popular base in the commune, but essentially operated in secret.[81] The supporters of the PL essentially, but not entirely, consisted of Tutsis. Because of this trend of majority Tutsi support, many people equated the PL with the internal support for the RPF.[82] Some Tutsi PL supporters themselves openly affirmed as much.[83]

The fight between the MDR and the MRND for influence was slightly muffled among intellectuals but became increasingly heated among the lower classes and in the countryside, especially as a result of the fusion of party disputes and the numerous court cases and settling of personal scores among peasants.[84] For some Gitesi residents, the lingering memory of the multiparty era consisted of chaos and unending fights. Usabyumuremyi, from Bwishyura Sector, put it this way: "In reality, they were not constructive parties; they were there to destroy. Everywhere they went, they did not have a language other than that of conflict, accusing each other of anything. So personally, I saw all that from a distance; I could not give support to what was going on."[85]

Serugendo, of Burunga Sector, ended up resigning from the MDR:

> Violence began to appear with these political parties. People attacked each other because of their political affiliations; one could not go to such and such a bar because it had been declared supportive of a certain party, and so on. This was happening before the war of 1994. I saw that things were not good at all. That is why I resigned from the party [MDR]. I became a simple observer. We had joined political parties believing that they would bring us good things, but we ended up realizing that the parties were not good at all.[86]

At the end of 1993, mass political activities were suspended; there were no more political rallies in Rwanda because of the anarchy eventually created by the war and political party activities.

From late 1993 into early 1994, the extremist Radio télévision libre des mille collines (Thousand Hills Free Radio Television, RTLM) became the most important source of information and formation of political opinion in Gitesi Commune. It helped reinforce the Hutu-power wave and radicalize Hutus' opinions in the commune. In Gitesi also, each of the opposition political parties, led by the MDR, split into a moderate and a Hutu-power faction. According to Karara, the new burgomaster at the time, the split within the MDR was not a result of ideological differences but rather of a war between leaders. The MDR-power faction in Gitesi had succeeded in rallying the majority of MDR supporters, and it was the most powerful political faction in the commune.[87]

Genocide in Gitesi Commune

In Gitesi, the genocide had two distinct dynamics: one internal to the commune and the other coming from nearby communes. In Mabanza and Gishyita Communes, which had a large Tutsi population, the massacres began the day after Habyarimana's death. Thousands of Tutsi refugees came to Kibuye Town on the misleading instructions of the prefect. The town as well as the whole commune remained calm until April 10, 1994, four days after the massacres began elsewhere. Thousands of killers arrived from the neighboring communes in pursuit of Tutsis from their areas but also at the invitation of prefecture authorities to give support to the Gitesi population, not big enough to accomplish the anticipated task. Thus, Tutsis from within and outside the commune were massacred in different areas, on different days, and by different killers. The Tutsis of Gitesi were killed throughout the commune, in the hills next to their homes, and on Karongi Mountain, where thousands of them had gathered. Fewer were killed in the major massacre sites in Kibuye Town. Thousands of Tutsis of Mabanza, Gishyita, and other communes were killed at the three massacre sites in Kibuye Parish, the Saint Jean Catholic Church and Home adjacent to the Kibuye Church, and in Gatwaro Regional Stadium.

The Beginning

April 7, 1994. In the days immediately following the death of President Habyarimana, Gitesi Commune remained peaceful. However, civil servants and soldiers, originally from the north of the prefecture, in conversations and small gatherings started to demand revenge, stating that Tutsis had killed the president.[88]

April 8. Tutsis and Hutu members of the moderate MDR-Twagiramungu faction fled toward Karongi Mountain.[89]

April 9. Tutsi refugees from Mabanza Commune as well as from Rutsiro and Kayove Communes of Gisenyi Prefecture arrived in Kibuye Town and were guided toward the stadium, under the supervision of Prefect Clément Kayishema.[90] The arrival of thousands of these Tutsis, many of them seriously injured, raised tensions in the town. From April 9 to 17, thousands of refugees from Mabanza and to a lesser extent from Gitesi and Gishyita Communes filled the four main massacre sites in Kibuye Town, namely, Gatwaro Regional Stadium, the Kibuye Church, the Saint Jean Catholic Church and Home, and the Nyamishaba agricultural school. Until April 14, refugees could leave these areas to go buy food.

April 10. The first burnings of Tutsi houses began in Bwishyura Sector, at the instigation of the civil servants in the commune. The arson then spread throughout the commune.[91]

April 12. As a result of the arson and the attacks against them to steal their cattle, the Tutsis of Gitesi Commune began to leave their homes; those from Burunga Sector sought refuge in Kibuye Town, at the Gataro Regional Stadium, and at the Kibuye Church.[92]

April 13. The first attacks on Tutsis gathered on Karongi Mountain began. The burgomaster, who could see the scene from his office, went there to intervene. A Tutsi who had sneaked into the crowd of Hutu attackers was killed under the nose of the burgomaster, who did not intervene. After the burgomaster left, the attacks against Tutsis resumed. The Tutsis defended themselves and pushed back the peasants attacking them. Faced with this resistance, the military, Kibuye Prison guards, commune police, and army reservists arrived to attack the Tutsis gathered there.[93]

April 15. Boats filled with killers arrived from the Kayove, Rutsiro (Gisenyi Prefecture), and Mabanza Communes. From April 15 on, the Tutsi refugees at Gatwaro Regional Stadium could no longer leave to buy food, and those who risked going out were immediately killed with machetes. In the Saint Jean Catholic Church and Home, a church leader counted the refugees and cited a total of 7,200.[94]

On that day, a soldier called Afrika was killed by Tutsis on Karongi Mountain. Several gendarmes and killers from Rutsiro and Mabanza Communes and Gisenyi Town were called to provide reinforcement. On Karongi Mountain, thousands of Tutsis gathered from different sectors of the commune. The massacres on the mountain required an organized effort: the participation of members of various security forces, killers from Rutsiro, and the mobilization of peasants from the surrounding areas motivated mainly by the desire to take cows and loot other property Tutsis had brought with them to the hill.[95] The attacks as well as the search for survivors on Karongi Mountain continued until June 1994. Faced with this growing pressure from the attackers, some Tutsis headed for the Bisesero Hills in Gishyita Commune, where major resistance had been organized by Tutsis from the area.[96]

April 16. An attack was launched against the Kibuye Church, located in the town. The killers shot and threw grenades into the church courtyard, where the refugees had poured into the parish.[97]

April 17. A combined attack was launched against Gatwaro Regional Stadium, the Kibuye Parish, and the Nyamishaba agricultural institute. Gendarmes, prison guards, armed militias, and peasants participated in the carnage at each of these sites, and thousands of Tutsis were exterminated on April 17 and over the next few days.[98]

In 1999, the genocide survivors' umbrella organization, Ibuka, published a dictionary of names of people killed in Kibuye.[99] Philip Verwimp made a quantitative analysis of the list and estimated that 10,850 Tutsis were killed in Gitesi Commune, and 1,664 survived.[100] Of these, 2,298 people were killed in their cell of residence, 3,182 in the hills across the commune, and 2,432 in unidentified areas. The remaining 2,938 people would have been killed in the different large-scale massacre sites, in Kibuye Town and on Karongi Mountain. According to this count, the majority of refugees exterminated in the sites in Kibuye Town came from Mabanza Commune.

The operations to exterminate Tutsis at the five largest massacre sites in Gitesi Commune were organized at the prefecture level. On April 11, the interim government summoned the prefects to Kigali. During the meeting, the prefects reported on the situation in their prefectures, especially the killings, but according to Human Rights Watch, this meeting did not yield a definite plan of action. The implication is that the prefects understood that the agenda was to continue and expand the massacres.[101] Upon leaving the meetings, Prefect Kayishema made plans for Tutsis to be rounded up in the sites in the administrative center of the prefecture, Kibuye Town.[102] Several testimonies accuse Kayishema of being the main organizer of large-scale massacres in the prefecture. A survivor who escaped the massacre at Gatwaro Regional Stadium told African Rights, "On Sunday April 17, a man who escaped death at the hands of Clément Kayishema, the prefect, ran to the stadium. He told us: 'It's all over.' He said that the prefect had personally killed five people he had previously arrested and detained in the prison. The same prefect came to the stadium to carry out a census on Sunday. He had the people counted by cells; I don't know what the total came to."[103]

Alison Des Forges wrote that in early May, Prefect Kayishema reviewed again the data burgomasters had sent him for the last trimester of 1993, and he identified errors in the tallying of Tutsis in different communes.[104] In the year 2000, Kayishema was eventually condemned to life in prison by the International Criminal Tribunal for Rwanda for his role in the genocide in Kibuye. This demonstrates the organized nature and the primary role played by state authorities, largely through the use of the gendarmes. However, other dynamics were also at play in the mobilization of the population to exterminate Tutsis at the large massacre sites. The minority of the Gitesi population who participated in the massacres at the very beginning was mobilized through the political parties. Taking stock of the massacres in the whole prefecture, former burgomaster Karara states, "Even during the war in 1994, it was not the Interahamwe who carried out the killings; it was the MDR-power faction. The MRND was not there."[105] Regarding Gitesi Commune in particular, a survivor in the town during the genocide explained,

> On Friday April 15, we saw boats full of Interahamwe coming from Gisenyi Prefecture and Mabanza Commune. After they arrived here, they gathered all the Hutus who belonged to Pawa [the Hutu-power coalition], who pointed out the houses to encircle on the basis that some young Tutsi had preferred to remain indoors. . . . On Sunday [April 17], at about 10:00 a.m., there was an attack on a huge scale. There were soldiers, communal policemen, prison wardens, and members of Pawa and their allies.[106]

Like Burgomaster Karara, this survivor makes a clear distinction between the MRND Interahamwe militias coming from outside the prefecture and the Hutu-power faction, which in Gitesi Commune and most of Kibuye Prefecture belonged to the MDR. The different political affiliations of the killers seemed clear and important to those who experienced the tragedy. These testimonies show that, apart from members of the state security organs and the Interahamwe coming from Gisenyi Prefecture and Rutsiro Commune, the inhabitants of Gitesi who spontaneously mobilized and who zealously participated in the extermination were essentially supporters of the MDR-power faction.

An important proportion of the general population in the commune was part of the dynamics of the massacres at the large sites, especially on Karongi Mountain. As Usabyumuremyi, who played an important role in organizing the massacres on the hill, explained, thousands of Hutu residents from the six neighboring sectors were mobilized to encircle the mountain and prevent the Tutsis from escaping.[107]

Genocide in the Sectors

Many Tutsis in sectors of Gitesi Commune were killed by their neighbors. Even though the Ibuka's "dictionary" analyzed by Verwimp underestimated the number of genocide victims in the commune, this study gave significant indications of the major patterns and methods of the killings. Thus, according to this study, 21 percent of Tutsis living in Gitesi were killed in their cell of residence, 29 percent in the mountains of the commune, and 22 percent at an unidentified location. A vague category, "in the mountains" suggests that the victims did not die at the major massacre sites, and that means at least some of those victims were killed by ordinary people from Gitesi. The same is true of the people killed at an unidentified location. Some might have been killed at the big massacre sites in town largely by organized killers coming from outside the commune, other in other places by ordinary residents of Gitesi. The following captures the internal dynamics that unfolded at the sector and cell levels.

Burunga Sector. Serugendo recounts how things happened in his cell, Kabuga:

> When the war broke out in 1994, we united, Hutus and Tutsis, and formed a coalition in the cell. In the cell next to ours, where our farmers' association and our prayer group were based, acts similar to the kubohoza of 1993 began. I saw people take others' cows. I saw it. I thought that was a very bad thing; I tried to advise my friends not to take part in such behavior, I had not yet been overcome by the desire to commit evil. The following day, they planned an attack against our cell because, they said, we were allies with the Tutsis. A delegation that included Tutsis went to negotiate peace with the attackers. The others were armed with fishnets. A few days later, they organized a

major attack to hit three cells: ours, the adjacent one beyond the small river in Mabanza Commune, and the next one over. It was a huge attack carried out by a crowd of people. When they arrived in our cell, they made a diversion to go to the side where Tutsi families lived; they took cows, drove them to a spot, torched the houses, and so forth. They killed two people, and none of us reacted. . . . The attackers came from three cells: Nyamarebe, Mbogo, and another of Mabanza Commune. Most of them were known for being troublemakers: they were simple peasants organized according to cells, each with a president and vice president. The group from Nyamarebe Cell was led by Fabien Shyerezo, assisted by Damien Gahunga. The group from Mbogo was led by Damien Rugeruza and Mathias Mucumbitsi. Mabanza was led by César Kabahizi. There were many people, just like in 1993 during kubohoza, when people took over the valley from the state during the multiparty period. After taking our cows and burning our homes, they sent us a message that they would come to kill us because we supported the Tutsis although they were the ones who had killed the president. We said to each other: "We cannot accept that people come to our cell and eat our cows and our goats." Moreover, they had just killed someone, so we said to ourselves: "Things are beginning to get worse!" So we began to secretly form groups. . . . After the attacks and the looting, hatred began to appear among us, and that is how the massacres of Tutsis were introduced in our area. This hatred emerged between people fighting over property.[108]

Serugendo went on to explain that an old land dispute between a Tutsi and a Hutu family became the motive that sparked the massacre of Tutsis in Kabuga Cell by his Hutu neighbors. The testimony of Kanani, who lived in the same cell, was similar to Serugendo's point by point. Regarding the Nyamarebe Cell, referred to in this testimony as the origin of some of the killers, the former burgomaster explains that before April 13, when the first massacres occurred in Gitesi Commune, people from Nyamarebe Cell went to neighboring Mabanza Commune to kill Tutsis because the peace still prevailing in Gitesi did not allow killing. This killing campaign in Mabanza and in Burunga Sector completed Nyamarebe residents' path to extremism, which began with the establishment of political pluralism. The cell, of which the population was almost entirely Hutu, came under complete MDR control. As we have seen, in this cell at the instigation of the local MDR the residents sought to attack neighboring Ruyenzi Cell by appealing to groups of killers from Kayove Commune in Gisenyi Prefecture.[109] In 1993 in this sector, the local MDR led a kubohoza of the commune marshlands, using physical threats to expel the farmers' groups working there.[110] Also in this same cell, a group of people burned down someone's house, accusing him of theft and forcing the burgomaster to call in the gendarmes to restore order.[111]

Gitarama Sector. Nyampuza's testimony tells about the attacks in Gitarama:

Three days after the shooting down of Habyarimana's plane, attacks began in my neighborhood. The Tutsis gathered, intending to defend themselves, and

Hutus who did not know what was going on joined them. They fought back by throwing stones at the attackers. The next day, the attacks resumed, and Tutsis threw stones once again. On April 11, things worsened. This time there was a huge attack; they had called for reinforcement from other sectors. They said Gitarama had resisted because there were many inyenzi. When the Tutsis saw that the attack was too strong, some escaped and left for Gitwa Hill on Karongi Mountain next to the FM antenna. That was where everybody gathered.[112]

Mbonabande, also a survivor from Gitarama Sector, gave a more detailed account of the attacks:

When Habyarimana died, the top authorities in Kigali said on RTLM that nobody should move. We stayed at home as people organized to kill us. We were able to prepare our meals and we fetched water; we were under the impression that this was a war as simple as the previous one [in 1973], but people said that this war would be the final one. They started to throw stones at us; we resisted, supported by some Hutus. We united with some Hutus who trusted us, and we fought together; they did not have those politics, they knew nothing about that, and some had Tutsi wives. Their brothers warned them, telling them that this was the final war and that no one would survive, that they were risking their own lives as well. The brothers said they were going to get soldiers, and if the Hutus did not change their minds, they were risking their lives. "Leave them before things get worse!" they said to the Hutus. That is how they left us. We climbed the mountain. Those who attacked us were our brothers, our Hutu neighbors. They were not strangers; they were people of the sector. All of a sudden, we saw that they had taken up spears and machetes. We also took our machetes and fled, heading for the mountain. When they caught someone, they killed that person with machetes. They were led by a man called Gasana, another called Mashyaka, and another called Mossi, political party leaders. They brought young people here. On the hill, they followed us, and we also threw stones. They surrounded us, and when they caught someone, they killed him, and we buried him. The chiefs were simple peasants, but they knew the history of what had happened. They knew that they had to kill. Here and in Kibuye Town as well, there were meetings in which people also said that everyone had to kill. They were members of the MDR-power. Mashyaka was the MDR councilor for the sector. He appointed himself party chief, assumed the role of sector councilor, and issued orders. Mashyaka was seventy years old; before 1973, under the First Republic, he had been sector councilor. Gasana, his deputy, was about thirty years old. They recruited young people and ordered them to enter houses to evict and kill Tutsis. . . . When they attacked us and ate the first cows, we thought they were just thieves. We did not think they were going to kill us. We were saying: "It does not matter if they kill only cows," but we soon saw they were secretly killing anyone who dared to leave. We started to notice that certain people were disappearing, so we left the area and headed for Karongi Mountain. . . . On Karongi there were many of us, and we occupied Mukuba, a beautiful hill, quite tall. We were thousands; just imagine, someone who could not hear another, even close by, because of the racket. That was when we saw the soldiers on top of vehicles coming from Kibuye

Town with guns. They shot at us, we threw stones, we got tired, and we would see about twenty people fall with one blast. So after they pelted us with bullets, when we saw that all of us could die, we ran, some headed for the Bisesero Hills [Gishyita Commune] and others for Gisenyi Prefecture. It was everyone for himself; we do not know where our children perished; we do not know where our wives were killed; they chased us as they shot. That was how it was.[113]

Mbonabande's testimony suggests that Mashyaka, the MDR head of Gitarama Sector, acted in continuity with the violence of the PARMEHUTU era. In 1973, at the end of the PARMEHUTU regime, Mashyaka as councilor organized the attacks against Tutsis; in 1994, it was again he who led the massacres in the sector, this time as an MDR-power leader who had taken control of his sector.[114] To do so, he ousted the legitimate sector councilor. Nyampuza highlights the leading role played by MDR supporters in the killings in Gitarama Sector, at one point in defiance of the local state representative, the legitimate councilor:

At one point during the killings, the councilor said to the killers: "You have killed enough, can you not let the young girls live, so that they at least become your servants?" They violently condemned him, calling him an Inkotanyi. He was in the MRND, but he was not for the massacres. . . . In our village, our Hutu neighbors were the ones who led the first attacks. They were led by Gasana and Mashyaka, who were MDR and MDR-power members. Others belonged to the MRND. There were many of them. . . . During the attacks, they were singing: "Let's exterminate them, we are power, exterminate them, expel them all from the forest so that the name Tutsi is forgotten.[115]

Bwishyura Sector. Catherine Kandamutsa, condemned for participation in the genocide, insisted that in her village good relations between Hutus and Tutsis prevailed until the last minute.

There was no problem between Hutus and Tutsis of our area. Really, there was no suspicion. We lived side by side harmoniously as usual. . . . We continued to hear rumors here and there; we saw people fleeing and going to this [Kibuye] Church, the [Saint Jean Catholic Church and] Home, and the [Gatwaro Regional] Stadium. In our areas we remained united, Tutsis did not flee, and they were not suspicious of us. Then all of a sudden, we saw boats arriving full of people. The people were scary; they were armed with traditional weapons. When people saw them, they started to run, and among those fleeing were our people, whom I could call Hutu, who fled with Tutsis toward the Saint Jean complex, but they later returned. That is how we got separated.[116]

In these witness accounts, two facts stand out: on the one hand, the several cases of unity between Hutus and Tutsis faced with the first attacks; on the other, the fact that the instigators of the massacres were most often members of the local MDR-power branches and that during the massacres, this distinct political identity was the source for leadership.

The Causes of Mass Participation, According to Those Involved

When the actors in this genocide were asked why, in their opinion, simple peasants went out to kill their neighbors, with whom they had lived peacefully, their diverse answers converged.

Kanani, of Kabuga Cell in Burunga Sector, who confessed to killing three people, explained:

> The attackers asked us, "Why do you support Tutsis when they have to die; they are already condemned. You are supporting people who killed our chief?" Then they only looted, but nobody from our cell took part in the looting. Then, after a meeting held there, the people told themselves, "These things are being done in public. The soldiers are shooting from the other side where they are with the killers, so these are orders; we also must begin killing." That was how we set out to start killing in our cell. We did it believing that it was an order given all over the country because no authority condemned the act, and the killings were not going on at night but in broad daylight. People started killing the others, and on the radio it was said that the enemy was nobody other than one's neighbor and that because of this word "accomplice," the Tutsis were the accomplices of the RPF, so the confrontation began. This sensitization was often broadcast on the radio. So that is how we began—we took part in events without knowing how they began. We hurt our former brothers with whom we lived, who invited us to their ceremonies and vice versa; we betrayed our friendships.[117]

In these uncertain moments of the first attacks against Tutsis, several Hutu communities called upon by the politicized killers had to make a choice. Some of the interviewees mentioned the radio as an important guide whose calls to massacre were legitimate and helped them with their betrayal of Tutsi neighbors. Serugendo, in the same gang of killers as Kanani, completed the latter's response by evoking other reasons that pushed communities to commit murder.

> The deaths of Tutsis in our area were caused primarily by people wanting their land. These were the neighboring cells from where the first attacks against our cell were launched. There were few Tutsis in those cells, so that is why they came to our area to look for Tutsis, and those who did not join in solidarity with the Hutu murderers could get in trouble and be treated like Tutsis. As a result, the killings spread like an epidemic. . . . I became evil because of land. As Tutsis were being massacred, people redistributed their land and property. I was given responsibility as secretary of this operation. I was put in charge of writing: this land, this field, this banana plantation, this coffee plantation in such an area belongs to such and such a person. . . . We had to ensure that the owner was really dead. When the property was being redis-

tributed, it could be said that so-and-so was still alive or hiding at Serugendo's home, for example. That is how my friends and I became involved
in carrying out patrols in search of people who were still living, confirming
that they were dead, and killing them if necessary. I got involved in this
crime. I remember one day, I was in Matyazo Cell at Ruganda. I was with the
others at the main trading center, and a man came and said to me, "You know,
Gaspard is hiding at his grandmother's." He said that to the councilor as well
as to the leaders of the killing gangs who had now made themselves important. Everyone was alerted, and we all headed there.[118]

Nyampuza also insisted that looting and land-grabbing were the motives
for participating in the killings.

When the murderers were assured that the massacres had really been completed, they started to share the land belonging to Tutsis as well as the
sorghum that was already ripe. The leaders of the attacks were the ones in
charge of the redistribution. For example, whoever had not "worked" or who
had not been exemplary would not receive a good portion. The most enthu-
siastic participant could choose the best land given that the soil was not all
equally fertile. This participant could choose the fertile field known for its
abundant harvest—the same for the banana plantation. There would be times
when someone would demand a portion of the loot, and he would be told:
"You did not do anything. We told you to kill these people to take their property because there is no other means of survival." They even said at the beginning that there would be compensation: that is, whoever killed the most
would be rewarded. That was what was being said. There were those who
participated in order to get something.[119]

The testimonies of Serugendo and Nyampuza show how the distribution
of the loot was institutionalized, that it was before the community and through
negotiation. The killers deferred to the higher authorities, either the sector
councilors or the political party leaders, who led the massacres. These socialized processes reflect how the massacres evolved. The massacres were started
by usually violent, politically and materially motivated, smaller groups, and
after a while they were committed in the name of the community under the
leadership of political parties' leaders and sometimes of state local authorities.
The organization and institutionalization of looting was not enough to completely prevent violent competition among the killers, as Nyampuza narrates:
"Sometimes there were problems during distribution, especially when there
was a productive banana plantation, a fertile field involved; people resorted to
fighting with machetes, and the strongest won. Many Hutus died in this manner. This was also the perfect moment to kill one's enemy. This was the time
to settle scores."[120]

As elsewhere in the country, the large massacres in April were followed
by violent disputes over Tutsi property that set the killers against each other.
Burgomaster Karara organized a public meeting on May 9, 1994, at the sta-

dium, where he asked the people to put an end to these quarrels but not the killings.[121]

On another note still related to the causes of mass participation, Nyampuza mentions the dimension of manipulation:

> The people had been sensitized by the authorities. The leaders benefited the most. They carried out sensitization in meetings and rallies, and they told people to kill Tutsis so that they could acquire the Tutsis' property. They told the people that the Inkotanyi would kill them instead if they won. The majority of killers took it as revenge. The people were saying: "We must kill them before they kill us."[122]

On his part, Burgomaster Karara excluded hatred between communities and explained mass participation as motivated by the search for gain, especially among the youths. It was also out of some form of selfish fatalism:

> Here in Gitesi, I would say that it was possible for the massacres not to have happened. I would say that generally, there was no animosity among the population. There was not any. There was support for a movement. The people joined a movement, and because they saw that these things were happening everywhere, they took part in it. However, when I held a public meeting, the people were generally hostile to these things. The problem that remained was knowing what was to be done, what we could do to help them. Then, one can also point to the problem of the young people. The youths in general were very agitated. . . . When we held meetings, even in May, it was always possible to maintain order and security, but there were external forces, and because their interests were served by taking part, people got involved. However, to say there was hatred in Gitesi, I do not think that is true.[123]

In this extract, the former burgomaster demonstrates that some communities were initially not inclined to participate in the massacres; the question of what to do arose when the sentiment that the killings were the order of the day started. This was a case of exterior pressure that had not become coercive as such. This testimony allows us to see that the moment of indecision because of lack of direction did not last long. Forces internal to the communities eventually prevailed, namely, the desire of seizing the opportunity to grab the property of Tutsis. The youths of the community were the most determined in this regard.

Alongside opportunistic greed as a cause of mass participation in the killings, Usabyumuremyi, in contrast to the burgomaster, advanced the idea of profound ideological and political antagonism between the Hutus and Tutsis. This view is from an intellectual, someone who finished secondary school and was a white-collar employee.

> In my view, two reasons might explain mass participation in the attacks: Tutsis had climbed the mountain with their property, especially their live-

stock. Some peasants were saying to themselves: "Maybe I can come back with a cow or a goat, or I could take a metal sheet." There was also another motive behind this; we cannot forget that the Hutus were not happy with the Tutsis. So I can tell you this, maybe considering history from a long time ago until today, I can tell you that maybe in the heart of the Hutus there were some who were not happy with Tutsis and who took advantage of the situation to settle scores. It is possible. Maybe the history that I learned in primary and secondary school was not completely true, but in any case this was history that my teachers, all of them Tutsi, taught me. What I know is that in this country, there were historical upheavals of society. Tutsis were in power for a long time, Hutus later took over power, and now the Tutsis have returned. That means that these things cannot leave some people's hearts. So if some have wronged others, when the others come to power, they can take their revenge. That is what I have seen, and not only intellectuals are affected. History, the life of this country during previous eras, is known also by those who cannot read or write. Someone can say to you: "I was the servant in the royal court. It was like this. As for me, I lived in the area of a certain chief somewhere, and it used to be like this." One can notice that many people have kept this history engraved in their memory. When such a person finds the opportunity, I do not see how that person will not take advantage and seek his revenge.

Take me for example—you see how old I am. I do not know much about the past, but when people were talking, I speak of elderly men, when they talked of their life in the royal court, the way in which they worked so hard to get a cow, for example, and how at any moment that cow could be snatched from them; when they explained how you could own something without really becoming its owner, when someone from your family committed an offense, a member of this family had to be sacrificed so that you could be saved, those are the elements of history passed down for generations. My father was not a court attendant, and I never personally heard him talk about that, but when we were young, our uncles would tell us those things. I cannot say that I have concrete evidence to support all of this with certainty. For example, Tutsis can say that Habyarimana oppressed them; would I be able to find proof of that? However, they saw it clearly. When someone holds power and does not want to share it—I can give the example of our commune where there was no Tutsi councilor, no Tutsi head of a commune department, no Tutsi police officer—it becomes clear that an ethnic group is marginalized. Under Habyarimana, Hutus were the ones in power. It is possible that with the power, Tutsis will behave the same way toward the Hutus. At the time, I was not yet born. So you understand the issue is some kind of revenge; they would say: "You oppressed us; let us also oppress you." Maybe that is the cause of that hostility. What I want to tell you is that if an ordinary citizen notices that the state itself is marginalizing an ethnic group, I do not see how that citizen can support that ethnic group because the citizen also follows the example of the leaders; in all that he does, he imitates what the state does. How can you explain to me that on the list of candidates at the election of councilors, there was not even one name of a Tutsi? Does that probably require some level of education? If there can be a regime in which that balance is possible, where the citizen himself sees that the balance exists up to the highest levels, without any ill intention displayed by the authorities, nobody, Hutu or Tutsi, would mind. In that case, coexistence would be peaceful. However, when the citizen sees that his party is supported by those in power, he also begins to behave like an important person even if he is a poor man. For example, a family may be rich and have a family member who is poor, but that will not stop the poor person from being proud of his rich family even if the rich relatives do not help him at all. He will say to others: "Know that I belong to such and such a family!" That is the same thing with the people. When they see that everywhere, in the government, in parliament, in the ministries down to the level of the communes and sector councils, the positions are fairly distributed, nothing can prevent that citizen from living peacefully side by side with his neighbor. The residents can share everything, but when at the higher levels nothing is going right, someone will say: "We may share everything, but who will support me?" The other will reply, "You see, we share but know that so-and-so is related to me in this way. Look, the parliament, the ministers, and the commune, those are us. Even if we quarrel, you cannot go to the commune council because it belongs to my people." I am thirty-nine years old, which means that in general, I don't know much about the things that happened during the time of Kayibanda. But me, now, I have killed Tutsis. If someone asked me to explain all that, it would be difficult. What did they do to me that I can say to explain? In fact, the problem has its origin in the state, and the state obviously did not want these people to live. Is that not right? So what about me? How would I be able to claim to support them? In whose country? In my country of me alone? What I want to say to you is that if the regime is against a section of the population, an individual cannot support such people in such a manner. That is why, besides greed, I can say that the greed can also lead people to kill. A family may refuse to give me a wife, but I am able to kill that family to take their property away. Overall, the population noticed that the state was against Tutsis, so their previous peaceful coexistence was thrown into oblivion because of the small advantages the population hoped to get out of it.[124]

Despite coming from the same living conditions Karara did, Usabyumuremyi subtly illustrates here the notion of Hutu and Tutsi political identity, disconnected from the daily social relationships between the two communities, of which the determining factor was the state. Usabyumuremyi, who confessed to killing thirteen people, some of them children, explains the people's participation in the massacres by evoking historical resentment, the reproduction of the Hutu and Tutsi antagonistic political identities by the state, the "authorizing" force that allowed those who participated in the killings to satisfy their greed.

All the witnesses I interviewed cited looting and seizure of the victims' land as the main reasons for mass popular participation in the genocide. By contrast, there was an apparent contradiction when it came to the ideological causes, with some saying that such causes existed and others denying that they did. This contradiction was only apparent because, as the testimonies have shown, there were two profoundly different motives depending on the group of killers in question. Based on the facts cited above, one may say that on the one hand, some groups initiated and led the massacres. These were the more narrowly defined groups of peasants and lower-ranking community leaders, politically and ideologically organized and materially motivated. Belonging to these groups were intellectuals, the local heads of political parties, local government authorities, peasants, and violent criminals. At the other level were larger groups, entire neighborhood communities. After a short period of ambivalence, these larger groups, less politically motivated, felt that there was a large movement leading toward the massacres, presenting an opportunity to loot and seize Tutsi property. Many then decided to take advantage of the opportunity. During the first killings, mass participation in the massacres was played out in the interface between the two groups. What is striking is how swiftly and radically those in the second category decided to side with the zealous killers.

Whatever reason pushed people to participate in the extermination of their neighbors, be it ideology, greed, or conformity, the survivors could not distinguish anyone from the others after the threshold was crossed, and the survivors often highlighted the killers' wild euphoria. Nyampuza described the phenomenon:

> People had gone crazy. You would meet a person you knew, and you could not recognize him; you would wonder if you were looking at a human being. There was a friend of ours to whom my husband said: "You are my friend, what do you really gain from these killings? Look, you have just killed so many people." When this man met a Tutsi child, he killed; an old woman, he killed. The other responded, "Me too, I am beginning to sense the evil I have done. I am going to the priest to confess so that I stop killing." We therefore thought he had been convinced of his sin, but the next day, we learned that he had killed another two children. Yet these two were the children of a certain Kabalira, also his friend. They visited each other, they shared things, but he killed Kabalira's children. So we said to ourselves that those people no longer have a human heart. Those people were no longer human.[125]

The delayed start of the genocide in Gitesi Commune, a few days after it began in the other Kibuye Prefecture communes at the instigation of MDR supporters in the sectors and cells as well as of the prefect in the capital, reflected the moderate politics of the commune residents before and during political pluralism, which had denied the MDR hegemonic control.

There were two main dynamics to the genocide in the commune: one produced large-scale massacres at specially designated sites and the other occurred in the cells and sectors. The main organizer of the massacres at the large sites was Prefect Kayishema. He largely used the resources of the state, including the gendarmes and other security forces, but he also used peasants from other communes in Kibuye and the Interahamwe from Gisenyi Prefecture. MDR-power supporters actively participated in the massacres at the large sites. The general population of Gitesi also contributed greatly to the massacres, especially in controlling the movement of Tutsis by preventing them from fleeing, combing the forests and buses for them, surrounding certain sites, and being part of a human fence around Karongi Mountain. The population at the margins was also killed. At the large massacre sites, the action of the state was crucial, supported at the local level by the MDR-power structures. In the sectors, MDR-power groups were the main actors in the extermination of Tutsis, doing the main physical action themselves, taking control of different communities and mobilizing and organizing other groups and individuals among the population. In many communities, Hutus and Tutsis initially stayed united against the attacks often led by MDR-power supporters. When they met such resistance, the assailants often attempted and succeeded in convincing Hutus to abandon the Tutsis, pointing out that they were fighting a losing battle and that those who did not disown the Tutsis were to share their fate. The attackers' resolve and organization, the prospect of the property to be amassed, and the fact that they counted among their ranks many hardened criminals seem to have contributed to dampening the will of Hutu groups—sometimes whole communities—who had united with Tutsis. The messages of discouragement from the attackers often provoked uncertainty and arguments on what these groups in solidarity with Tutsis should do. Communities or sections of communities made their decisions. The analysis of the political context at the national, prefecture, and commune level, along with exhortations from the radio, eventually convinced these communities of the futility of their resistance. Finally, the opportunity to grab their neighbors' property eventually convinced sections of these communities to turn against their former allies. Young Hutus who had the most to gain by participating in the massacres contributed the most in radically changing the attitudes of their communities. Also the youths, often MDR-power supporters, formed the bulk of the groups of the first attackers. The MDR-power structures at the core of the first groups of attackers brought together former prominent MDR-PARMEHUTU leaders as well as criminals.

The influence of the MDR-PARMEHUTU ideology was especially heavy on the educated members of the Hutu community. Usabyumuremyi's case was illuminating. He was a modest, rural, public figure who had good relations with Tutsis and stayed away from political trouble for religious reasons. When he got convinced to participate in the massacres, he became a particularly zealous and ideologically motivated killer. By his own confession, he killed thirteen people. He justified his actions by reproducing the main arguments of the PARMEHUTU ideology, essentially based on the memory of a *ressentiment* history and on his feeling of belonging to the Hutu political identity.

With Usabyumuremyi's case, one can contrast that of former burgomaster Karara. Even though he had no sympathy for the RPF and was convinced of the necessity of fighting it, he seemed not to have associated the war against the RPF with the massacre of his Tutsi constituents, at least at the beginning. During the democratization period, he did his best to protect his commune from violence. During the genocide, he seemed to be relatively ambivalent, stepping aside when the killings intensified but at the same time cooperating with Prefect Kayishema, the main architect of the genocide in Kibuye Prefecture and Gitesi Commune.

The comparison between the two personalities can be enlightening. Both men were of the same age, that is, in general they followed the same process of political socialization by the MDR-PARMEHUTU as well as by the Habyarimana regime. Despite their different socioprofessional status, both were intellectuals in the Rwandan sense: that is, educated people working for the local administration. The men, each in their own way, enjoyed the status of prominent figures and behaved like people who held some responsibility in society. The main difference between them was their level of education and exposure to the world. Usabyumuremyi just finished secondary school and never left the commune. Karara had a high level of university education abroad, which, according to him, opened his mind to many more horizons and allowed him to develop a critical distance from the prevailing social and ideological context in Rwanda. By contrast, the weakness of Usabyumuremyi's education seems not to have given him the tools necessary to distance himself from ideologically charged knowledge spread at school and in the political speeches aimed at intellectuals such as him. This factor, combined with his social status, may have explained his drift toward participation in the genocide. Poorly educated community intellectuals such as Usabyumuremyi were more flexible to the ideological conditioning of the "Hutu Republic" than were, for example, the illiterate peasants.

The state authorities and the MDR-power supporters seem not to have had significant authority or real means of coercing the population into the killings. These communities had proven their capacity for resistance when in the late 1980s and early 1990s they subverted the authority of the MRND party-state. For the most part, communities in Gitesi Commune had been persuaded to participate in the killings.

After communities were won over, however, groups of ideologically motivated people and hard-core killers assumed control of the communities, and the killings were done in the name of the community, even if, individually, a number of people did not necessarily agree. At a more profound level, deep poverty, recurrent periods of hunger since the end of the 1980s, and lack of prospects due to acute land shortage explain this turnaround. However, it is also the lack of an available political alternative that must have pushed so many to eventually welcome the season of killings.

Notes

1. République rwandaise, *Recensement administratif de la population rwandaise durant la période de 1960–1987*, 1987, p. 56.

2. République rwandaise, *Recensement général de la population et de l'habitat au 15/08/91*, p. 14.

3. Préfecture de Kibuye, *Rapport portant sur la situation alimentaire dans la préfecture durant le mois de septembre 1984.*

4. Préfecture de Kibuye, *Procès-verbal de la réunion du conseil préfectoral de sécurité du 10/10/84.*

5. Préfecture de Kibuye, *Procès-verbal de la réunion du conseil préfectoral de sécurité du 27/08/84.*

6. Préfecture de Kibuye, *Procès-verbal de la réunion du conseil préfectoral de sécurité du 19/07/85.*

7. Préfecture de Kibuye, *Procès-verbal de la réunion du conseil préfectoral de sécurité du 03/09/85.*

8. Préfecture de Kibuye, *Procès-verbal de la réunion du conseil préfectoral de sécurité du 11/11/85.*

9. Préfecture de Kibuye, *Procès-verbal de la réunion du conseil préfectoral de sécurité du 03/12/85.* With rumors of disputes within the top government leadership, a former local personality from the Kayibanda regime soon saw an opportunity to speak out and took on the role of reviving the anti-Tutsi ideology.

10. Préfecture de Kibuye, *Procès-verbal de la réunion du conseil préfectoral de sécurité du 13/03/87.*

11. Commune Gitesi, *Procès-verbal de la réunion du conseil communal du 06/11/87.*

12. Commune Gitesi, *Procès-verbal de la réunion du conseil communal de sécurité du 06/01/88.*

13. Commune Gitesi, *Procès-verbal de la réunion des membres et responsables de cellules du 14/11/88.*

14. Ibid.

15. Commune Gitesi, *Procès-verbal de la réunion des dirigeants des bureaux de vote pour l'élection du président Habyarimana du 19/11/88.*

16. Commune Gitesi, *Lettre du Bourgmestre au Préfet concernant la tournée du 11/09/89.*

17. Commune Gitesi, *Procès-verbal de l'assemblée des habitants de la ville de Kibuye, des agents de la commune ainsi que des fonctionnaires des cellules Interahamwe du 29/06/89.*

18. Commune Gitesi, *Lettre du Bourgmestre au Préfet concernant la tournée du 11/09/89.*

19. Commune Gitesi, *Lettre du Bourgmestre au Préfet concernant la situation de sécurité de la commune du 26/09/89.*

20. Commune Gitesi, *Lettre du Bourgmestre au Préfet concernant la tournée du 14/03/90.*

21. Ibid.

22. This defiance was in the form of the establishment of the first independent newspapers and the first activist initiatives for human rights, dating from the second

half of 1989. On July 5, 1990, President Habyarimana declared an *aggiornamento politique* ("new political era"). See Reyntjens, *L'Afrique des Grands Lacs en crise*, 1994, pp. 90–91.

23. Augustin Karara, interview with author, June 1, 2001, Kibuye Prison.
24. Anne-Marie Nyampuza, interview with author, June 8, 2001, Kibuye Town.
25. Edouard Serugendo, interview with author, June 1, 2001, Kibuye Prison.
26. Benoît Usabyumuremyi, interview with author, June 6, 2001, Kibuye Prison.
27. In 1994, Mashyaka once again led the killings in the sector despite his age of seventy.
28. Eliezer Mbonabande, interview with author, June 8, 2001, Kibuye Prison.
29. Nyampuza interview.
30. Ibid.
31. Usabyumuremyi interview.
32. Ibid.
33. Karara interview.
34. Préfecture de Kibuye, *Procès-verbal de la réunion du conseil préfectoral de sécurité du 03/12/85*.
35. Catherine Kandamutsa, interview with author, June 10, 2001, Kibuye Prison.
36. Alphonse Nsengimana, interview with author, June 5, 2001, Kibuye Prison.
37. Mbonabande interview.
38. Serugendo interview; Usabyumuremyi interview.
39. Karara interview.
40. Commune Gitesi, *Lettre du Bourgmestre au Préfet concernant l'assistance aux nécessiteux du 10/01/94*.
41. République rwandaise, *Recensement administratif de la population rwandaise durant la période de 1960–1987*, 1987, p. 56.
42. Commune Gitesi, *Lettre du Bourgmestre au Conseiller des secteurs Gasura, Bwishyura et Kagabiro concernant le litige entre l'Église évangélique et Mme Uzamuranga du 03/05/91*.
43. Commune Gitesi, *Lettre du Bourgmestre au Responsable du cadastre de la ville de Kibuye du 27/01/94*.
44. Commune Gitesi, *Lettre du Bourgmestre au Conseiller du secteur Gitesi du 21/03/94*.
45. Commune Gitesi, *Procès-verbal de la réunion du conseil communal de sécurité du 07/09/93*.
46. Commune Gitesi, *Lettre du Bourgmestre au Procureur de la République demandant son intervention pour mettre fin à la situation de violence dans la localité de Mbabara du 25/03/94*.
47. Préfecture de Kibuye, *Rapport de sécurité du mois de mars 1991*.
48. Ibid.
49. Commune Gitesi, *Procès-verbal de la réunion du conseil communal de sécurité du 07/09/93*.
50. Commune Gitesi, *Lettre du Bourgmestre au Préfet concernant des problèmes de sécurité du 01/10/93*.
51. Ibid.
52. Commune Gitesi, *Lettre du Bourgmestre au Préfet concernant des problèmes de sécurité du 04/02/94*.
53. Commune Gitesi, *Lettre du Bourgmestre au Préfet concernant la mort d'Edison Ndahimana du secteur Gitesi du 04/02/94*.
54. Commune Gitesi, *Lettre du Bourgmestre au Procureur de la République l'informant de ce qui s'est passé dans le secteur Burunga du 25/03/94*.

55. See Karara interview; Serugendo interview; Commune Gitesi, *Procès-verbal de la réunion du conseil communal de sécurité du 07/09/93*.

56. Chrétien et al., *Rwanda: les médias du génocide*, 1995.

57. Usabyumuremyi interview.

58. Nyampuza interview.

59. Préfecture de Kibuye, *Rapport de sécurité du mois de novembre 1990*.

60. Until the genocide in April 1994, this measure was never implemented because of resistance it drew.

61. Préfecture de Kibuye, *Rapport de sécurité du mois de novembre 1990*.

62. Ibid.

63. Usabyumuremyi interview.

64. Karara interview.

65. Ibid.

66. Ibid.

67. Préfecture de Kibuye, *Résolutions dégagées de la réunion du conseil de sécurité du 28 août 1991*.

68. This refers to the fire used to burn Tutsi houses from 1959 onward. Préfecture de Kibuye, *Résolutions dégagées de la réunion du conseil de sécurité du 28 août 1991*.

69. Ibid.

70. Silas Kanani, interview with author, June 6, 2001, Kibuye Prison.

71. Serugendo interview.

72. Karara interview.

73. Ibid.

74. Préfecture de Kibuye, *Rapport portant sur l'évolution de la situation politique en préfecture de Kibuye du 28/08/91*.

75. These incidents, reported by former burgomaster Augustin Karara, took place in Nyamarebe Cell of Burunga Sector, in a border sector of Gishyita Commune, as well as in Gasura Sector. The prime minister then was Nsengiyaremye, a member of the MDR. Karara interview.

76. Commune Gitesi, *Procès-verbal de la réunion du conseil communal de sécurité du 07/09/93*.

77. Karara interview; Serugendo interview.

78. Nyampuza interview.

79. Karara interview.

80. Préfecture de Kibuye, *Rapport portant sur l'évolution de la situation politique en préfecture de Kibuye du 28/08/91*.

81. Karara interview.

82. Ildefonse Muderere, interview with author, June 5, 2001, Kibuye Prison.

83. Usabyumuremyi interview.

84. Préfecture de Kibuye, *Rapport de sécurité du mois d'août 1991*.

85. Usabyumuremyi interview.

86. Serugendo interview.

87. Karara interview.

88. Ibid.

89. Préfecture de Kibuye, *Rapport portant sur la sécurité dans la préfecture de Kibuye du 10/04/94*.

90. Des Forges, *Leave None to Tell the Story*, p. 161.

91. Karara interview; Usabyumuremyi interview.

92. Préfecture de Kibuye, *Rapport portant sur la sécurité dans la préfecture de Kibuye du 10/04/94*.

93. Usabyumuremyi interview.

94. Testimony of a survivor of the massacre at Kibuye Church, quoted in African Rights, *Rwanda,* 1995, p. 418.

95. Usabyumuremyi interview.

96. Mbonabande interview.

97. African Rights, *Rwanda*, p. 420.

98. Ibid., pp. 416, 424.

99. According to Ibuka, *Dictionnaire nominatif*, 1999, 59,050 Tutsis were killed, and 12,175 survived. Philip Verwimp contended this figure was smaller than the reality because not all the Tutsi victims or even all the Hutu victims were identified. Verwimp also presented data from the 1991 national census, which put the number of Tutsis in Kibuye Prefecture at 71,225; that is, 15 percent of the population. The administrative census of 1987 on one hand presents general population figures reasonably close to the 1991 general population census if one factors in the growth of the population over time, but on the other give quite different figures for the Tutsi population. The 1987 administrative census estimated Tutsis to be 19.3 percent of the Kibuye Prefecture population. It is probable that the number of Tutsis in the 1991 census was underestimated for political reasons. In the case of Gikongoro prefecture see Verpoorten, "Death Toll of the Rwandan Genocide," 2005, pp. 331–367. Ibuka, *Dictionnaire nominatif*; République rwandaise, *Recensement général de la population et de l'habitat au 15/08/91*, pp. 9, 14; Verwimp, "A Quantitative Analysis of Genocide in Kibuye Prefecture," 2001; République rwandaise, *Recensement administratif de la population rwandaise*, p. 56.

100. I think this figure is far from the real number of Tutsi victims in Gitesi Commune for the following reasons. The general population census of 1991 did not provide the ethnic breakdown of the population by commune, but the administrative census of 1987 put the number of Tutsis at 17,315 for Gitesi out of a population of 49,946, or 34.7 percent of the population. The 1991 census numbered Gitesi residents at 60,030; using the 1987 administrative census percentage of Tutsis to estimate the population in 1991 comes to 20,830 Tutsis, almost double the number of victims plus survivors recorded in the Ibuka dictionary.

101. Des Forges, *Leave None to Tell the Story*, p. 156.

102. Ibid., p. 161; Kamanzi, *Rwanda: du génocide à la défaite*, 1997, p. 109.

103. African Rights, *Rwanda*, pp. 396–397.

104. Des Forges, *Leave None to Tell the Story*, p. 156.

105. Karara interview.

106. "Pawa" is the Kinyarwanda pronunciation of "power." African Rights, *Rwanda*, p. 418.

107. Usabyumuremyi interview.

108. Serugendo interview.

109. Karara interview.

110. Commune Gitesi, *Procès-verbal de la réunion du conseil communal de sécurité du 07/09/93*.

111. Ibid.

112. Nyampuza interview.

113. Mbonabande interview.

114. Ibid.

115. Nyampuza interview.

116. Kandamutsa interview.

117. Kanani interview.

118. Serugendo interview.

119. Nyampuza interview.

120. Ibid.

121. Usabyumuremyi interview; Commune Gitesi, *Lettre du Bourgmestre au Préfet du 17/05/94.*

122. Ibid.

123. Karara interview.

124. Usabyumuremyi interview.

125. Nyampuza interview.

10

Understanding Mass Participation in the Genocide

My study of Kigembe and Gitesi Communes demonstrates that they both experienced mass participation in the genocide of Tutsis—in the actual killings, but even more so in terms of the physical control of the Tutsi population, a necessary condition for its successful execution. In a country as crowded as Rwanda, and without prearranged concentration camps or systems for transporting and watching over both the people designated for extermination and the killers, the data collected indicate that a large part of the general Hutu population was responsible for blocking Tutsis' escape. This physical control was enforced by setting up impenetrable human circles around areas where Tutsis were concentrated, erecting roadblocks on various routes, and participating in organized searches to flush people out of hiding. Even when attempting to escape, the odds of a Tutsi running into a Hutu woman, child, or elder on a path, in a field, in a thicket, or even at the home of a formerly sympathetic Hutu neighbor often turned out to be fatal. Many, rather than look the other way, preferred to call out to the killers. The proliferation of such acts seems to have facilitated the almost total physical control of the Tutsi population and the subsequent intensity with which the Tutsis were executed. However, one must also emphasize that the vast many of those who survived did so thanks to some form of help they received from a Hutu or a Hutu family.

In southwest Butare Prefecture, home to one of the highest concentrations of Tutsis in the country, alongside the local people, Burundian refugees on the Rwandan side of the border with Burundi played a significant role in the massacres in the communes along the border. However, the highest concentration of Tutsis in the southwest of Butare was located a little farther north of the Burundian refugee camps. Thousands of people were killed near the border with Burundi, but the numbers of the victims who perished farther north far exceeded those. The farther one moved away from the border, the less the Burundian refugees were involved in the genocide.

Another fact to consider is that a large number of Tutsis had chosen to heed the local authorities' advice to assemble at locations close to their place of residence, in spaces that were fairly open, which made it easier for the Hutus to surround them. Again, in areas where widespread massacres took place, such as in Maraba, Runyinya, Gishamvu, Nyakizu, Kigembe, and Nyaruhengeri Communes, to mention just a few in southwest Butare, the thousands of people who besieged the large gatherings of Tutsis were not members of Interahamwe, the National Revolutionary Movement for Development (MRND) militia, but rather members of the general population. Similarly, in Kibuye Prefecture, with the other major concentration of Tutsis in the country, those who trapped the Tutsi refugees in the Bisesero Hills (Gishyita Commune) and Karongi Mountain (Gitesi Commune) were essentially the residents of the surrounding neighborhoods.[1]

In both Butare and Kibuye Prefectures, especially in regions with large Tutsi populations, the killers needed actual firearms to overcome the last-ditch resistance of thousands of Tutsis gathered at specific sites. At these large killing sites, a part of the genocide was thus carried out by soldiers and policemen, another by groups of trained killers, and the last part by the people themselves. However, one important aspect of this genocide was its decentralized nature, and when targeted groups were smaller, neighboring communities played a bigger role in the killings. According to Philip Verwimp's calculations, about 5,500 of the 10,850 Tutsi genocide victims in Gitesi Commune were killed in a residential area or in the mountains close by, that is, away from major sites of massacres where trained killers from outside played a crucial part.[2]

Human hedges, roadblocks, physical checkpoints, and tracking down of escapees and hiders were also entrusted to the surrounding communities with women and children participating. In Gitesi Commune, six sectors had been mobilized to encircle Karongi Mountain, where thousands of Tutsis had gathered. In Kigembe Commune (Butare Prefecture), a large part of the male population of Kivuru Sector accompanied the victims to the killing sites in Nyaruteja Sector. In Murama Sector, a mob of locals—men, women, and children gripped by extreme euphoria—rounded up Tutsis and then accompanied them to Kigembe Sector. From there, the Kigembe Sector residents transferred the Tutsis to the public in Nyanza Sector. From there the Tutsis were transferred to the people of Nyaruteja Sector, who in turn accompanied the Tutsis to the commune office building, where Rwandan men, women, and children as well as many Burundian refugees waited to kill them. The same process took place with the Tutsis of Ngera Sector, farther north of Murama Sector and therefore farther away from the commune headquarters in Nyaruteja Sector. The Tutsis in Kigembe generally lived mostly in the northern part of the commune, in historical Nyakare Region, where there were almost no Burundian refugees. Most of the Tutsis of the commune were transferred to the commune office, in the extreme south of the commune near the border, with surrounding local communities relaying one another because of the distance. Recall that the Kigembe Commune stretched over 114 square kilometers (44 square miles).

The areas with the larger Tutsi populations were almost all located in the prefectures most defiant of the MRND, such as Butare and Kibuye, studied in detail in this book, but also Gitarama and Gikongoro.[3] In the section on political developments at the national level, I found that in Gitarama and Gikongoro Prefectures the MRND suffered the same popular rejection as in Butare. This means that in these two prefectures as well, the rise of the militias from the presidential clique, that is, of the Interahamwe and Impuzamugambi, was held in check. One may reasonably assume that in the absence of militia to carry out the killings, a large number of the killings were carried out by the people themselves. Butare Prefecture was a good illustration of this, where most of the killings were carried out by a combination of soldiers and locals with almost no involvement of Interahamwe. When Interahamwe were much implicated like in Kigali, there is also good reason to ask whether, during the massacres, the Interahamwe were all well-defined groups of trained killers following orders, or whether at some point a number of young men just linked up with the militias more or less spontaneously, thereby making it difficult to distinguish between organized militias and the general population.

Mass participation was the main instrument for physical control of the Tutsi population. From the testimonies of survivors from Kigembe Commune but also elsewhere in Butare Prefecture, it appears that fleeing to Burundi provided the greatest chance for survival, and this despite the presence of Burundian refugees and Burundian Hutu killers working from the other side of the border. Similarly, the largest numbers of survivors in Kibuye Prefecture were those able to escape the physical control enforced by the local population, to run away or hide in forests. In a small country where nine out of eleven prefectures shared a long border with a foreign country and where logistical resources and an established infrastructure to support the killings were completely lacking, the issue of physical control of the victims scattered across the country was of capital importance in the successful execution of the total genocide against the Rwandan Tutsis. This control was provided by a large part of the Hutu population.

Social Factors Behind the Mass Participation

From this research, I can identify two types of factors favoring the mass participation in the genocide against the Tutsis: those linked to the socioeconomic and cultural context and those linked to the dynamics of politics, ideology, and the war.

The mass participation in the genocide can, in part, be interpreted as a desperate move to adapt, an attempt to break away from unbearable circumstances. In this respect, Luc Bonneaux refers to the notion of "demographic entrapment," when "the young and dynamic—peasants without land, shepherds without herds, workers without labor—choose to fight their way out of the trap, with the scarce farmlands of their competitors."[4] Maybe one of the main contributions of this book is employing an ideographical approach to show the depth of the socioeconomic crisis starting in the late 1980s and its devastating social consequences. The drop of life expectancy to 32.6 years in 1990, the lowest ever reported in Africa since 1968, before the Rwandan Patriotic Front (RPF) war and the ensuing genocide, captured the peasants' dire situation at the time.[5]

Subsequently, this study has drawn a strong link between poverty and violence and showed important continuities in the processes and nature of the peasant violence before and during the genocide. The multiple causes of the socioeconomic crisis starting in the late 1980s are well known, a combination of structural and contextual factors such as sustained population growth, shortage of land, soil exhaustion and erosion, falling producer prices of coffee and tea, devaluation of currency because of the structural adjustment programs, unpredictable weather, and crop diseases. This multifaceted crisis had severe effects on food security, such as recurring food shortages, famines in certain regions, and widespread endemic hunger in Butare and Kibuye Prefectures. The hunger and land shortage caused a rise in social violence and murders, which worsened every time there was a further shortage of food. In an insidious fashion, the hunger undermined family and neighborly relations through the increase in murders within families and bloody physical attacks between neighbors living on adjacent tracts of land. When political parties were permitted to function, people in Kigembe and Gitesi used them as a pretext to grab commune land. The crimes committed during times of near famine before the genocide were not very different from many of the first attacks against Tutsis during the genocide, mostly motivated by the opportunity for looting, grabbing land, and a compulsive appetite for meat.[6] On a broader level, the social crisis in the late 1980s also gave way to a spectacular rise in violent crime that struck families and villages in many parts of Butare Prefecture but even more so in Kibuye Prefecture.[7]

This phenomenon was more than just simply crime; it also targeted the relatively richer neighborhoods of Butare and spread more and more to the local authorities, members of cell committees, cell leaders, and sector councilors in both Butare and Kibuye. The violence evolved into a low-intensity underground rebellion by masking its true appearance, but acts of violence and disobedience increased toward the late 1980s. From my study, it appears that the people who revolted were, indeed, the poor, but not the poorest. The level of education seemed to have made the phenomenon more acute; the young respondents who were poor but not destitute, who had attended primary school and more specifically had completed their studies at the vocational schools, seemed to articulate the harshest criticism of the MRND in the late 1980s. To us, the poorest interviewees seemed resigned, physically weak and often sick, but above all, unable to affect their immediate social environment. Although my study cannot provide a definitive position on this question, the notion of "structural violence" developed by Peter Uvin to explain the frustration of the Rwandan peasantry appears problematic because it gives the impression that the people living in extreme poverty formed the majority of those likely to give in to violence.[8] In its place, I propose the notion of "relative deprivation," which Ted Gurr defines as an individual's perception of the difference between one's aspirations and the extent of one's fulfillment.[9] In order to explain frustration among the peasants of that time, one would therefore need to take into account not only the economic and social crisis but also the promises of development persistently repeated but never honored by the Habyarimana government. The rise in the level of schooling, not accompanied by an increase in opportunities and chances in life, must have increased the frustration and rebellious behavior.

This infrapolitical development in the late 1980s and its blossoming with the fervent popular support for opposition parties during the democratization process in Butare and Kibuye Prefectures differ with the obedience to the state theory when it comes to explaining mass participation in the genocide.[10] Studies on social banditry take into account certain aspects of the social reality of Butare and Kibuye Prefectures during the late 1980s and the early 1990s. Eric Hobsbawm explains that social banditry is a movement of peasant protest against oppression and poverty. According to him, social crime is not organized and has no ideology; it is prepolitical and primitive and cannot gain political meaning other than in being against authorities under the influence of ideas and organizational resources coming from beyond the peasant world.[11] Whereas in Hobsbawm's view social criminals spare the poor by targeting the rich and the powerful, the criminals of Butare and Kibuye Prefectures, whose attitudes of revolt evolved in a different ethical context, directed their crimes toward their own social circles and against members of the less wealthy social classes.

The concept of *anomie* used by Gurr seems to better capture the normative framework in which the peasants of the prefectures studied evolved. Gurr explained that anomie is a breakdown in norms that govern social behavior. Anomie leads to widespread uncertainty, to which is attributed several types of deviant behavior such as crime, suicide, drug addiction, and gangs. Gurr suggested that anomie can lead to collective deviant behavior and establish alternative norms of rebellion. "When rebellion becomes endemic in a substantial part of the society, it provides a potential for revolution, which reshapes both the normative and social structure."[12]

This theoretical understanding allows us to see in the serious crises of the late 1980s a desire, both widespread and deep-rooted, for social change, probably because the status quo was simply not sustainable for the youths within the peasantry. As we shall see further on in this conclusion, this desire for change was first invested in multiple parties before attempting to find its fulfillment in the genocide, while at the same time offering the political elites great potential for the mobilization of peasants.

The authorizing influence coming from the political elites and state institutions in both Butare and Kibuye Prefectures, especially on communities and groups that initially resisted the call for killing, led them to evaluate their next course of action in terms of perceived utility of political violence. This phenomenon comes across clearly in the reports about members of the communities in northeastern Butare or in some parts of Gitesi Commune who in the beginning desisted from participating in the massacres or who had initially united with Tutsis against the politicized groups of killers. In the end, they felt their struggle was in vain because the directive to kill was the generally accepted and executed norm. Similarly, the news that the violence was going on in other surrounding areas seemed to have encouraged many hesitant groups to also start committing violence. More than that, the immediate observation that some people were receiving material gains from the massacres acted as a strong incitement to the youths of hesitant communities.[13]

More than just circumstantial opportunity, the perceived utility of political violence was profoundly ingrained in members of the society in both Butare and Kibuye Prefectures who wished that killings had happened well before they did. In early 1990, Danielle de Lame heard people on Murundi Hill in Bwakira Commune (east of Kibuye Prefecture) talking about the need to eliminate again part of the population: "The precarious food situation of 1989 was a source of urgent concern. By mid-1990, propaganda began to produce effects in Murundi, and ethnic splits had formed again. Some people viewed the conflict as a way to cut down an oversized population and proceed to a second division of land parcels that had become much too small."[14]

During the first months of democratization, particularly in March 1992, people on the other end of Kibuye Prefecture in Gitesi Commune impatiently awaited the *rukokoma*, the national conference demanded primarily by the Republican Democratic Movement (MDR), imagining that it would be a "time when they can eat, when they can take others' property by force, obtain land, when many people would die, thereby making land available."[15] During the initial massacres in Kivuru Sector (Kigembe Commune, Butare Prefecture), people shouted along the way that the Hutu revolution had begun. The elder Antoine Kabutura, from Kivuru Sector, made the link between the 1994 killings and legacy of the 1959 revolution: "The people knew, given what had happened in 1959. Those who had been chased away in 1959, 1960, and 1961 had not returned. And their land was redistributed in 1962. They feared nothing because they wanted to grab these pieces of land whose owners would not return."[16]

One must not see this desire to use violence and murder to tackle problems of socioeconomic hardships as simply individual deviance created by the opportune moment. This out-of-the-ordinary behavior was possible because it was achieved in a specific cultural context, defined by the precedent of the 1959 revolution. The revolution appears to have established a habitus of violence, an aspect of the popular political culture that pushed the repetition of predatory violence against the Tutsis.[17] On this Gurr's work provided useful interpretative insights:

> Probably the most potent determinant of perceived utility of political violence is people's previous success in attaining their ends by such means. Psychological and comparative evidence cited above suggests that people who obtain their demands through aggression are likely to use it as a tactic in the future. Intermittent rewards for aggression lead to establishment of very persistent aggressive habits. . . .[18]
>
> The intensity and scope of utilitarian justifications for political violence vary strongly with the extent to which a collectivity has increased its average value position in the past through political violence. . . .[19]
>
> Scope as well as intensity is said to be affected, on the assumption that the greater the average value gain through political violence, the greater the proportion of people in the collectivity who are likely to have gotten direct benefit. No specific time span is suggested for the operation of the effect. Value gains in the immediate past are probably recalled more clearly than remote gains. But dramatic successes of previous generations are likely to be enshrined in group traditions, more than losses or failures, and to be invoked to justify future rebellion decades and even centuries hence.[20]

The desire for a repeat of the rapacious anti-Tutsi violence of the revolution is not surprising, given that these events were not so distant in time and because of the resurgence of land pressures thirty-five years later, interrupted by a brief lull. The revolution allowed individuals and families to climb the social ladder through acquiring land, obtaining administrative and political appointments, and being able to send their children to school. The impact of these rapid social promotions was reinforced by the fact that they occurred within rural communities and not simply in the distant towns.

Despite the acute economic and social crisis in Rwanda, at the grassroots level the ethnic tensions by the late 1980s were nevertheless more of a residual phenomenon—I found few such cases during that period. These tensions were probably growing, as De Lame suggests, but they seemed to be utilitarian rather than experienced as a form of a fervor tied to identity. In fact, the opposite was true: there was a definite move toward assimilating the Tutsi minority through notable, relatively frequent, interethnic mating.

Nevertheless, it would be a mistake to attribute the bitterness of social relations as it could be perceived during the late 1980s and early 1990s solely to the effects of the 1959 revolution or to the serious deterioration of living conditions in the late 1980s. One must also consider more long-term historical determinants that seem to have contributed to the peculiar rigidity and harshness of the culture of social and political relations. When one considers the history of Rwanda over a longer period, and from this perspective, the invaluable contributions of Jan Vansina, Catharine Newbury, Alison des Forges, Emmanuel Ntezimana, and Jean Rumiya, one is struck by how far back one can trace the rigidity of social relations not only between Hutu and Tutsi political identities undergoing crystallization but also relations within the groups themselves.[21]

The tipping point seems to have been the establishment of *ibikingi* and *uburetwa* in the second half of the nineteenth century. Although these innovations in sociopolitical relations were already the manifestation of land pressure resulting from the relative increase in human and animal populations, historical studies are more focused on the effects of these new institutions in crystallizing antagonistic Hutu and Tutsi identities. It is important to also emphasize that the effects were not limited to the Hutu-Tutsi antagonism; they also seemed to have produced a peculiar national political culture and social relations over a long time. The atmosphere of rapacious greed seemed to have long locked Rwandan society into a widespread struggle for survival and wealth that in the late nineteenth and early twentieth century progressively became more openly violent. The widespread greed that defined social relations ended up emptying traditional institutions of their social mediating significance, such as lineage structures, clan solidarity, and family relations upheld by rituals such as *ubuse* (ties between clans); *kubandwa* (traditional worship ceremony); *kunywana* (blood pact); the notions of *ubufura* (honor) and of *ubuntu* (humanity); and at the top levels of government *ubwiru,* keepers of the esoteric code, *ubuhake* (the cattle clientship system); in short, all the institutions that regulated social relations.[22] These social constraints could explain the failure of these institutions to resist the tabula rasa policy of the Catholic Church; this lack of resistance distinguished Rwanda from many African societies that did not completely lose their traditional beliefs. The same corroding forces could account for the failure of Western churches and modern civil society to provide alternative sources of ethical norms that could have hampered mass participation in the genocide and the genocide itself. Thus, an attempt to comprehend the success in mobilizing many people to commit genocide must also include the long-term erosion of the Rwandan moral fabric, partly resulting from the steady environmental degradation that sharply accelerated in the 1980s.

The Political Factors Behind the Mass Participation

Earlier, I cited Hobsbawm's notion of social banditry regarding the primitive nature and thus the lack of organization, political orientation, or ideology in the revolts by the peasants against their oppression and the severity of their living conditions. Hobsbawm explained that the political orientation and organizational resources of such movements to achieve their confused, desired goals can only come from outside the peasants' world. This theory partly supports the results of my research indicating that the genocidal path the peasants adopted as a strategy for change in Rwanda was largely inspired by a radical faction of the national, regional, and local elites. Although the dire socioeconomic conditions of the late 1980s provided the *necessary* fertile ground for political violence on the part of the peasants, the political and ideological leadership seemed to better explain the peculiar process of mobilizing the peasants onto the narrow path of total genocide.

My research has shown that the former opposition political parties played a critical role in mobilizing people for committing genocide in Butare and Kibuye Prefectures, at the grassroots superseding state structures in the process. Against the regional backdrop of declining loyalty to the MRND party-state the political parties, especially the MDR, replaced the state as the force of mobilization and political control of the killings while taking over or collaborating with its structures at the local level.[23] An appreciation of this process requires understanding the political dynamics that transferred control of the people at the grassroots to the opposition parties in these two regions and how the opposition joined the former MRND party-state and its genocidal agenda.

Comprehending the political process leading up to the mass participation in the genocide in Butare and Kibuye Prefectures requires understanding the larger national political context. That context was shaped by the reaction of the party-state and a large part of Hutu public opinion to the war led by the RPF, the internal political contest against the former party-state itself, the direction the Arusha accords were taking, and the assassination of Burundian president Ndadaye. The former party-state decided that its response to these dramatic developments would be genocide against the Tutsi minority for its own sake but also as a means to stop a wider political change. However, the loss of influence in the center, south, and some of the west—regions where most of the Tutsi population lived—meant that for the genocide in whole to be successfully implemented by the population, the MRND needed a political process capable of mobilizing the people and the state structures. This is where the important role of the opposition parties in the genocide comes in.

After multiple parties were established in June 1991, the country was divided into three political zones: the northern zone comprising Gisenyi, Ruhengeri, and Byumba Prefectures remained loyal to the former MRND party-state; the center, south, and part of the west covering Gitarama, Butare, Gikongoro, and most of Kibuye Prefectures were almost completely cut off from the MRND and came under opposition control; and finally, a politically less united zone, in which the political influence was shared between the opposition and the MRND, comprising Cyangugu, Kigali-rural, Kigali-town, and Kibungo Prefectures.

Butare and Kibuye Prefectures were in the zone that resolutely rejected the MRND because of the socioeconomic crisis already discussed but also for ideological reasons.

The ideological dimension became evident when the MDR party was engaging in the debate between the conservatives and the reformists on whether to change the name of the party or revive the name MDR-PARMEHUTU. The return to the old party name symbolized an endorsement of the party's violent anti-Tutsi legacy under the First Republic. Ideology was again reflected in the Social Democratic Party (PSD) choice to define itself as against ethnic discrimination. At the regional level, in Butare Prefecture, the concordance between the geographical spread of the Rwanda National Union (UNAR), Association for the Social Welfare of the Masses (APROSOMA), and the MDR-PARMEHUTU in June 1960 and the distribution of influence of the Liberal Party (PL), PSD, and MDR in March 1993 clearly showed the ideological continuities between the political pluralism of 1959–1963 and that of 1991–1993. At the local level, in Kigembe Commune, we saw how ideological loyalty transformed into the reactivation of loyalty to MDR-PARMEHUTU among the party's former supporters and the handing down of this ideology across generations within families. In Gitesi Commune, we also identified this phenomenon among those who had chosen to join the MDR in the 1990s out of their loyalty to the MDR-PARMEHUTU.

The fact that in 1991 the MDR received its earliest support from Gitarama Prefecture, the birthplace of the party, not to mention in southwest Butare, manifests this political and ideological continuity nationwide. My study shows that even the reformists in the new MDR, when they spoke to the rural population uncritically promoted the historical memory of the MDR-PARMEHUTU among the peasants. The revival of the memory of the MDR-PARMEHUTU "liberation" cause within the context of the RPF war reaffirmed the fundamental Hutu-Tutsi enmity and legitimized anti-Tutsi violence among MDR followers.

The question therefore arises as to why these opposition parties changed their political orientation by abandoning their fierce opposition to the MRND and joined MRND's leadership in the genocide plan to reassert MRND political dominance. The response revisits the debate on context or ideology as the major cause of the outbreak of genocide. The data I have collected at the regional and local levels provide an empirical contribution to the debate.

Hutu Ideology Versus the Context of War

In Butare Prefecture, the first popular reactions to the October 1, 1990, RPF attack were muted, yet ethnic tension rose among the urban elites of Butare and Nyabisindu Towns as well as in the secondary schools. At the grassroots level, reactions varied in the Butare and Kibuye Prefectures. Although there was no ethnic tension reported in Butare, tensions emerged in Mabanza and Gishyita Communes on the one hand and in the Rutsiro and Kivumu Communes on the other (Kibuye Prefecture). The tensions in the first two seemed linked to their significant Tutsi population and perhaps to their previous history of closeness to the monarchy considering that Rwamatamu and Gitesi Communes also with large Tutsi populations were not affected. Meanwhile, the tensions in Rutsiro and Kivumu emerged from the communes' political and culture proximity to Gisenyi Prefecture, the MRND political stronghold. Finally, tensions in Kivumu echoed the massacres of Tutsis in neighboring Kibilira Commune (Gisenyi Prefecture) led by the local authorities. Generally, though, these tensions were relatively local; there was no major hostility from Hutus toward their Tutsi neighbors.

Interviewees from Butare and Kibuye Prefectures said that the real tipping point for ethnic tension to appear in the communities was the advent of multiple political parties in mid-1991.

Overall, nationwide, prior to the genocide, the more serious episodes of violence, killing dozens of Tutsi civilians, occurred in regions under MRND control and were either related to the evolution of the war against the RPF or advancements in the Arusha peace process. Butare Prefecture did not experience any bout of ethnic violence before the genocide. In Kibuye Prefecture the highest tension and open ethnic violence did not erupt at the beginning of the RPF war, rather, ethnic tensions and violence as serious as the killings in August 1992 in Gishyita and Rwamatamu Communes were instigated by the MRND.

My research has demonstrated that the pace of the population in entering into the genocide in the communes of Butare was determined by the dominant party in the communes. In Butare Prefecture, there was clear continuity from regional political preferences displayed during the commune elections of June 1960 to those reenacted after the return of the political parties in 1991.

As a result, the region southwest of Butare, which had chosen overwhelmingly the MDR-PARMEHUTU in 1960 and the MDR in 1991, was the area where the political violence was greatest and the ethnic tensions the highest. In the end, this continuity led that region to become the first to plunge into the genocide despite its location in a prefecture unfavorably disposed to the killing. The same political and ideological continuities also applied to the PSD, which seemed to follow the footsteps of APROSOMA, and to the PL, which followed UNAR. These three lines of heritage determined the three distinct behaviors at the start of the genocide: the first a rapid entry into the genocide (MDR/MDR-PARMEHUTU), the next a delayed entry into the genocide after pressure from the top levels of the state (PSD/APROSOMA), and the third characterized by organized resistance by Hutus and Tutsi together (PL/UNAR and PSD/APROSOMA).

My study did not record this kind of direct line to the past for Kibuye Prefecture; instead, the line of continuity leading to the genocide was shorter: it started mainly from the membership in the MDR when multiple parties were established in 1991, passed through the ethnopolitical violence before the formation of the MDR-power faction, and culminated in the early entry into the genocide. In Butare and Kibuye Prefectures, generally hostile to the MRND, the main factor that could explain the early entry into the genocide at the grassroots is affiliation to the MDR-power faction.[24] Thus in Butare Prefecture and to a lesser extent in Kibuye Prefecture, it was not simply Hutus who first delved into the genocide but rather the Hutu supporters of the Hutu-power coalition. It was their groups, made up of local party leaders, intellectuals, simple peasants, and thugs, that pressured local communities into participating in the genocide.

The importance of ideological leanings and their long persistence, such as in the case of Butare Prefecture, tend to relativize the importance of the propaganda diffused in the media, particularly on the radio. The media definitely played an insidious role in radicalizing minds, and during the genocide it became one of the important actors guiding the killing, as several respondents from Gitesi testify. However, this impact needs to be placed into local dynamics, which had a more direct effect on the actors.

The impact of earlier political and ideological leanings on the political mobilization of the 1990s and on the genocide mitigates the instrumentalist theory of the national elites manipulating the people from above. My study has shown that Butare Prefecture was particularly receptive to various parties as a result of, among other reasons, the similarities people drew between the parties of the 1960s for which their families or their village opted. This shows that the ideology of these parties had retained real influence among the rural people, thus partly affirming the constructivist assertion, which suggests that ideological discourses still had a strong resonance in the communities even though the context in which the discourses were initially produced had changed. Thus my study supports to a large extent Uvin's constructivist theory regarding deeply entrenched racial prejudice in Rwandan society, considering that historically the more ideologically potent antecedent was the MDR-PARMEHUTU narrative that reshaped Rwanda national identity.[25] But this racial prejudice did not influence much of the grassroots population in Butare and Kibuye, rather the intellectuals and some groups of peasants faithful to the legacy of the MDR-PARMEHUTU.

Finally, I need to confront my findings with the last argument of the proponents of the contextual explanation for the mass participation in the genocide: the fear, anger, and combativeness caused by President Habyarimana's sudden death attributed to the RPF, or the fear of returning to Tutsi hegemony, which led to the direct association of all Tutsis with the RPF in incitement.[26] At this point, to avoid teleological arguments, it is again crucial to consider the chronology of events. The interviewees from Gitesi and Kigembe Communes stated that when they heard the news of Habyarimana's death, they were seized with anxiety and doubt, but not with panic about the RPF. In the two communes, except in Nyamarebe Cell of Gitesi, people were generally peaceful, and in several areas Hutus and Tutsis went on patrol together. In various villages of Gitesi, Hutus and Tutsis formed a common front against the killers. In Kigembe, the social environment deteriorated but not because of the radio propaganda about the threat of the RPF and Tutsis within the country; rather, it was a result of the news that the killings had begun in neighboring Nyakizu Commune and that Hutus were eating their cows. The first anti-Tutsi violence by the peasants was driven by the motivation to loot, not by the intent to kill Tutsis. In Gitesi Commune and in most areas, the solidarity between Hutus and Tutsis broke under pressure from the killers working within the local MDR structures or from killers sent by the state authorities from Kibuye and Gisenyi Prefectures. There was no mention of fear aroused specifically by the RPF or direct association between local Tutsis and the RPF during the first days of the genocide by non-politicized people. By contrast, the opportunity to loot and to take land seemed to have been the determining factor in the change of attitude among initially peaceful communities.

In a broader dimension, Tutsi survivors from Kigembe Commune and elsewhere in Butare Prefecture explained that they did not head for Burundi during the initial days of the genocide because they felt safe, and they never thought that their neighbors might attack them. This confidence would be difficult to explain if the Hutus of Butare were already gripped with panic about the RPF and had directly linked it to local Tutsis, as the radio propaganda had consistently done. Finally, the way in which various communes of Butare Prefecture carried out the genocide, following the three patterns already explained according to the orientation of the dominant political party, largely refutes the thesis of the president's death or the radio propaganda interpretation of the death having sowed panic among the Hutus and pushed them to kill Tutsis.

When it came to Kibuye Prefecture, in Mabanza and Gishyita Communes for which I have sufficient data, at the grassroots, the first to start to kill were members of MDR-power. This suggests that in Kibuye and in Butare Prefecture, fear and combativeness against the RPF may have mobilized people to kill only selectively, according to specific preexisting political and ideological leanings.

The same dynamics were also at play in Kigali in the first days of the genocide; the first wave of Hutu fear appeared to be sparked by the Interahamwe and Impuzamugambi militias of the MRND and the CDR, respectively, because of the extremely violent atmosphere these militias had created in the preceding months, not by the RPF.[27]

Nevertheless, the fear at the level of both the organizers and the grassroots increased to real panic as the RPF continued to advance. The fear factor as one of the causes of the massacres should therefore be analyzed diachronically and be contrasted with the chronological progress of the RPF. From this perspective, the HRW report shows that the bulk of the massacres were carried out in the first three weeks after the death of Habyarimana, that is, before the end of April and before the RPF started to get the upper hand and the defeat of the government became imminent.[28]

Up to now, I have limited this chapter to the causes of the mass participation in the genocide. My analysis of the regional and local case studies should nevertheless furnish elements that might contribute insight into the motivations of the initiators and architects of the genocide at the central level.

The political dimensions of the genocide were so strong that it is difficult to separate the political from the other motives. However, analyzing ideological motives and distinguishing them from the political ones, especially in the total genocide against the Rwandan Tutsis, is crucial. According to Robert Melson, the difference between partial and total genocide is that the former seeks to massacre a large portion of a collective, to diminish its social importance or its political power without necessarily exterminating all of its members or destroying the group's cultural institutions, whereas total genocide seeks to exterminate the group targeted by a particular state or society. In his comparison of two genocides in whole—the Armenian genocide and the Holocaust—according to the degree of physical annihilation, the degree of cultural destruction, and its worldwide scale, Melson explains that even though total genocides imply the physical and cultural destruction of a group, those genocides can in some cases allow the people targeted to change their identities and then be spared. Thus, in the case of the Armenian genocide, some people survived by converting to Islam. This was not possible during the Holocaust, in which Hitler sought to kill all identified as Jews, even those who had converted to Christianity or who did not consider themselves Jews. Finally, the Holocaust had a unique spiritual dimension in which Jews were identified as evil, and their elimination from the earth meant the redemption of the world. Thus Nazism "was not only a political ideology; it was a theodicy whose scope was global."[29]

The genocide against the Tutsis of Rwanda, more maybe than the Armenian genocide, had no remission; its goal was the extermination all Tutsis living in the territory controlled by the Rwandan Armed Forces (FAR). The impossibility of survival through some change in attitude, the expansion of the circle of people to be killed, the moving from men and young male children to women and little girls, the genealogical enquiries on "dubitous Hutus," and the killing of Hutus who looked like Tutsis all attested to the determination to annihilate the Tutsi population.

Melson identified revolutions as the specific historical events that favored the advent of total genocides. According to him, revolutionary regimes need to mobilize a political base to secure their vision of the new society they wish to create. To do so, they must construct a new system of legitimacy and seek support from a new authentic political community they have redefined as the people, the nation, the class, or the race:

> The new authentic political community is that subset of the territorial state's inhabitants who are expected to fulfill the ideological vision of the revolutionary regime and to support the postrevolutionary state. By the same token there exist members of the old order who were either opposed to the revolution or whose identities cannot be made to fit into the new postrevolutionary political community. These others are likely to be excluded from the new political community and declared "enemies of the revolution." It is just such "enemies," that is, those excluded from the postrevolutionary community, who may become victims of repression and even genocide.[30]

Melson finally indicates as other conditions for genocide to be committed, a totalitarian state and a society under stress by passing through a crisis.[31]

It is hard not to recognize in Melson's observations the mobilizing ideology the MDR-PARMEHUTU used after the 1959 revolution. One can identify the new political community installed by the PARMEHUTU in the form of Hutu Rubanda Nyamwinshi (popular majority), whose legitimacy was based on their presumed status as the indigenous majority and the fact that they presumably lived in servitude under the Tutsis for four centuries. The illegitimate community was identified as the entire Tutsi population, considered foreigners, Hamitic people from Ethiopia, a minority, and the oppressors.[32] This redefinition of the national community corresponded with the production of "hegemonic myths identifying the victims as outside the sanctioned universe of obligation," which Helen Fein identifies as a necessary condition for ideological genocides.[33]

Melson's work provided an insightful explanation of the theory of provocation, which in the case of Rwanda is the basis of those who perceived the genocide as a result of the RPF 1990 war and/or the shooting down of President Habyarimana's plane. Melson illustrated the theory of provocation in genocides principally using the case of the Armenian genocide. In this line of thinking, the Armenians provoked their own killing, because of the actions of the armed nationalist groups demanding greater internal autonomy from Turkey in 1915, considered an existential threat to the creation of the new Turkey. Furthermore, some Armenians allied with Russia in the war against

Turkey, and some Russian army units had Armenian soldiers and commanders.[34] Showing that the threat presented by Armenian nationalists was minor, Melson argued that this threat did not require the extermination and destruction of the Turkish Armenians. In refuting this thesis, Melson explained that it is better to look for the reasons for the Armenian genocide in the way revolutionary young Turks, influenced by their Turkish nationalism, came to *perceive* the Armenian community as an existential threat to the new state in the dire political and military context of the time.[35]

A striking parallel can be drawn here with the Rwandan situation. The genocide of Rwandan Tutsis opposed a revolutionary regime at war with an "external" enemy threatening the revolutionary order, which since 1959 had labeled the internal Tutsi community illegitimate and intrinsically opposed to the revolutionary order. To assess the validity of this comparison, one has to analyze the actions of internal Tutsis during the RPF war (1990–1993) and the level of threat the Tutsis represented. Two factors could objectively justify the hostility against the local Tutsis: some Tutsi elites inside Rwanda who publicly supported the RPF and the fact that young Tutsis were leaving the country to enlist with the RPF. When it came to the real threat posed by the internal Tutsi population, the weight of its contribution to the RPF war was real but not significant.[36] In the context of the RPF war, the fact that the victim community of the genocide was not completely innocent of the accusation of providing support to the enemy, to some extent, could have justified significant retaliation, if not politicide, a partial genocide of which the rationale would have been instrumentalist. Its goal would have been to disorganize the Tutsi community, punish its active elements, and terrorize it in order to induce changes in behavior or attitudes.

After President Habyarimana's death, during the concomitant war and genocide, one could argue that the massacres were a means to pressure the RPF. However, even then, the interim government requested a cease-fire in exchange for an end to the massacres only because it was not able to contain the RPF, but then it refused to first end the massacres as the precondition demanded by the RPF. This move suggests that for the architects of the genocide, it was more important to continue with the massacres than to stop the war they were about to lose. The HRW report suggests that genocide was an integral part of the war.[37] Kamanzi took the argument further by implying that the genocide organizers appeared to have considered the massacre of Tutsis the war itself.[38] He emphasized that the leaders of the genocide wanted to resume the war they had already lost in February 1993, with no supplemental preparations other than the genocide plan and without French military support.

It is difficult to avoid seeing some form of magical thinking in the logic seeming to link the war to the genocide. One can argue that the internal Tutsi community, harmless, defenseless, largely innocent, submissive to the Hutu regime, and on the path to assimilation by the Hutu majority, was the victim of total genocide because in the mental framework of the killers it was considered the enemy.[39] Thus the war launched in 1990 by the RPF did play a major role in establishing an atmosphere of open violence that, in and of itself, could have led to a politicide, or a partial genocide targeting Tutsi elites even broadly defined. However, the extreme nature of the total genocide seemed to stem from the ideological universe of the planners. Lemarchand echoed this distinction between partial and total genocides in his suggestion that the downslide toward the total genocide of the Tutsis was a result of the contribution of the more ideologically driven members of the Hutu-power coalition, whose epicenter was the MDR-power faction, as opposed to the political and military structure of the former MRND party-state. Members of the former party-state may have planned a partial genocide before the death of Habyarimana.[40]

The crucial role of the MDR-power faction in massively mobilizing people for the killing of their neighbors in two prefectures far away from the war zones concurs with this theory.

In hindsight, the extraordinary nature of the total genocide was evident in the manner in which literally all the analysts and commentators were surprised by the turn of events. It was even more tragic that the large section of the Tutsis within the country did not expect it either. Few could have imagined that the war would lead to the near extinction of the physical and social presence of peasants belonging to the lowest stratum of Rwandan society.

In conclusion, Melson's theory linking genocide, revolution, war, and social crisis provides a good explanation for the mass participation in the genocide in Rwanda. The Tutsi genocide was perpetrated by a Hutu totalitarian revolutionary regime facing an armed challenge on the political identity of the new Rwandan state by a section of the population excluded. Sought to be the main executor of the massacres by elites who had anticipated its answer, an important part of the Hutu population complied all the more strongly as it was experiencing an extreme survival crisis, and hoped for benefit. The precedent of the ethnic cleansing of the 1959 revolution provided the political and cultural framework that legitimized the ethical and utility rationale for participating in the massacres.[41]

The uncommon nature of a total genocide largely executed by the population in three months is due to the combination of these elements at one time in one place constituting a sort of perfect storm. The severity of the peasant crisis, part of a wider and older national crisis that this book has tried to portray, best demonstrated by the 1990 lowest life expectancy ever in Africa since 1968, has further accentuated the fatal combination.

Tracing the deepest roots of the genocide of Tutsis to the 1959 revolution corroborates Mahmood Mamdani's theory of the categories of Rwandan identity as political identities linked to the building of the state, as opposed to the ancient categories based on traditional culture or socioeconomic divisions.[42] Mamdani's constructivist framework for analyzing "Hutu" and "Tutsi" as polarized political identities was more convincing and is closer to the results of this research when he gave the framework a more limited scope, involving particularly the Hutu and Tutsi elites, as low as they might have been.[43]

The question of the role of traditional culture, or rather of its memory, is crucial to understanding the dynamics of conflict that led to the 1994 genocide. My research shows that at the national and local levels, before the 1990 war, the Hutu and Tutsi communities witnessed a strong trend toward integration. This integration was characterized by, among other things, a rise in the number of interethnic marriages and friendly coexistence based on several traditional practices regulating neighbor relations. In some poorer rural areas, despite the extreme poverty, these practices seemed to have resisted the political redefinition of the Hutu and Tutsi identities. The practices could account for the resistance and reluctance of some communities toward the genocidal violence. This was the dynamic in Nyanza Region—the former royal capital—and in Mayaga Region in the northeast Butare Prefecture, when Hutus and Tutsis joined forces after the start of the genocide and decisively fought the killers. The role of this culture among the poor of the region and elsewhere is distinct from the primordial and essentialist explanations of the Rwandan conflict such as those proposed by Pierre Erny and Bernard Lugan or implied by Filip Reyntjens.[44] In this part of the country and elsewhere, traditional popular culture seemed to have been a uniting factor rather than a cause of division. When all is said and done, the fixist "ethnicity" theory, such as the one proposed by Reyntjens, and the constructivist ethnic ideology I have attempted to present here, resemble each other and are difficult to distinguish. One of the differences can be found at the level of the interpretation of their respective origins, based on communal and antagonistic ancient cultural and political relations or being an integral part of the construction of the modern Rwandan state. In more tangible terms, the most important difference between these two conceptions is in the identification of agency and historical responsibility for the genocide.

From this difference in conceptions of the nature of the ethnic conflict in Rwanda and in the root causes of the genocide emerges a normative corollary: the cultural conceptions of Rwandan ethnicity and conflict tend to diminish the moral and political responsibility of the leaders who drove the genocide by using the argument that ultimately it was an ethnic war pitting against each other two different entities in an age-old conflict.

The fact that the Tutsi minority had in other times been associated with the traditional ruling class, and that decades later these very poor people were suspected of harboring feelings of cultural superiority, also contributed to some assigning a measure of democratic legitimacy to the genocide of the Tutsis.[45]

Notes

1. For more specifics on the Bisesero Hills, see African Rights, "Bisesero: Résistance au génocide," 1995.

2. Verwimp, "A Quantitative Analysis of Genocide in Kibuye," p. 45.

3. Based on the 1991 census, these four of the eleven existing prefectures were home to 57 percent of the total national Tutsi population.

4. Bonneaux, "Rwanda: A Case of Demographic Entrapment," 1994.

5. World Bank, World Development Indicators, 2014.

6. According to Norbert Elias, poverty, hunger, and fear form the most powerful factors behind instinctual violence. The rarity of meat can culminate in the development of a desire for meat that seeks to be satisfied through violence. "When, in the Middle Ages, a peasant renounced all meat because he was too poor or because the livestock was reserved for the meals of the landlords, he acted under physical constraint and gave up his desire to eat meat until he was able to do it without exposing himself to external danger." Elias, *La dynamique de l'Occident*, 1975, p. 208.

7. See also André and Platteau, "Land Tenure Under Unbearable Stress"; De Lame, *A Hill Among a Thousand*, p. 309.

8. Uvin, *Aiding Violence*.

9. Gurr, *Why Men Rebel*, 1970, p. 13.

10. Prunier, *Rwanda Crisis*, pp. 141, 248 ; Gourevitch, *We Wish*, p. 23; Willame, *Aux sources*, p. 105.

11. Hobsbawm, *Primitive Rebels*.

12. Gurr, *Why Men Rebel*, p. 42.

13. Many relentless killers also hid their Tutsi friends. One such person was Thaddée Karengera, one of the main organizers and active participants in the massacres in the Nyakare region of Kigembe Prefecture.

14. De Lame, *A Hill Among a Thousand*, p. 98.

15. Préfecture de Kibuye, *Lettre du Préfet au Ministre de l'Intérieur et du Développement communal du 13/03/92*.

16. Antoine Kabutura, interview with author, May 18, 2001, Kigembe.

17. Des Forges observes this progression from a few years after the revolution: "At this time, Hutu politicians also established the link between 'patriotism' and profit. In attacking the supposed enemies of the nation and the revolution, the Hutus stood to gain, both in the short term from goods pillaged and in the long term from lands appropriated from Tutsis driven away. Given the political and material gains from anti-Tutsi violence, officials and others had strong incentives to widen the circle of people targeted from the narrow group of former powerholders to all Tutsis. By 1967, when both the incursions and the attacks on Tutsis within Rwanda ended, Tutsis were at risk of attack for the simple fact of being Tutsi." Des Forges, *Leave None to Tell the Story*, p. 39.

18. Gurr, *Why Men Rebel*, p. 218.

19. Gurr defines values as the "desired events, objects, and conditions for which men strive." Ibid., p. 25.

20. Ibid., p. 222.

21. Vansina, *Antecedents to Modern Rwanda*; Newbury, *Cohesion of Oppression*; Rumiya, *Le Rwanda sous;* Ntezimana, "Le Rwanda social."

22. Mbonimana, "Les institutions traditionnelles."

23. Vincent Ntezimana was a university professor imprisoned in Belgium for participating in the genocide. In a book published just before his trial, he wrote, "At that time, I was myself a member of the MDR and therefore able to closely follow the

events shaking my party. I am convinced that the breakup of the MDR was fatal for Rwanda." Ntezimana, *La justice belge*, p. 95.

24. A large section of the rural communities that had joined the MDR in 1991 naturally became the MDR-power faction, at least in part because of promotion by MDR conservatives as well as reformers of the historical memory of the MDR-PARMEHUTU as a tool to politically mobilize the rural communities.

25. Uvin wrote, "The most profound factor fueling the transmission of genocidal ideology from the regime to the masses, however, was the long-standing and deeply ingrained racism of Rwandan society. . . . For decades, Rwandan society had been profoundly racist. The image of the Tutsis as inherently evil and exploitative was, and still is, deeply rooted in the mind of most Rwandans; this image was a founding pillar of the genocide to come. Although ethnic peace had prevailed during most of the regime, the racist nature of Rwandan society had not changed." Uvin, "Tragedy in Rwanda," *Environment* (April 1996): 13, cited in Mamdani, *When Victims Become Killers*, p. 199.

26. Lemarchand's articulation of the same idea merits citation: "By contrast, in Rwanda under Habyarimana, the threat of Tutsis taking power, either through the Arusha accords or by force, was a scary reality for many. The crash of the president's plane on April 6, 1994, introduced a major breakdown in people's perceptions: the widespread anxiety about the return of Tutsi hegemony gave way to a collective psychosis that the media only inflamed and channeled toward paroxysmal violence. Fear and ethnic hatred evolved into panic, and panic into murder." Lemarchand, "Les génocides se suivent," p. 28.

27. "By Monday, April 11, an estimated 20,000 Rwandans had been slain, the vast majority of them Tutsis. However, because some of the first victims had been highly visible Hutus and because assailants continued to target Hutu adversaries of the MRND and the CDR, many Hutus also feared for their lives. They saw the killings as broader than a genocide and also as constituting an extreme form of kubohoza, with victims chosen on partisan, regional, or economic grounds. Both in Kigali and elsewhere, Hutus cooperated with Tutsis in fighting off militia attacks or fled with Tutsis to places of refuge. Often, Hutus made such decisions not only because of their political beliefs but also because of ties of family or friendship with Tutsis." Des Forges, *Leave None to Tell the Story*, p. 201. Ntaribi Kamanzi explains that in Kigali, Hutus and Tutsis were afraid and sought refuge together in places such as schools, churches, and hostels. The militias and their commanders then sent the message ordering all the Hutus to leave the area because they were all going to be attacked, and yet only Tutsis were the target. Kamanzi, *Rwanda: Du génocide à la défaite*, pp. 103–104.

28. Ibid.

29. Melson, *Revolution and Genocide,* pp. 27–29.

30. Ibid., pp. 18–19.

31. Ibid., p. 13.

32. Des Forges, "The Ideology of Genocide," 1995.

33. Fein, "Scenarios of Genocide," 1984, p. 18. When the monarchist party reacted strongly against the November 1959 revolt, the future president, Grégoire Kayibanda, sent a telegram to the UN demanding the division of the country into Tutsi and Hutu zones. *Dispatch from Ruanda-Urundi, November 13, 1959, no. 426: Telegram sent to the UN by a Hutu leader of Ruanda.* Lemarchand reports on another call Kayibanda made for separate zones for Hutus and Tutsis: "Citing Disraeli, Kayibanda compared the communities of Rwanda to 'two nations in a single state . . . two nations between whom there is no intercourse and no sympathy, who are as ignorant of each other's habits, thoughts, and feelings as if they were dwellers of different zones, or inhabitants of different planets.'" Lemarchand, *Rwanda and Burundi*, p. 169.

34. Melson, *Revolution and Genocide*, pp. 152–159.

35. Ibid.

36. According to Des Forges, from September 1992 to around August 1993, burgomasters drew up lists of people who had joined the RPF ranks and sent them to the prefects. When the commander of the army had an accident around February 1993, a list of 331 persons suspected of being RPF supporters was found in his car. Human Rights Watch (HRW) also stated that in 1993, hundreds of secret RPF cells made up of six to twelve members, including Hutus and Tutsis, were set up. According to HRW, the young Tutsis joining the RPF were neither a military nor a political threat to the regime. Des Forges, *Leave None to Tell the Story*, pp. 99–100, 130.

37. "Diplomatic hopes of halting the genocide by ending the war could not produce results as long as the organizers of the slaughter saw the genocide as a way of winning the war." Ibid., p. 21.

38. Under the heading "The Month [May] of the Defeat and Bitterness for the Ex-FAR," Ntaribi Kamanzi wrote, "The government side is desperate; it badly wants a ceasefire. It plunged into the massacre of the innocent instead of engaging in war, and now that the civilians to kill are finished, it finds itself face to face with what it had hoped to avoid by killing the Tutsis." Kamanzi, *Rwanda*, p. 148.

39. In September 1992, the army chief of staff sent a circular identifying the RPF as the principal enemy, but in other parts of the document, he identified the enemy as the Tutsis. Des Forges, *Leave None to Tell the Story*, pp. 62–63. After the assassination of Hutu leaders opposed to the Hutu-power coalition on the day after Habyarimana was killed, the top army officers formed on April 8, 1994, an interim government that gave many positions to the Hutu-power leaders of the former opposition. The first task of the government in its plan of mobilization for the genocide was to explain that the times of partisan and regional conflict had ended and that the sole enemy was the Tutsis, who had to be eliminated. Later, groups of killers sang in the streets of Kigali, "We have only one enemy, and we know him, it is the Tutsi." Ibid., 203.

40. "There is no doubt that the death of Habyarimana was the signal for putting the genocide plan into action. But did it target all Tutsis, without distinction, or only opposition leaders? This is the hypothesis maintained by Hutus who were not known for extremism. According to them, this initial plan transformed into the extermination of all Tutsis when the most implacable members of the Hutu-power faction themselves inspired the violence." Lemarchand, "Les génocides," p. 32.

41. See note 18.

42. Certain passages of his arguments are important to keep in mind: "Political identities exist in their own right. They are a direct consequence of the history of state formation and not of market or cultural formation. . . . When it comes to the modern state, political identities are inscribed in law. . . . Political identities are the consequence of how power is organized. The organization of power not only defines the parameters of the political community, telling us who is included and who is left out, it also differentiates the bounded political community internally." Mamdani, *When Victims Become Killers*, p. 22.

43. Ibid., pp. 217, 229–230.

44. Erny, *Rwanda 1994*; Lugan, *Histoire du Rwanda*; Reyntjens, *L'Afrique des Grands Lacs en Crise*.

45. Among the victims, not the executioners, a collective consciousness of belonging to a culturally superior group existed. Lemarchand, "Les génocides," p. 24. "Some policymakers, particularly in France and in Belgium, were wedded to the notion that an ethnic majority was necessarily the same as a democratic majority. They could not bring themselves to condemn the genocide because they feared increasing the likelihood of an RPF victory and the subsequent establishment of a government dominated by the minority." Des Forges, *Leave None to Tell the Story*, p. 21.

Acronyms

ADERWA	Alliance for Democracy in Rwanda (Association pour la démocratie au Rwanda)
ADL	Rwandan Association for Individual Rights and Civil Liberties (Association rwandaise pour la défense des droits de la personne et libertés publiques)
AGEUNR	General Association of Students of the National University of Rwanda (Association générale des etudiants de l'Universite nationale du Rwanda)
AMASASU	Alliance of Military Officers Provoked by the Age-Old Underhanded Acts of the UNAR Sympathizers (Alliance de militaires agacés par les séculaires actes sournois des unaristes)
APROSOMA	Association for the Social Welfare of the Masses (Association pour la promotion de la masse)
AVP	Association of Peace Volunteers (Association des Volontaires pour la Paix)
CDR	Coalition for the Defense of the Republic (Coalition pour la défence de la République)
CERAI	integrated rural vocational and training school (Centre d'enseignement rural et artisanal intégré)
CSP	Country Supreme Council (Conseil Superieur du Pays)
ESO	school for noncommissioned officers (Ecole des Sous-Officiers)
FAR	Rwandan Armed Forces (Forces armées rwandaises)
GDP	gross domestic product

GTBE	broad-based transitional government (Gouvernement de transition à base élargie)
HRW	Human Rights Watch
JDR	Youth for a Democratic Republic (Jeunesse démocratique républicaine)
LIDER	League of Students of Rwanda (Ligue des Étudiants du Rwanda)
MDR	Republican Democratic Movement (Mouvement démocratique républicain)
MRND	National Revolutionary Movement for Development (Mouvement révolutionnaire national pour le développement)
MSM	Hutu Social Movement (Mouvement Social Muhutu)
ONAPO	National Office for Population (Office National de la Population)
ORINFOR	Rwanda Office for Information (Office rwandais d'information)
PARMEHUTU	Party of the Hutu Emancipation Movement (Parti du mouvement de l'émancipation hutu)
PDC	Christian Democratic Party (Parti démocratique chrétien)
PL	Liberal Party (Parti libéral)
PSD	Social Democratic Party (Parti social démocrate)
PSR	Rwandan Socialist Party (Parti socialiste rwandais)
RADER	Rwandan Democratic Rally (Rassemblement démocratique rwandais)
RPA	Rwandan Patriotic Army
RPF	Rwandan Patriotic Front
RTLM	Free Radio and Television of the Thousand Hills (Radio télévision libre des mille collines)
SAP	structural adjustment program
UEBR	Union of Baptist Churches in Rwanda (Union des Eglises Baptistes au Rwanda)
UNAMIR	UN Assistance Mission in Rwanda

UNAR   Rwanda National Union (Union nationale rwandaise)

UNHCR   UN High Commission for Refugees

Bibliography

African Rights. *Rwanda: Death, Despair, and Defiance*. London: African Rights, 1995.
———. *Not So Innocent: When Women Become Killers*. London: African Rights, 1995.
———. "Bisesero: Résistance au génocide, avril–juin 1994." *Témoins* 8, n.d.
Amselle, Jean-Loup, and Elikia M'Bokolo, eds. *Au coeur de l'ethnie: Ethnie, tribalisme et État en Afrique*. Paris: La Découverte, 1985.
André, Catherine, and Jean-Philippe Platteau. "Land Tenure Under Unbearable Stress: Rwanda Caught in the Malthusian Trap." *Journal of Economic Behavior and Organisation* 34, no. 1 (1998): 29–47.
Andreopoulos, George J., ed. *Genocide: Conceptual and Historical Dimensions*. Philadelphia: University of Pennsylvania Press, 1994.
Ashford, Douglas E. *Ideology and Participation*. Beverly Hills, CA: Sage, 1969.
Azarya, Victor, and Naomi Chazan. "Disengagement from the State in Africa: Reflections on the Experience of Ghana and Guinea." *Comparative Studies in Society and History* 29, no. 1 (1987): 105–131.
Bangamwabo, François-Xavier. *Les relations interethniques au Rwanda à la lumière de l'agression d'octobre 1990: Genèse, soubassements et perspectives*. Ruhengeri: Éditions Universitaires du Rwanda, 1991.
Bart, Jean-François. *Montagnes d'Afrique, terres paysannes*. Bordeaux: Presses Universitaires de Bordeaux, 1993.
———. *L'État en Afrique: La politique du ventre*. Paris: Fayard, 1988.
Bayart, Jean-François, Achille Mbembe, and Comi M. Toulabor. *Le politique par le bas en Afrique noire*. Paris: Karthala, 1992.
Berger, Iris. *Religion and Resistance: East African Kingdoms in the Precolonial Period*. Tervuren: Musée Royal de l'Afrique Centrale, 1981.
Bertrand, Jordane. *Rwanda: Le piège de l'histoire*. Paris: Karthala, 2000.
Bézy, Fernand. *Rwanda, Bilan socio-économique d'un régime, 1962–1989*. Louvain-la-Neuve: Université Catholique de Louvain, 1990, p. 17.
Bonneaux, Luc. "Rwanda: A Case of Demographic Entrapment." *Lancet* 344, no. 8938 (1994): 1689–1690.
Braeckman, Colette. *Rwanda: Histoire d'un génocide*. Paris: Fayard, 1994.
Cambrezy, Luc. *Le surpeuplement en question*. Paris: Éditions de l'Orstom, 1992.
Chossudovsky, Michel. "Economic Genocide in Rwanda." *Economic and Political Weekly* 31, no. 15 (April 13, 1996): 938–941.
Chrétien, Jean-Pierre. "La révolte de Ndugutse, 1912: Forces traditionnelles et pression coloniale au Rwanda allemand." *Revue française d'histoire d'outre-mer* 59, no.4 (1972): 645–680.
———. "Des sédentaires devenus migrants: Les motifs de départs des Burundais et des Rwandais vers l'Ouganda (1920–1960)." *Cultures et développement* 10, no.1 (1978): 71–101.

———. "Hutu et Tutsi au Rwanda et au Burundi." In Jean-Loup Amselle and Elikia M'Bokolo, eds., *Au coeur de l'ethnie: Ethnie, tribalisme et État en Afrique*, pp. 129–166. Paris: La Découverte, 1985.

———. *Le défi de l'ethnisme: Rwanda et Burundi, 1990–1996*. Paris: Karthala, 1997.

———. *The Great Lakes of Africa: Two Thousand Years of History*. Translated by Scott Straus. New York: Zone Books, 2006.

Chrétien, Jean-Pierre, Jean-François Dupaquier, Marcel Kabanda, and Joseph Ngarambe. *Rwanda: Les médias du génocide*. Paris: Karthala, 1995.

Chrétien, Jean-Pierre, André Guichaoua, Gabriel Le Jeune. *La crise d'août 1988 au Burundi*. Paris: Afera-Karthala, Cahiers du CRA, n° 6, 1989.

———. Annual reports, 1982, 1985, 1987, 1988, 1989.

———. *Résultats du recensement mené en août 1989*, n.d.

———. *Note du Bourgmestre au Préfet du 26/01/87, Renseignements sur 25 ans de l'Indépendance nationale.*

———. *Lettre du Bourgmestre au Préfet du 13/01/87*, Renseignements sur le Guide du Bourgmestre.

Cox, Joseph A., and Francis G. Elliott. "Primary Adult Lactose Intolerance in the Kivu Lake Area: Rwanda and the Bushi." *American Journal of Digestive Diseases* 19, no. 8 (1974): 714–724.

De Heusch, Luc. "Anthropologie d'un génocide: le Rwanda." *Les Temps Modernes* 49, no. 579 (1994): 1–19.

De Lame, Danielle. *A Hill Among a Thousand: Transformations and Ruptures in Rural Rwanda*. Translated by Helen Arnold. Madison: University of Wisconsin Press, 2004.

Des Forges, Alison. "The Ideology of Genocide." *Issue: A Journal of Opinion* 23, no. 2 (1995): 44–47.

———. *Defeat Is the Only Bad News: Rwanda Under Musinga, 1896–1931*. Edited by David Newbury. Madison: University of Wisconsin Press, 2011.

———. *Leave None to Tell the Story: Genocide in Rwanda*. New York: Human Rights Watch, 1999.

D'Hertefelt, Marcel. "Les élections communales et le consensus politique au Rwanda." *Zaïre* 14, no. 5–6 (1960): 503–438.

Economist Intelligence Unit. "Zaïre, Rwanda, Burundi." Country Profile, 1980–1990.

Elias, Norbert. *La dynamique de l'Occident*. Paris: Calmann-Lévis, 1975.

Erny, Pierre, *Rwanda 1994: Clés pour comprendre le calvaire d'un people*. Paris: L'Harmattan, 1994.

Fein, Helen. "Genocide: A Sociological Perspective." *Current Sociology* 38, no. 1 (1990).

———, ed. *Genocide Watch*. New Haven, CT: Yale University Press, 1992.

———. "Scenarios of Genocide: Models of Genocide and Critical Responses." In *Toward the Understanding and Prevention of Genocide: Proceedings of the International Conference on the Holocaust and Genocide*, pp. 3–31. Boulder, CO: Westview Press, 1984.

Foucault, Michel. "How Is Power Exercised?" Translated by Leslie Sawyer. In Israel W. Charny, ed., *Michel Foucault: Beyond Structuralism and Hermeneutics*, 216–226. Edited by Hubert L. Dreyfus and Paul Rabinow. Chicago: University of Chicago Press, 1982.

Fujii, Lee Ann. *Killing Neighbors: Webs of Violence in Rwanda*. Ithaca, NY: Cornell University Press, 2009.

Giddens, Anthony. *Central Problems in Social Theory, Action, Structure, and Contradictions in Social Analysis*. London: Macmillan, 1979.

Gourevitch, Philip. *We Wish to Inform You That Tomorrow We Will Be Killed with Our Families: Stories from Rwanda.* New York: Farrar, Straus and Giroux, 1998.

Guichaoua, André. "L'ordre paysan des hautes terres centrales du Burundi et du Rwanda." In *T. 1 de Destins paysans et politiques agraires en Afrique centrale.* Paris: L'Harmattan, 1989.

———. *The Problem of the Rwandese Refugees and the Banyarwanda Populations in the Great Lakes Region.* Geneva: Office of the UN High Commissioner for Refugees, 1992.

———. *Rwanda 1994: Les politiques du génocide à Butare.* Paris: Karthala, 2005.

———. *Rwanda: de la guerre au génocide: Les politiques criminelles au Rwanda (1990–1994).* Paris : La Découverte (Cahiers libres), 2010.

Gurr, Ted R. *Why Men Rebel.* Princeton, NJ: Princeton University Press, 1970.

Hanssen, Alain. *Le désenchantement de la coopération: Enquête au pays des mille coopérants.* Paris: L'Harmattan, 1989.

Harroy, Jean-Paul. *Rwanda: de la féodalité à la démocratie, 1955–1962. Souvenirs d'un compagnon de la marche vers la démocratie et l'indépendance.* Bruxelles: Hayez, Acádeemie des sciences d'outre-mer, 1984.

Hobsbawn, Eric J. *Primitive Rebels: Studies in Archaic Forms of Social Movement in the l9th and 20th Centuries.* Manchester, UK: Manchester University Press, 1970.

Horowitz, Irving Louis. *Genocide: State Power and Mass Murder.* New Brunswick, NJ: Transaction, 1976.

Ibuka. *Dictionnaire nominatif des victimes du génocide en préfecture de Kibuye.* Kigali: Ibuka, 1999.

International Criminal Tribunal for Rwanda. Prosecutor versus Jean Kambanda, Case No. ICTR-97-23-1.Arusha: 1997.

International Federation of Human Rights (Paris), Africa Watch (Washington), the Inter-African Union on Human and Peoples' Rights (Ouagadougou), and Center for Human Rights and Democratic Development (Montreal). *Report of the International Commission of Investigation on the Violations of Human Rights in Rwanda Since October 1, 1990.* March 1993.

International Federation of the Red Cross and Red Crescent Societies. "Under the Volcanoes: Special Focus on the Rwandan Refugee Crisis. "*World Disasters Report,* 1994.

Kagame, Alexis. *Un abrégé de l'histoire du Rwanda de 1893 à 1972.* Butare: Éditions Universitaires du Rwanda, 1975.

Kamanzi, Ntaribi. *Rwanda: Du génocide à la défaite.* Kigali: Éditions Rebero, 1997.

Kershaw, Ian. *The Nazi Dictatorship: Problems and Perspectives of Interpretation.* London: Arnold, 1992.

Kimonyo, Jean-Paul. *Revue critique des interprétations du conflit rwandais.* Butare: Éditions de l'Université nationale du Rwanda, 2000.

King, Maurice. "Rwanda: Malthus and Medicus Mundi." *Medicus Mundi Bulletin* 54 (August 1994): 11–19.

Kuper, Leo. *Genocide: Its Political Use in the Twentieth Century.* New Haven, CT: Yale University Press, 1981.

Lemarchand, René. *Rwanda and Burundi.* New York: Praeger, 1970.

———. "The Coup in Rwanda." In Robert Rotberg and Ali Mazrui, eds., *Protest and Power in Black Africa,* pp. 877–924. New York: Oxford University Press, 1970.

———. "Les génocides se suivent mais ne se ressemblent pas: l'Holocaust et le Rwanda." In *L'Afrique des Grands Lacs: Annuaire 2001–2002.* Anvers: Centre d'étude de la région des Grands Lacs d'Afrique, 2002.

Leurquin, Pierre. *Le niveau de vie des populations rurales du Ruanda-Urundi.* Leuven: Éditions Nauwelaerts, 1960.

Linden, Ian, and Jane Linden. *Church and Revolution in Rwanda.* Manchester, UK: Manchester University Press, 1977.

Logiest, Guy. *Mission au Rwanda. Un Blanc dans la bagarre Hutu-Tutsi.* Bruxelles: Didier-Hatier, 1988.

Longman, Timothy P. "Genocide and Socio-political Change: Massacres in Two Rwandan Villages." *Issue: A Journal of Opinion* 23, no. 2 (1995): 18–21.

Lugan, Bernard. *Histoire du Rwanda: De la Préhistoire à nos jours.* Etrépilly: Éditions Bartillat, 1997.

Mamdani, Mahmood. *When Victims Become Killers: Colonialism, Nativism, and the Genocide in Rwanda.* Princeton, NJ: Princeton University Press, 2001.

Maquet, Jacques-Jérôme. *The Premises of Inequality in Ruanda: A Study of Political Relations in a Central African Kingdom.* London: Oxford University Press, 1961.

Maquet, Jacques-Jerôme, and Marcel d'Hertefelt, *Elections en société féodale: Une étude sur l'introduction du vote populaire au Ruanda-Urundi.* Brussels: Académie royale des sciences coloniales, 1959.

Marysse, Stefaan, Tom De Herdt, and Elie Ndayambaje. *Rwanda: Appauvrissement et ajustement structurel.* Paris: L'Harmattan, 1994.

Maton, Jef. *Développement économique et social au Rwanda entre 1980 et 1993: Le dixième décile en face de l'Apocalypse.* Ghent: State University of Ghent, 1994.

Mbembe, Achille. *Afriques indociles: Christianisme, pouvoir et État en société postcoloniale.* Paris: Karthala, 1988.

———. "Notes on the Postcolony," *Journal of the International African Institute* 62, no. 1 (1992): 3–37.]

Mbonimana, Gamaliel. "Les institutions traditionnelles constitutives de l'identité nationale." *Cahiers du Centre de gestion des conflits* 2 (2001): 5–31.

McDoom, Omar. "Rwanda's Ordinary Killers: Interpreting Popular Participation in the Rwandan Genocide." *Crisis States Research Centre Working Papers Series* 1, 77. London: Crisis States Research Centre, London School of Economics and Political Science, 2005.

Melson, Robert. *Revolution and Genocide: On the Origins of the Armenian Genocide and the Holocaust.* Chicago: University of Chicago Press, 1991.

Mouvement Révolutionnaire national pour le développement (MRND). "Manifeste." *Traits d'Union Rwanda 11, Forum pour le Dialogue Regional,* 1996.

Mugesera, Antoine. *Imiberero y'Abatutsi kuri republika yambere n'iyakabiri (1959–1990).* Kigali: Les Éditions Rwandaises, 2004.

Mulindwa, Zebron. "Les conséquences géographiques de la pression démographique sur le versant occidental de la Crête Zaïre-Nil en préfecture de Kibuye (Rwanda)." Master's thesis, Université d'Aix-Marseille, Marseille, 1985.

Munyangaju, Aloys. *L'actualité politique au Rwanda.* s.l., 1959.

Musangamfura, Sixbert. "Le parti MDR-Parmehutu: Information et propagande, 1959–1969." Unpublished master's Mémoire de maîtrise, Université nationale du Rwanda, Kigali, 1987.

Newbury, Catharine. *The Cohesion of Oppression: Clientship and Ethnicity in Rwanda, 1860–1960.* New York: Columbia University Press, 1988.

———. "Background to Genocide in Rwanda." *Issue: A Journal of Opinion* 23, no 2 (1995): 12–17.

Nkundabagenzi, Fidèle. *Le Rwanda politique (1958–1960).* Brussels: CRISP, 1961.

Nkurikiyimfura, Jean-Népomucène. *Le gros bétail et la société rwandaise évolution historique des XII–XIV siècles à 1958.* Paris: L'Harmattan, 1994.

Nsengiyaremye, Dismas. "La transition démocratique au Rwanda, 1989–1993." In André Guichaoua, ed., *Les crises politiques au Rwanda et au Burundi, 1993–1994*, pp. 239–263. Lille: Université des Sciences et Technologies de Lille, 1995.

Ntezimana, Emmanuel. "Le Rwanda social, administratif, et politique à la fin du dix-neuvième siècle." In Gudrun Honke, ed., *Au plus profond de l'Afrique: Le Rwanda et la colonisation allemande, 1885–1991*, pp. 73–80. Wuppertal: Verlag, 1990.

Ntezimana, Vincent. *La justice belge face au génocide rwandais.* Paris: L'Harmattan, 2000.

Nzisabira, Jean. "Accumulation du peuplement rural et ajustement agropastoraux au Rwanda." *Cahiers du CIDEP* 1, 1989.

Pabanel, Jean-Pierre. "Bilan de la Deuxième République rwandaise: Du modèle de développement à la violence générale." *Politique africaine* 57 (1995): 112–123.

Prunier, Gérard. *The Rwanda Crisis, 1959–1994: History of a Genocide.* London: Hurst, 1997.

Reid, Andrew. "The Role of Cattle in the Later Iron Age Communities of Southern Uganda." PhD diss., University of Cambridge, Cambridge, UK, 1991.

Republic of Rwanda, Ministry of the Interior. *Bilan des 25 ans d'indépendance du Rwanda: 1962–1987.* Kigali: République Rwandaise, 1987.

Republic of Rwanda, Ministry of the Interior, Division Recensement et Statistiques. *Recensement administratif de la population rwandaise durant la période de 1960–1987* (internal reference document). Kigali: République Rwandaise, October 1987.

Republic of Rwanda, Ministry of Planning,Service national de Recensement. *Recensement général de la population et de l'habitat au 15 août 1991.* Kigali: République Rwandaise, n.d.

Republic of Rwanda, Office of the President. *Ubumwe*, publication of discussions at Urugwiro Village, 1998.

Reyntjens, Filip. *Pouvoir et droit au Rwanda, droit public et evolution politique, 1916–1973.* Tervuren: Musée Royale de l'Afrique Central, 1985.

———. *L'Afrique des Grands Lacs en crise.* Paris: Karthala, 1994.

———. *Rwanda: Trois jours qui ont fait basculer l'histoire.* Brussells: Institut africaine-CEDAF, 1995.

Royaume de Belgique, Ministère des Colonies. *Rapport soumis par le Gouvernement belge à l'Assemblée générale des Nations unies au sujet de l'administration du Ruanda-Urundi pendant l'année 1959.* Brussells: Van Muysewinkel, 1960.

Ruanda-Urundi. *Supplément au Rudipresse* 184 (13 août), 1960.

Ruanda-Urundi, Conseil supérieur du pays (Rwanda). "Note de synthèse des débats du CSP sur le régime foncier," 1959.

———. "P.-V. de la 12e session," 26 septembre 1957.

———. "Compte rendu de la 10e session du CSP," 1957.

Rumiya, Jean. *Le Rwanda sous le régime du mandat belge, 1916–1931.* Paris: L'Harmattan, 1992.

Rutayisire, Paul. "Le remodelage de l'espace culturel rwandais par l'Église et la colonisation." *Cahiers du Centre de gestion des conflits* 2 (2001): 32–60.

Sanders, Edith R. "The Hamitic Hypothesis: Its Origin and Functions in Time Perspective." *Journal of African History* 10, no. 4 (1969): 521–532.

Saucier, Jean-François. "The Patron-Client Relationship in Traditional and Contemporary Southern Rwanda." PhD diss., Columbia University, New York, 1974.

Schoenbrun, David. "We Are What We Eat: Ancient Agriculture Between the Great Lakes." *Journal of African History* 34, no. 1 (1993): 1–31.

————. *A Green Place, a Good Place: Agrarian Change, Gender, and Social Identity in the Great Lakes Region to the 15th Century.* Oxford: James Currey, 1998.

Sebasoni, Servilien. *Les origines du Rwanda.* Paris: L'Harmattan, 2000.

Staub, Ervin. *The Roots of Evil: The Origin of Genocide and Other Group Violence.* Cambridge, UK: Cambridge University Press, 1989.

Straus, Scott. "How Many Perpetrators Were There in the Rwandan Genocide? An Estimate." *Journal of Genocide Research* 6, no. 1 (March 2004): 85–98.

————. *The Order of Genocide: Race, Power, and War in Rwanda.* Ithaca, NY: Cornell University Press, 2006.

Sutton, J. E. G. "The Antecedents of Interlacustrine Kingdoms." *Journal of African History* 34 (1993): 33–64.

Thibon, Christian. "Croissance et régimes démographiques anciens: Burundi, Rwanda et leurs marges 1800/1950." In *Histoire sociale de l'Afrique de l'Est, XIXe–Xe siècle,* pp. 207–229. Edited by Université de Burundi, Département de l'histoire. Paris: Karthala, 1992.

UN Development Program. *1990 Human Development Report: Rwanda.* Kigali: UNDP, 1990.

UN Security Council. 49th Year Supplement for July, August, and September 1994, Annexes I and II. Document S/1994/924. Official Record, 1994.

————. 49th Year Supplement for October, November, and December. Document S/1994/1125. Official Record, 1994.

Uvin, Peter. "Prejudice, Crisis, and Genocide in Rwanda." *African Studies Review* 40, no. 2 (1997): 91–115.

————. *Aiding Violence: The Development Enterprise in Rwanda.* West Hartford, CT: Kumarian, 1998.

Vansina, Jan. *L'évolution du royaume Rwanda des origines à 1900.* Brussells: Académie Royale des Sciences d'Outre-Mer, 1962.

————. *Antecedents to Modern Rwanda: The Nyiginya Kingdom.* Madison: University of Wisconsin Press, 2004.

Verpoorten, Marijke. "The Death Toll of the Rwandan Genocide: A Detailed Analysis for Gikongoro Province." *Population* 60, no. 4 (2005): 331–367.

————. "Leave None to Claim the Land: A Malthusian Catastrophe in Rwanda?" *Journal of Peace Research* 49 (July 2012): 547–563.

Verwimp, Philip. "A Quantitative Analysis of Genocide in Kibuye Prefecture, Rwanda." Discussion Paper. Leuven: Katholieke Universiteit Leuven, Center for Economic Studies, 2001.

————. "An Economic Profile of Peasant Perpetrators of Genocide: Micro-level Evidence from Rwanda." *Journal of Development Economics* 77, no. 2 (2005): 297–323.

Vidal, Claudine. *Sociologie des passions: Rwanda, Côte d'Ivoire.* Paris: Karthala, 1991.

Wagner, Michele D. "All the Bourgmestre's Men: Making Sense of Genocide in Rwanda." *Africa Today* 45, no. 1 (1998): 25–36.

Wallimann, Isidor, and Michael N. Dobkowski, eds.*Genocide and the Modern Age: Etiology and Case Studies of Mass Death.* New York: Greenwood, 1987.

Watson, Catharine. *Exile from Rwanda: Background to an Invasion.* Washington, DC: US Committee for Refugees, 1991.

Willame, Jean-Claude. *Aux sources de l'hécatombe rwandaise.* Paris: L'Harmattan, 1995.

World Bank. *World Development Indicators.* Washington, DC: World Bank, 2014.

————. *Rwanda : Agricultural Strategy Review.* Washington, DC: World Bank, 1985, 1991.

————. *Rwanda: Economic Memorandum of Sectoral Development and Current Policy Issues*. Kigali: World Bank, 1985.

————. Eastern African Regional Office. *Memorandum on the Economy of Rwanda*. Washington, DC: World Bank, 1976.

Young, Crawford, ed. *The Rising Tide of Cultural Pluralism*. Madison: University of Wisconsin Press, 1993.

Index

Abagizumwe, 128
Abakombozi, 157
Abakonde families, 37
Abstention, 114–117
ADERWA. *See* Alliance for Democracy in Rwanda
ADL. *See* Rwandan Association for Individual Rights and Civil Liberties
Agrarian groups, 11, 12, 15–16, 21, 76n85
Agriculture: cooperatives for, 191–192, 212n33; downfall of, 68–70; investment in, 37–38; in Kibuye, 270–272; in Kigembe, 193–196, 194tab, 195tab; shift from livestock to, 37
AIDS, 68, 72
Akanyaru River, 184, 217–218, 227, 255n15, 256n18, 260n156
Alcohol abuse, 209–210
Alliance for Democracy in Rwanda (ADERWA), 99
Amin Dada, Idi, 47–48
Animation, 192; anti-Tutsi behavior in, 233; consequences of, 204, 205; in education, 201; MDR control with, 224–225; MRND social control with, 62, 94, 190, 201, 207, 312
Anomie, 357
Anti-Semitism, 2
Anti-Tutsi ideology, 2, 74n34, 108n98, 304n126; in animation, 233; in Catholic Church, 22, 124; of CDR, 95, 156; from First Republic, 248; under Habyarimana, Juvénal, 55–56, 317; of Kanyarengwe, 124, 277; in mass mobilization and participation, 175, 342–344, 347, 370; of MDR,

150–151, 166, 233, 295, 296; of Nkundabakura, 233, 248; propaganda with, 35, 36, 105n35; in revolution of 1959, 300; spread of, 127–128; violence based on, 95, 124, 371n17, 372n25; in war of 1990, 218–219, 324–325, 362
APROSOMA. *See* Association for the Social Welfare of the Masses
Aristocracy, Tutsi, 16–17, 20, 21, 33, 138n37
Armenian genocide, 366–368
Arrests: for genocide participation, 335; migrant, in Burundi, 301n27; of religious movements, 278–280; reward for, 160; Tutsi, 144, 216–217, 255n11; in war of 1990, 216–218, 325
Arson: in Gikongoro, 97; in Kibuye, 97–98, 276–277, 288, 290, 291–292, 293, 298; of Tutsi property, 30, 114, 276–277, 316, 333
Arusha peace accords: demonstrations for, 95; Habyarimana, Juvénal and, 86–87, 91, 95, 99; MDR reactions to, 83, 91, 95, 289, 299; MRND reactions to, 83, 91, 289, 292, 298, 299, 363, 364; Nsengiyaremye and, 99; PL and, 83, 91, 95; PSD and, 83, 91, 95; refugee return and, 83; transitional government and, 82–83
Assassination, 16; of Burundi's president, 260n144, 262n234; of Gatabazi, 86, 161, 162, 165; of Habyarimana, Juvénal, 3, 4, 5, 86–87, 175, 332, 333, 338, 365, 368, 369, 373n40; of Hutu and Tutsi chiefs, 30

tion to prefect in, 156–157; PDC in, 147; political historical context of, 110, 112–113, 166–167, 174–176, 363–364; political pluralism in, 146–147, 162–165, 164*fig*, 259*n*124; political rallies in, 147–150, 155, 158; political trend in, 165–166, 168–169; population of, 139*n*70, 140*n*72; PSD in, 147, 150, 152, 161–163, 164, 164*fig*, 165, 259*n*124, 259*n*133; reaction to war of 1990, 143–146; revolution of 1959 influence on, 114; in Second Republic, 110, 124–129; security committee in, 140*n*78, 149, 157, 160, 161, 169, 179*n*66; socioeconomic crisis in, 132–133; Tutsi population in, 104, 109, 112*tab*, 124, 127, 137*n*2, 164, 165, 168, 353; Tutsi-Hutu cooperation in, 127, 168, 170; violence in, 132–137, 150–155, 159–160, 161–162, 363–364; voting patterns in, 61. *See also* Kigembe Commune

Buyenzi, Isaïe, 244–245, 255
Bwanakweri, Prosper, 25, 29, 30
Byumba Prefecture, 46, 102*fig*; demonstrations in, 99–101; development of, 63; under Habyarimana, Juvénal regime, 72; Interahamwe militias in, 95–96; political pluralism in, 94–95

Camouflage, 250
Cannabis, 206, 207, 209, 225, 314
Catholic Church, 42*n*94; anti-Tutsi ideology in, 22, 124; health care and, 136; in Kigembe, 191; monarchy conversion to, 18, 19; during nationalist movement, 24; schools run by, 19, 22, 124; support of PARMEHUTU, 28, 122; tabula rasa of, 18, 22, 360. *See also* Missionaries
Cattle-clientship system. *See* Ubuhake
CDR. *See* Coalition for the Defense of the Republic
Cell committees: in MDR takeover, 229, 230; peace keeping of, 291; power of, 202, 211*n*23, 211*n*28; Tutsi inclusion in, 213*n*65; violence to members of, 207, 208, 209; in war of 1990, 217
CERAI. *See* Integrated rural vocational and training school
Chief system, 14, 41*n*58; abuses in, 22;

assassinations in, 30; Belgian colonists against, 20; in CSP, 25; labor requirement under, 15–16; Tutsi aristocracy and, 138*n*37
Christian Democratic Party (PDC), 81, 92, 147
Christianity, 18
CIC. *See* Interministerial coordination committee
Citizens: education response from, 208; MRND control of, 200–205; MRND subscription fees for, 60, 201–203, 202*tab*; party-state reaction of, 203–205; sector councilors coercion of, 202; umuganda adherence by, 204–205, 207, 210; view of inyenzi, 50, 145
Civil disobedience. *See* Disobedience
Civil peace. *See* Peace efforts
Civilians: murder by ordinary, 274–275; role in genocide, 168, 236, 240–241, 242–244, 247, 303*n*72, 335, 336, 354, 358; use of media, 256*n*20
Clans, 13, 138*n*37, 360
Class structure: disobedience and, 356–357; herders over farmers in, 15–16; movement within, 15; oppression in, 14; political support differences and, 332; in Tutsi-Hutu divide, 120–122
Classe, Apostolic Léon, 18
Classist ideology, 28, 120–122
Coalition for the Defense of the Republic (CDR): alliance with Hutu-power movement, 86; anti-Tutsi ideology of, 95, 156; demonstrations by, 99–101; opposition to, 157–159; racist policy of, 83–84; regions dominated by, 95–96; sympathizers of, 160; violence against, 161–162; youth wing of, 94
CODAPAKI, 191, 212*n*33
Coercion: for mass mobilization, 4–6, 168, 173, 358; MDR membership and, 222; MRND control with, 202–203, 205; with political pluralism, 224–225
Coffee and tea market, 37–38; economic crisis and, 63; Kigembe income from, 193, 195, 195*tab*
Colonial rule, 39*n*2; Astrida and, 19, 23; challenge to, 22; elites aligning with, 18; floggings under, 41*n*58; hostility influenced by, 9, 10; labor require-

About the Book

Why did Rwanda's rural Hutus participate so massively, and so personally, in the country's 1994 genocide of its Tutsi population? Given all that has been written already about this horrific episode, is there still more that can be learned? Answering these questions, Jean-Paul Kimonyo's social and economic history explores at the deepest level the role both of power relations among Rwanda's grassroots citizens, political parties, and the state and of socioeconomic factors vs. politically/socially constructed ethnicity.

Jean-Paul Kimonyo is a senior adviser in the Office of the President of Rwanda and also a fellow at the Rift Valley Institute.

UNIVERSITY
OF
GLASGOW
LIBRARY